ADAPTATION

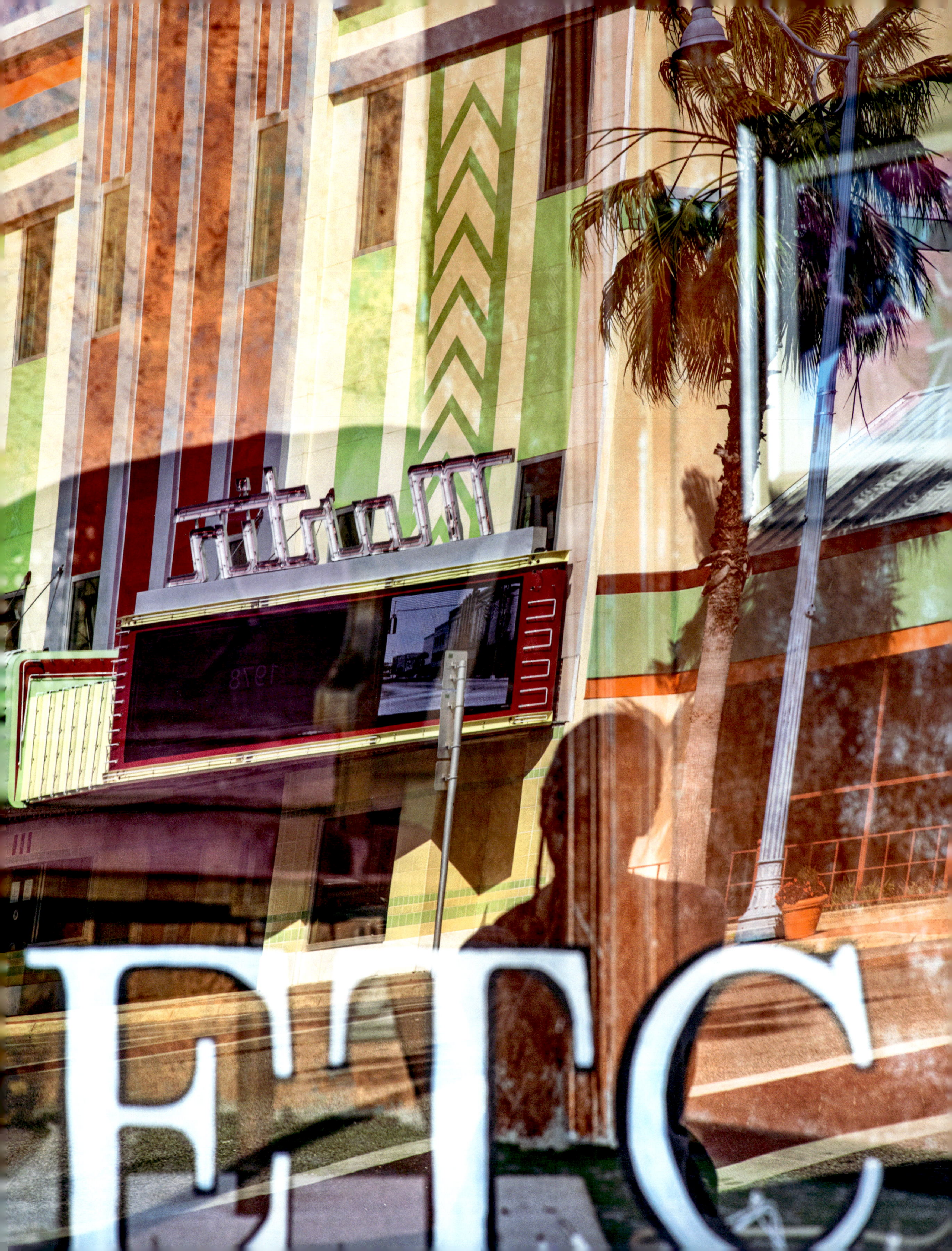
ETC

ANASTASIA SAMOYLOVA

ADAPTATION

EDITED BY
DAVID CAMPANY

with 195 illustrations

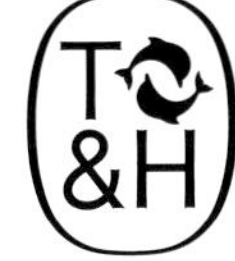

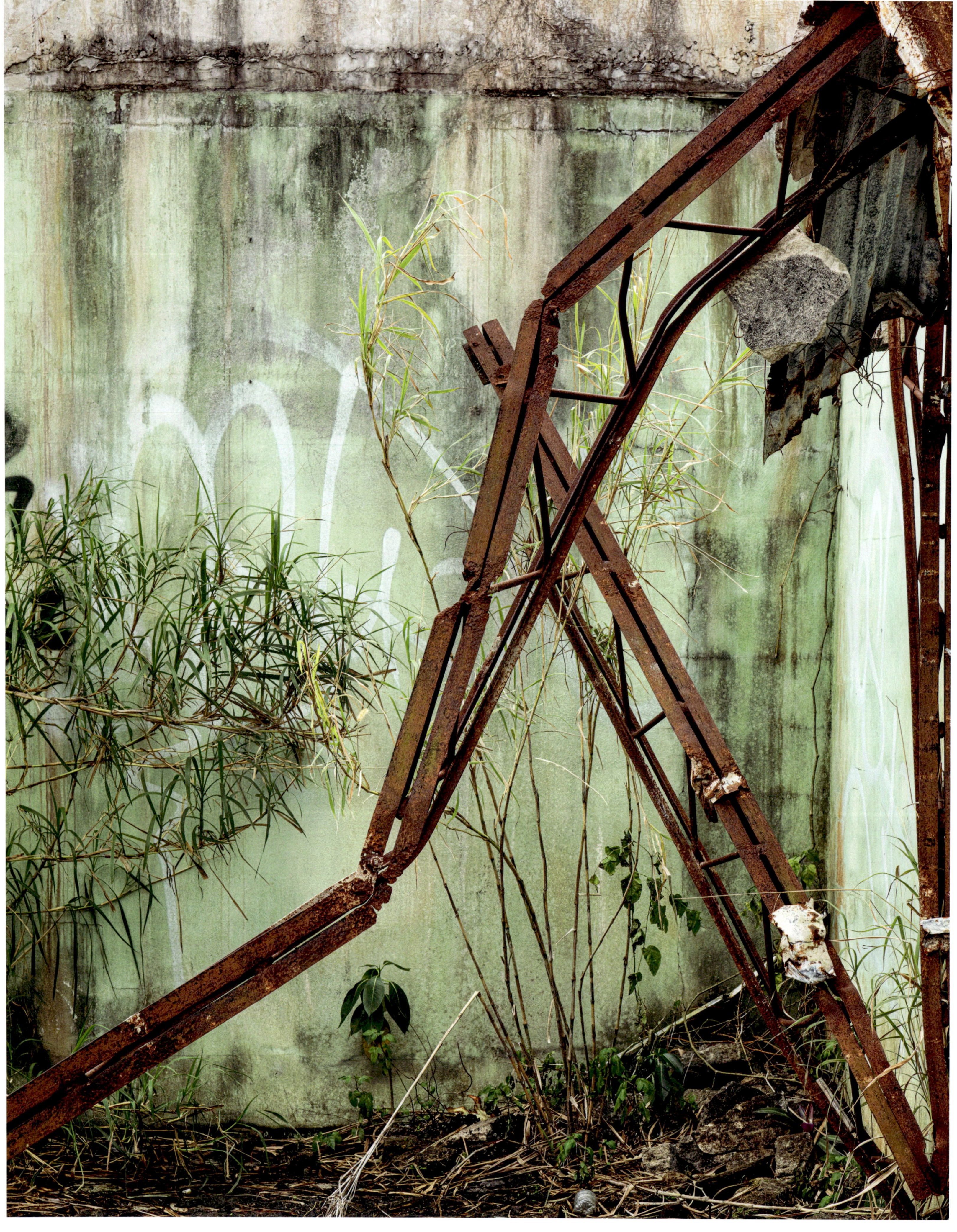

« ETC, Panama City, 2021 ⌃ Abandoned Tourist Attraction, Palmdale, 2020

CONTENTS

7 FOREWORD

8 LANDSCAPE SUBLIME

26 FLOODZONE

69 INCROYABLES FLORIDES
LUCY SANTE

72 BREAKFASTS

90 FLORIDAS

137 STATE OF THE STATE
MIA FINEMAN

140 PAINTINGS AND COLLAGES

166 IMAGE CITIES

213 THE WORLD'S IMAGE
DAVID CAMPANY

222 NOTES

222 PICTURE CREDITS

223 ACKNOWLEDGMENTS

223 AUTHOR BIOGRAPHIES

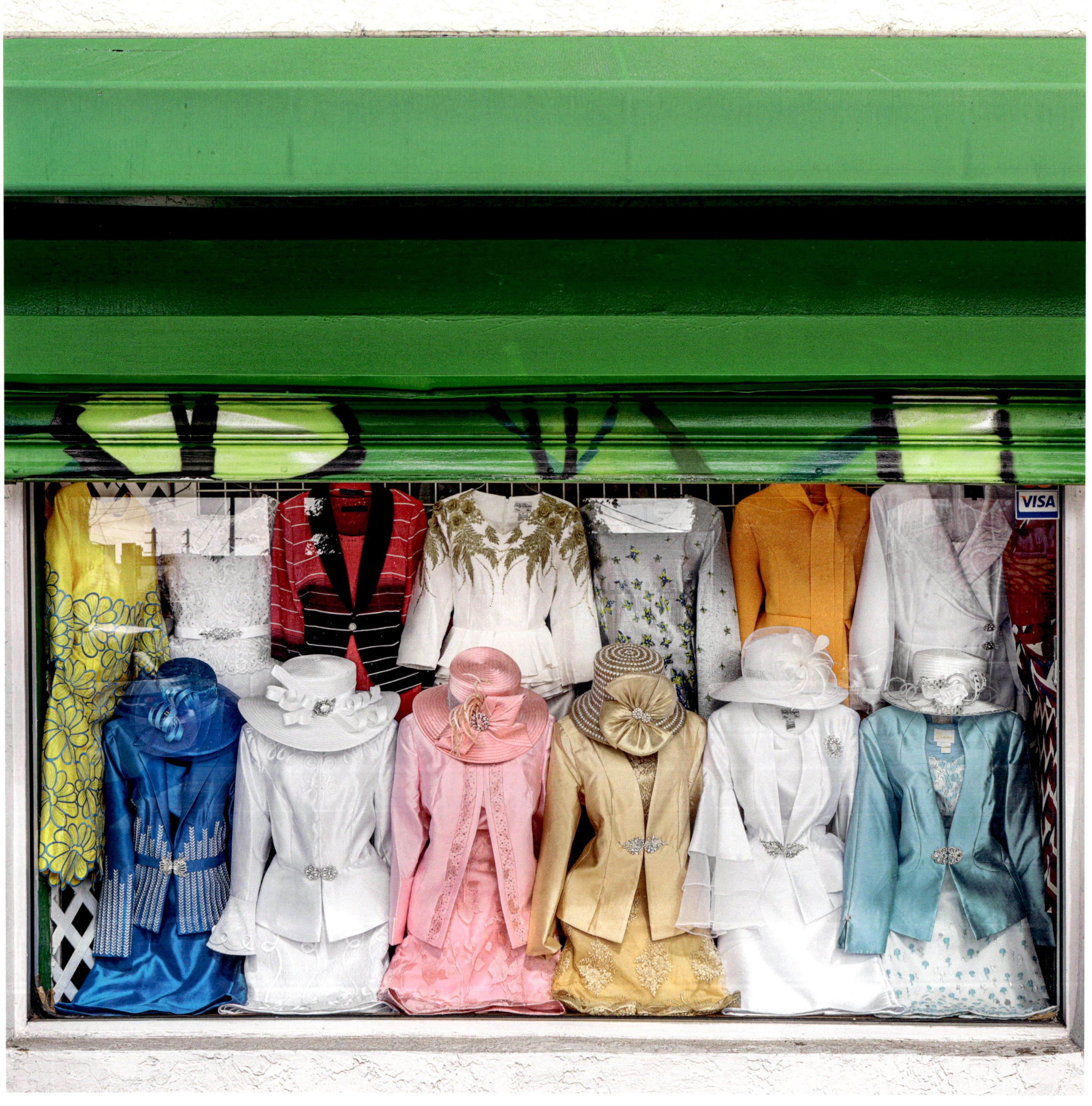

Looking, Miami, 2020

FOREWORD

DAVID CAMPANY

Adaptation is the first major survey of the art of Anastasia Samoylova, one of the most original image makers to have emerged in recent years. It brings together her six most important bodies of work. Each is very different, yet they all share the formal beauty, virtuoso use of colour and fascination with visual culture for which she is rightly celebrated.

Whether collaging and painting in her Miami Beach studio, documenting contemporary Florida or photographing cities around the globe, Samoylova is informed by the rapidly expanding image world in which we all now live. It seduces and shapes our perceptions, frames our sense of reality, informing and misleading all at once. She approaches it with a quizzical but engaged outlook, shaped first by her early years in post-Soviet Russia, then by the excessive spectacle of life in the USA. State propaganda and capitalist advertising are not so far apart.

Through her distinctive visual layering, Samoylova dramatizes the contradictions of a confusing 21st century. How can an artist deal with the internet's flood of images; or observe the flood-prone landscapes of climate change; or document the giant corporate visuals that dwarf the cities in which ever-more people now dwell? For Samoylova all these questions are deeply related. *Adaptation* allows us to see, for the first time, the threads of connection that unite her work, and to appreciate the enormous range of art and ideas that informs it. Russian Constructivism and Cubism, Pop and postmodernism rub shoulders with influences from cinema, literature and the greats of documentary photography. It is a provocative vision that invites us to think again about the predicament of the contemporary world and its representations.

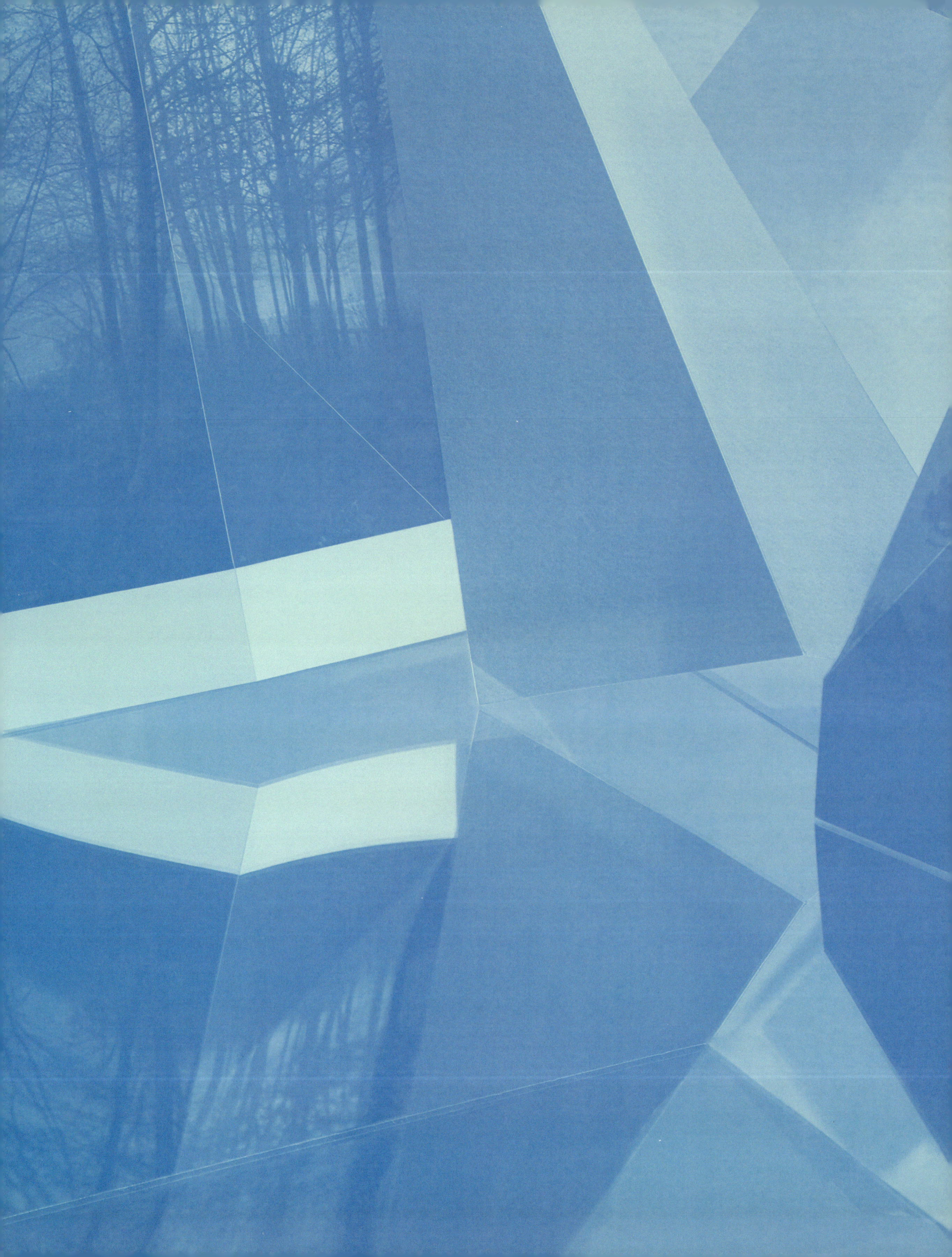

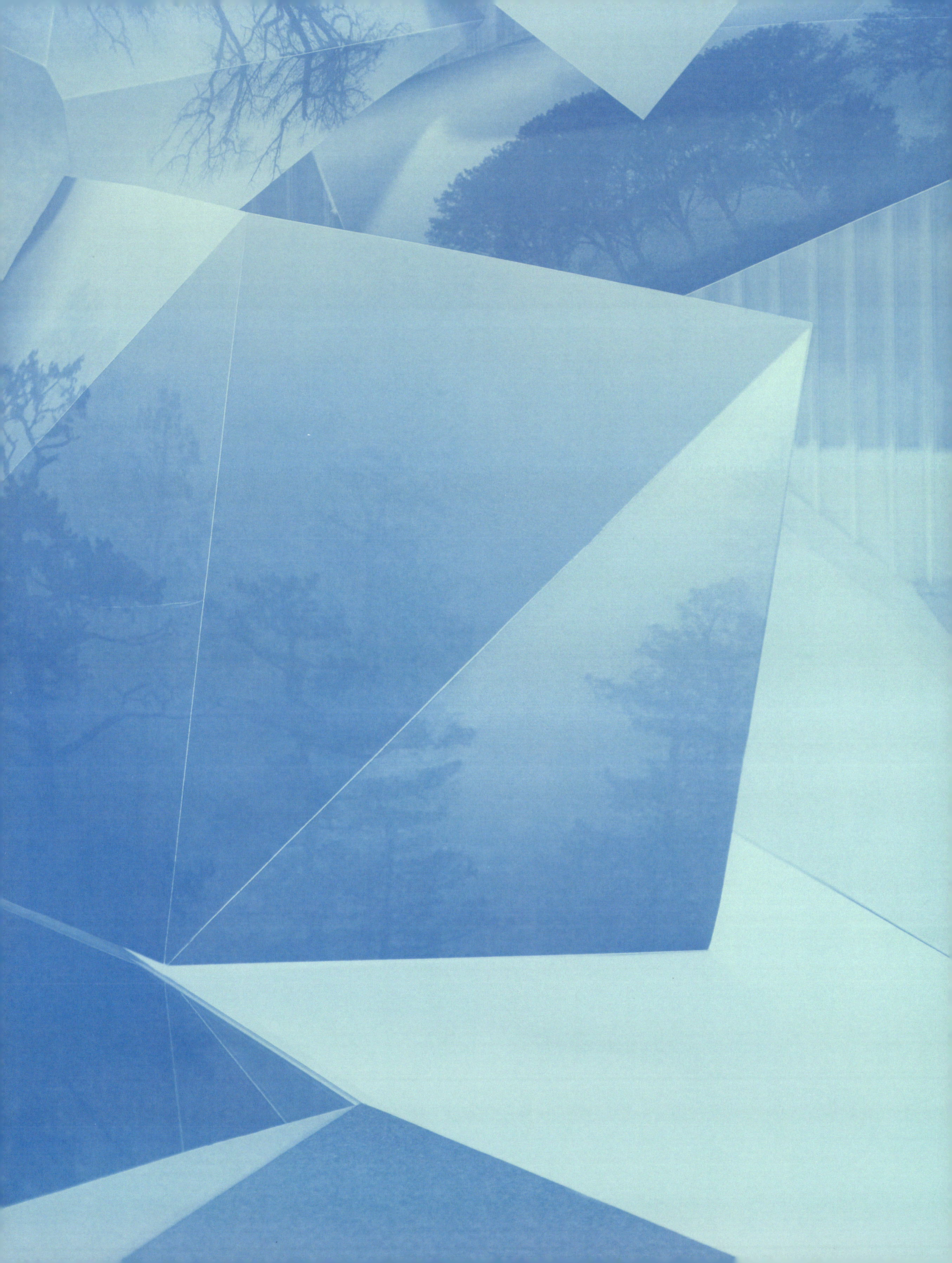

LANDSCAPE SUBLIME

A generation ago, the internet was fast becoming the place for the mass production and consumption of images. In 2004, the file-sharing website Flickr was established. YouTube arrived in 2005. What would global internet participation mean? A new era of individual expression, or conformity?

Samoylova has followed online visual culture closely since its popularization. She noticed not a great explosion of photographic freedom but the widespread adoption of strict visual forms. Landscape imagery mimicked pictorial ideals shaped by Western art history, advertising and cinema. Serious amateurs competed to make the most conventional views.

In 2013, Samoylova began the ongoing series *Landscape Sublime*. Searching Flickr using familiar landscape keywords – 'desert mirages', 'storms', 'trees in fog', 'canyons', 'tropics' – she would download copyright-free images, print them out in her studio, then fold and sculpt them into three-dimensional forms. These compositions, largely improvised before her camera, are indebted to the avant-gardes of the early 20th century. Constructivism and Cubism broke with single-point perspective, offering kaleidoscopic reconfigurations. Samoylova's assemblages may look 'digital' but all of the construction is done materially, emphasized through careful lighting. The camera is used only to document and present.

Traditionally the term 'sublime' has referred to our feelings of awe at the overwhelming and fearsome majesty of nature. However, what seems more sublime today is the vast number of similar images that fill the world's hard drives. And yet, something of that older sense of nature's uncontrollable power returns in the more recent works in this series that consider severe floods and fires caused by climate change.

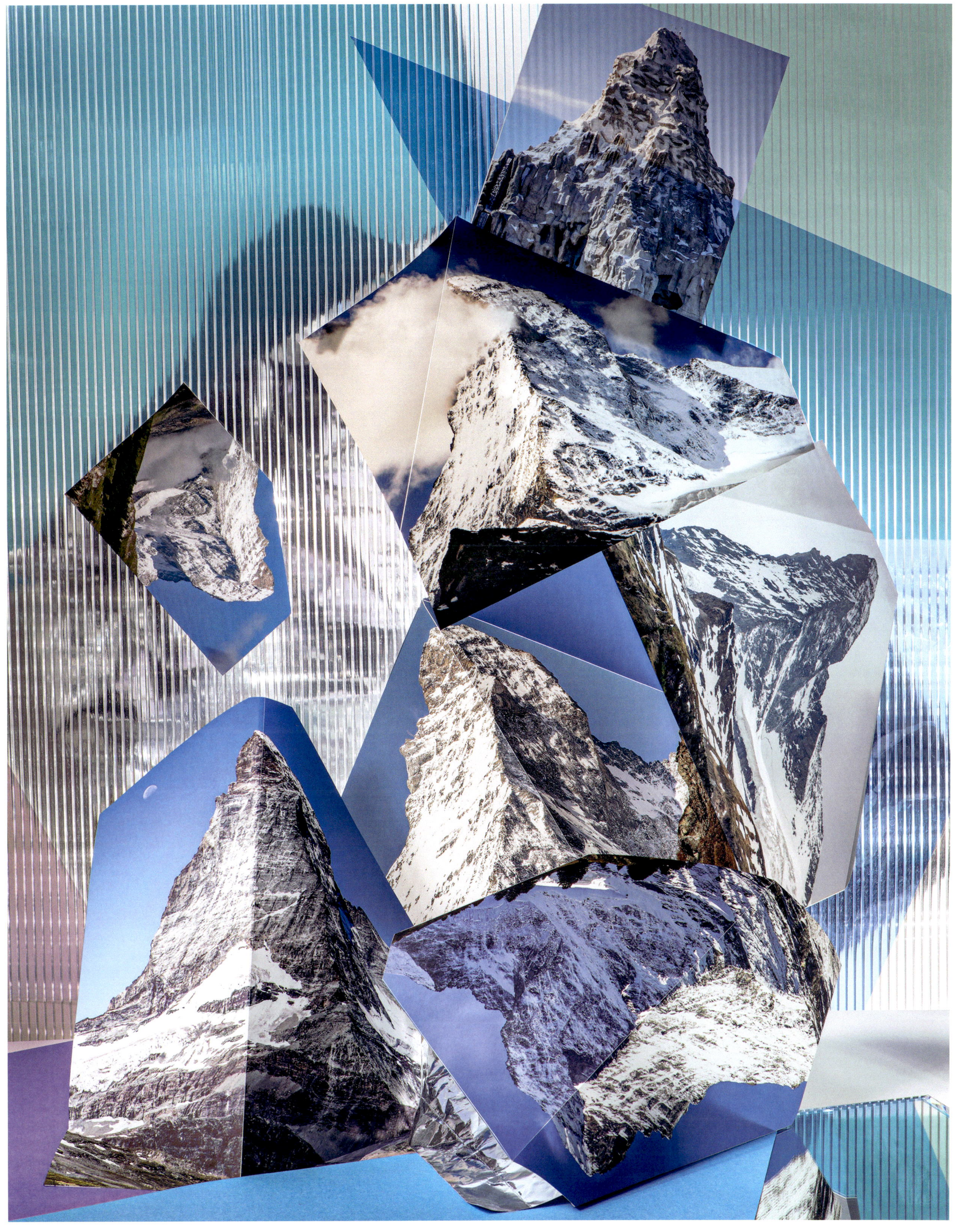

Six Real Matterhorns, 2019 ›› Rainbows, 2014

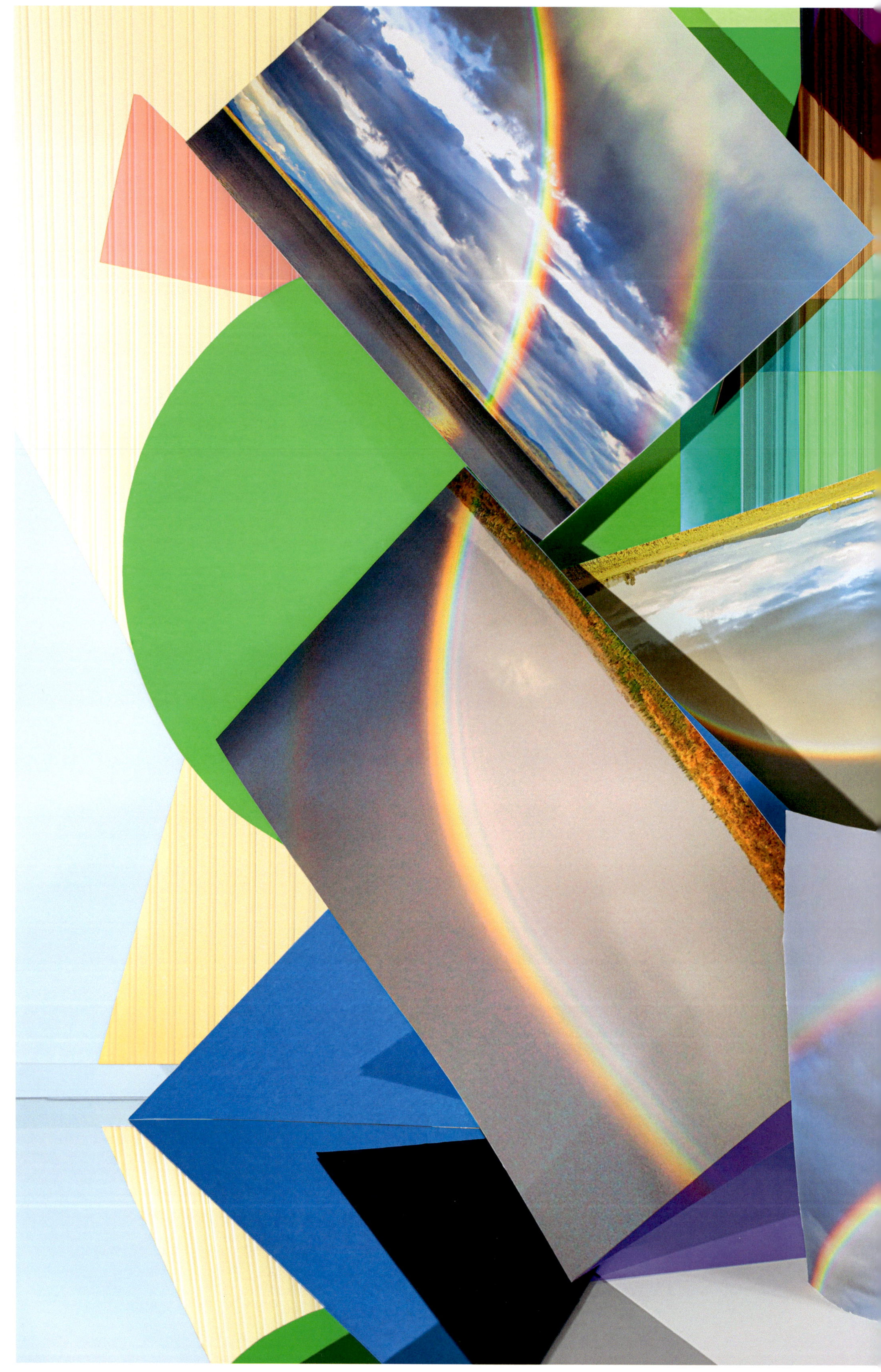

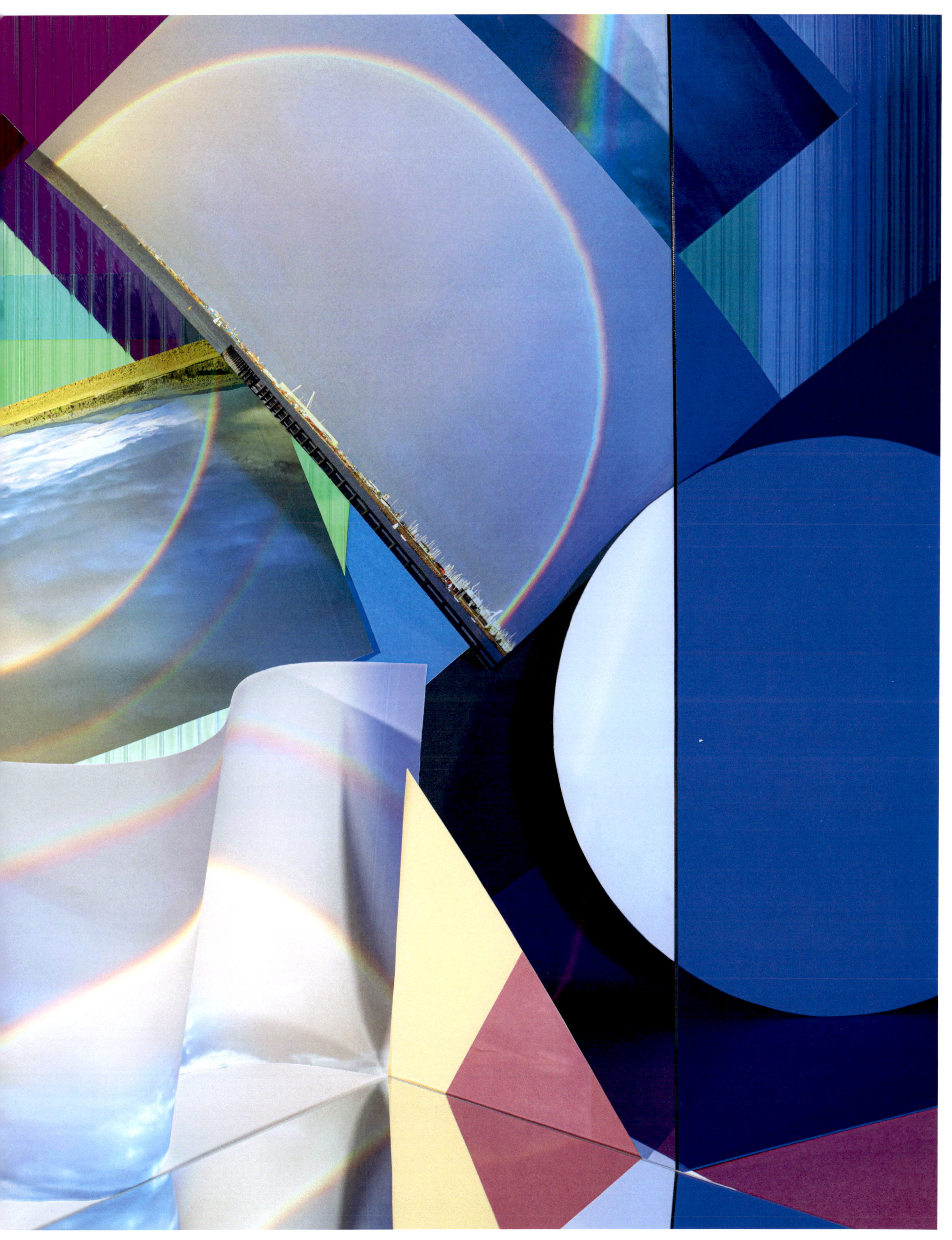

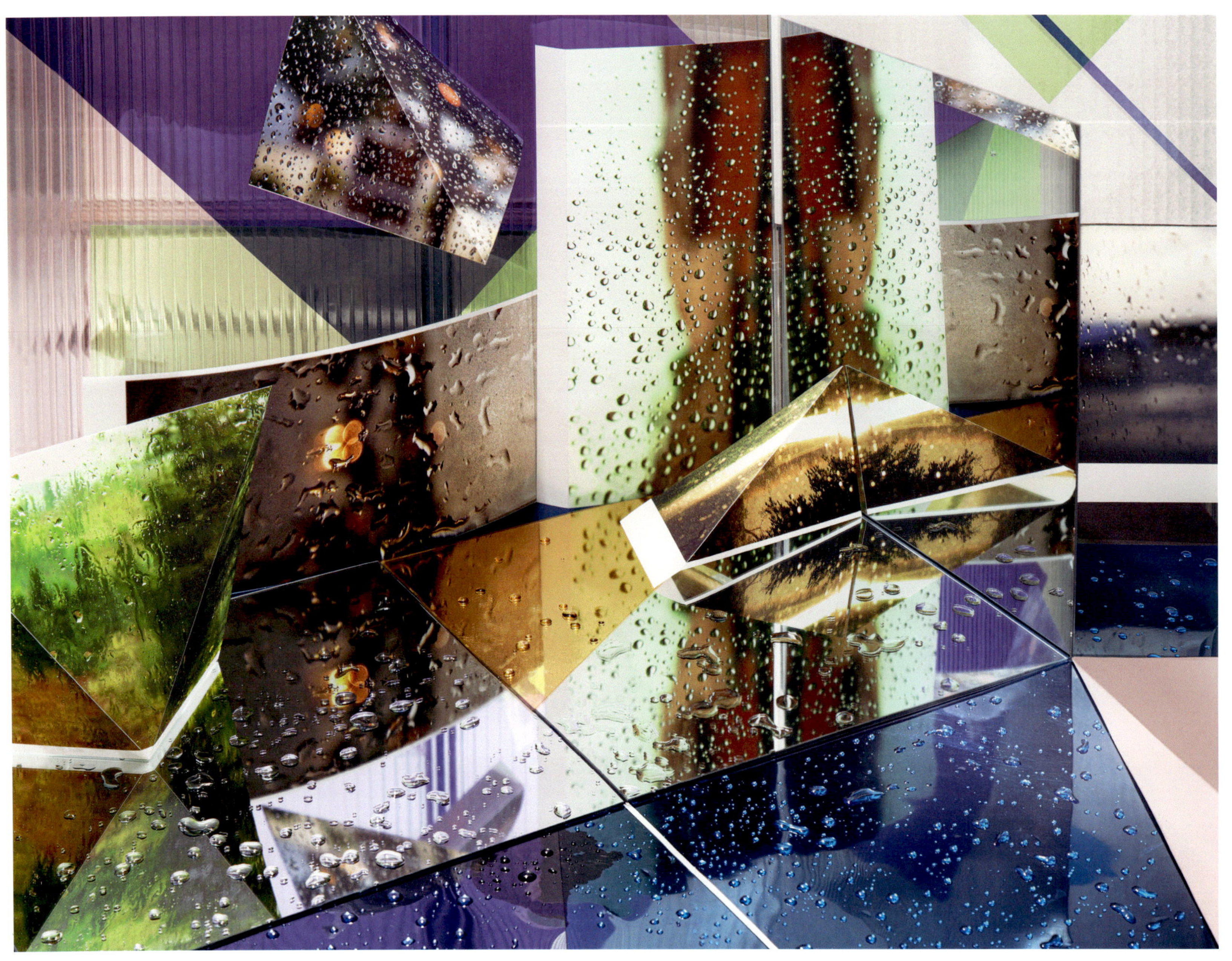

Rainy Windows, 2013

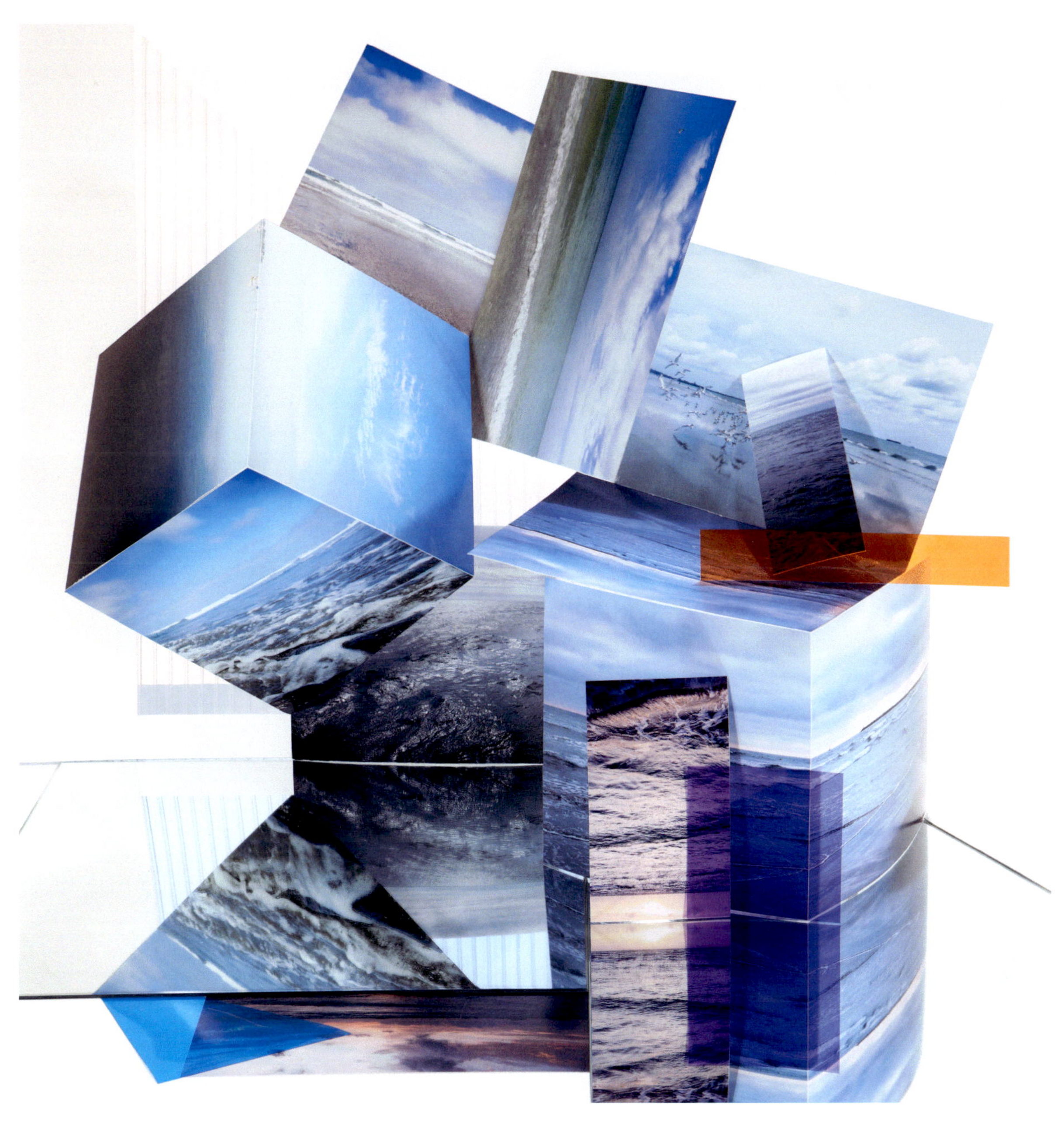

Beaches, 2014

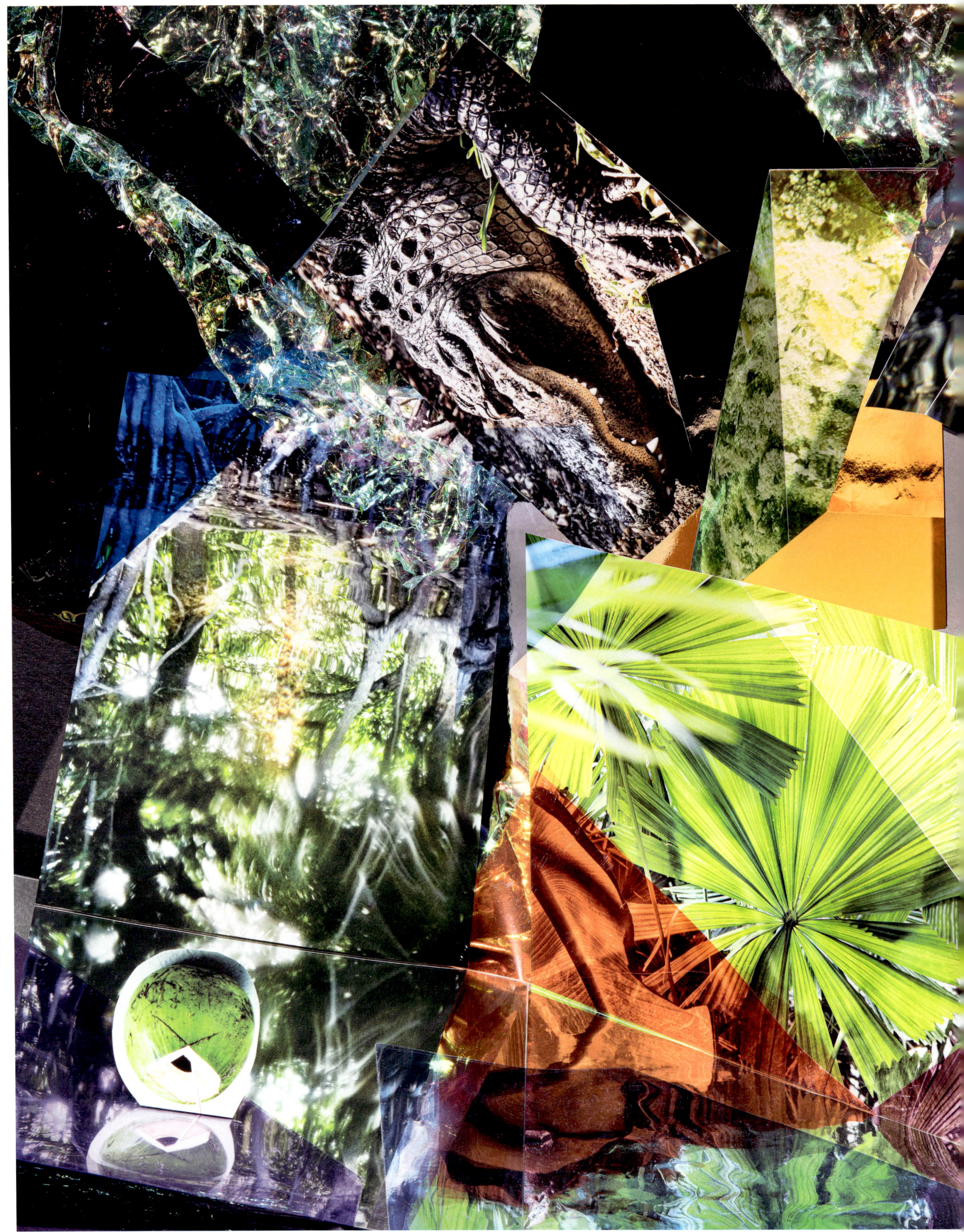

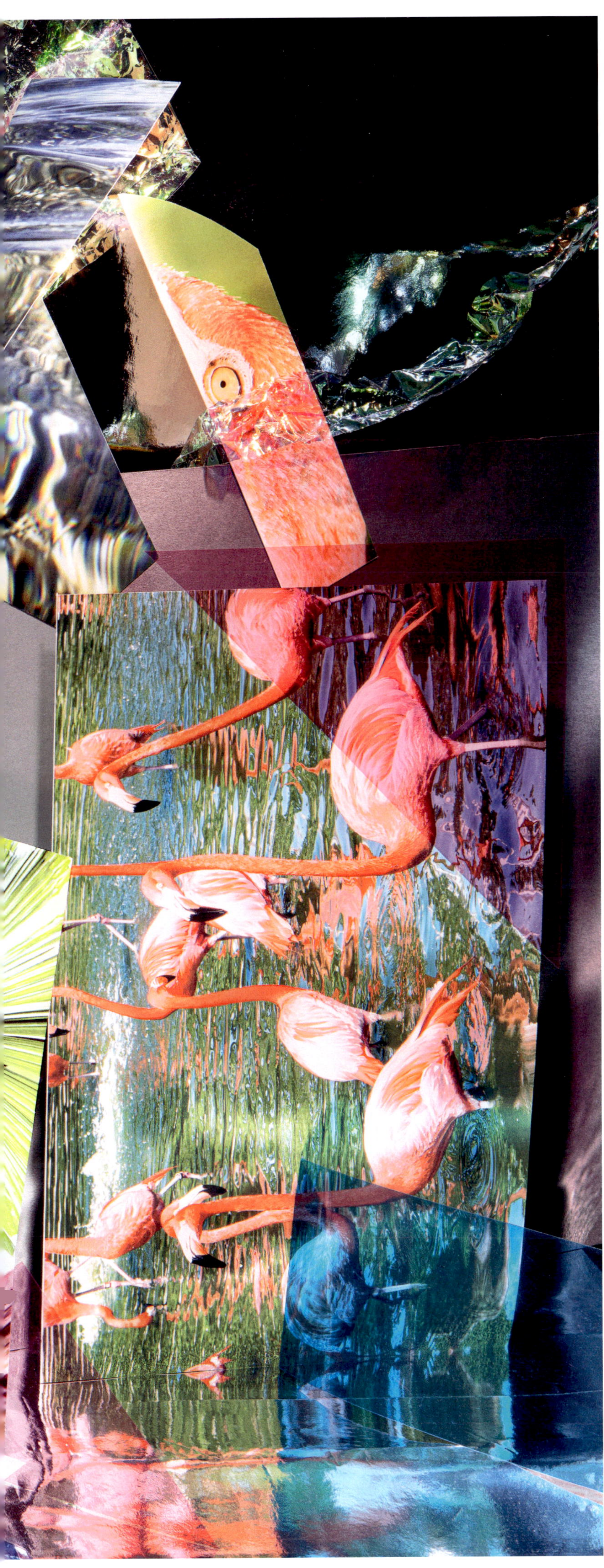

Mangroves, 2017

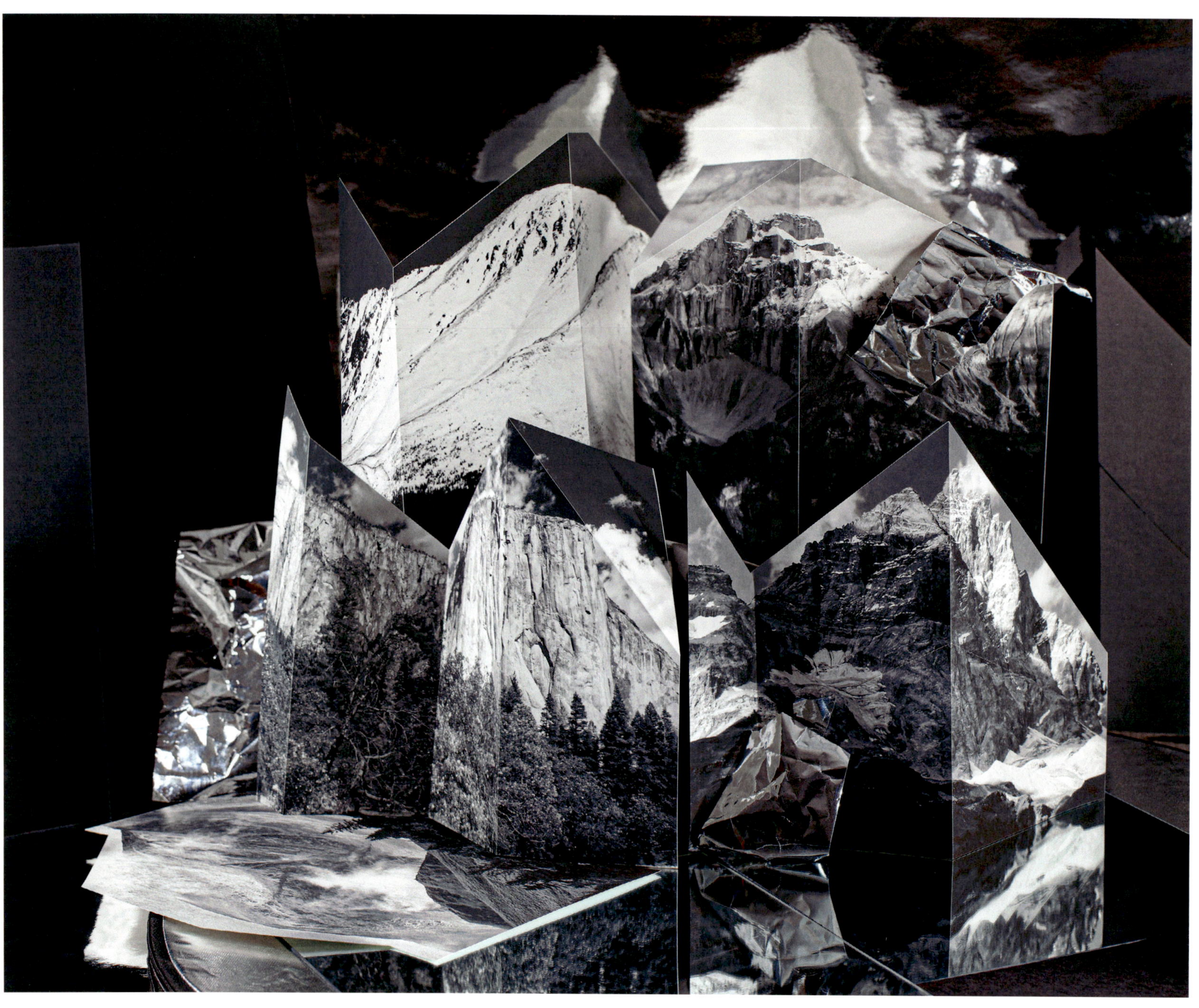

Black and White Mountains, 2015

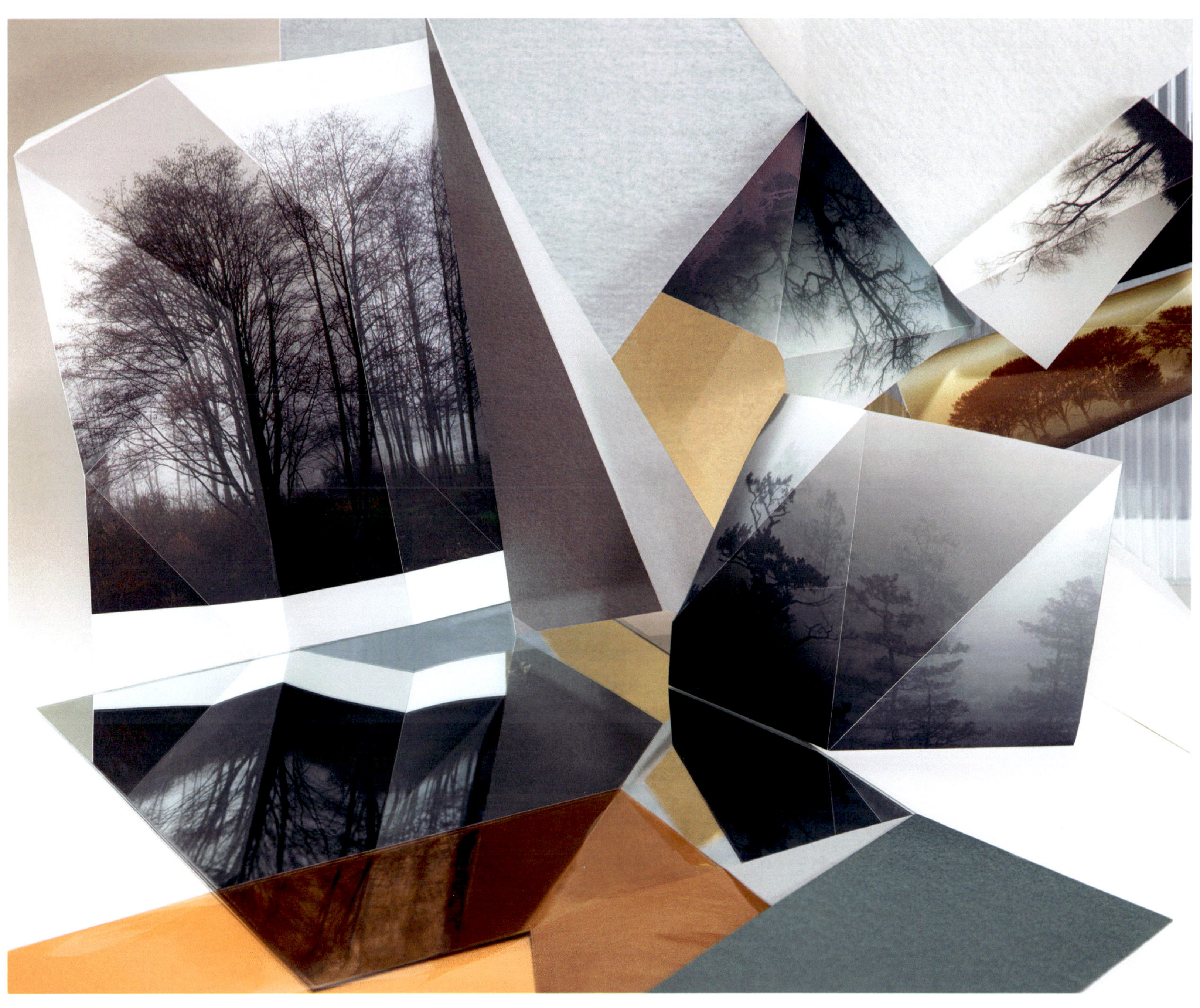

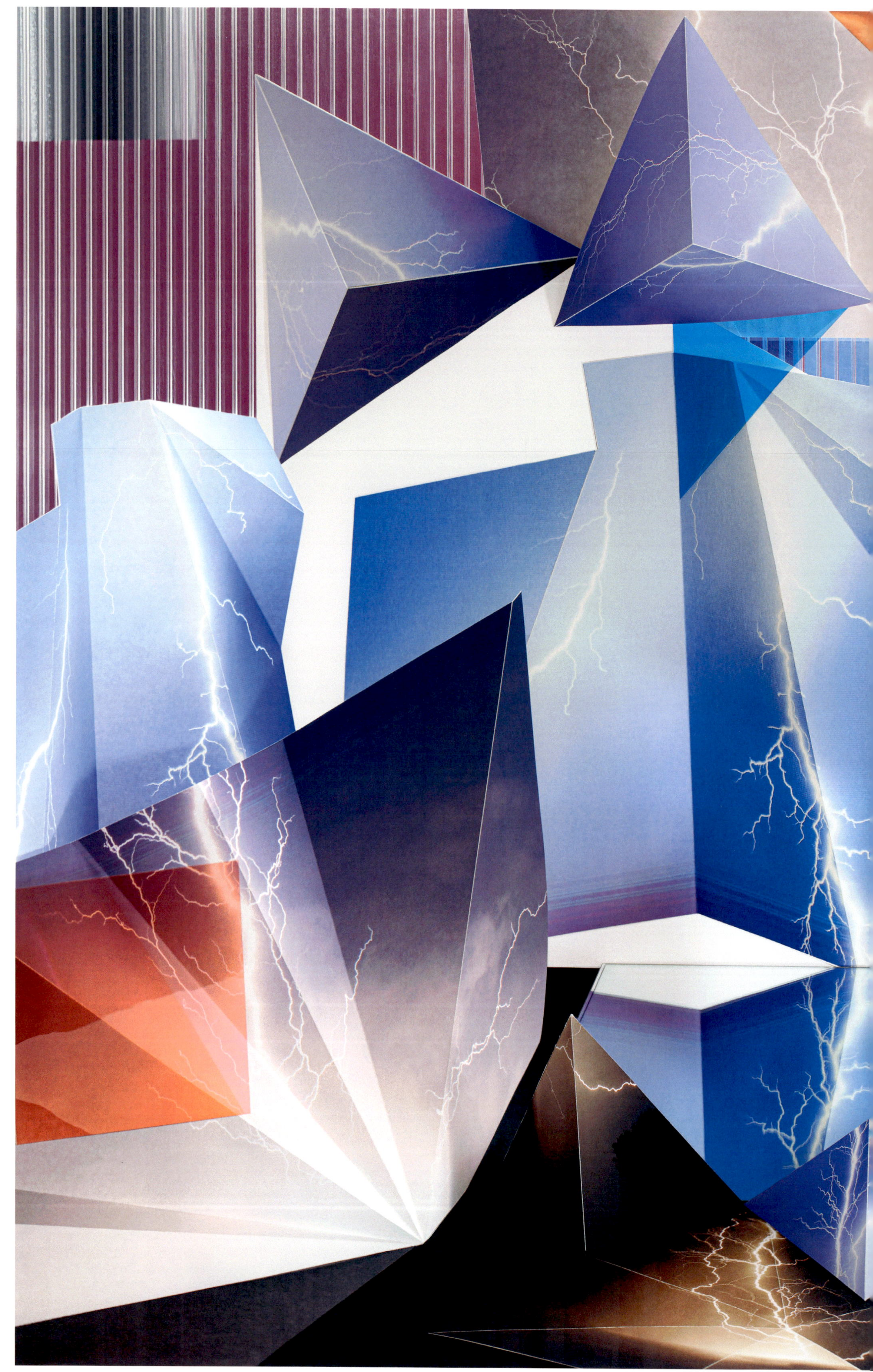

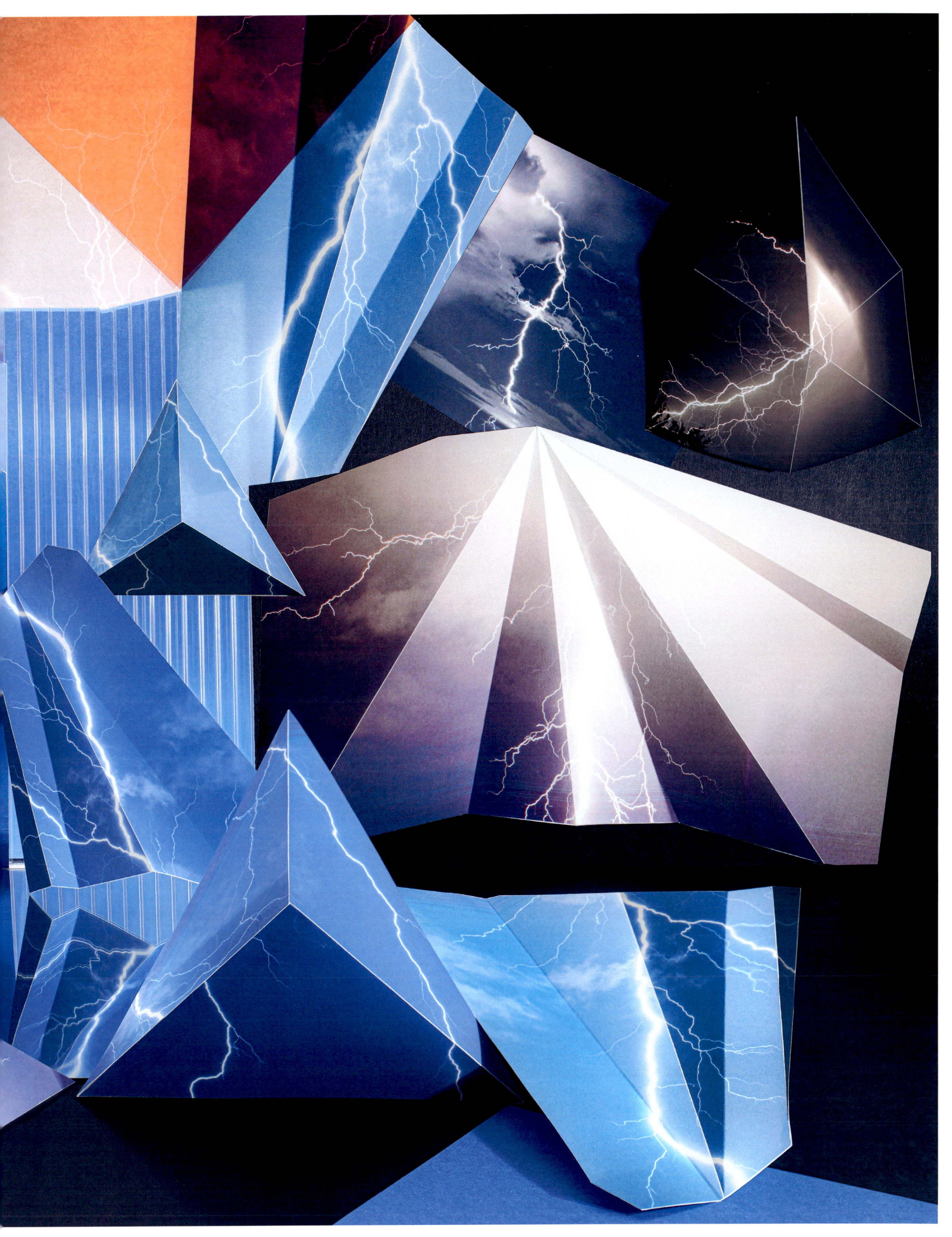

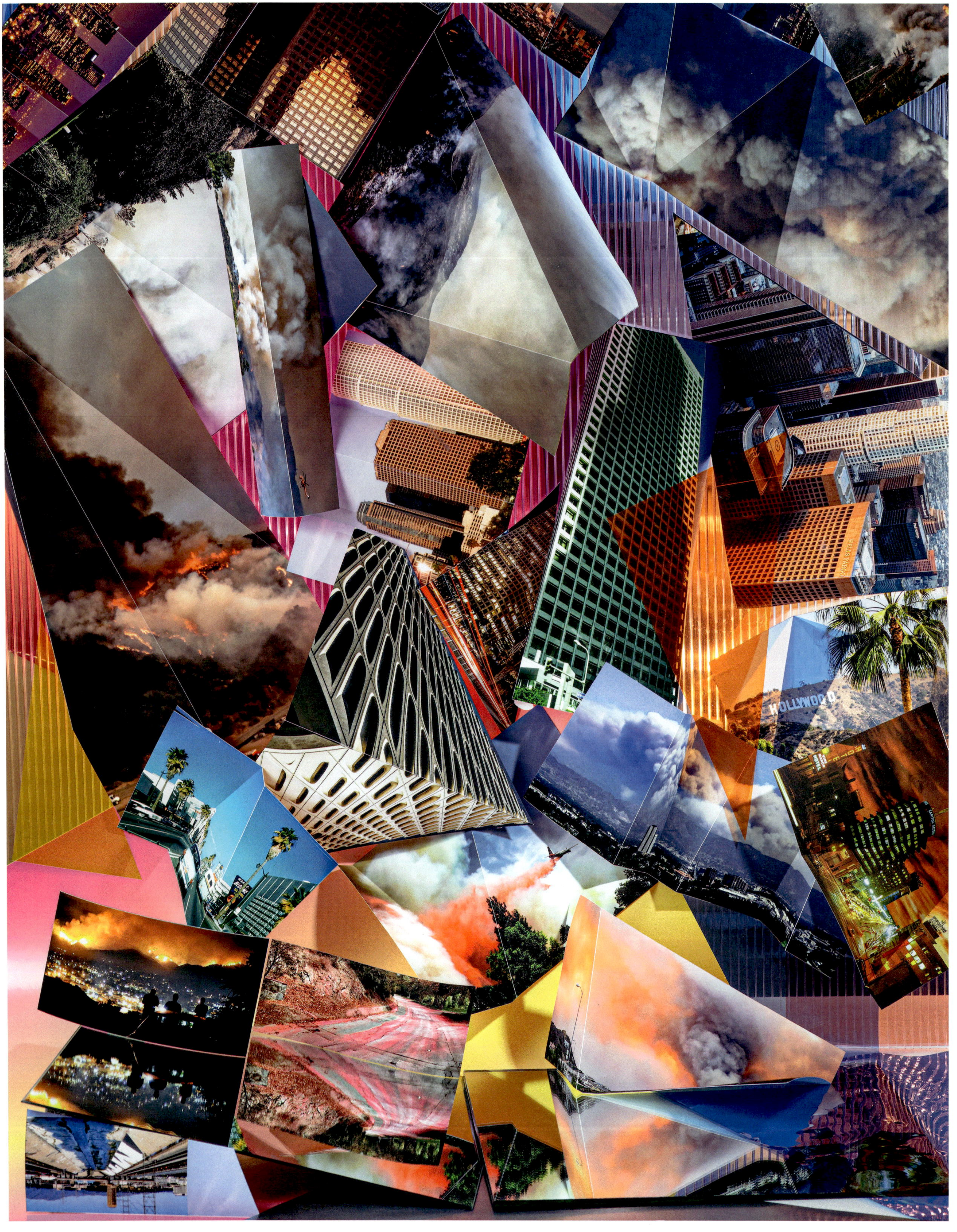

LA (On Fire), 2020

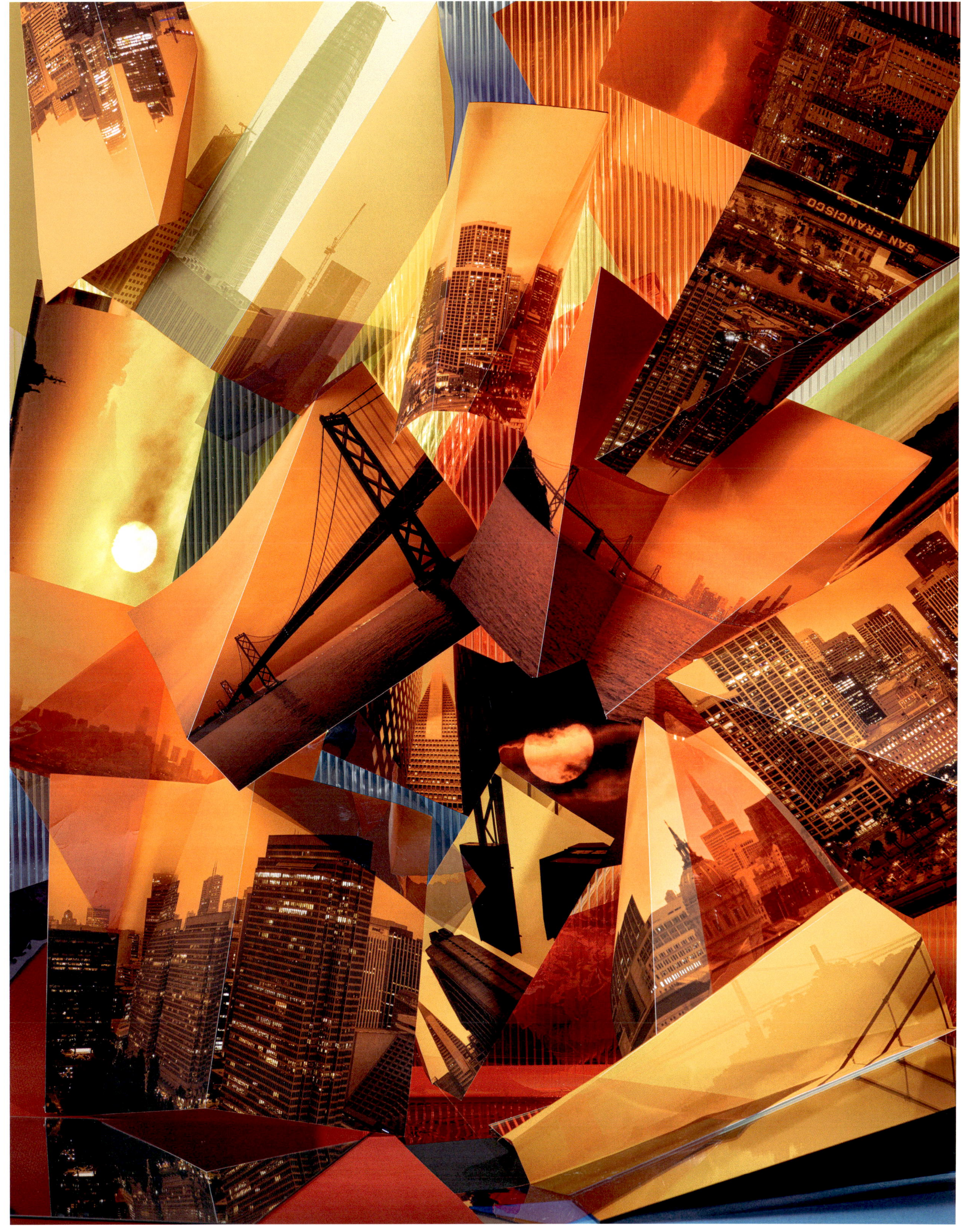

San Francisco Skies, 2020

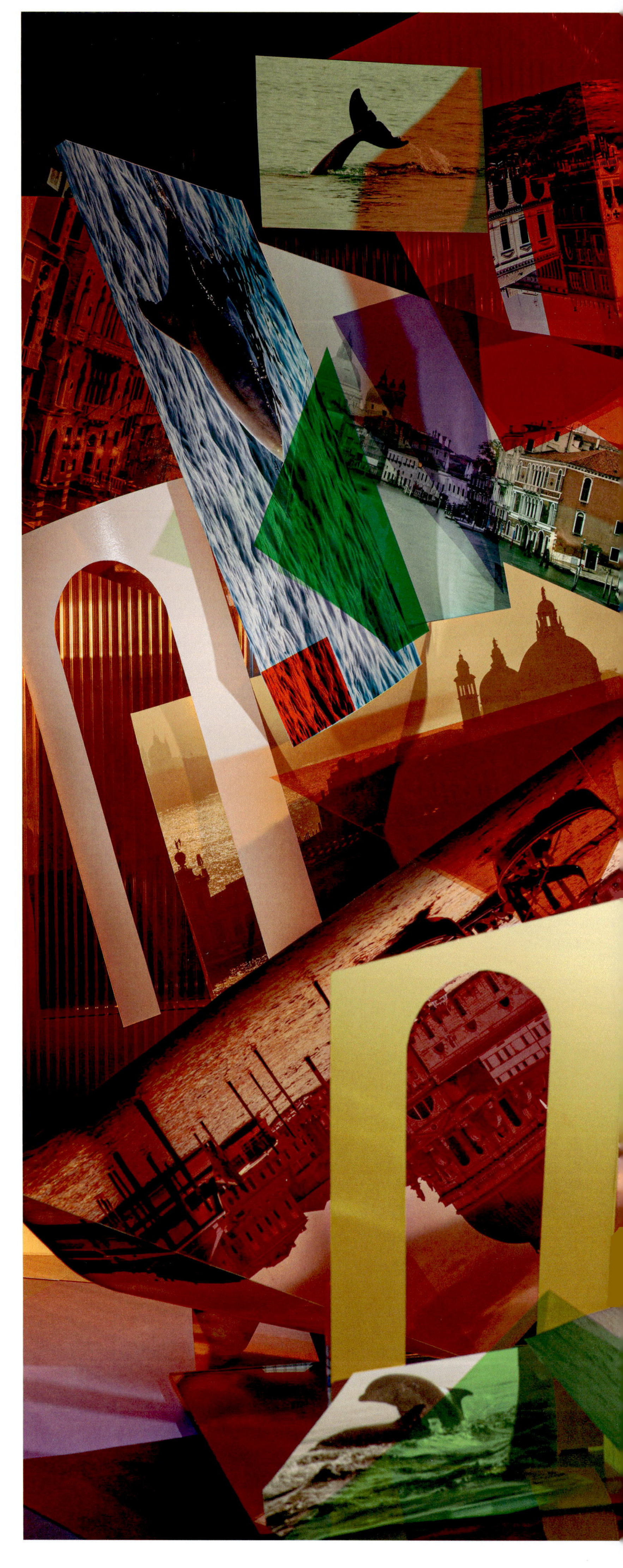

Dolphins in Venice, 2021

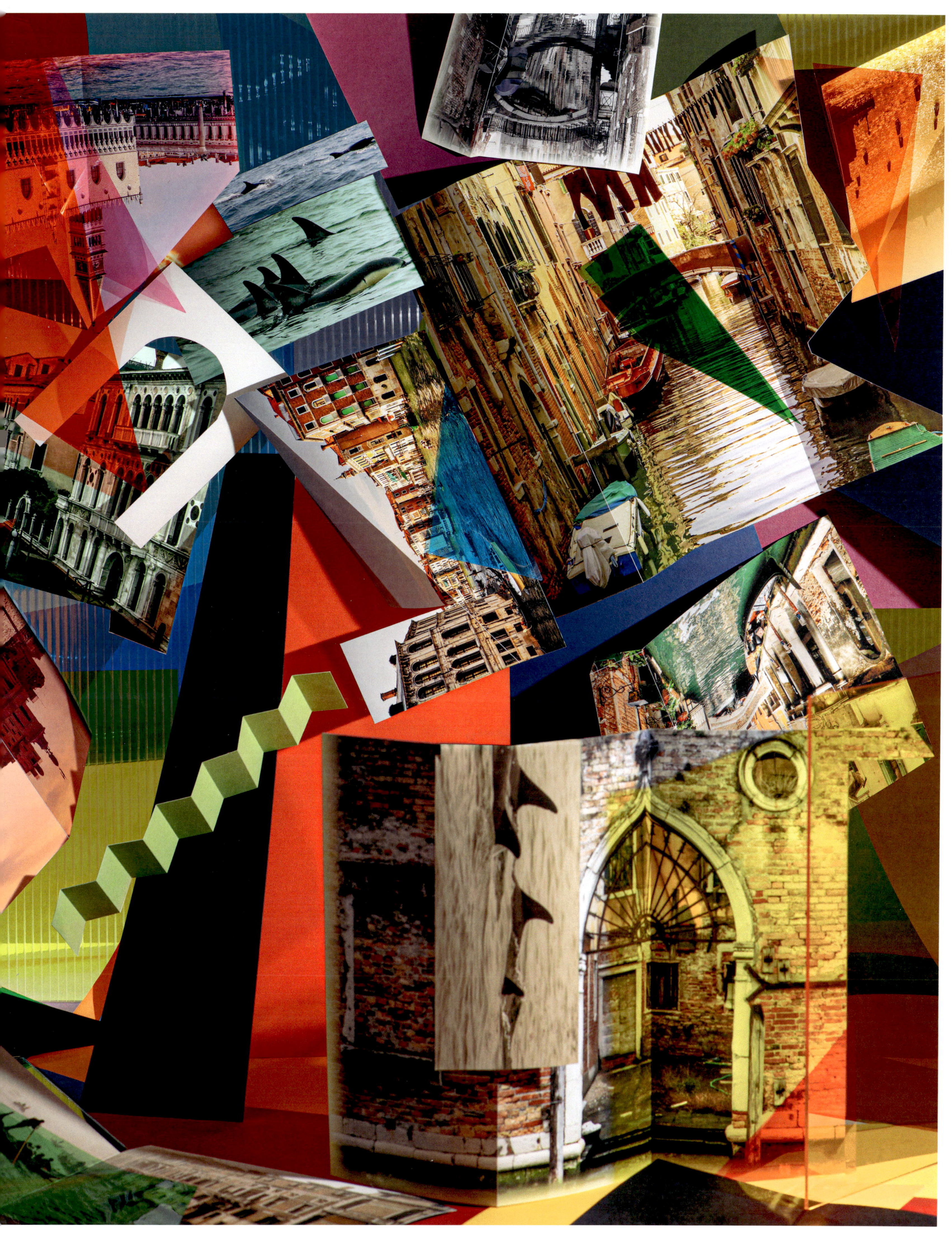

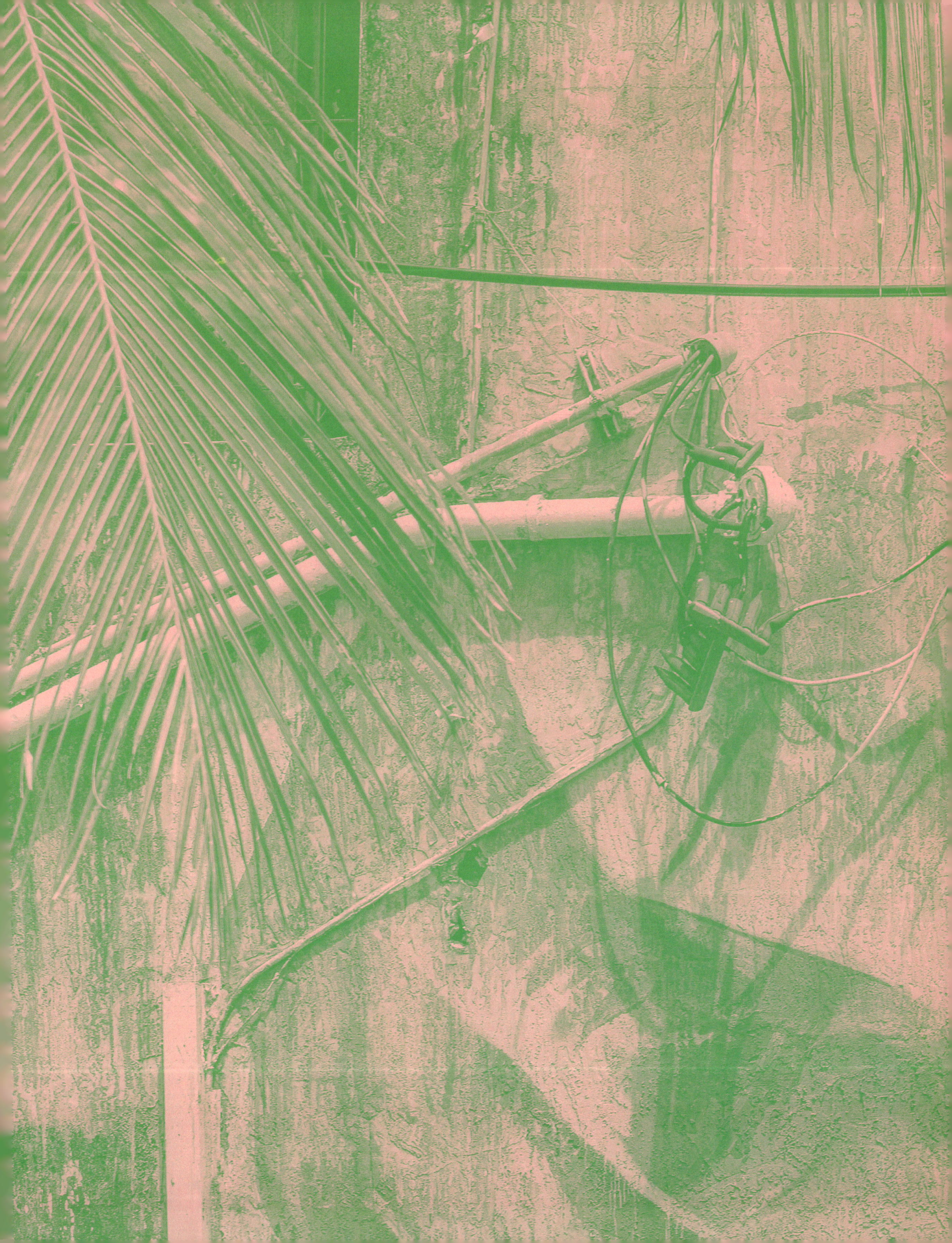

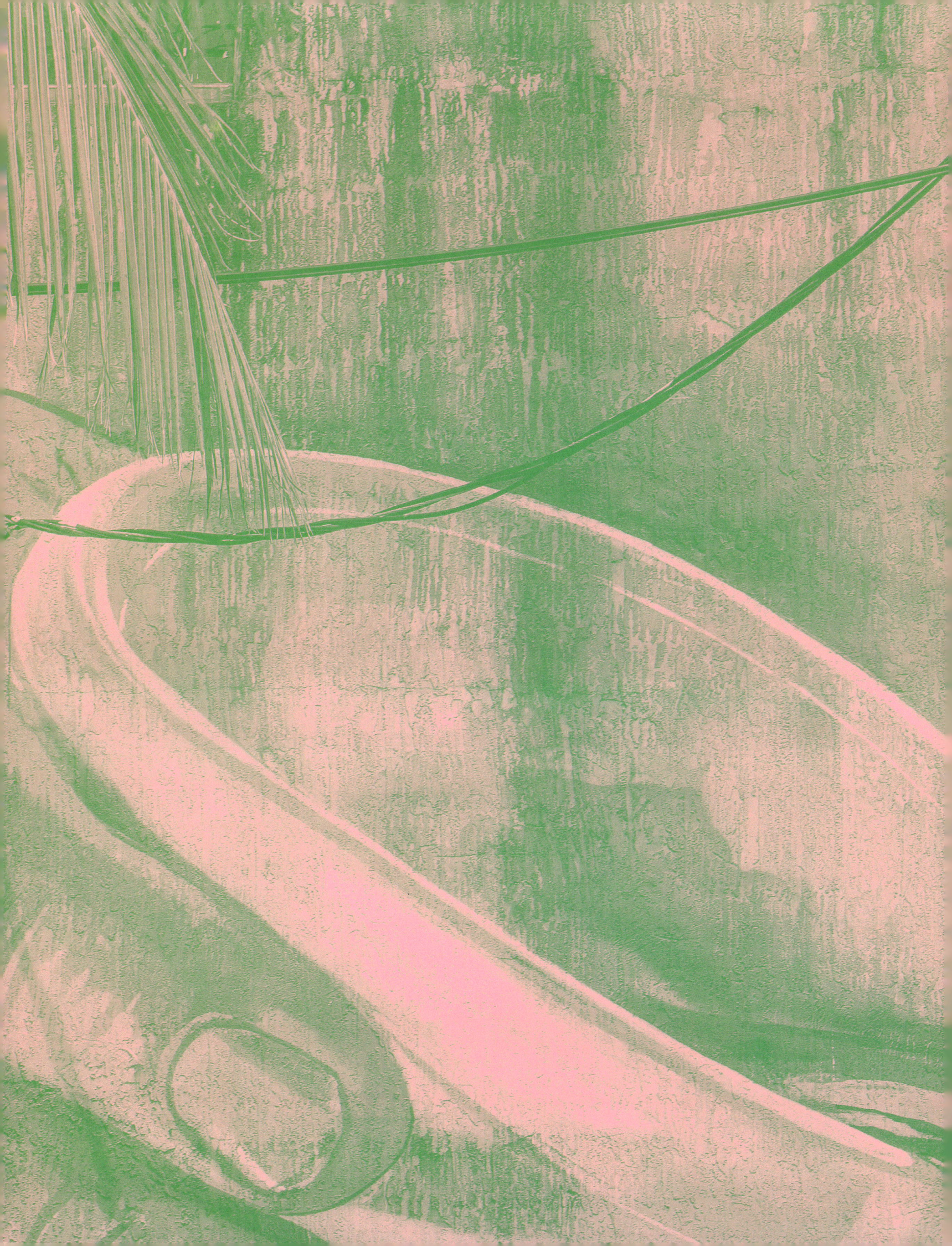

In 2016, Samoylova moved to Miami Beach on Florida's southeast coast. That summer, the city registered record high temperatures. Few places are more closely identified with 'the good life', but South Florida is a troubled paradise. Rising sea levels turn the limited fresh water salty and flood the foundations of a rampant real-estate boom. Gentrification pushes poorer communities aside. Culture wars rage and political debate is polarized. Through it all, the tropical flora and fauna threaten to return the region to swampland.

In August 2017, Hurricane Irma devastated parts of the Caribbean and southern United States, especially Florida. Samoylova witnessed it first hand, and saw how the mass media reported it with over-familiar visuals: storm-tossed streets, upturned cars and homes torn open. With the loose idea to gather imagery for her studio collages, she ventured into the aftermath with her camera, but realized this world was itself a kind of collage, of cognitive dissonance. The beauty of the region cannot dispel the gnawing unease that comes with life at the forefront of climate change. The glossy image promoted by tourism and advertising grows further and further from daily realities.

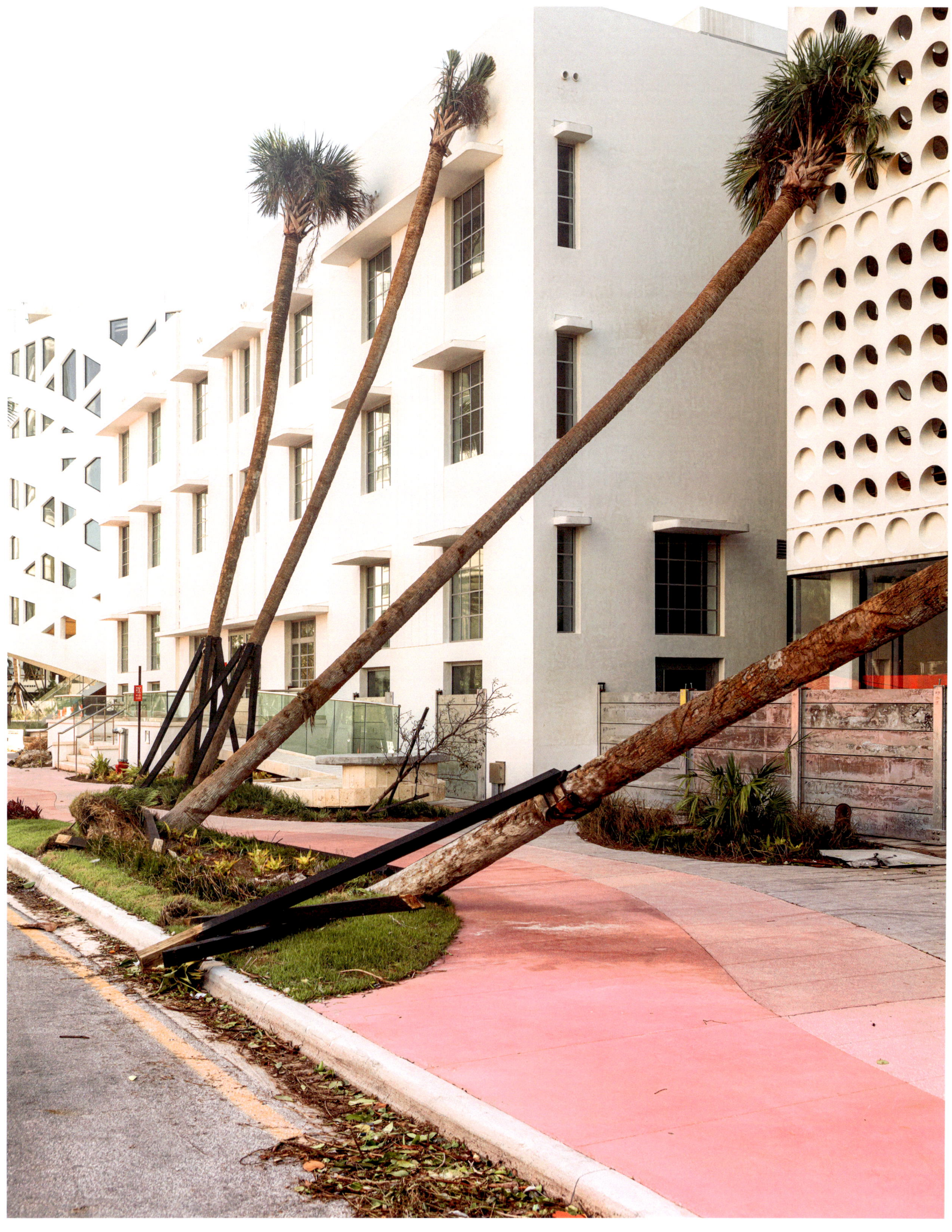

Pink Sidewalk, 2017

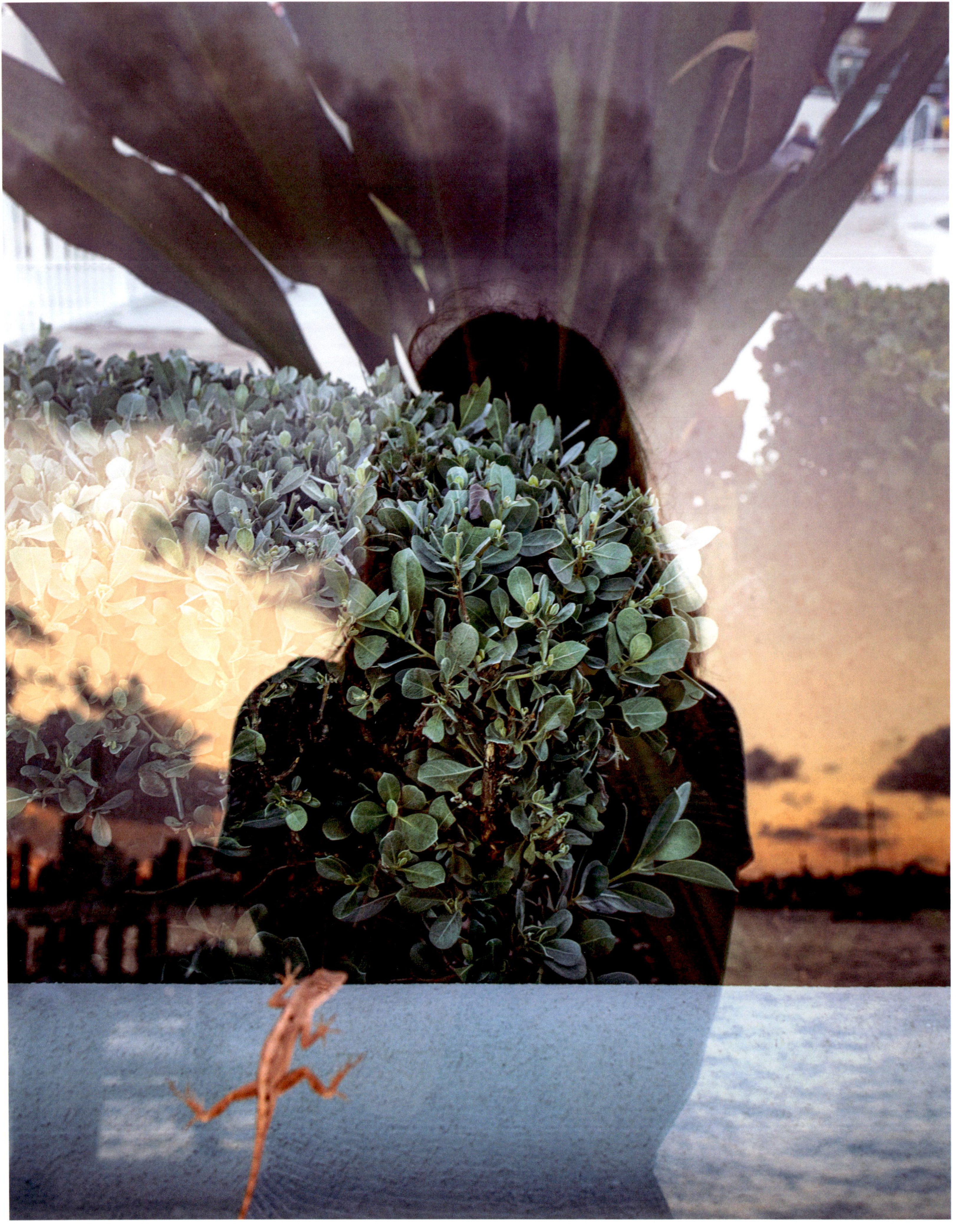

Biscayne Bay, 2018

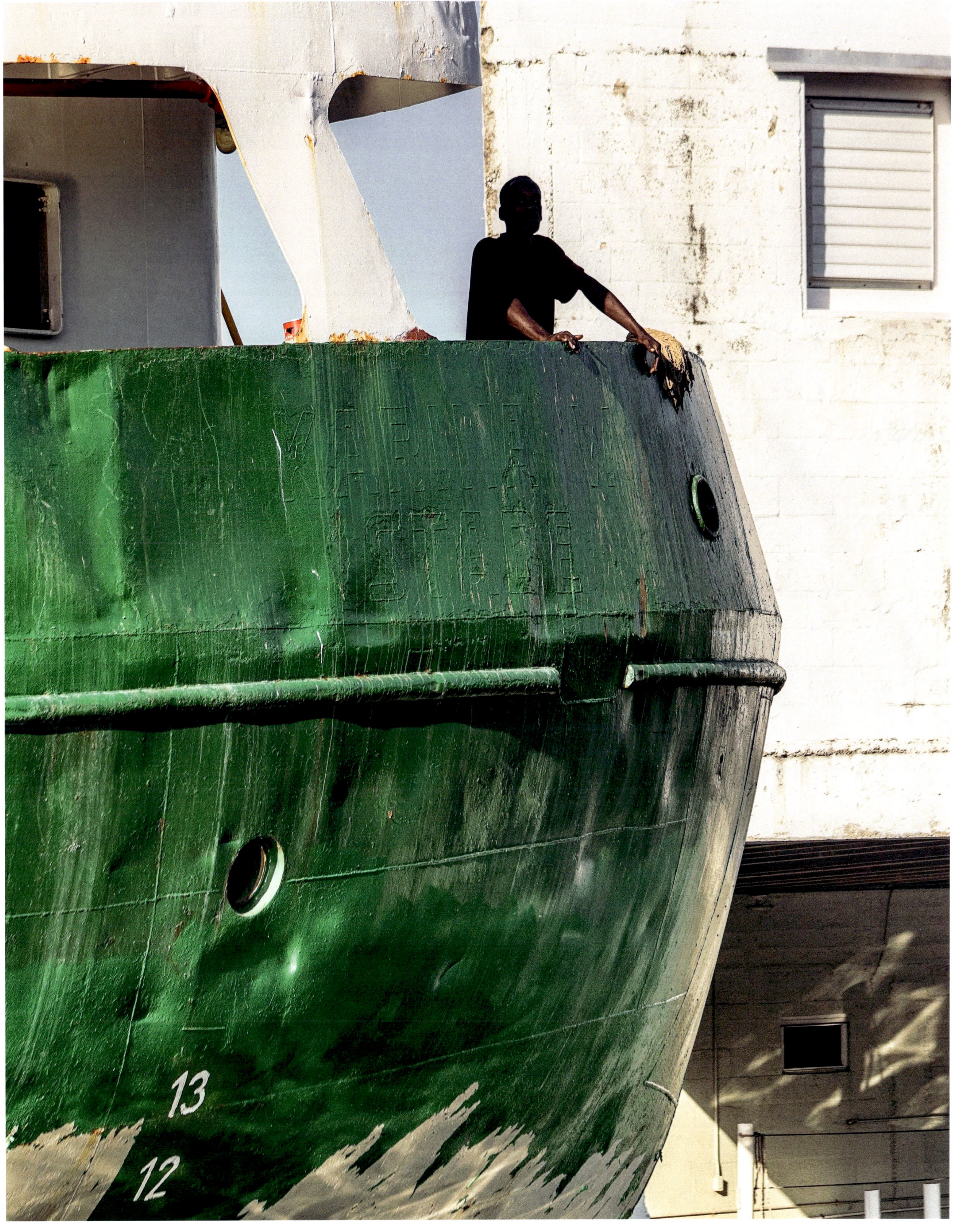

Miami River, 2018

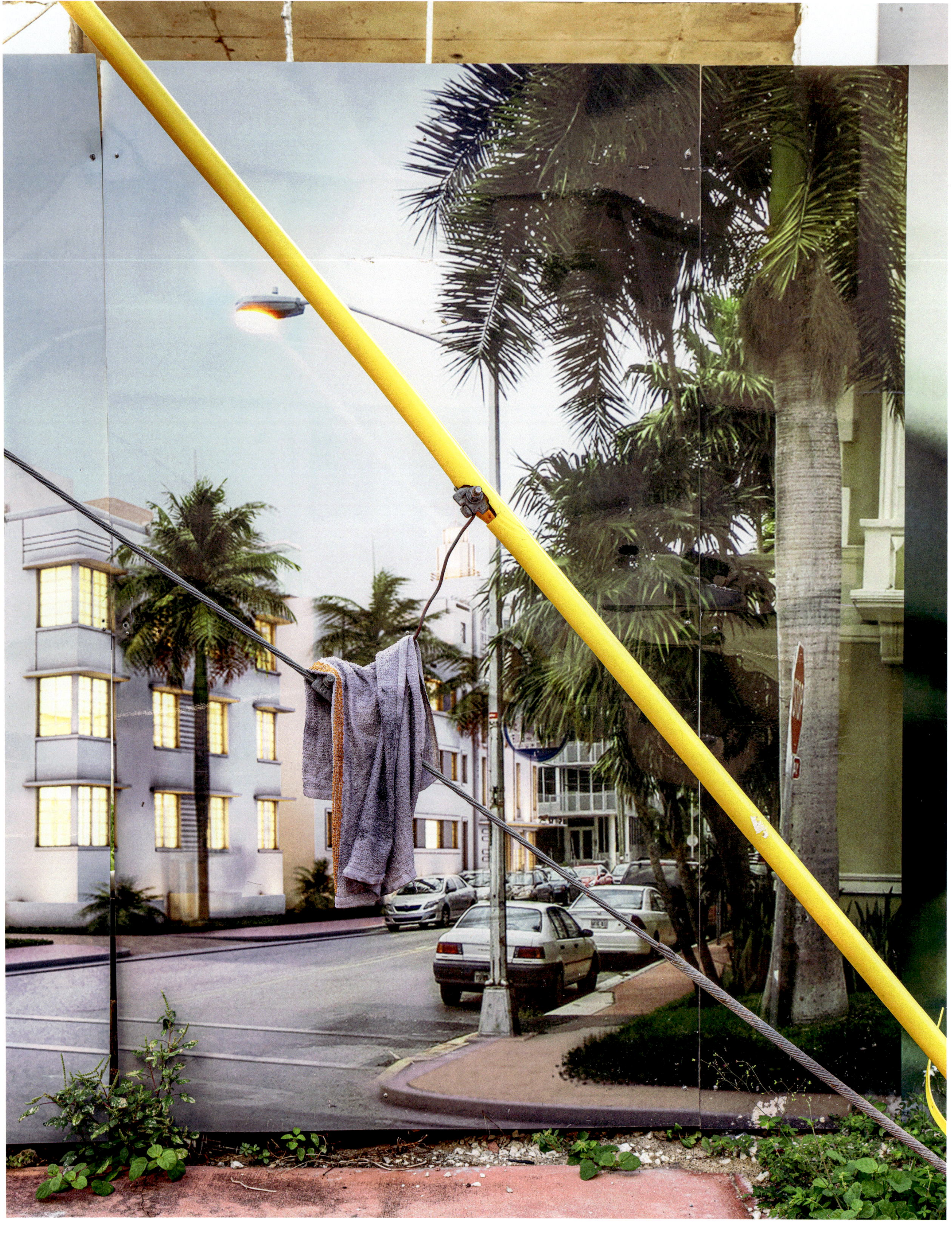

Construction in South Beach III, 2018

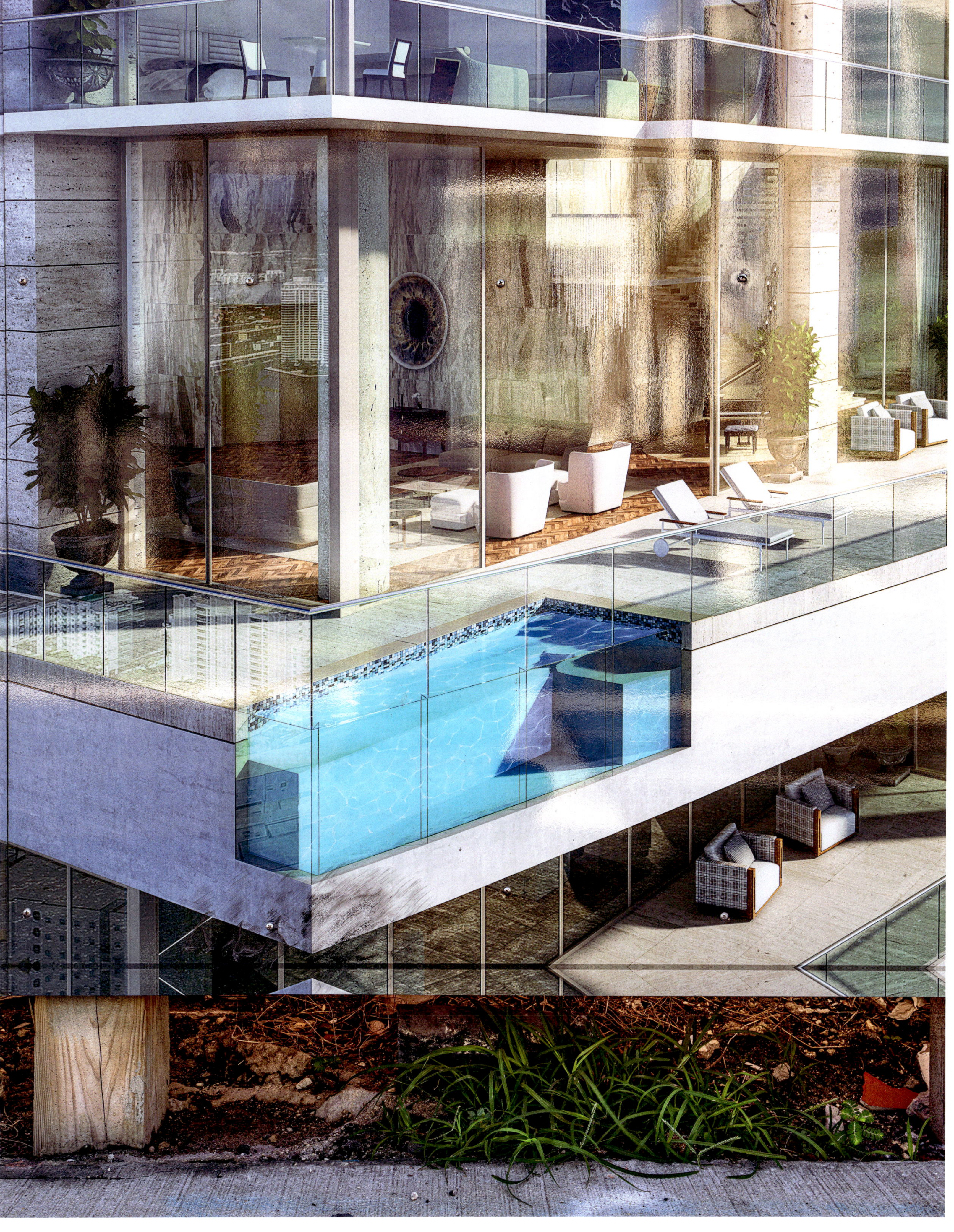

Construction in Sunny Isles, 2019 ›› Waterfront Houses, 2018

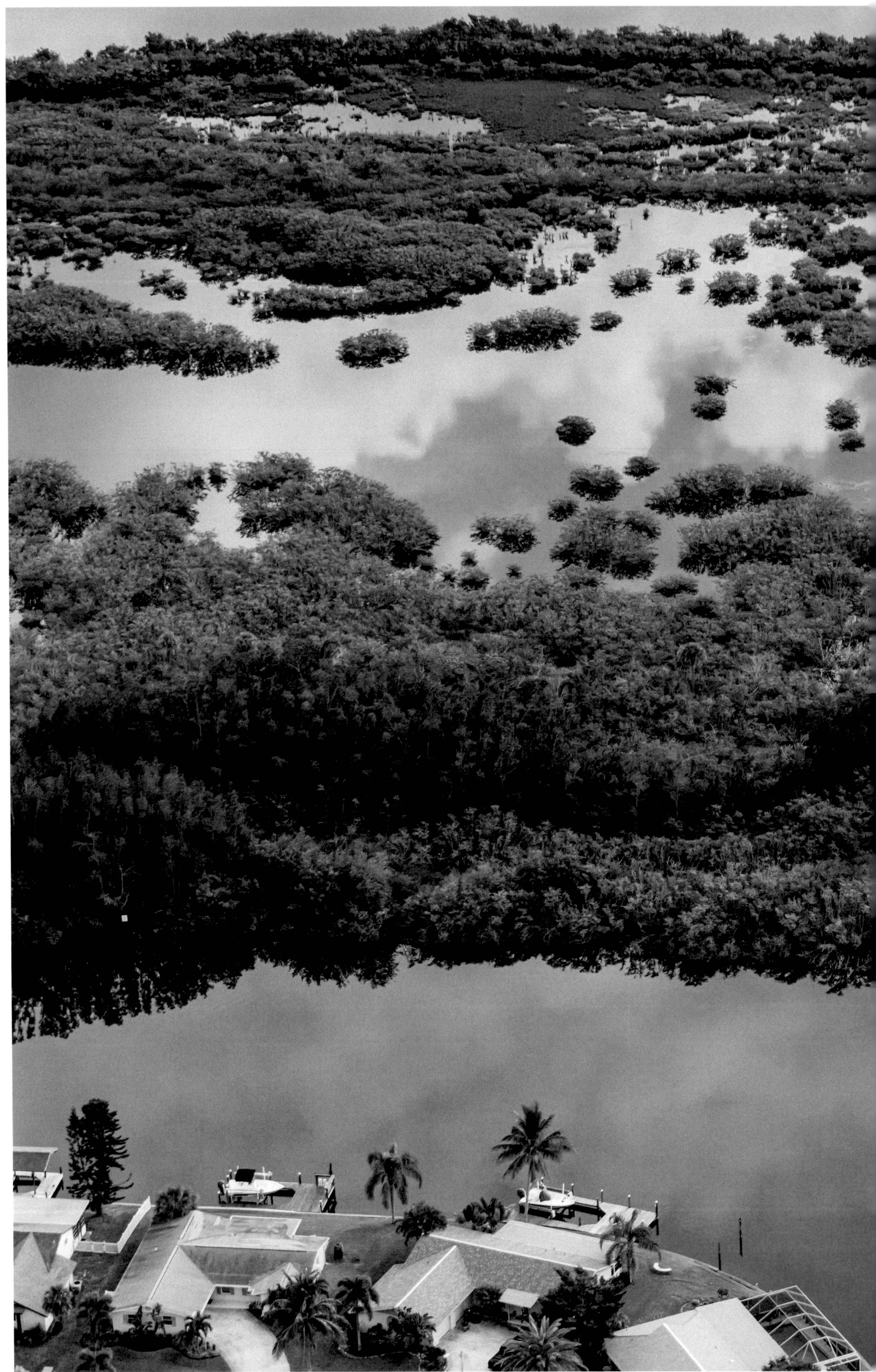

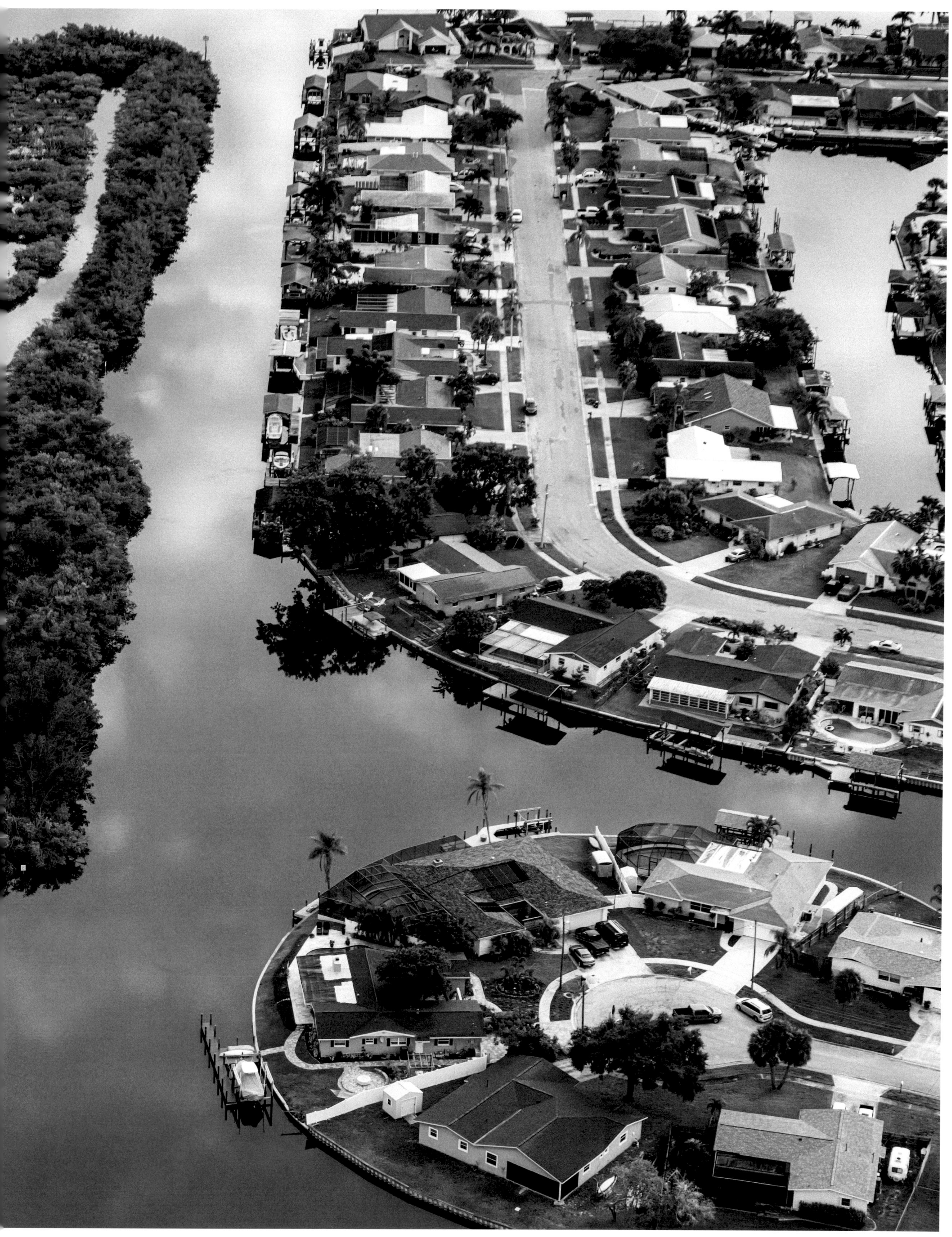

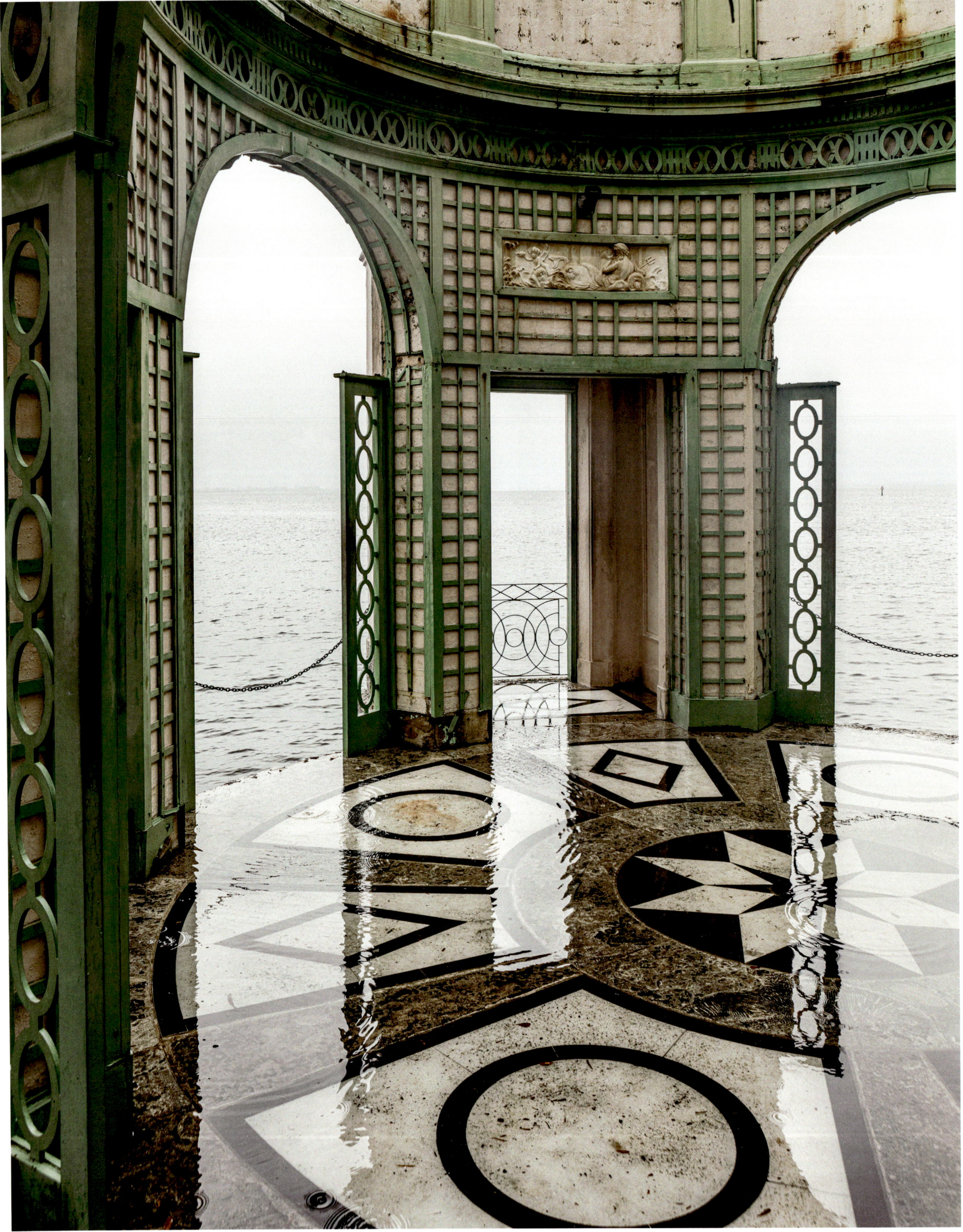

The Tea Room, Vizcaya, 2018

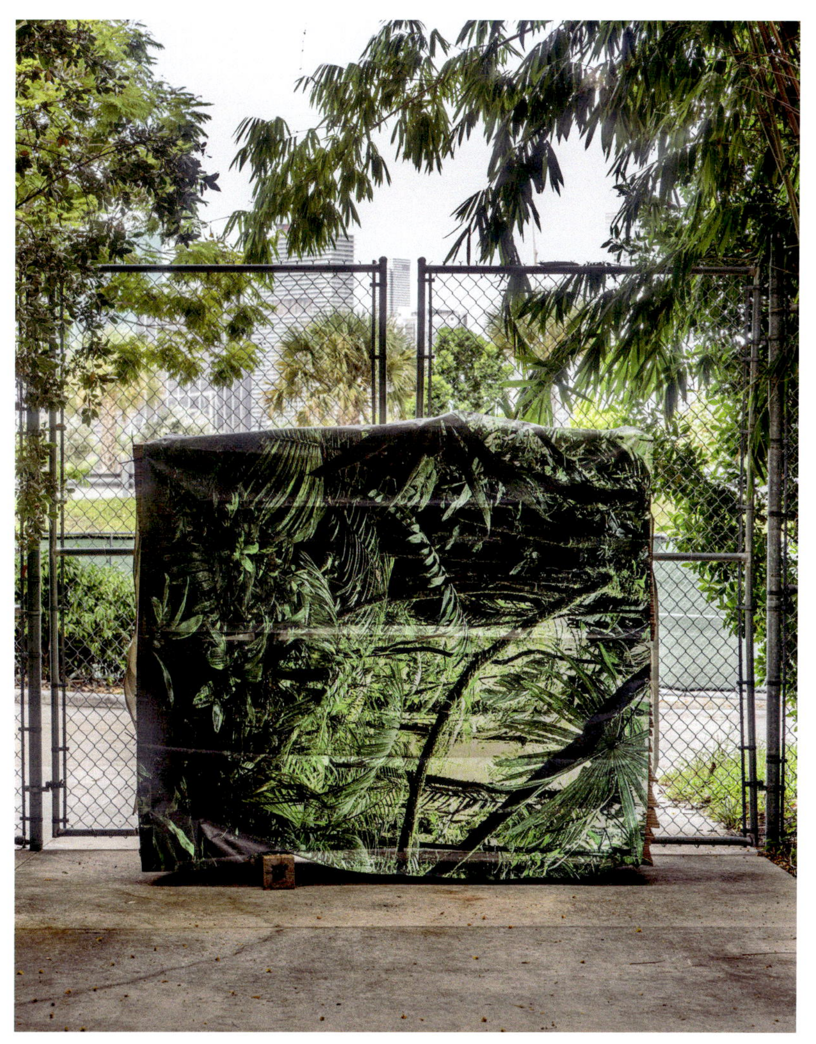

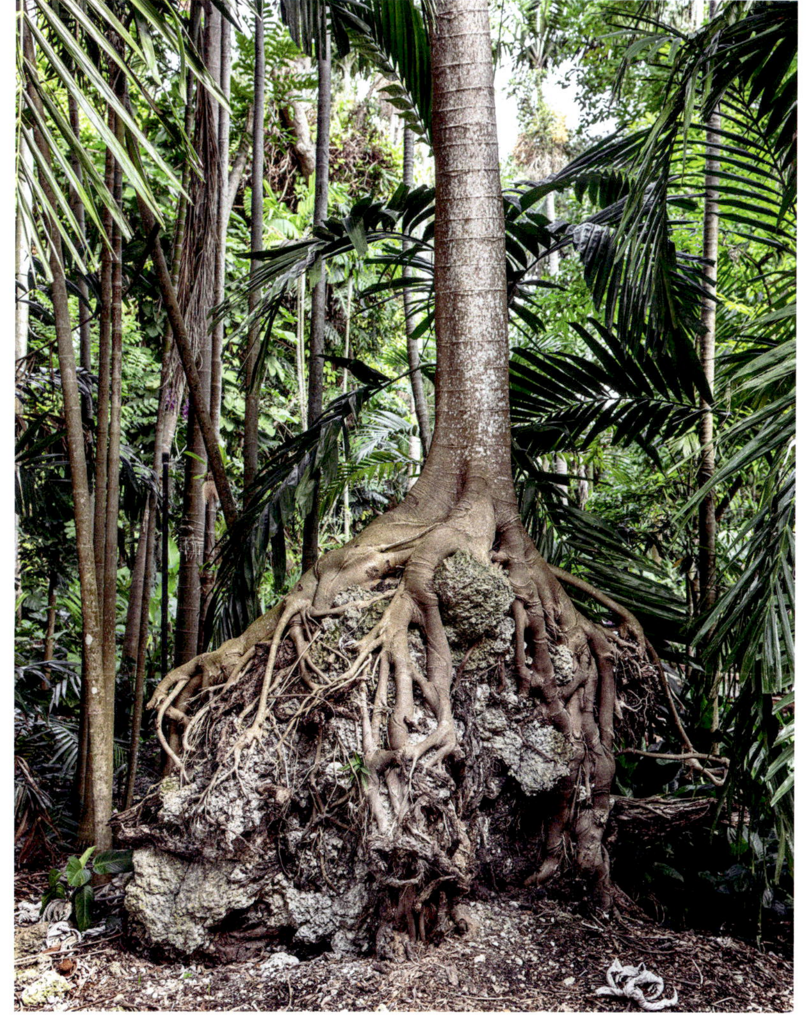

⌃ Camouflage, 2017 ⌄ Roots, 2018

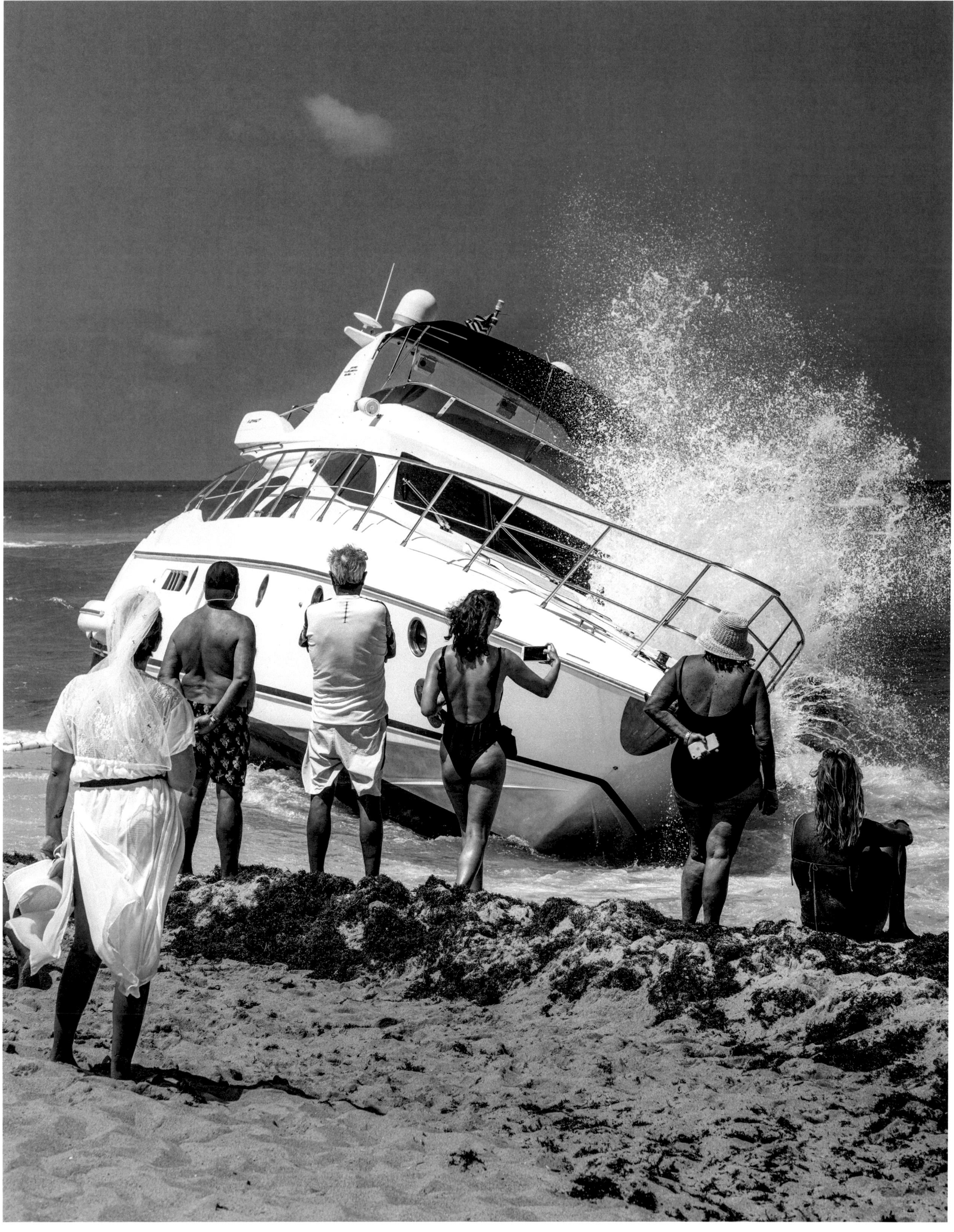

Beached Boat, 2019

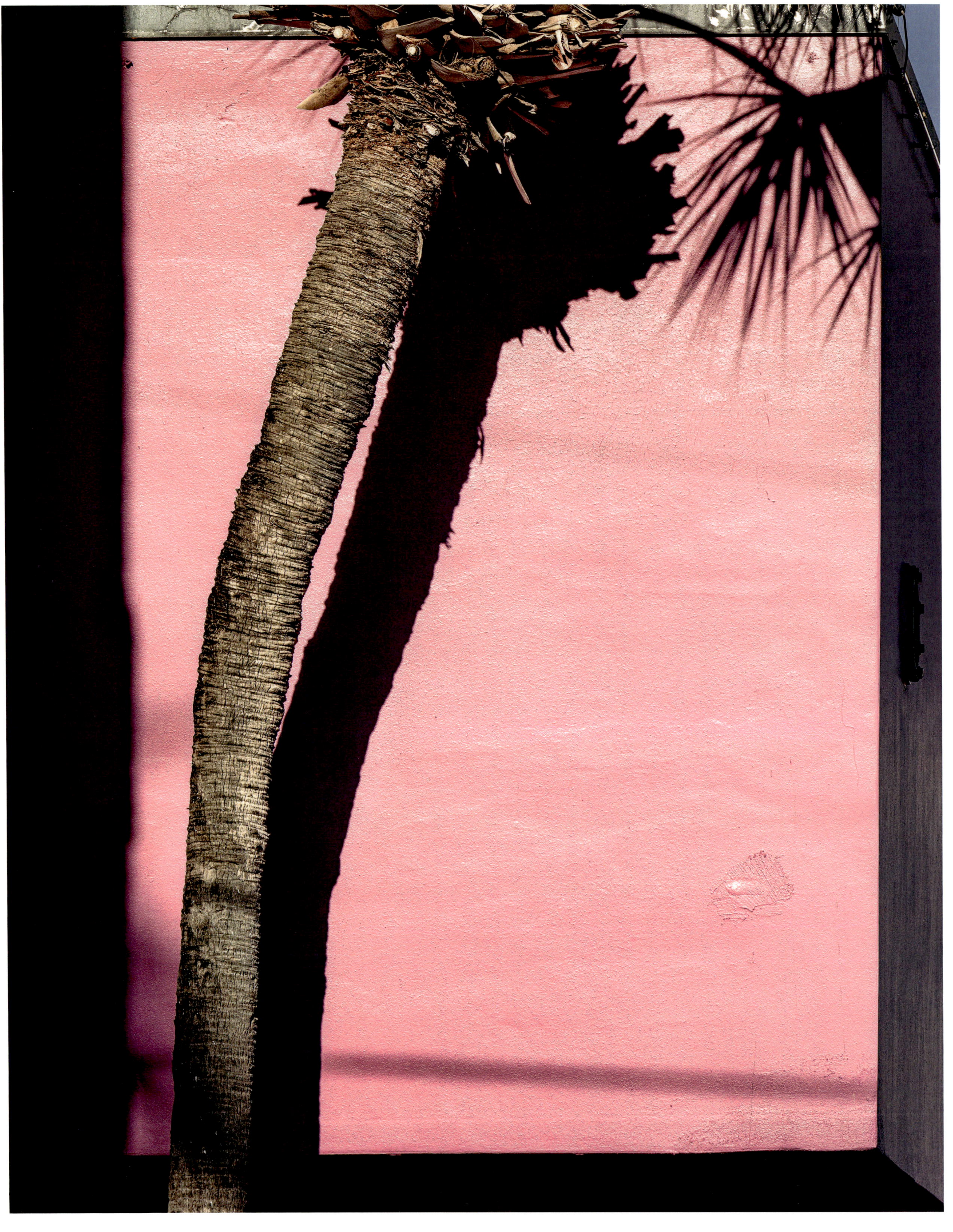

Miami Pink, 2019

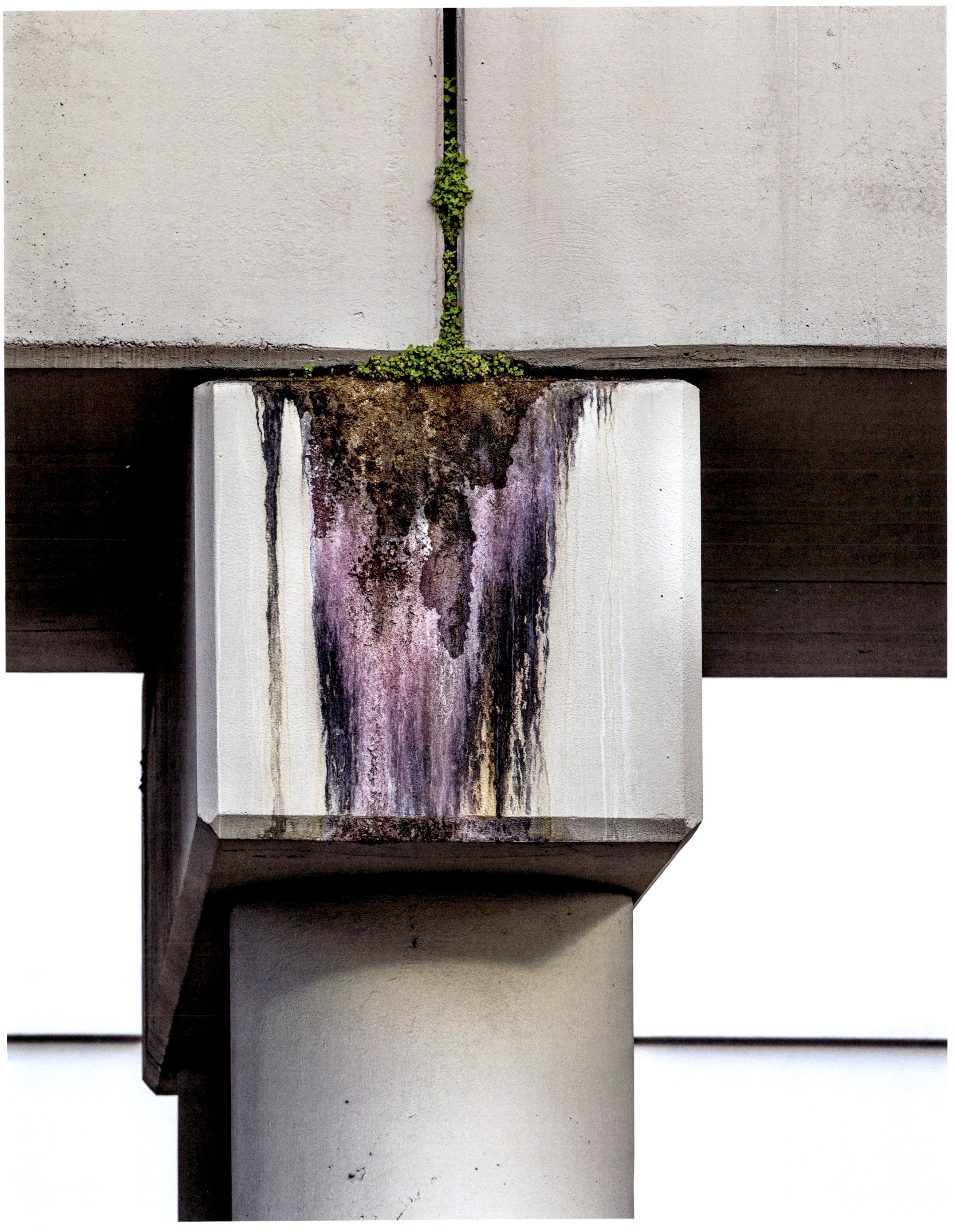

Concrete Erosion, 2019

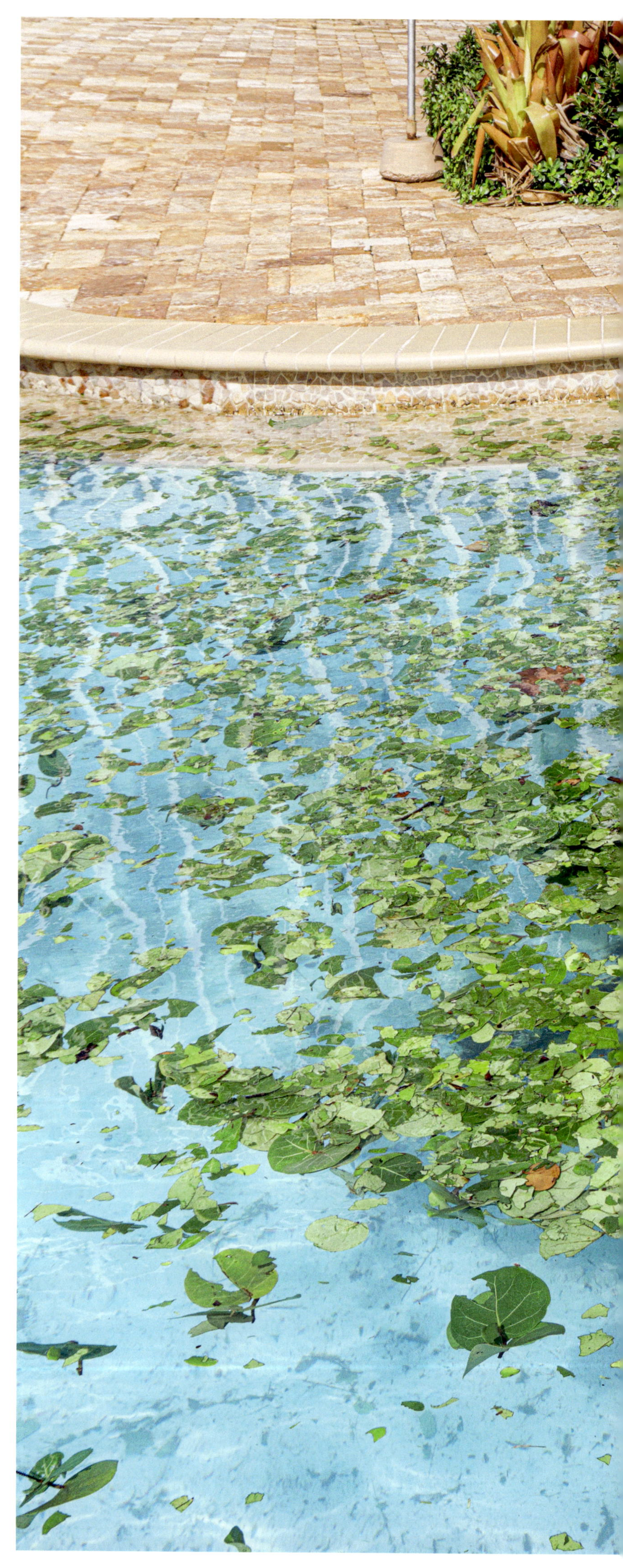

Pool after Hurricane, 2017

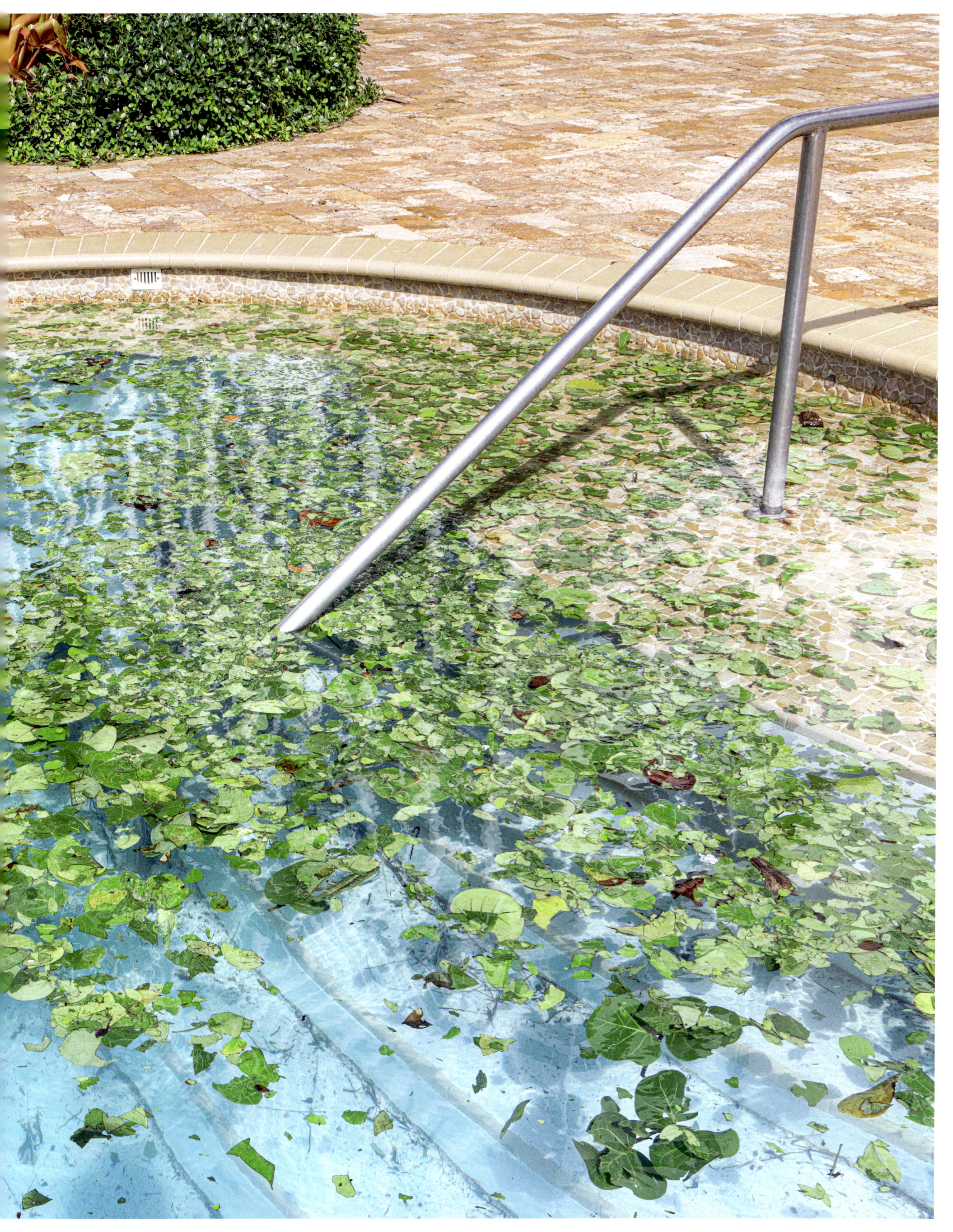

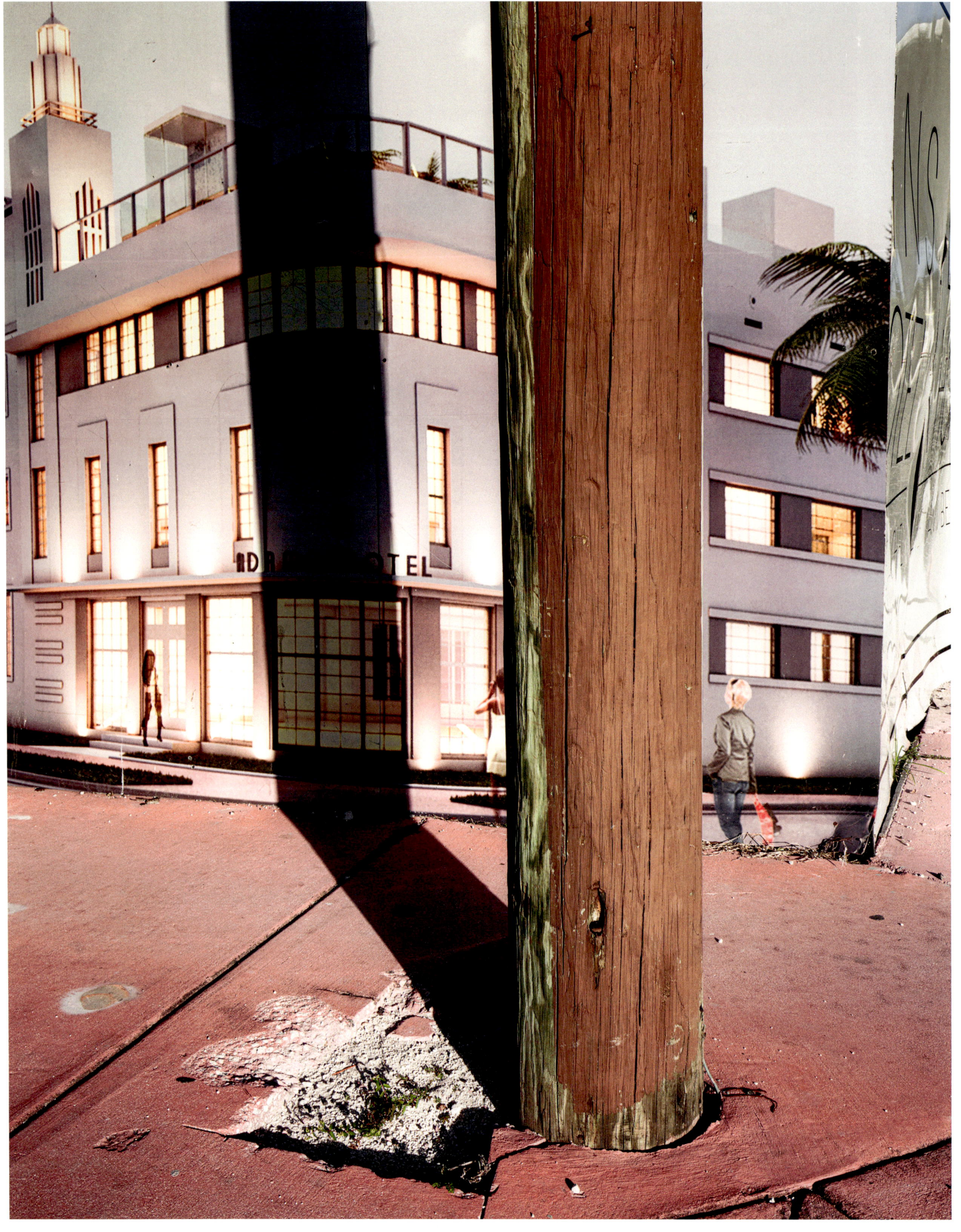

Park Avenue, 2018

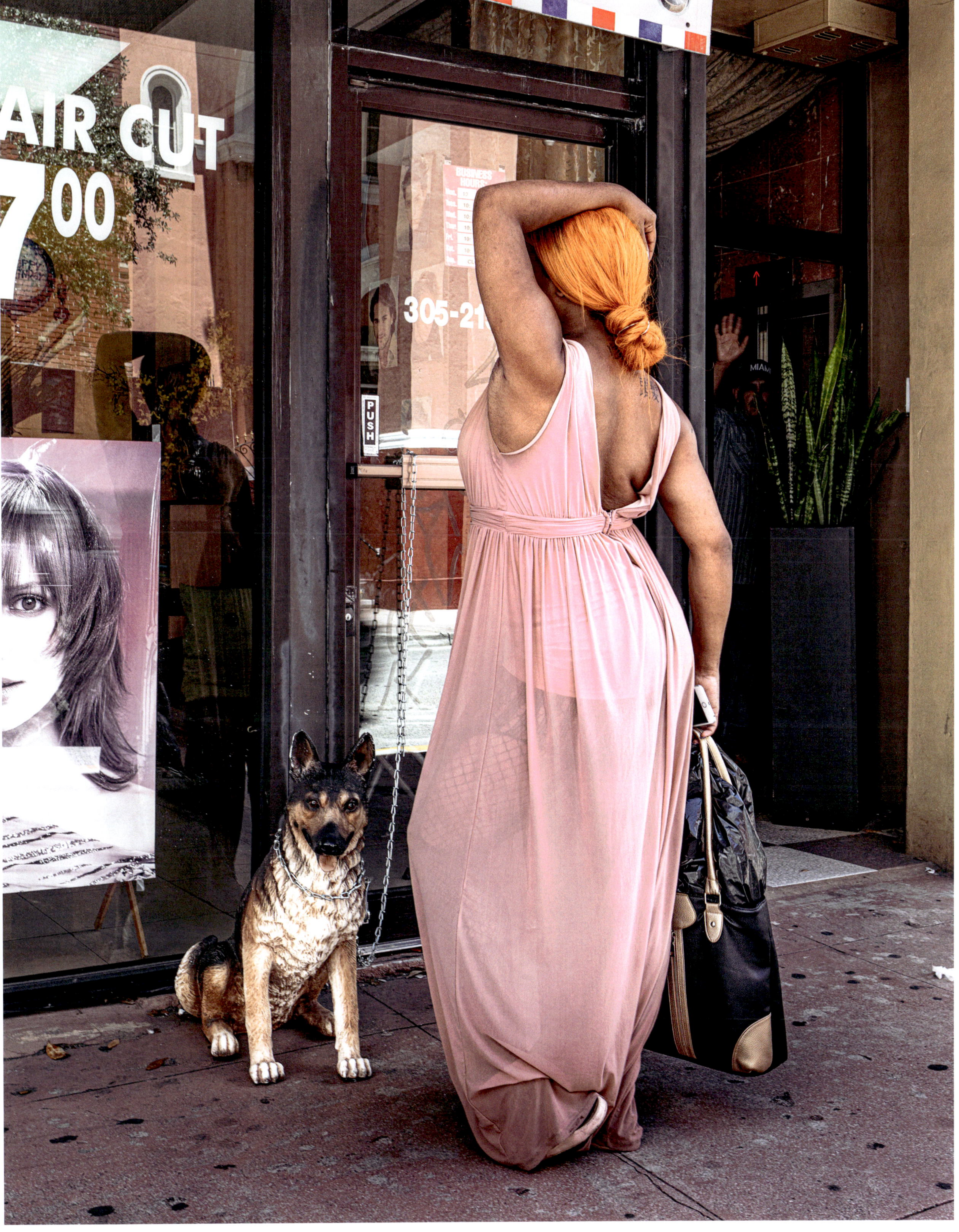

Barber Shop, 2018

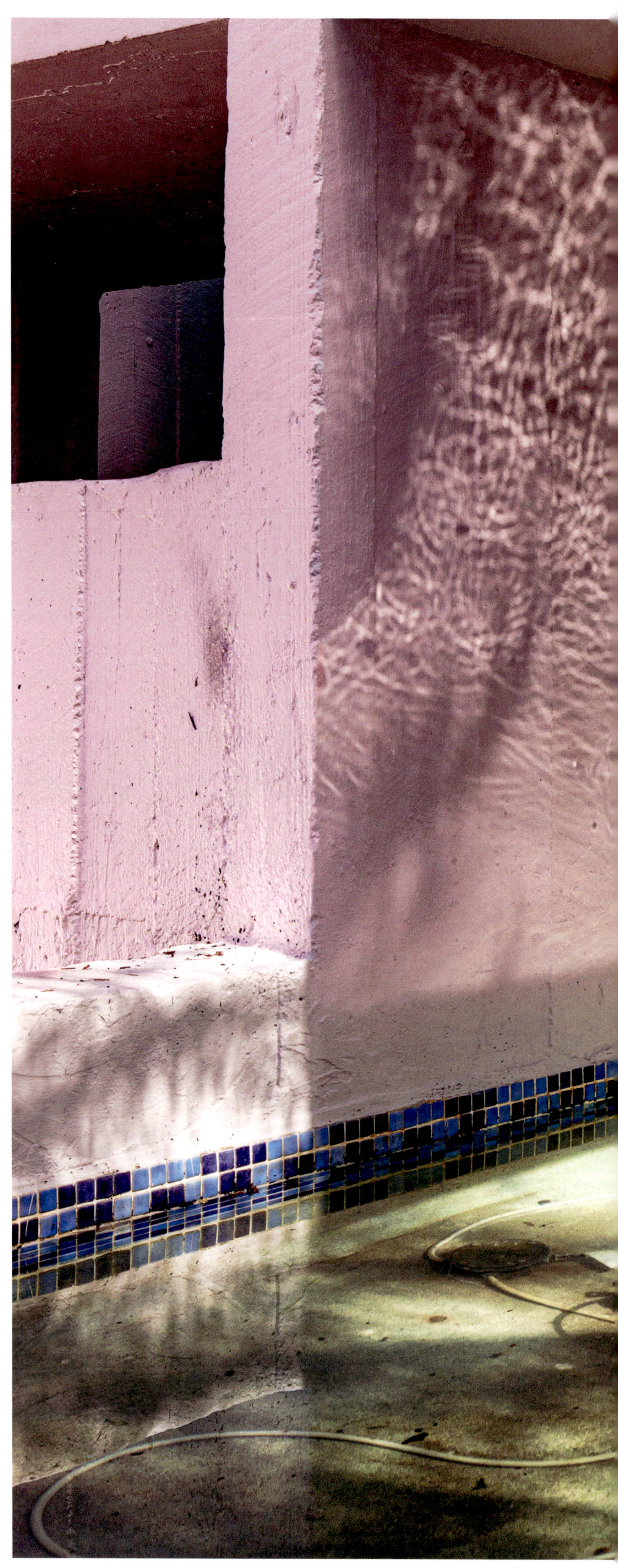

Fountain, 2017

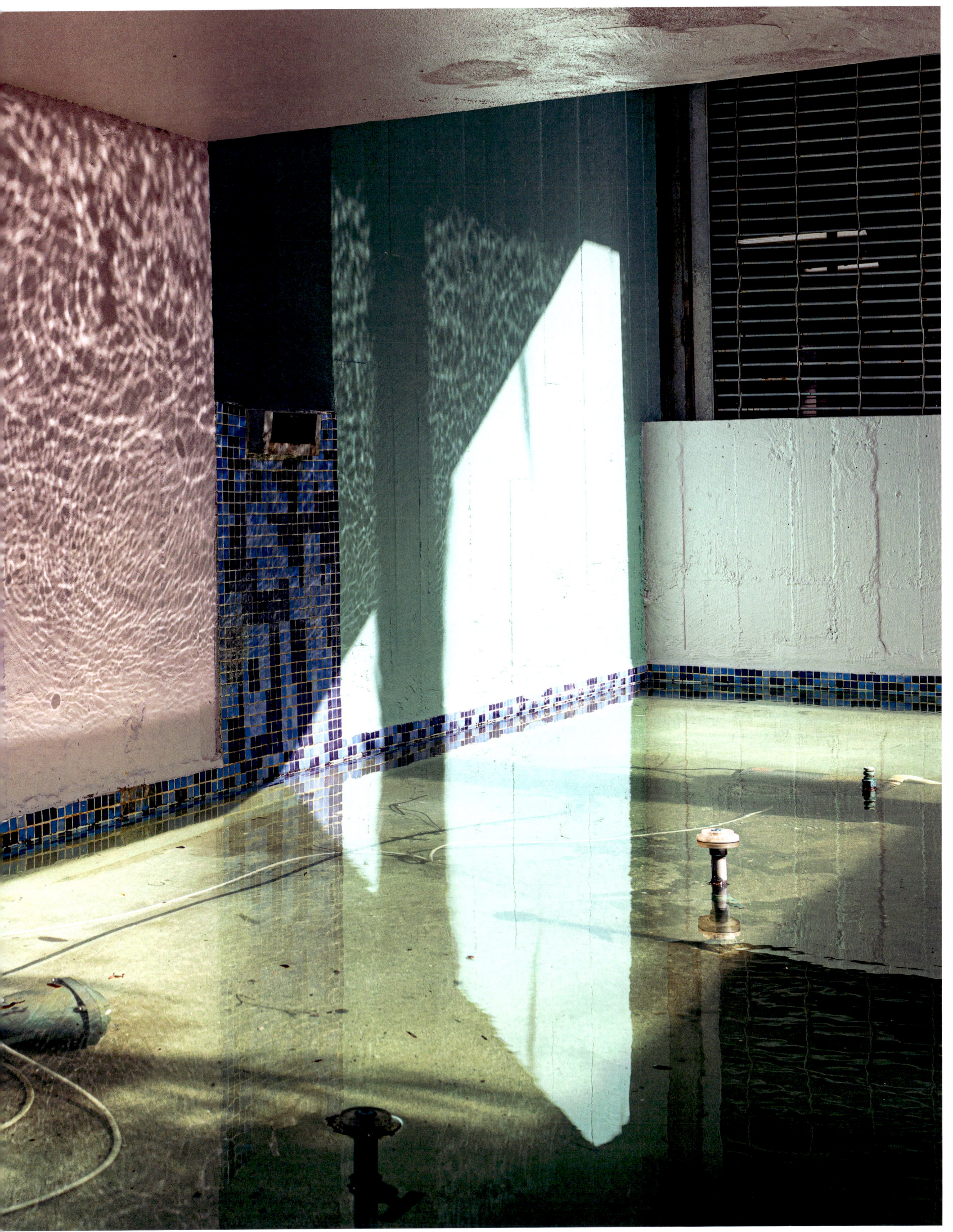

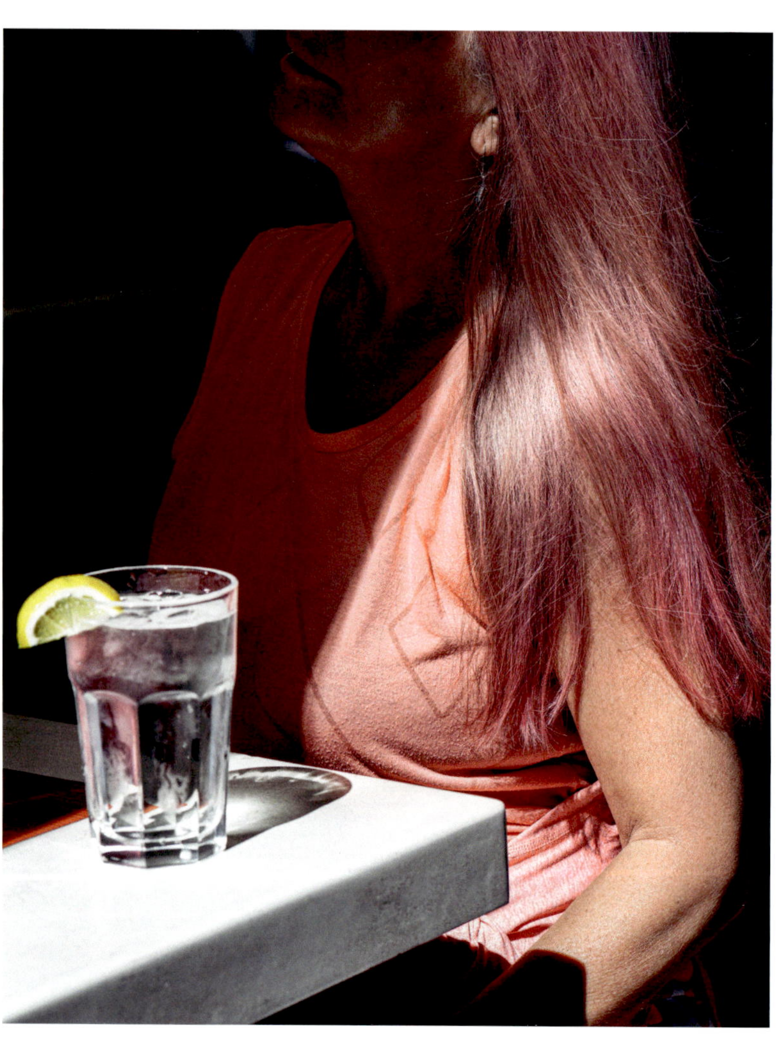

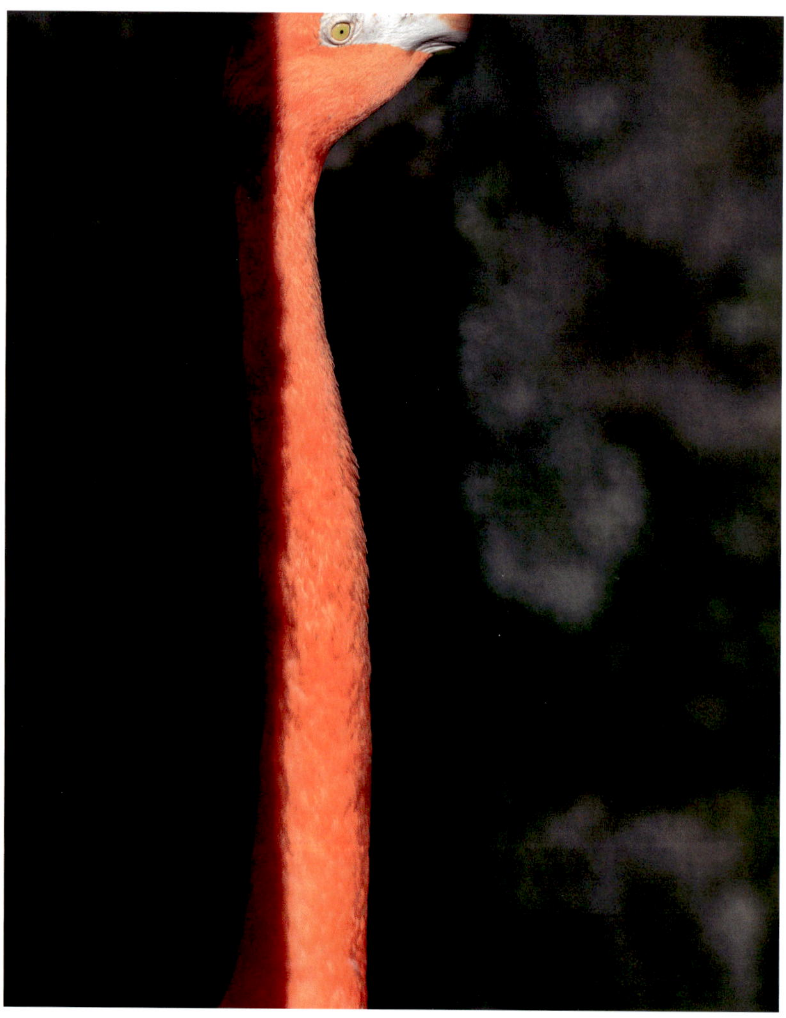

‹ Tourist in South Beach, 2019 › Flamingo, 2018

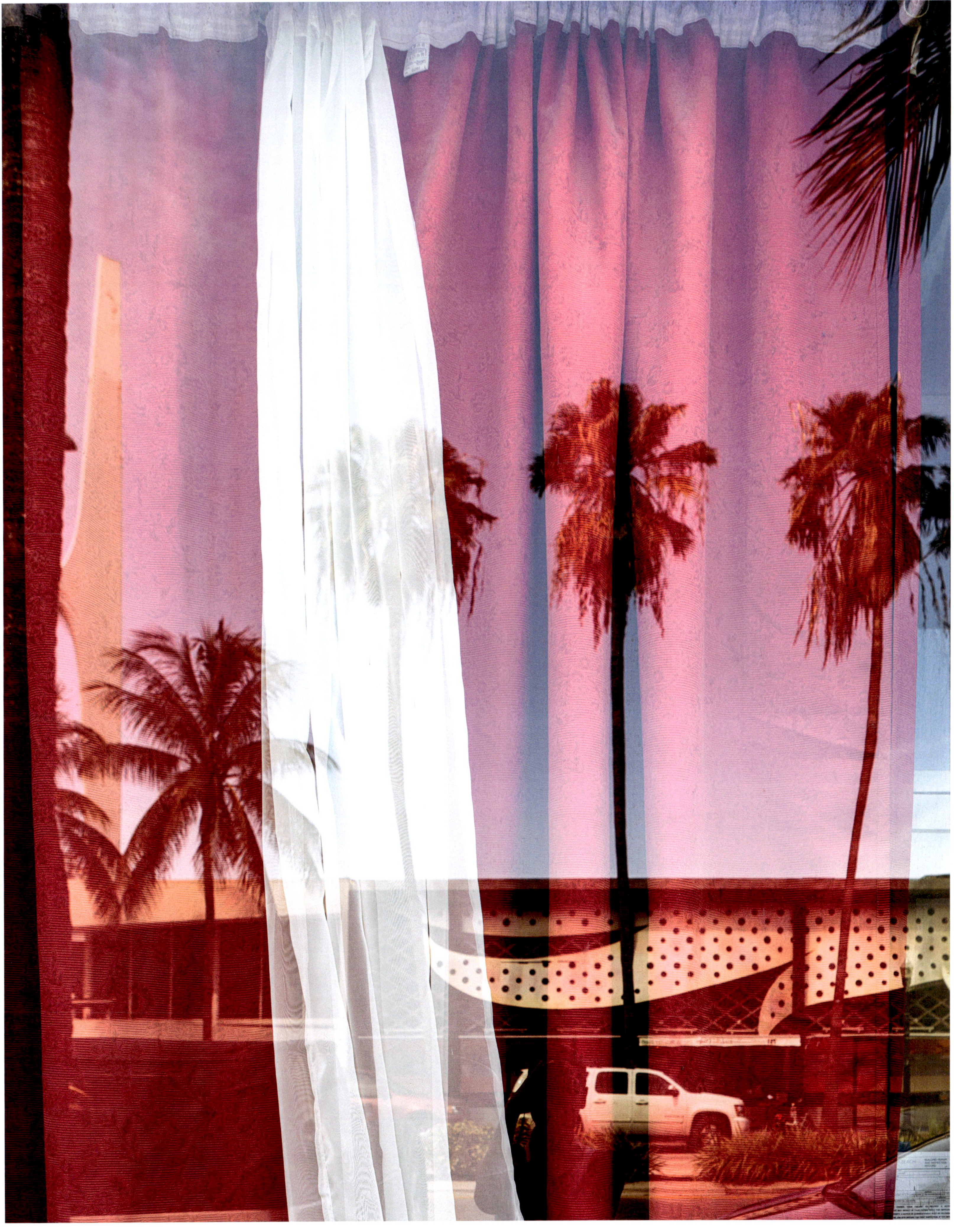

South Beach Reflection, 2017 » Gator, 2017

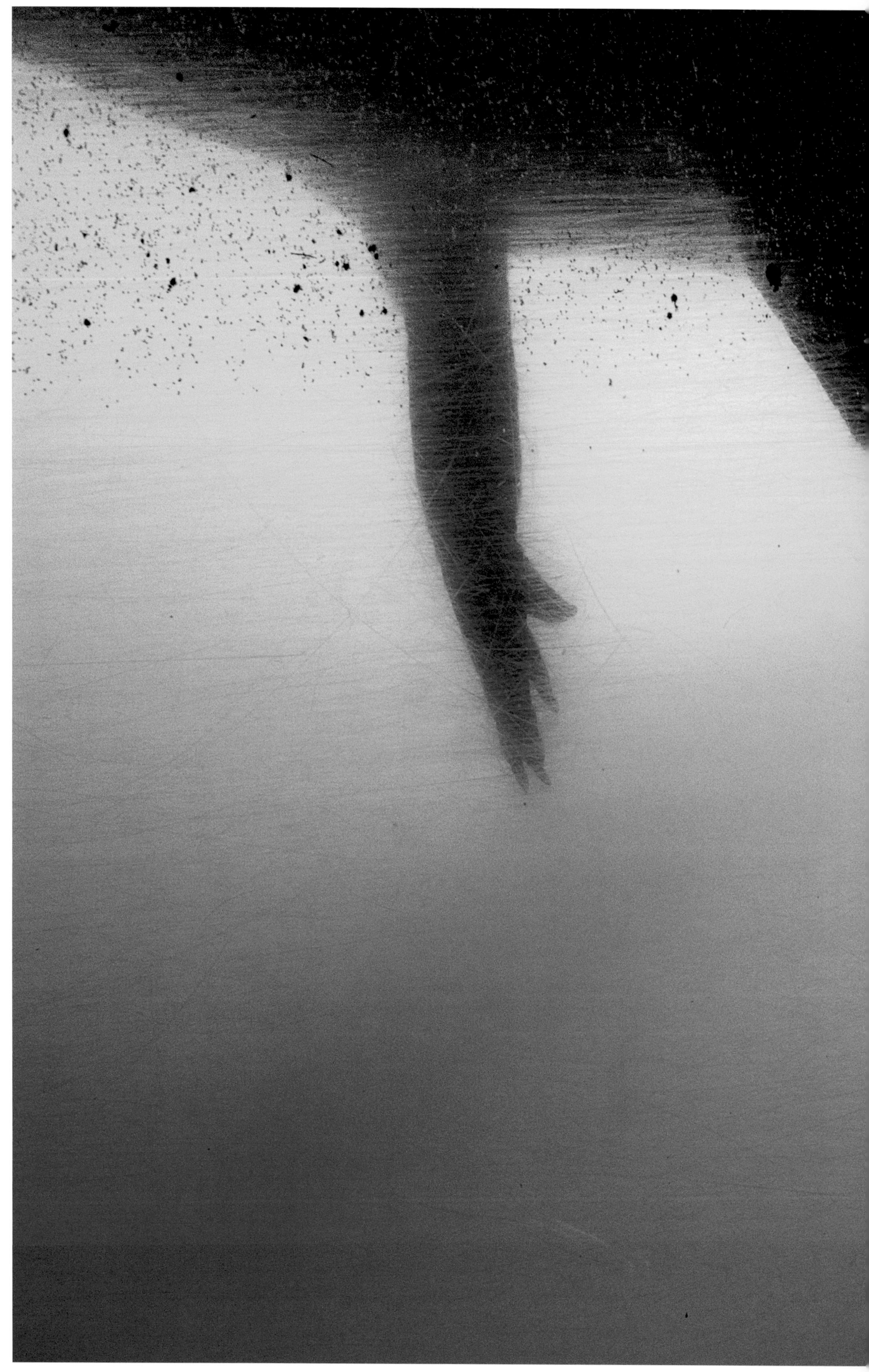

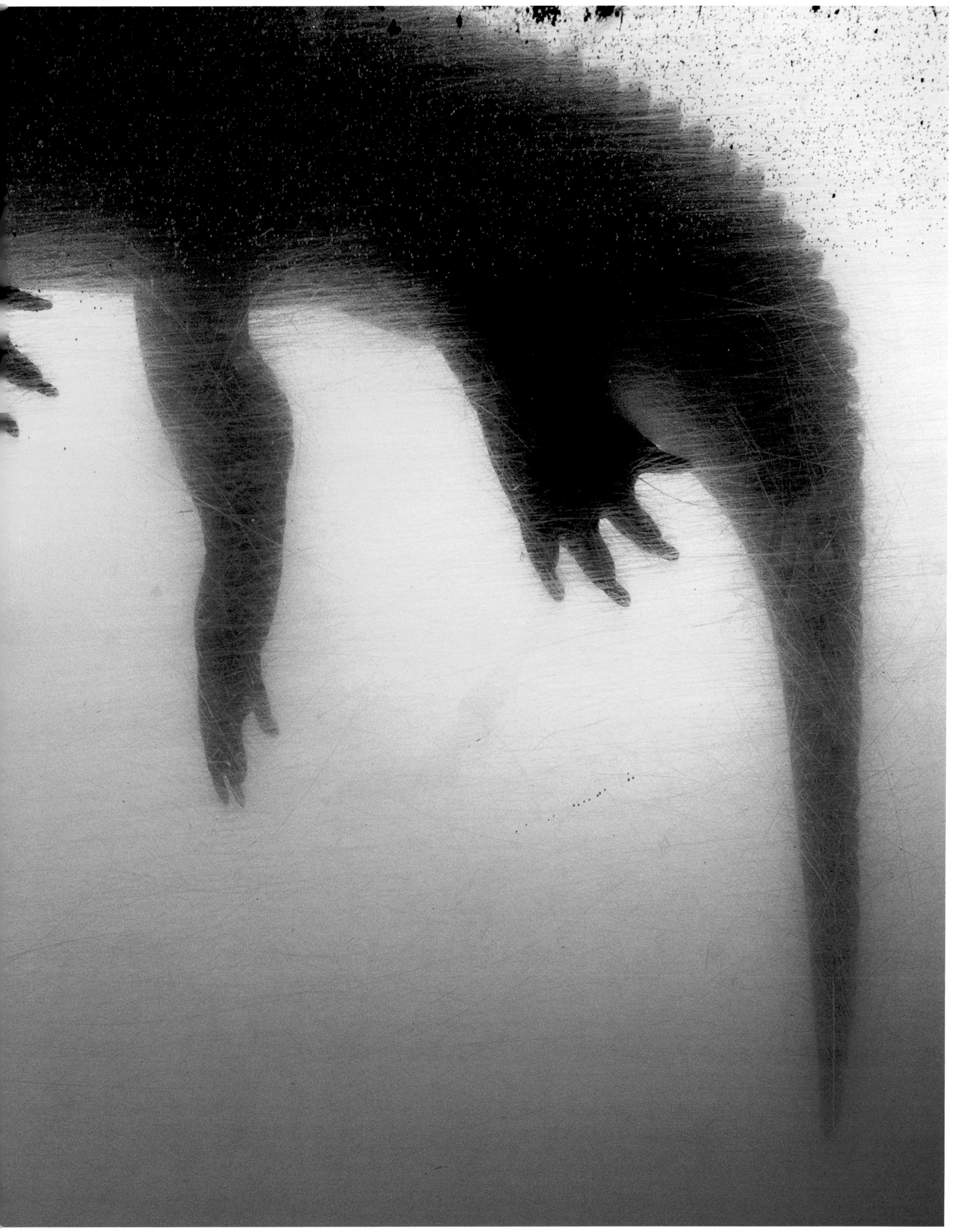

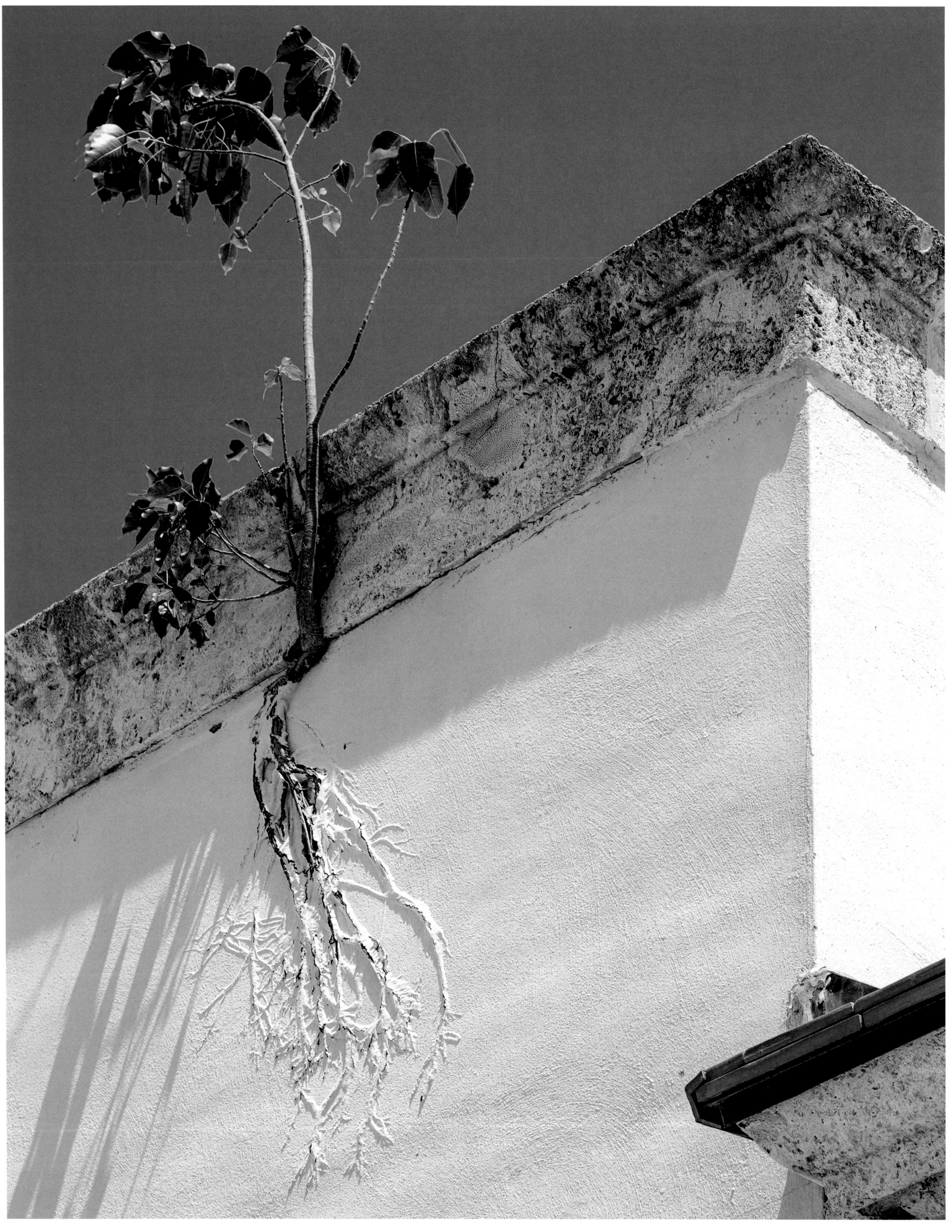

Painted Roots, 2017

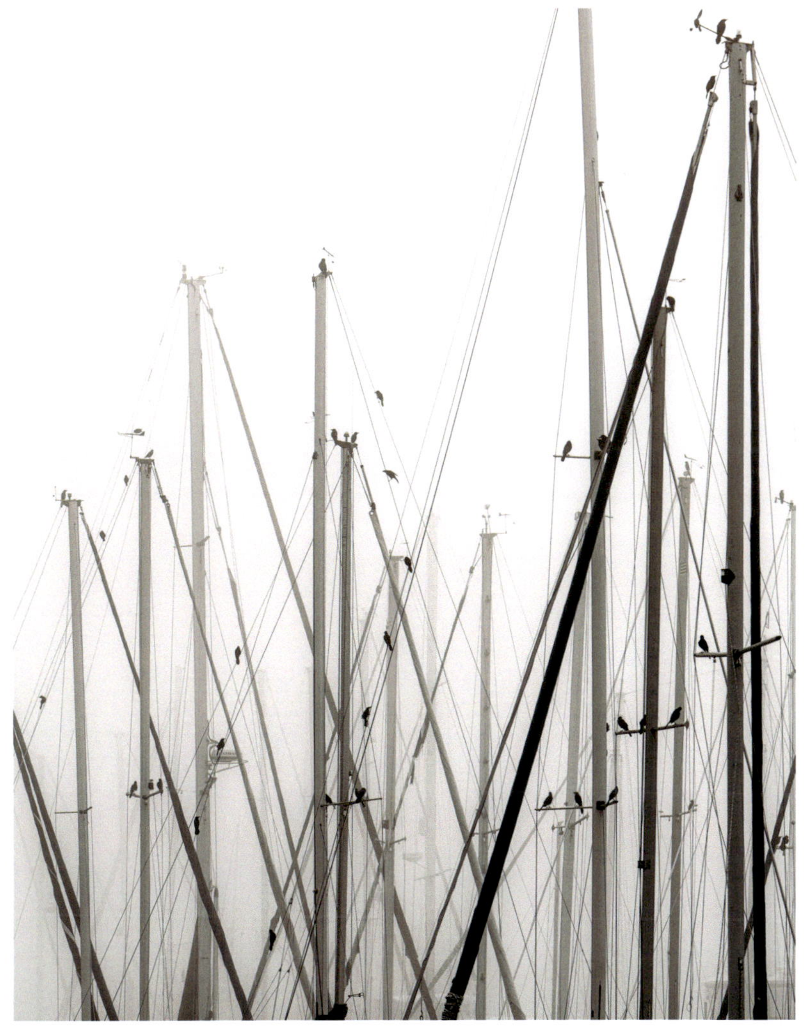

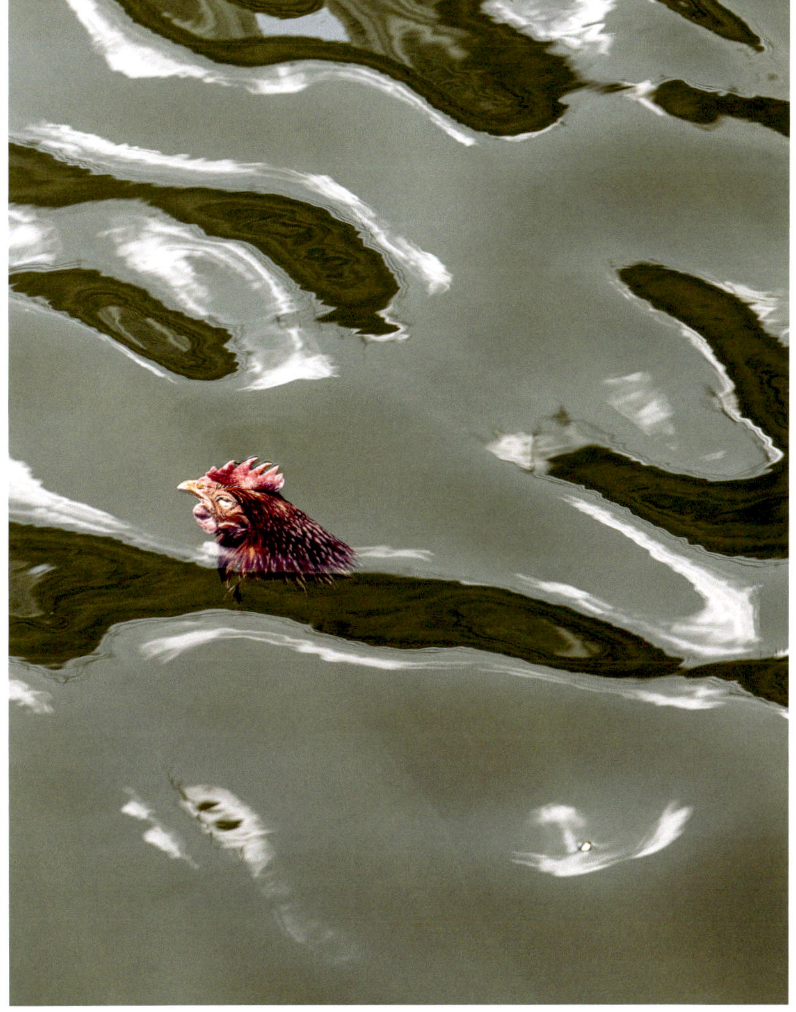

^ Masts, 2019
˅ Santeria Chicken, 2019

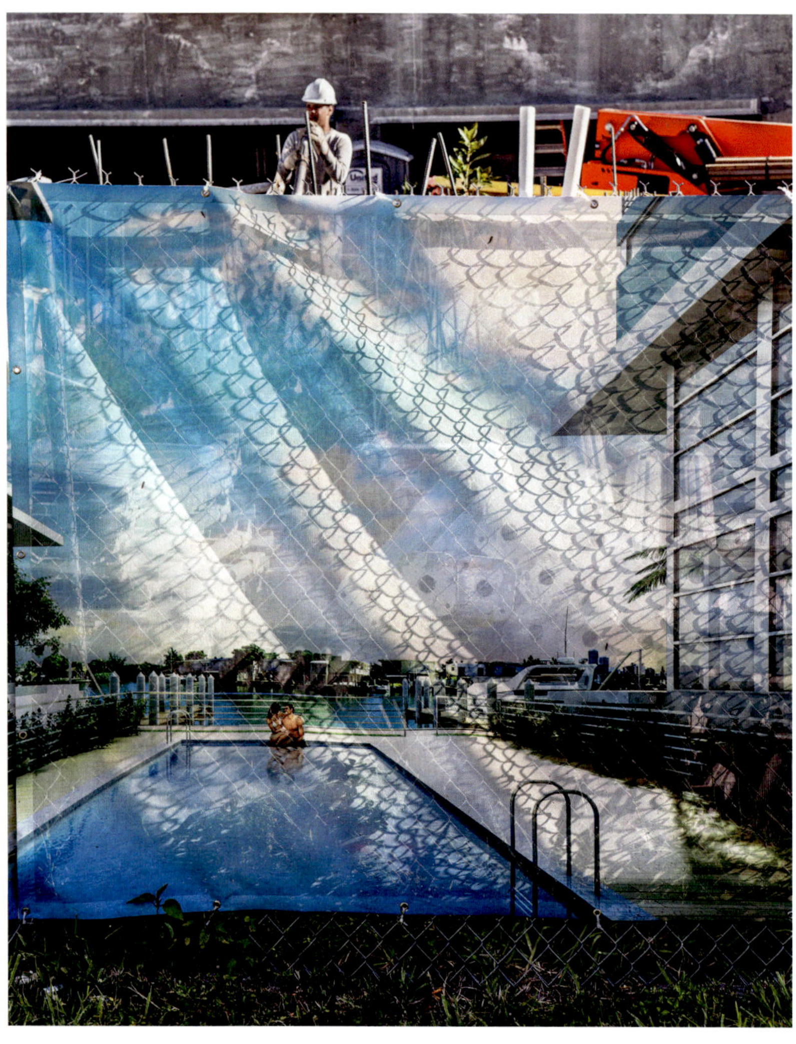

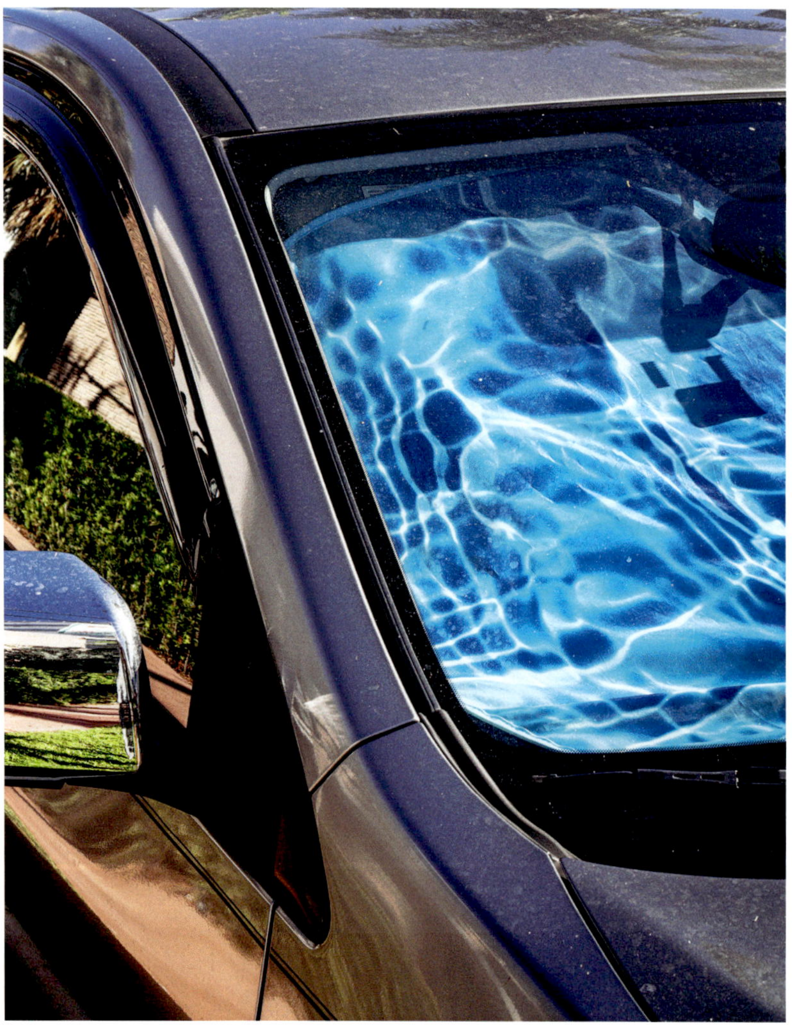

^ Construction in Normandy Shores, 2017

⌄ Water Shade, 2018

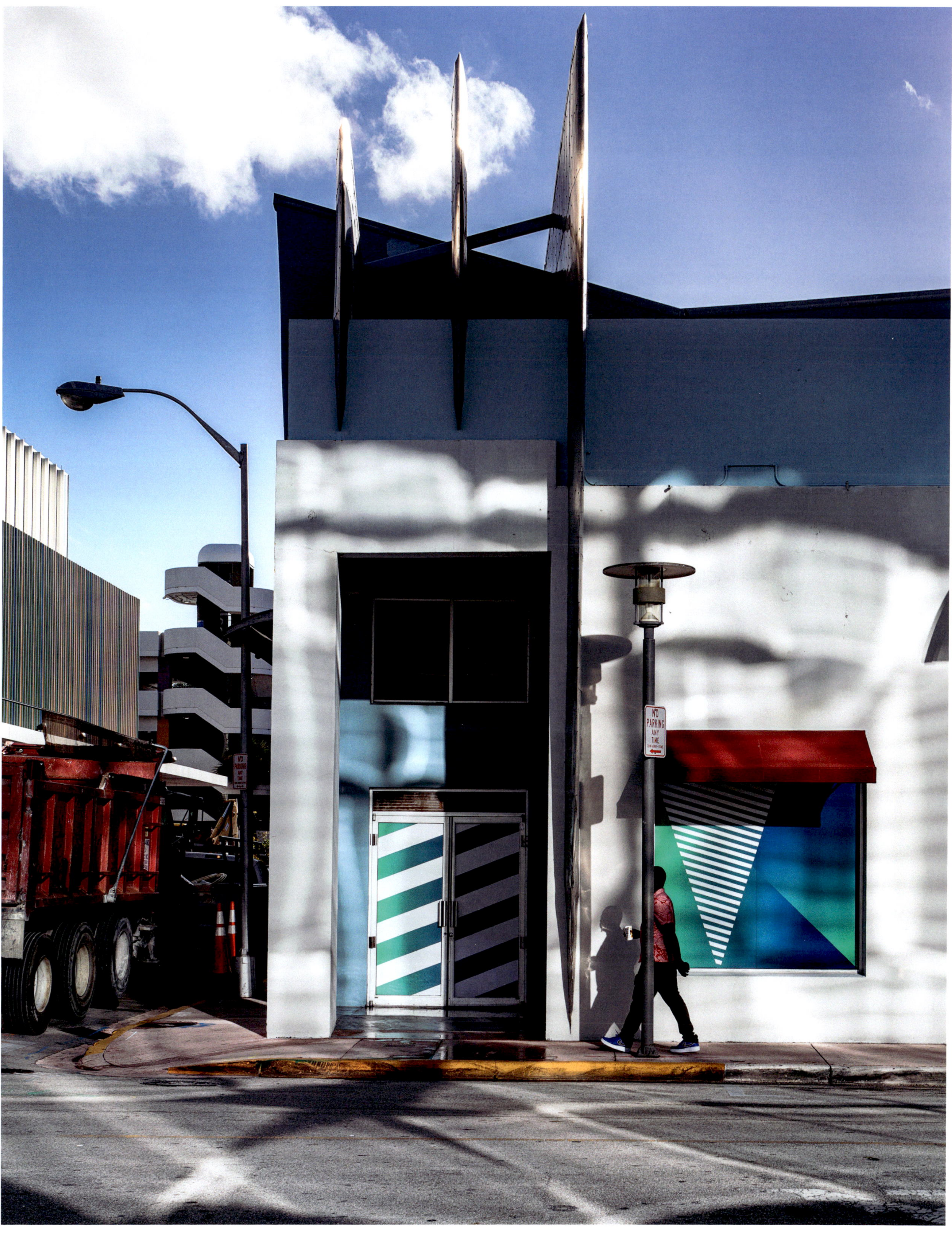

Street in South Beach, 2018

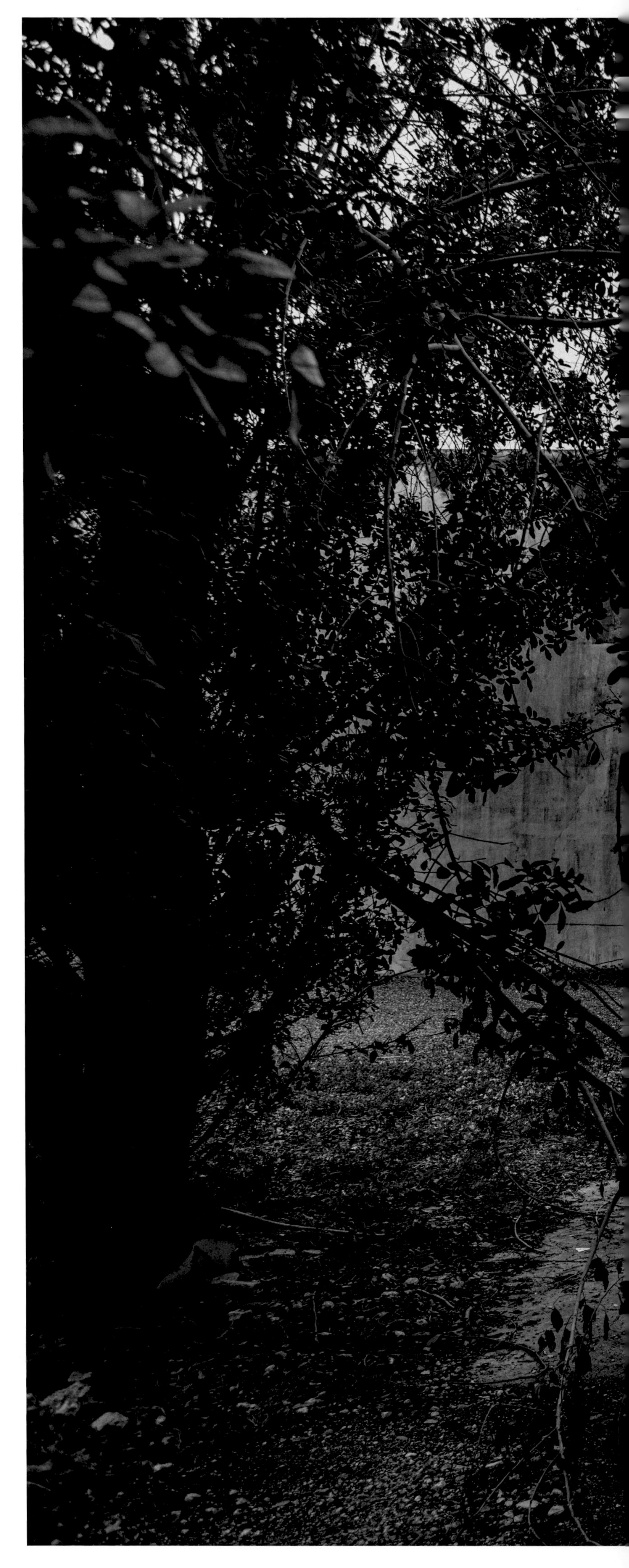

Little River, 2016

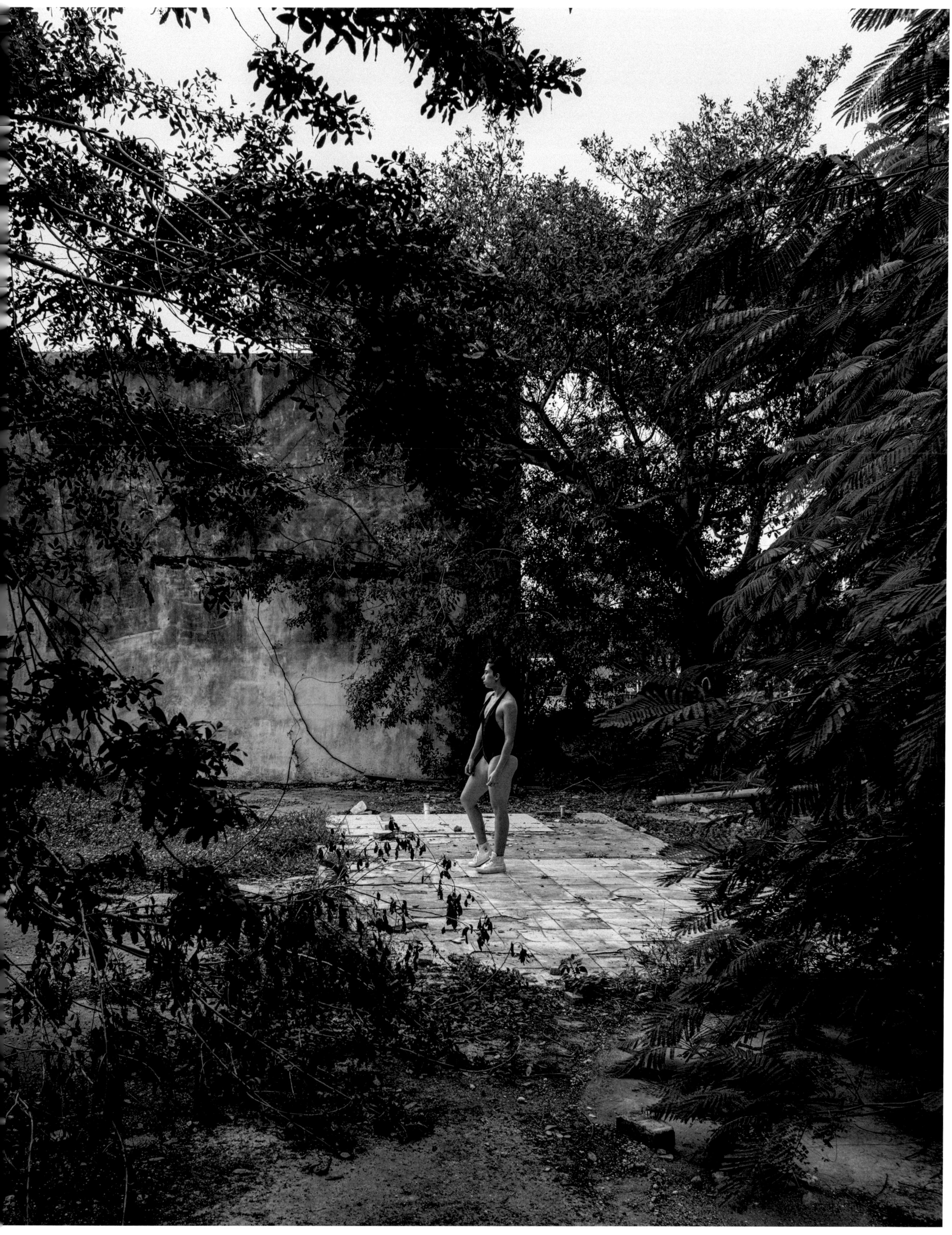

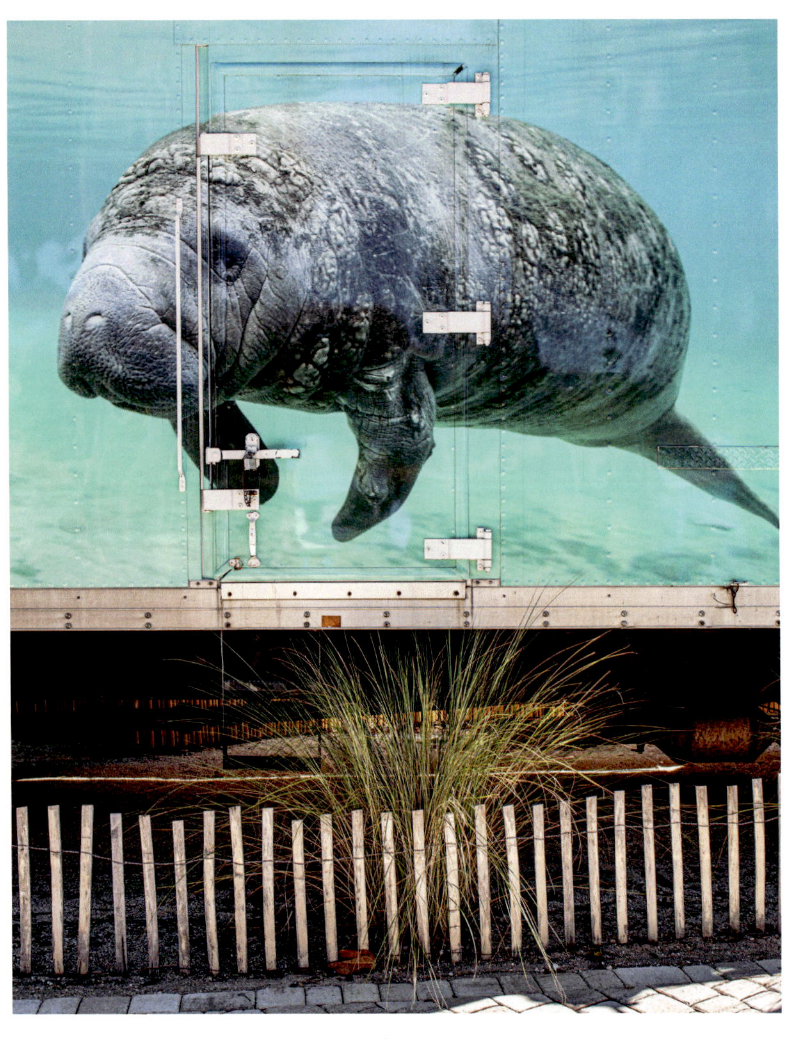

‹ Manatee Rescue Van, 2019

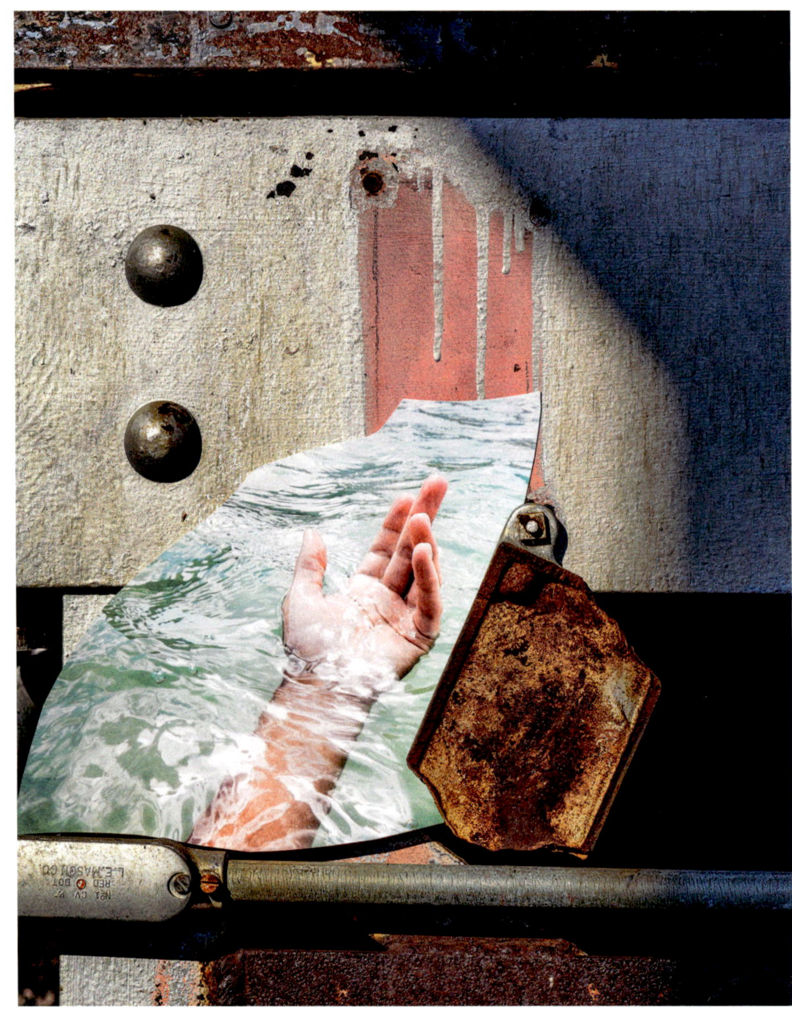

› Hand, 2017

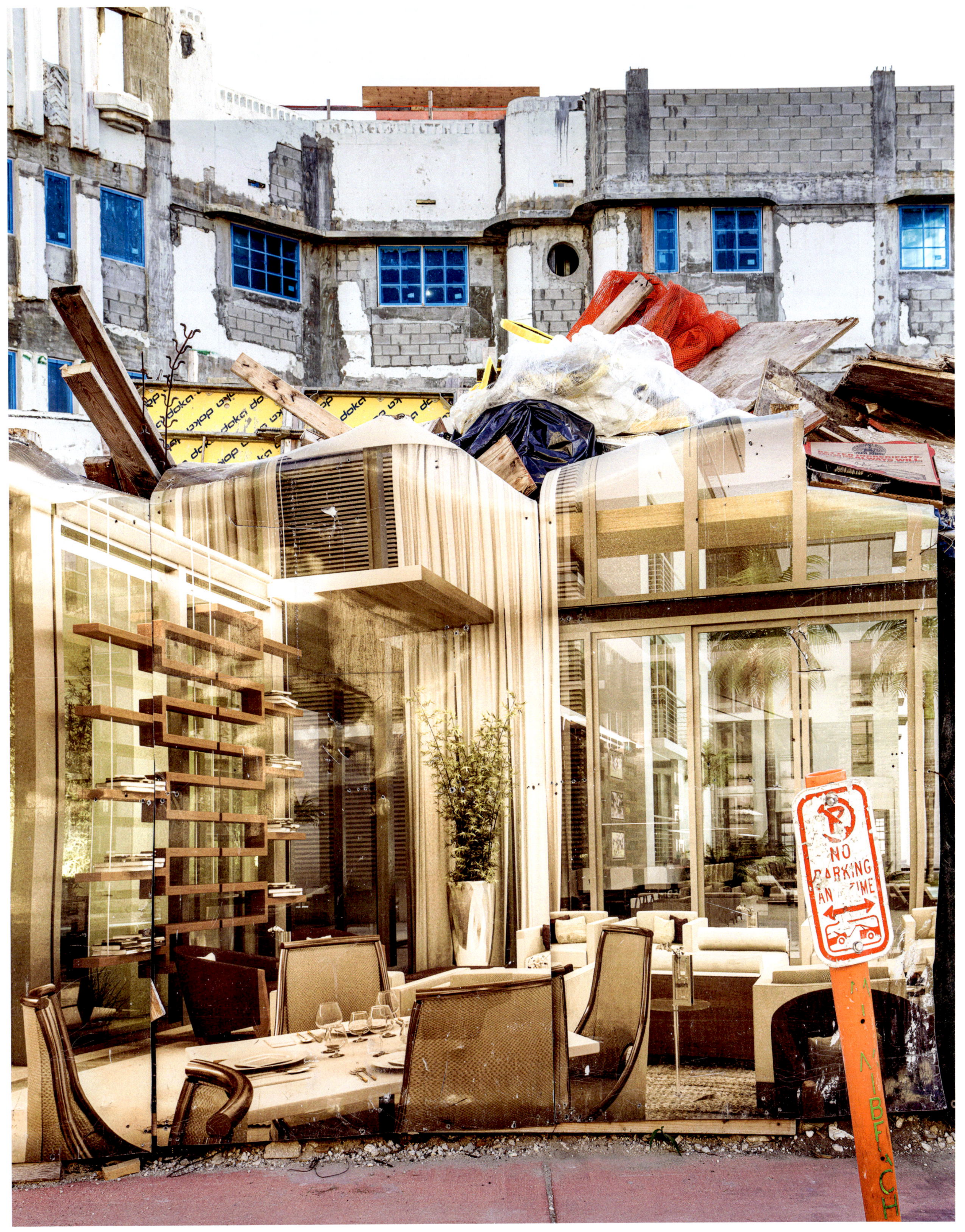

Construction in South Beach II, 2018

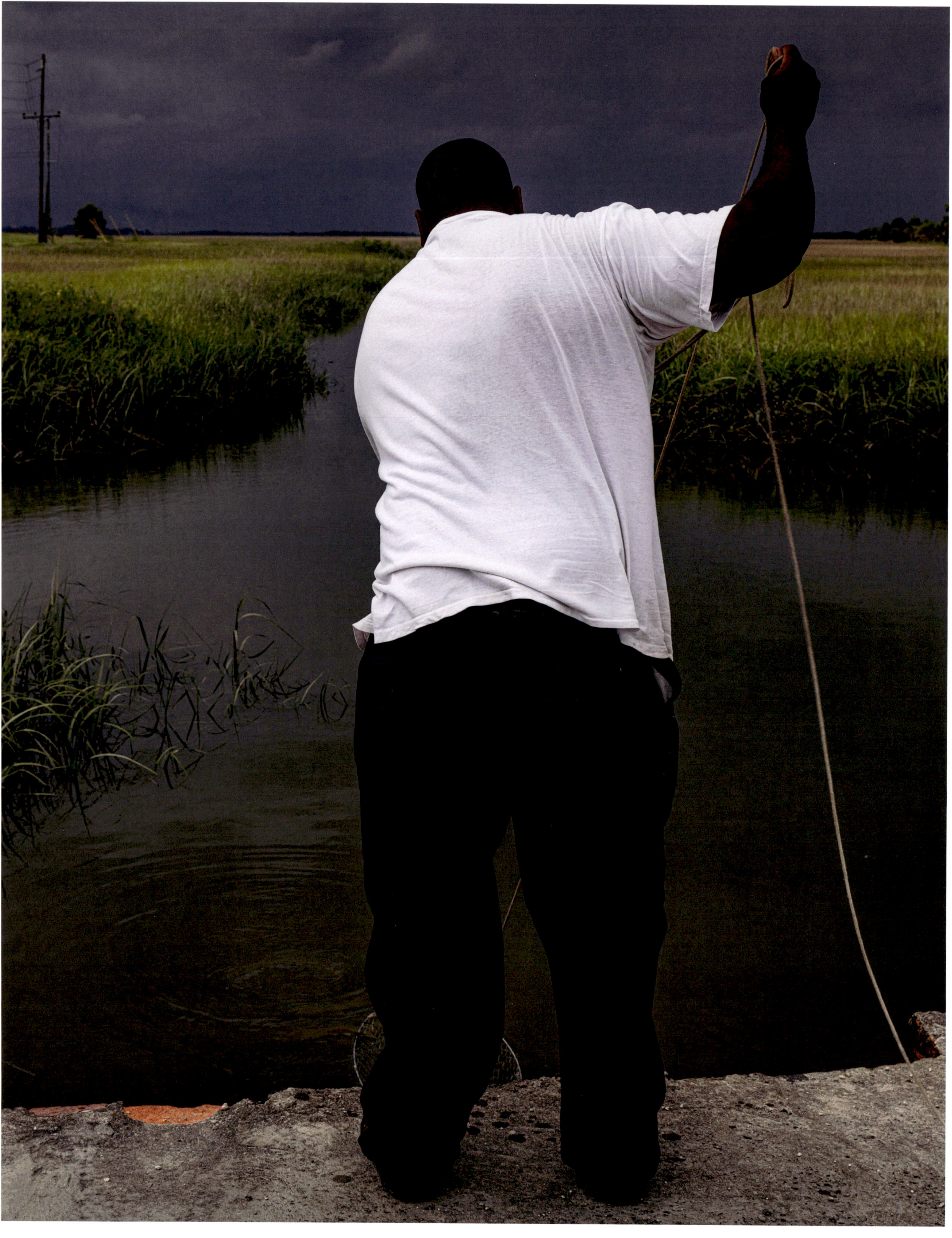

Crabbing, Georgia, 2018

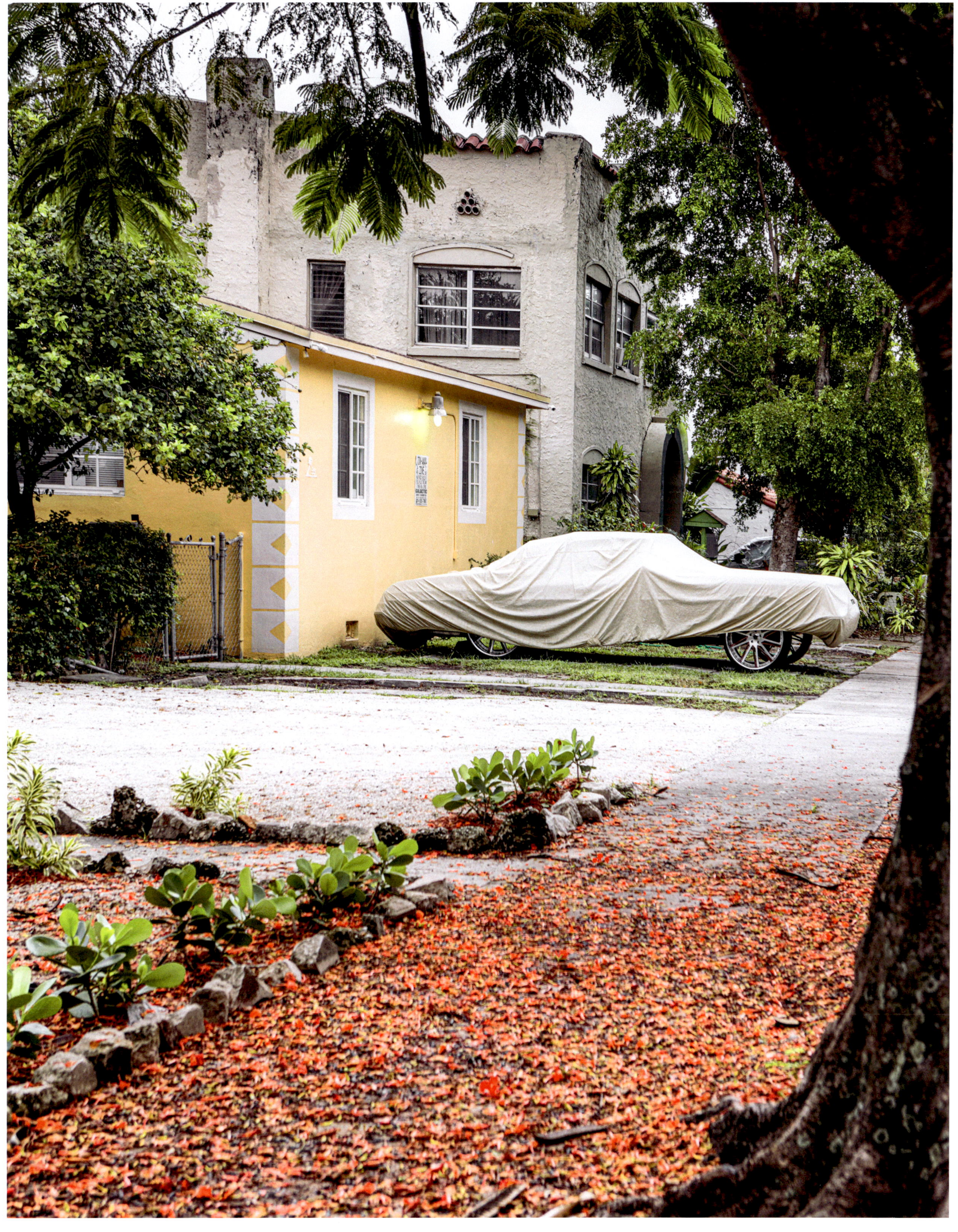

Morningside, 2017

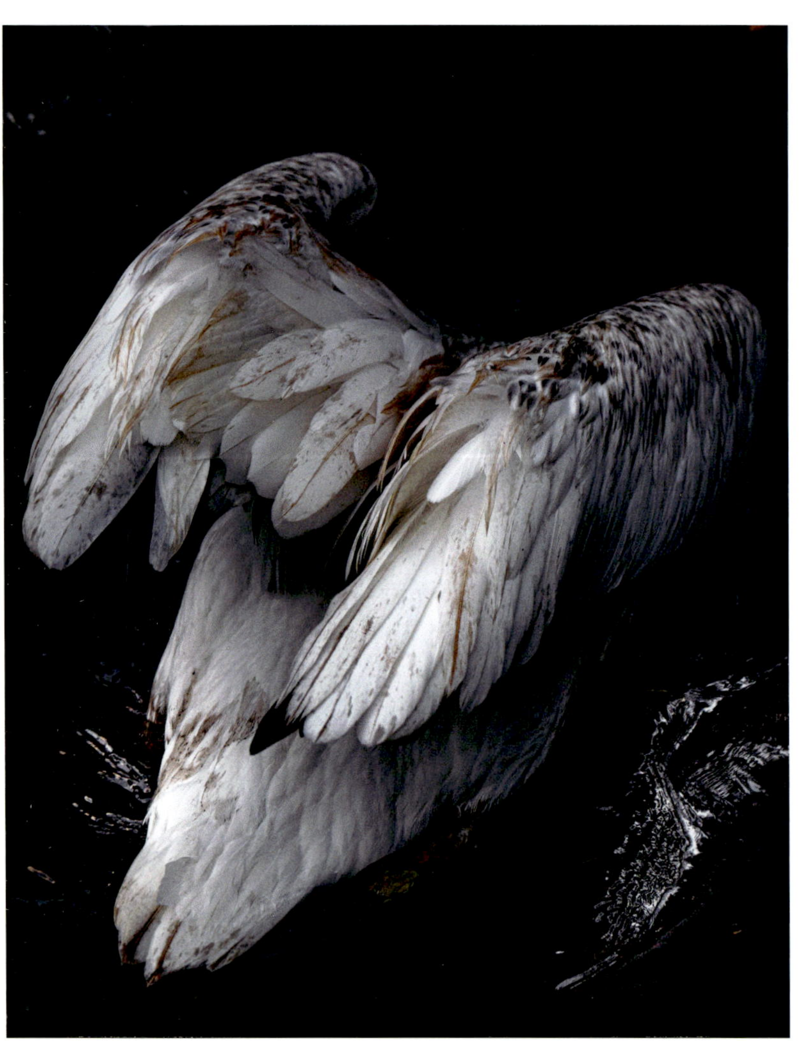

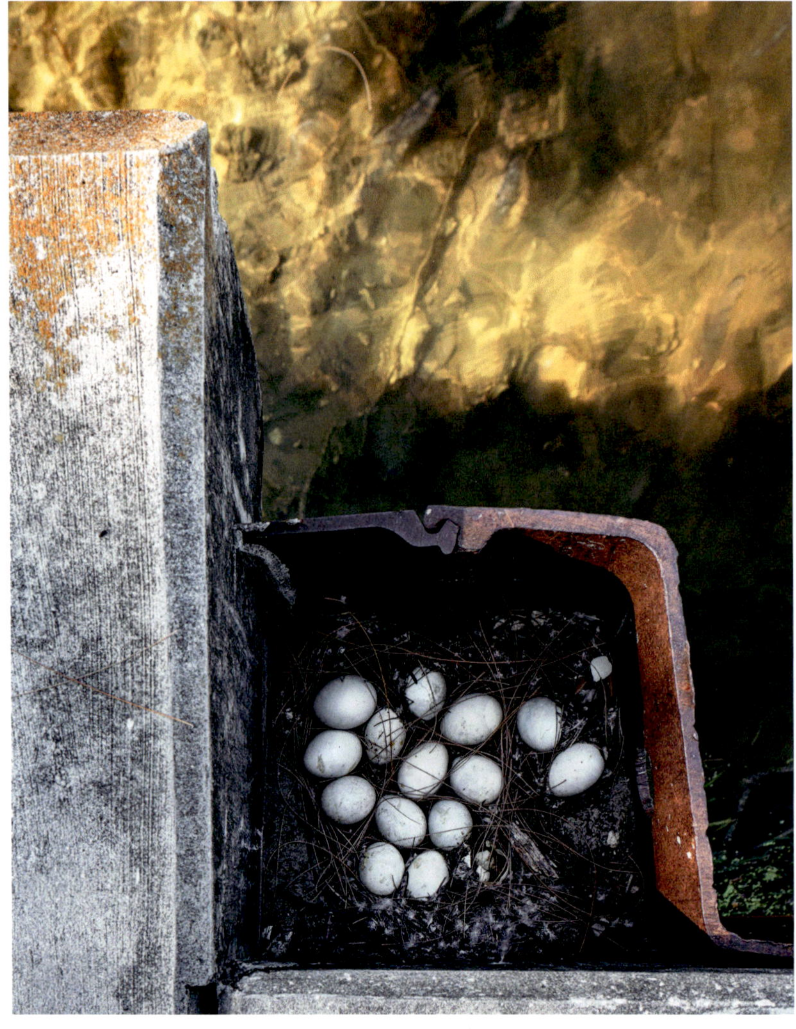

^ Diving Pelican, 2018
ˇ Eggs, 2019

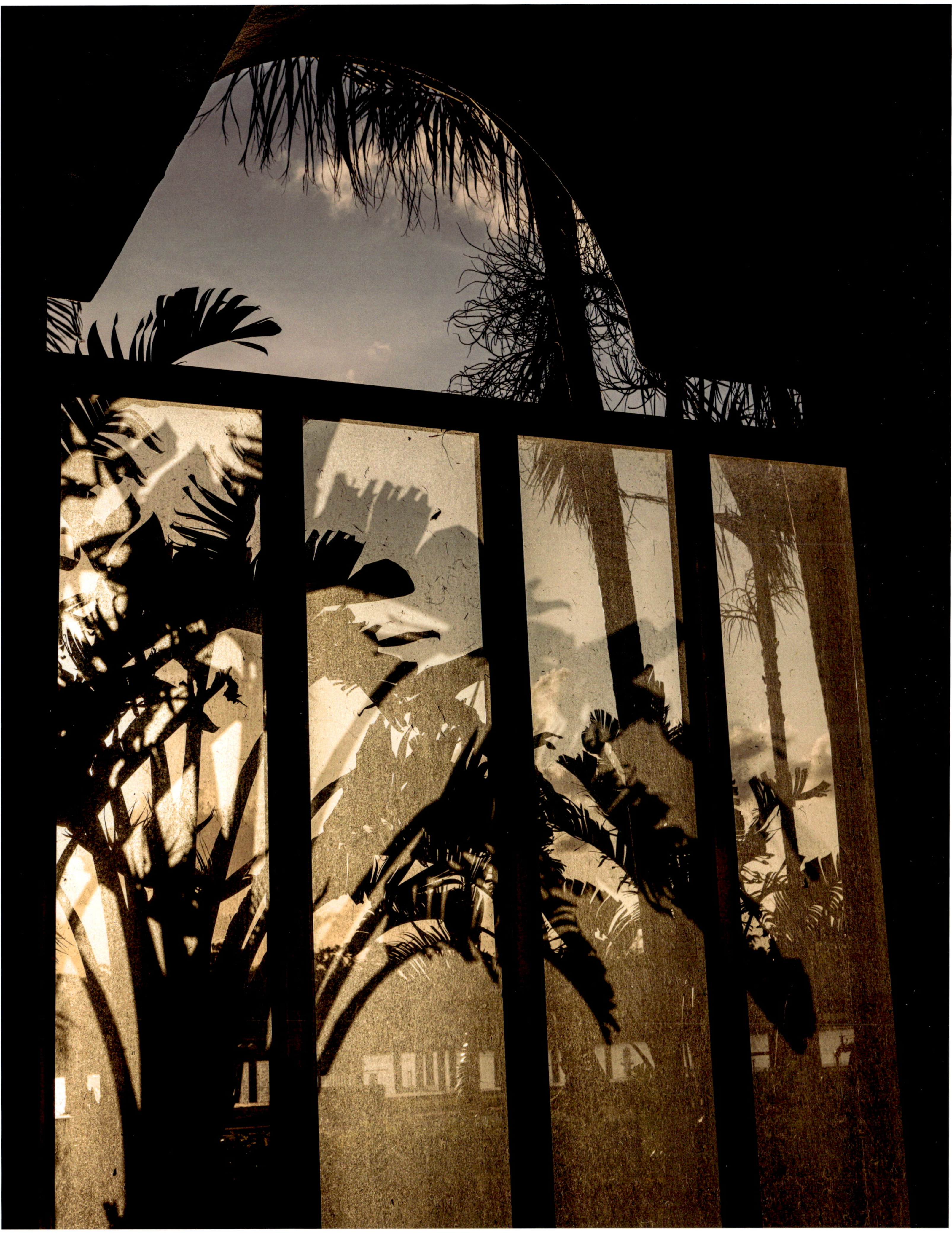

Sunset after Hurricane, 2017

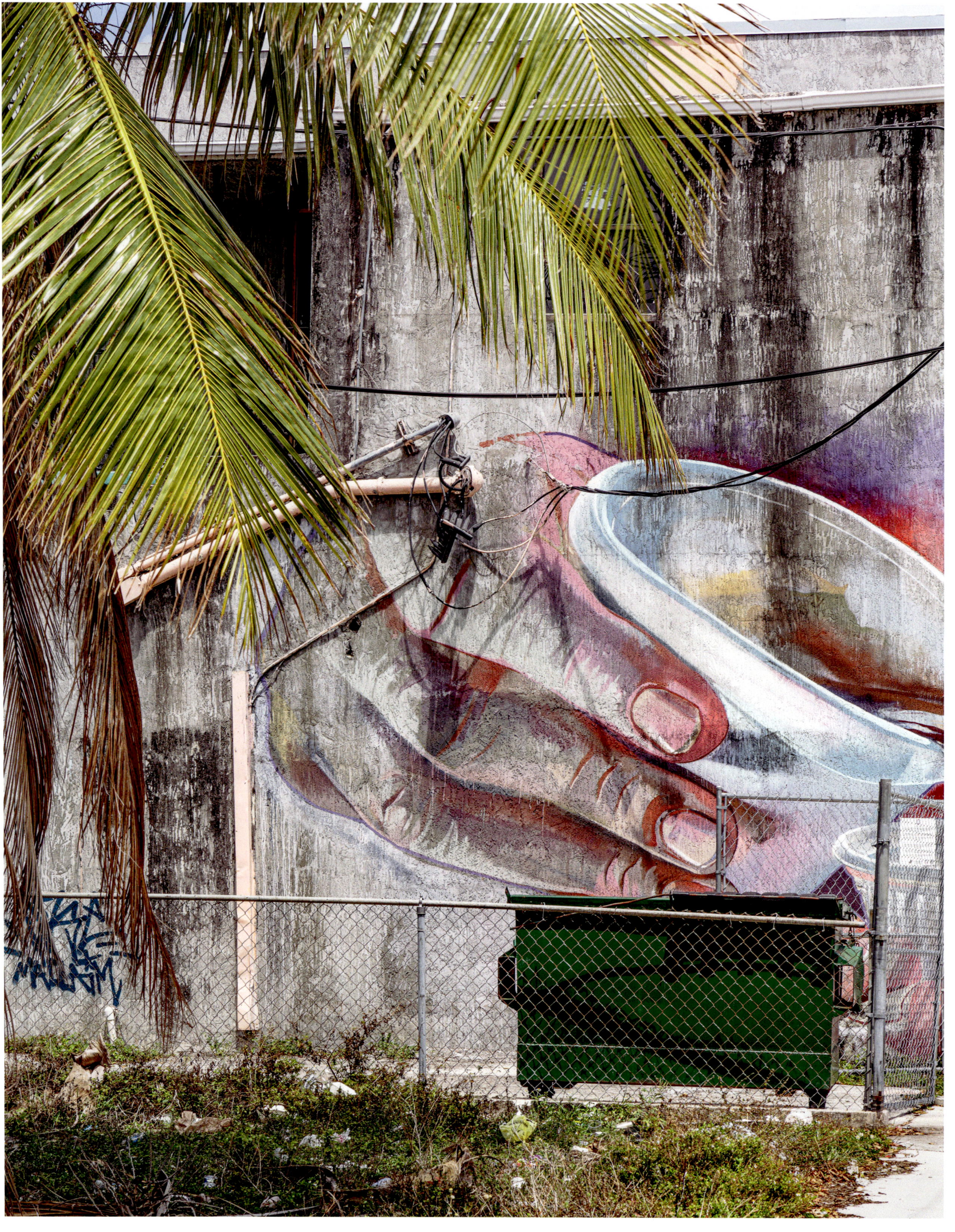

Graffiti Cup, 2018

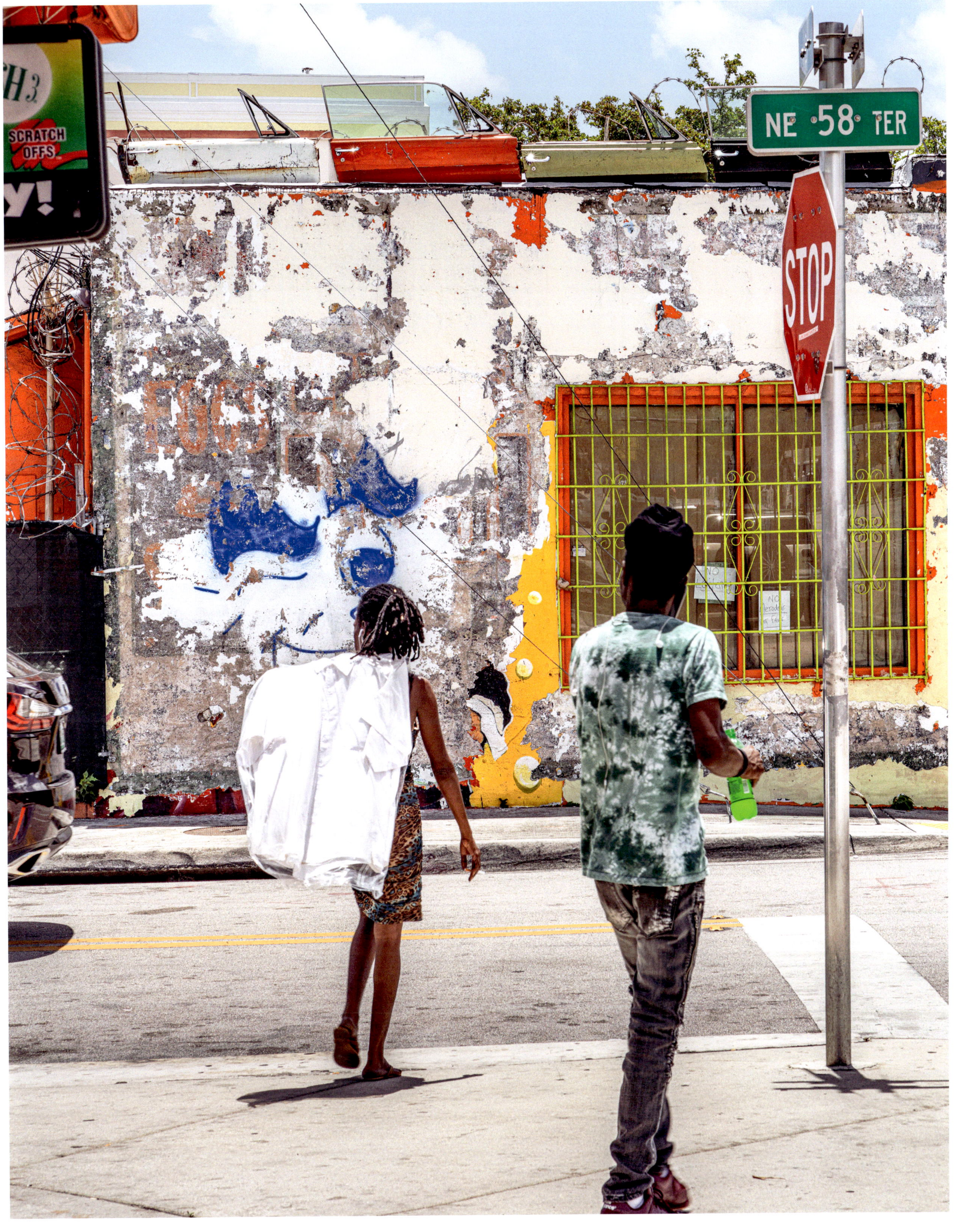

Street Crossing in Little Haiti, 2018 » Dome House, 2018

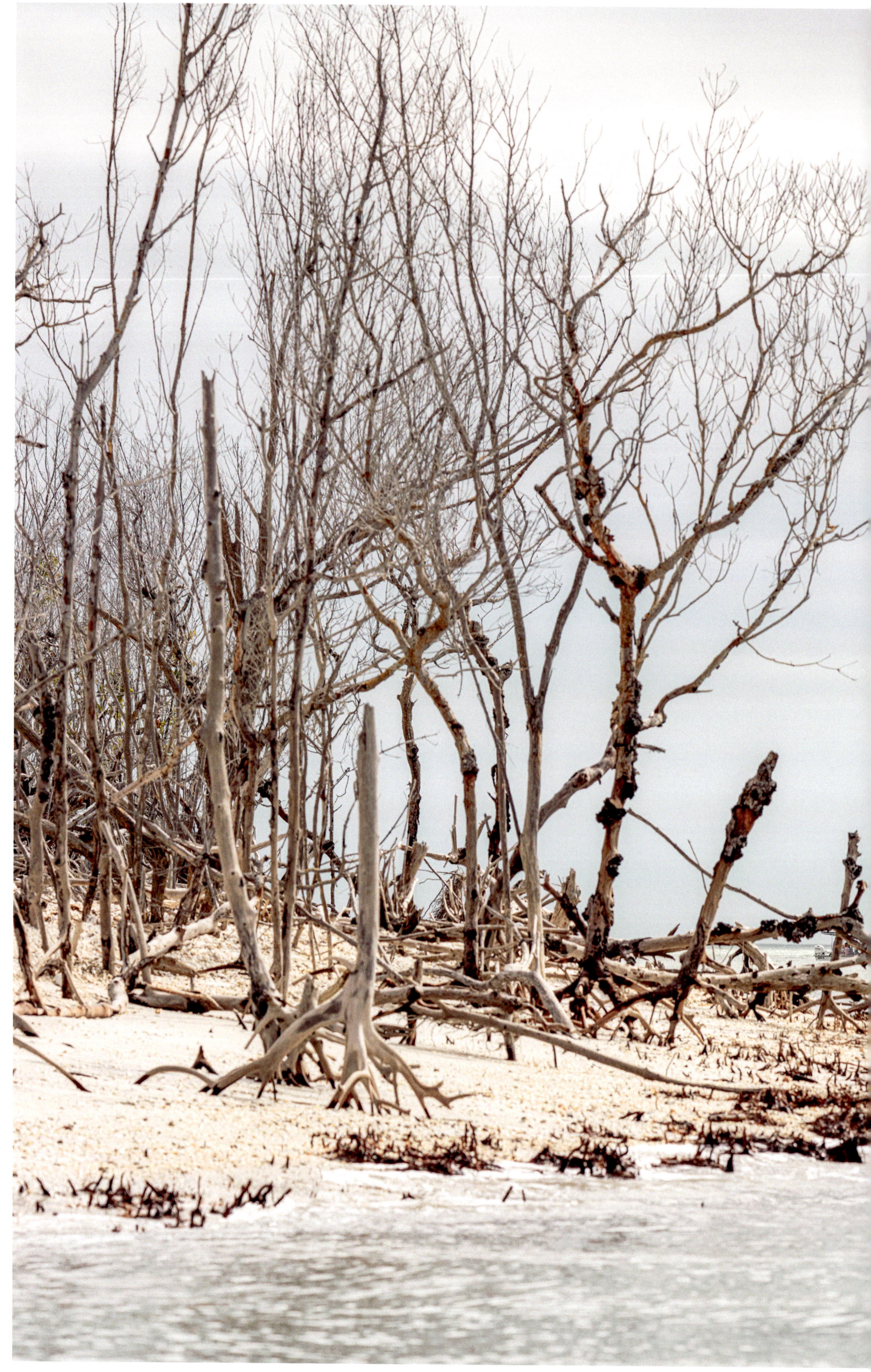

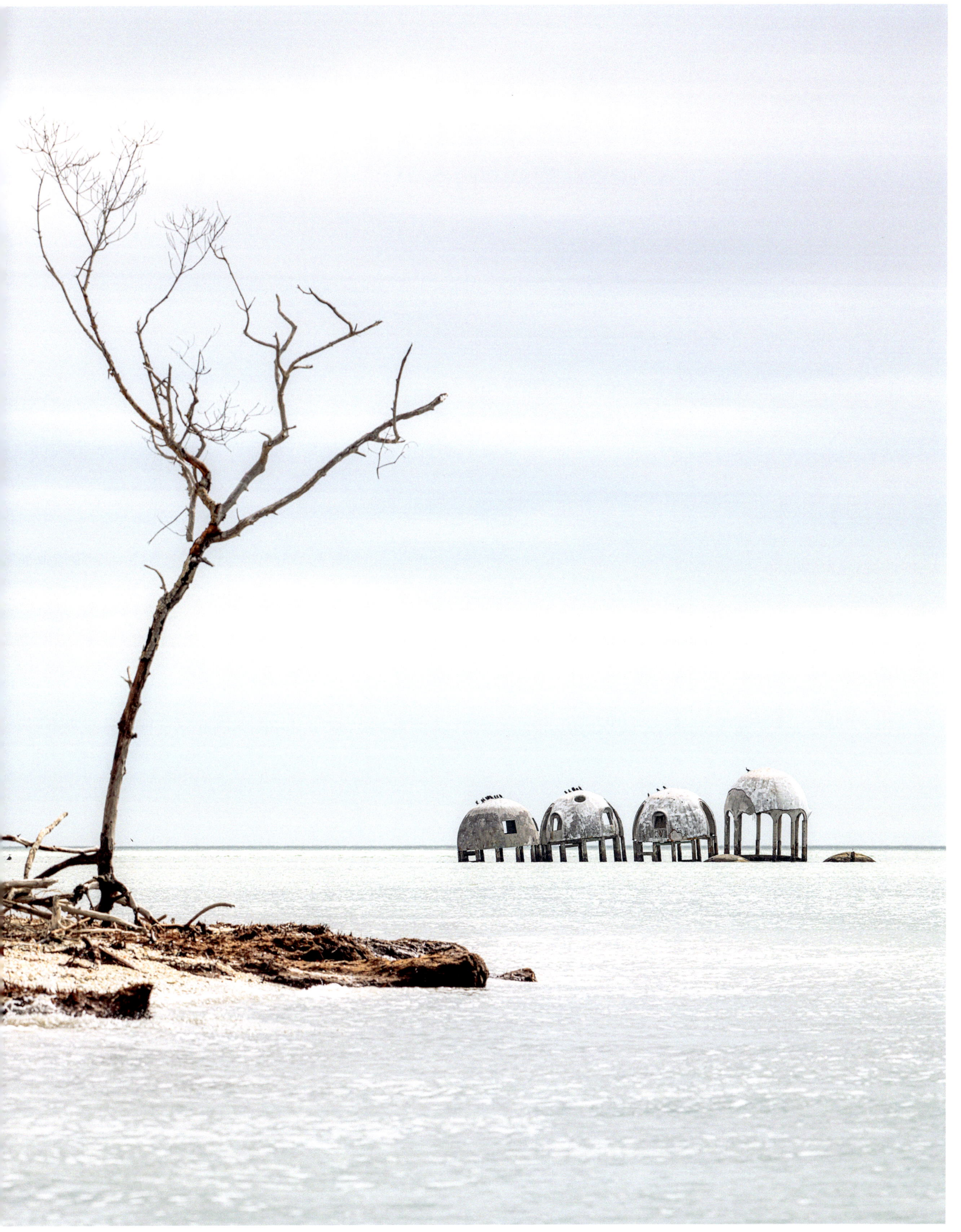

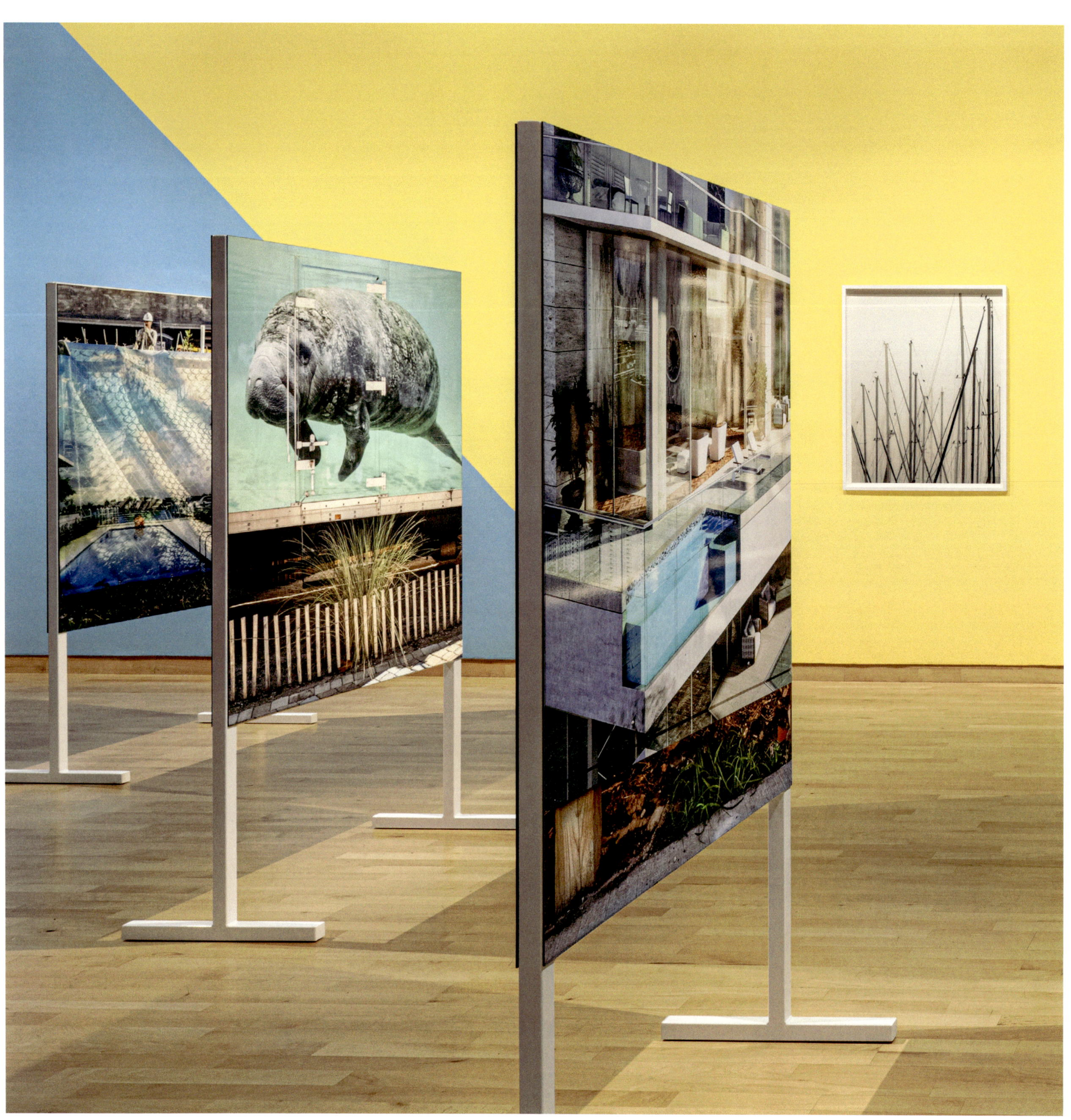

FloodZone exhibition, Contemporary Museum of Art, Tampa, 2020

INCROYABLES FLORIDES

LUCY SANTE

> I've grazed, you know, incredible Floridas
> Which sow among the flowers the eyes of panthers
> With human skins! Rainbows stretched like bridles,
> Under the marine horizon, for sea-green flocks.
>
> ARTHUR RIMBAUD, 'The Drunken Boat'

I can't speak with any authority about Florida. I've only been there twice, and the second time was a night and a day spent trudging around Palm Beach and its endless miles of privacy hedges. My Florida is a palimpsest of received images, travellers' tales, movies and crime novels and TV shows and supermarket tabloids, and the propaganda blitz the state generated in the 1960s, when I was a child (orange juice, retirement communities, sparkling white sands). There is also the montage of vivid and oddly matched scenes I carried away from my first trip to Florida, in the 1980s, when I drove south from Waycross, Georgia, down through the rural middle of the state, turned right to the Gulf Coast for a spell, then crossed over to Miami Beach; it was savage and superannuated, high-coloured and banal, cutting-edge and derelict. Florida was the dream of many high-school graduates of my vintage, who drifted south in search of jobs where they could wear shorts and flip-flops; of golden agers from the north who saw endlessly unrolling perfect days of golf; of every European taxi driver I ever chatted with.

Florida is the mysterious tropical appendix to the United States, a place that really shouldn't be there – as indeed it shouldn't quite, since it was stolen from the Seminoles by Andrew Jackson. It has exerted a powerful hypnotic spell on the country and the world for centuries, initially for the luxuriance of its vegetation, the secrets of its wildlife, the glamorous impenetrability of its swamps, the vast extent of its shoreline, not to mention its tropical or subtropical climate. The Florida legend made this allure comestible, mostly in the form of citrus fruits and dream vacations, in the 1920s, when it was burnished and broadcast by the railways and hotel chains. Until the Second World War the state was still considered underpopulated, but that swiftly changed after the war, when a mass exodus of retirees from the northern industrial states doubled the population in short order.

And now it is teeming, filled with all sorts of people from everywhere in the world who may or may not be contending with the fact that their domicile might not still be there in a year, the weather events being what they are. Florida is a collage unto itself, a mix of cultures, tempers, textures, colours, mores, fortunes, upkeep and decay. Anastasia Samoylova, raised and educated in Moscow, has been chronicling the state for a while now, and she has the uncanny eye required to do justice to its chance assemblages and yawning contrasts and sometimes grotesque ironies. Seeing Florida as it actually is cannot always be easy, since the place throws off such a blizzard of contradictions that the eye is strongly tempted to filter them, to make the daily passage easier. But Samoylova sees everything as if for the first time, while also remaining undeceived by any of it. She manages to combine the freshness of eye of the newly arrived with the gimlet-eyed scepticism of the habituée.

Her Florida does not lend itself to reductive views. It is gifted with as many contradictions as it has colours and textures. It is a sumptuously endowed place, romantic and evocative, at the same time that it is neglected and forlorn. Its human constructions seem to alternate between faceless glass and steel on the one hand and jury-rigged, hand-painted shacks on the other. The borderline between the realms is porous, though: chickens walk around within sight of those glass monoliths. It is brilliantly coloured, often in uncanny juxtapositions of colours: a wall displays a poster of the forty-fifth president with his facial features painted out, as well as scraps of other posters over fragments of graffiti lettering, an accidental accretion of colour and texture so casually perfect it almost looks intentional; a flooded garage interior is all blue except for a single pop of bright yellow. But it can also be black and white, as in the washed-out road that ends the sequence on a note of warning.

Well before she began photographing fashion billboards in major cities, their looming giant figures mocking passers-by, Samoylova was noticing the billboard culture of Florida, which often consists of large printed vinyl sheets hung low to the ground so that they can conceal ruin or demolition. They are generally artists' renditions of the architectural marvels promised instead, likely to contain two-bedroom flats with open kitchens and walls of glass. Sometimes they feature an entire idealized street scene, complete with decorous cars and pedestrians, failing to disguise the beaten-down, entropic streets they line. They are bisected by wires and telephone poles, and collect trash and weeds at their base. As Harold Rosenberg noted, 'American life is a billboard; individual life in the United States includes something nameless that takes place in the weeds behind it.'

There is no way to tell whether they are relics of financial ventures that have run aground or smiley-face threats to the communities that the projects they represent are about to displace, one day or another. Either way, they do what advertising tends to do in her photographs, which is to belittle the imperfect world that surrounds it. That makes the pictures sound as if they are all descended from the famous 'American Way' photograph by Dorothea Lange (1895–1965) for the Farm Security Administration, but with Samoylova there is always an additional wrinkle of disorientation: what if the posters show the real world, and we are merely the shadows that flit across it? In Florida you can't be too sure. The upside-down house was built that way, after all, and the seductive ripple of blue water in a swimming-pool advertisement hung on a wall turns out to be merely rippling vinyl. She reminds us what the signs of a poorer and more direct commerce look like: 'Florida Furniture', 'Except Sunday', 'Sandwich'. Those are all addressed to you, provided you have an interest, but the billboards are intended for some much wealthier person, perhaps passing behind you. But then the palm trees act as a permanent advertisement for the place you're actually standing in, unless a storm knocks them over.

In addition to sun, Florida has always been about water, nicely domesticated water lapping gently at sparkling white sands. Samoylova sees water rippling, glinting, beckoning, reflecting dappled light onto building facades even when it is not itself in the picture. Water has necessarily had its dark side, too, promoting rot and mould and seepage, but now water is increasingly making its presence felt in inconvenient ways. People deprived of beachfront property might have invited water into their homes in the form of pools, but now water is inviting itself into parts of habitations not designed for such purposes. It is at the gates, threatening the survival of the gazebo with its magnificent terrazzo floor, which looks stranded at the edge of the world.

The signs are clear: between rising ocean levels and ever more violent storms, much of Florida will be consumed by water in the coming decades. Shorelines recede and communities disappear, little by little or all at once. J. G. Ballard, in *The Drowned World* (1962), saw it coming: 'Just as psychoanalysis reconstructs the original traumatic situation in order to release the repressed material, so we are now being plunged back into the archaeopsychic past, uncovering the ancient taboos and drives that have been dormant for epochs.' Samoylova sees it coming: a desolate shore with dead trees faces a line of pods on legs, out in the ocean, like science-fiction survivors' huts; an overstuffed chair, which looks new, bobs in a pond that reflects windows as if it had floated out from a flooded lower storey. Already it is hard to tell where water is intended to be and where it is not. Soon enough the plazas and causeways and boulevards will be sunk in dirty green water like that which surrounds an alligator who, given the lighting, might or might not be alive.

And how are Floridians preparing for this impending cataclysm? By buying guns, Samoylova suggests, noting the family that cutely enumerates its members as representations of assault rifles in various sizes on the outside wall of their house. 'No Mercy' announces the tattooed chest of a man with two sidearms tattooed at his hips, so that he is armed even when he is naked and empty-handed. Those people are likely more concerned about looters than about the rising tide, because Florida is what they have achieved in life, and for their houses, cars and boats they are ready to go to war, assuming that involves a human enemy. Florida is a Xanadu of wishful thinking, and Samoylova shows us the how and the why in fantastically rich, complex, nuanced tableaux, at once sweet and poisonous.

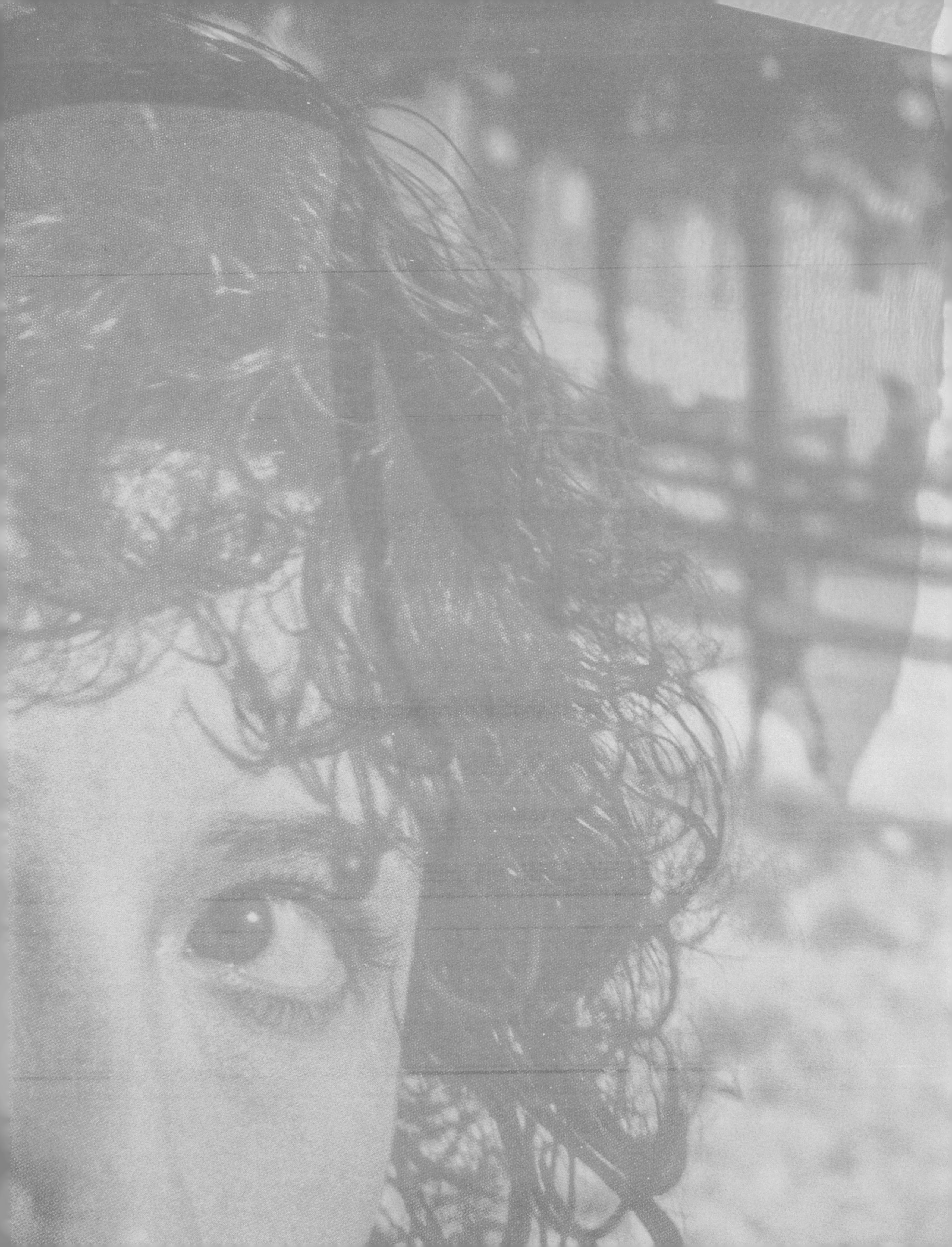

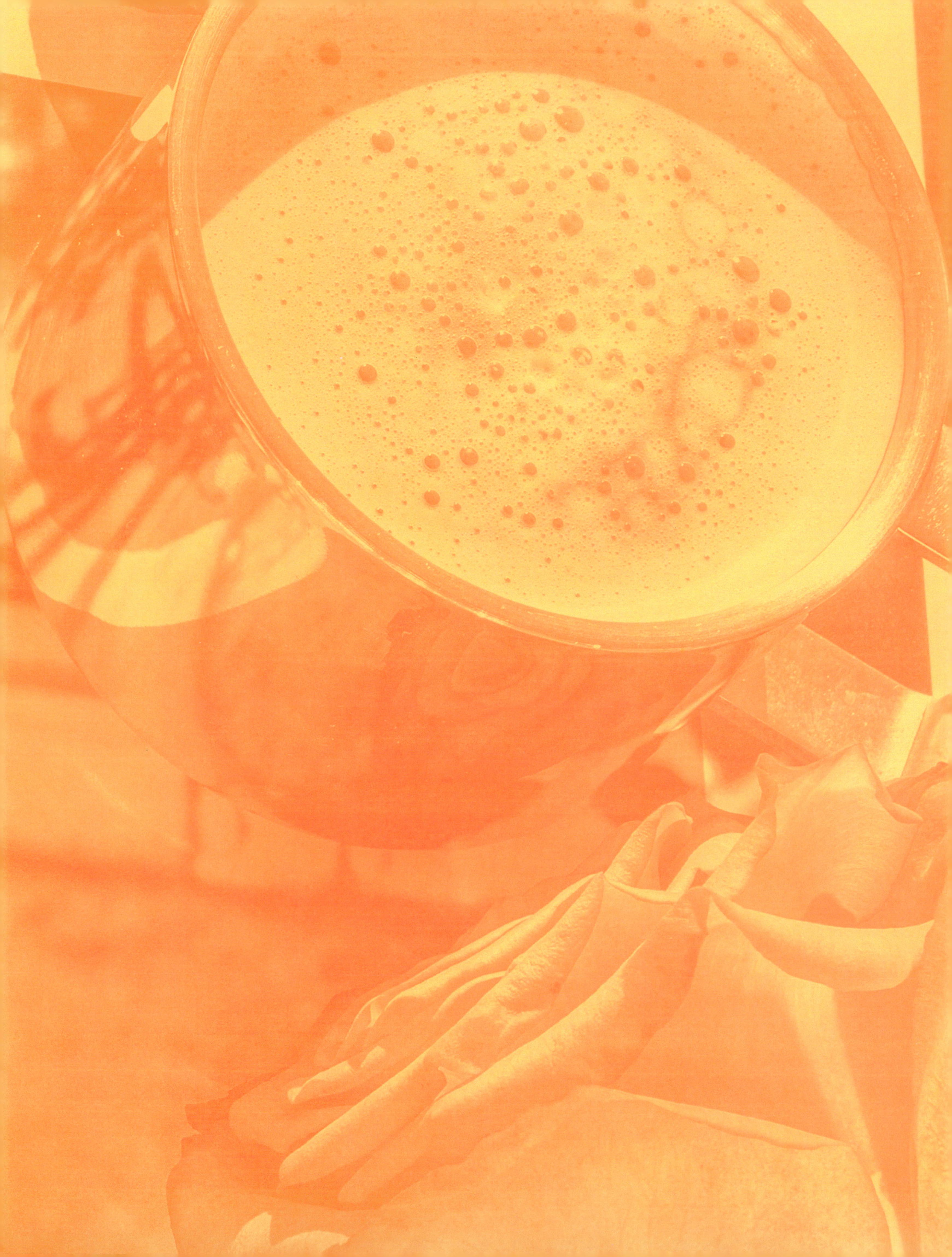

The printed page has been an important part of Samoylova's creative development. Like novels, art books and photobooks permit contemplative engagement. In this intimate setting, images can be studied and appreciated, and they enter into one's consciousness, shaping understanding, sharpening perception and clarifying artistic direction.

Samoylova looks at books in the morning, when her mind is open to inspiration and possibility. From here, she heads either to her studio or out into the observable world. Spending slow time with a book is a situation in which an imaginary artistic conversation can take place with the image makers she admires. Extending the ritual, the books sometimes lead to the making of a still-life photograph. An open page becomes part of the set-up, along with the accoutrements of the morning table.

Across all her work, Samoylova incorporates existing images. In *Breakfasts*, however, the images are not from the mass media, the internet or the commercial world. They are usually artworks in their own right, and for this reason the act of including them in her photographs comes with a degree of ambivalence. *Breakfasts* is not quite a gesture of 'appropriation', but it is not pure homage either. Rather, it is all part of an open and ongoing dialogue about images, their circulation and their influence.

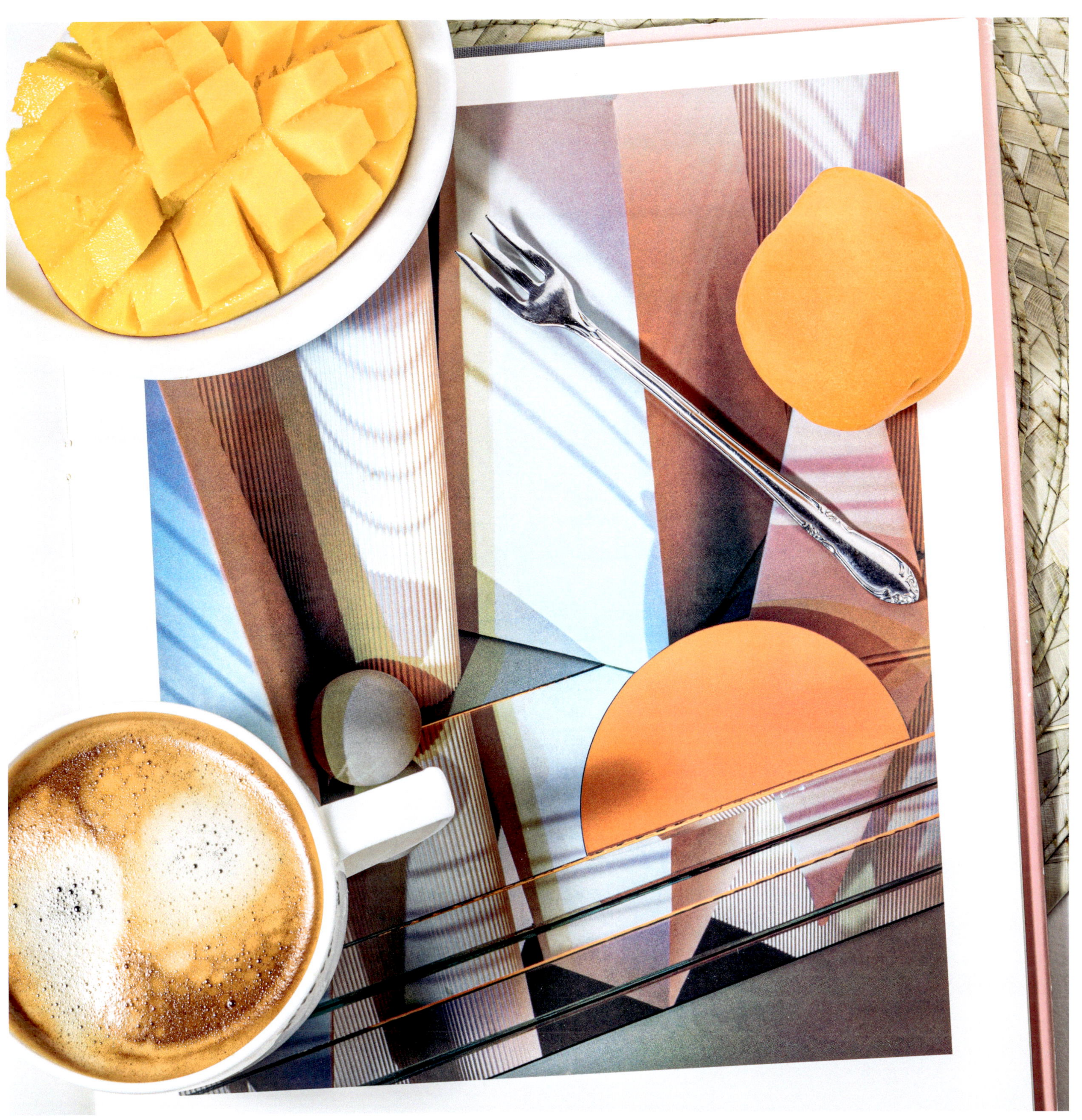

Breakfast with Barbara Kasten 1983, 2017

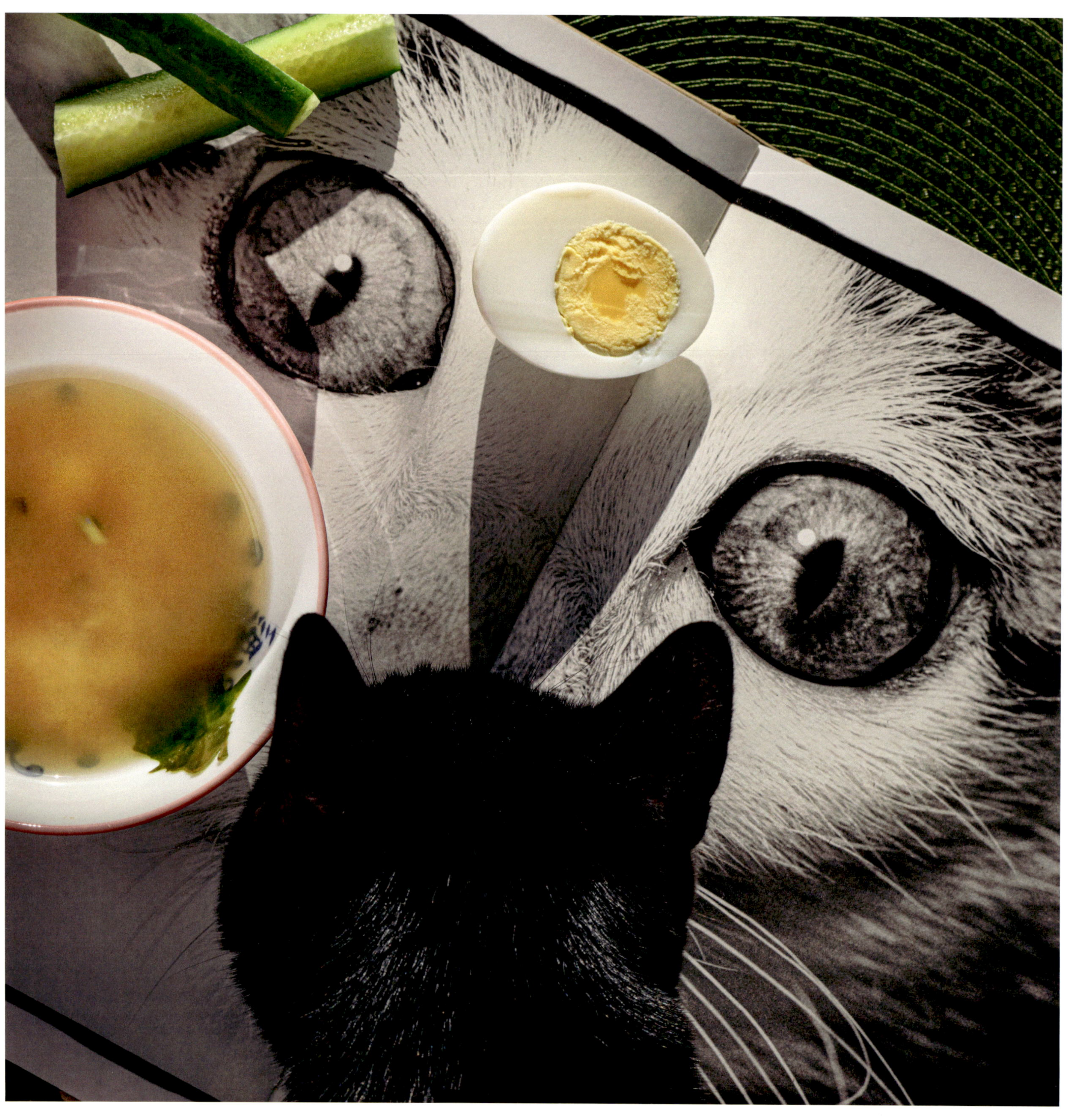

Breakfast with Masahisa Fukase 1978, 2023

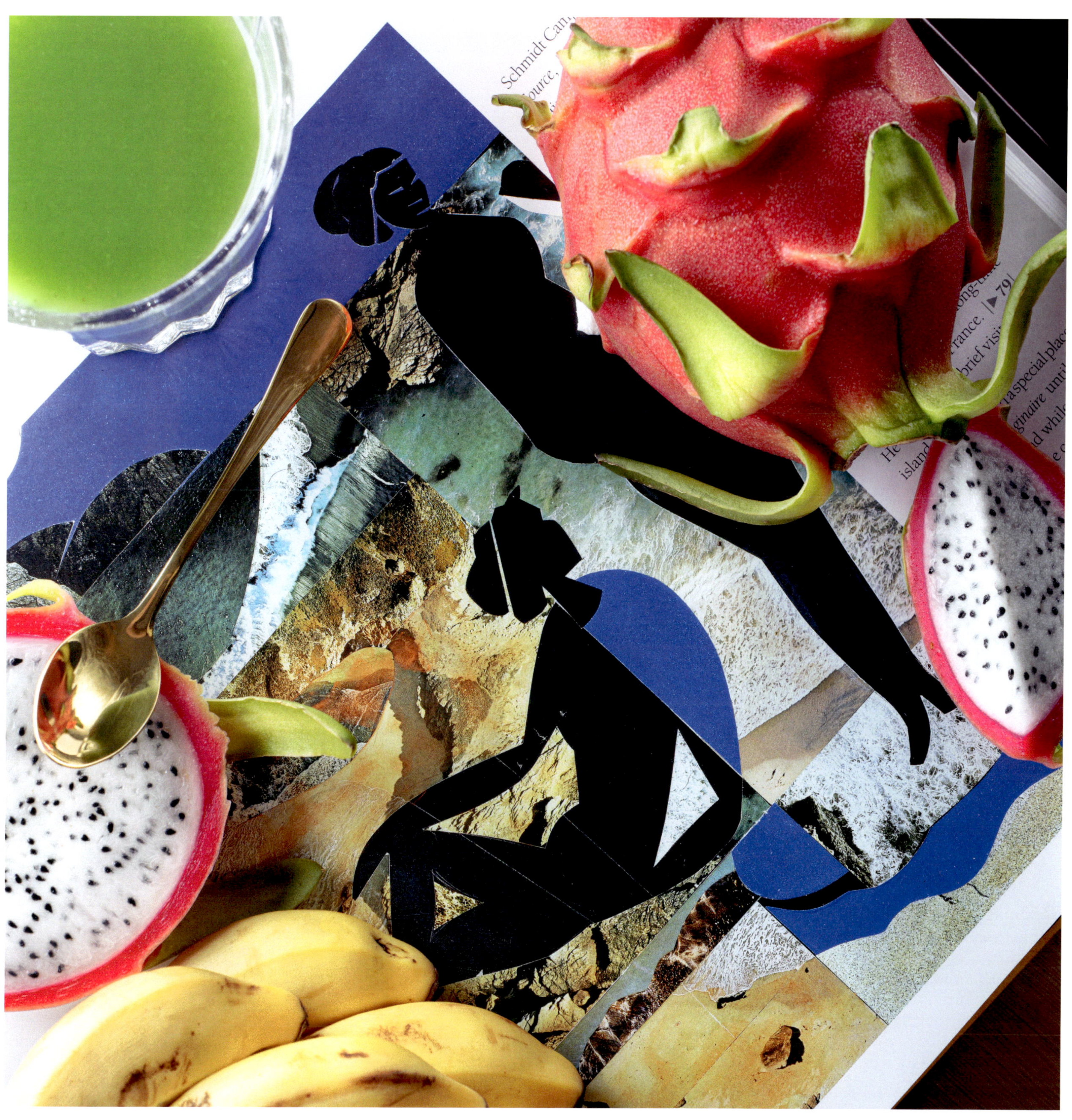

Breakfast with Romare Bearden 1952, 2024

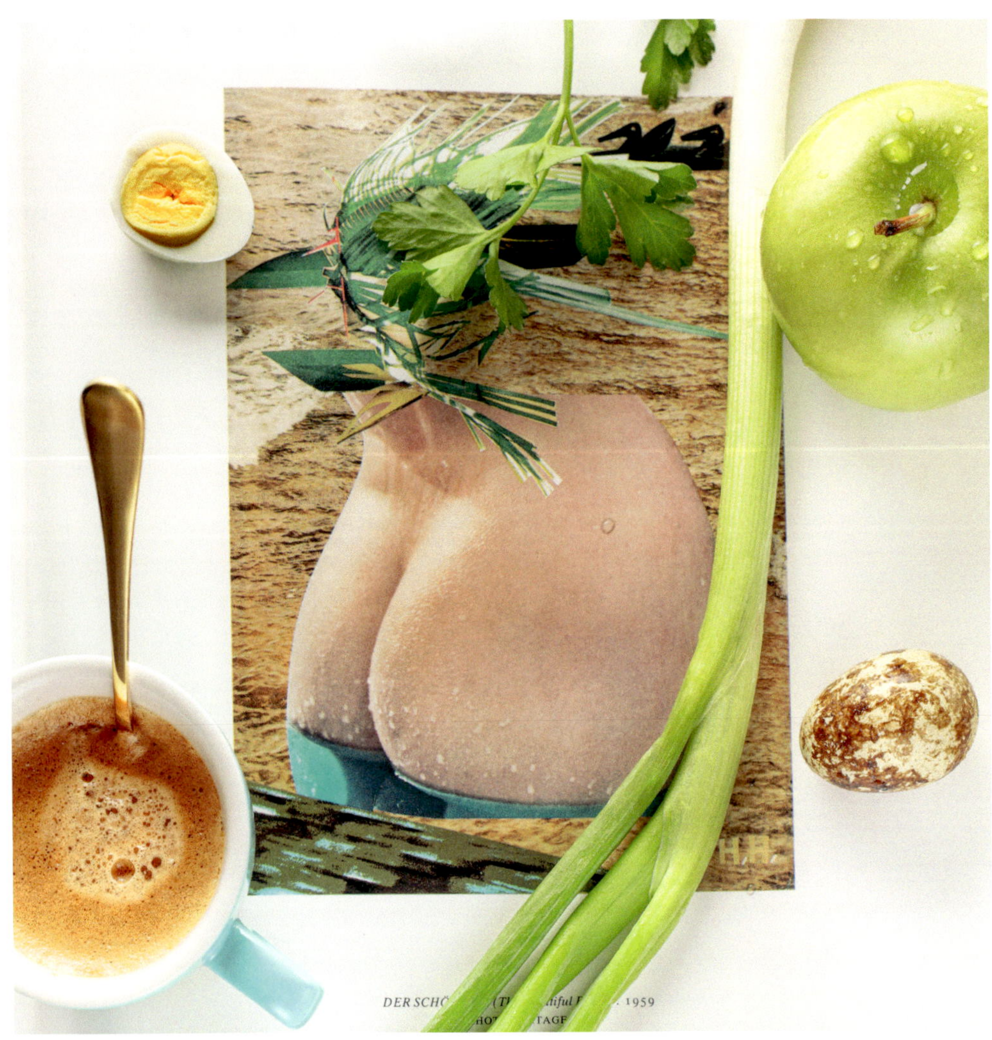

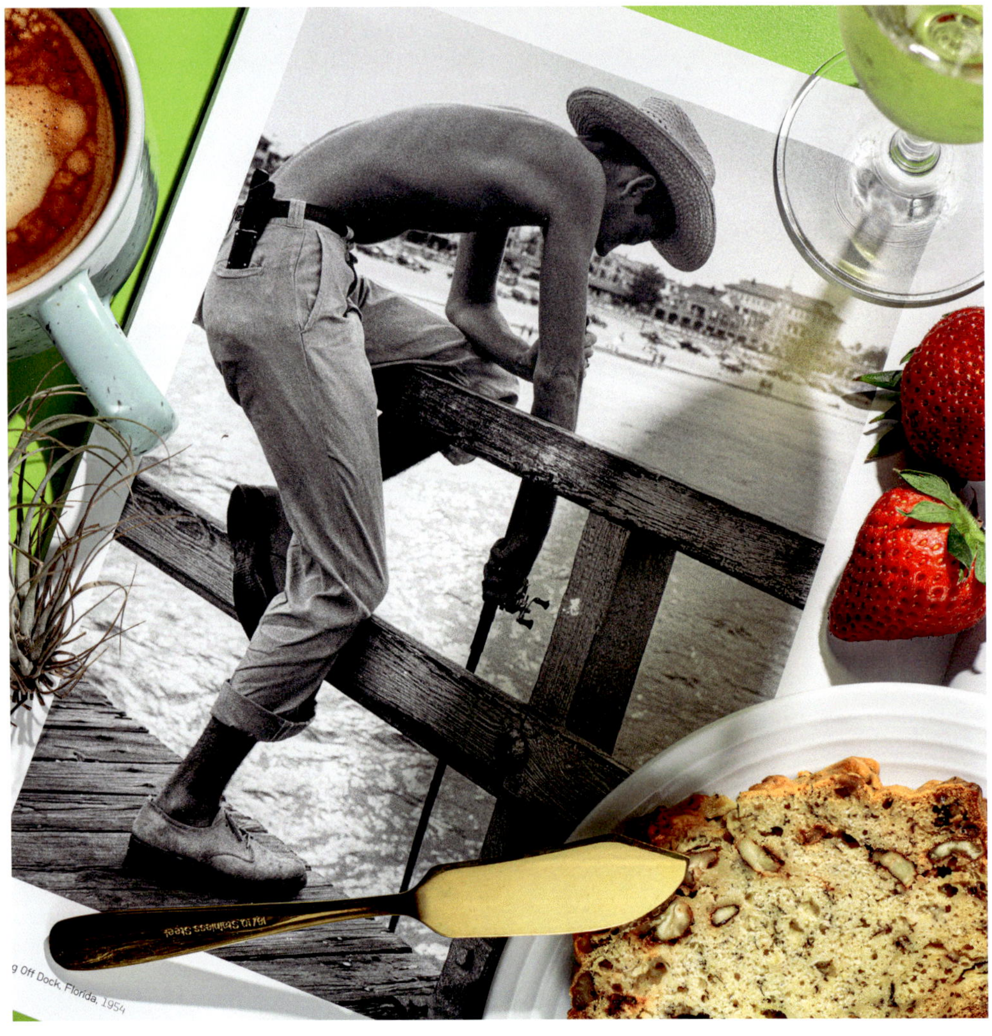

˄ Breakfast with Hannah Höch 1959, 2024
˅ Breakfast with Berenice Abbott 1954, 2020

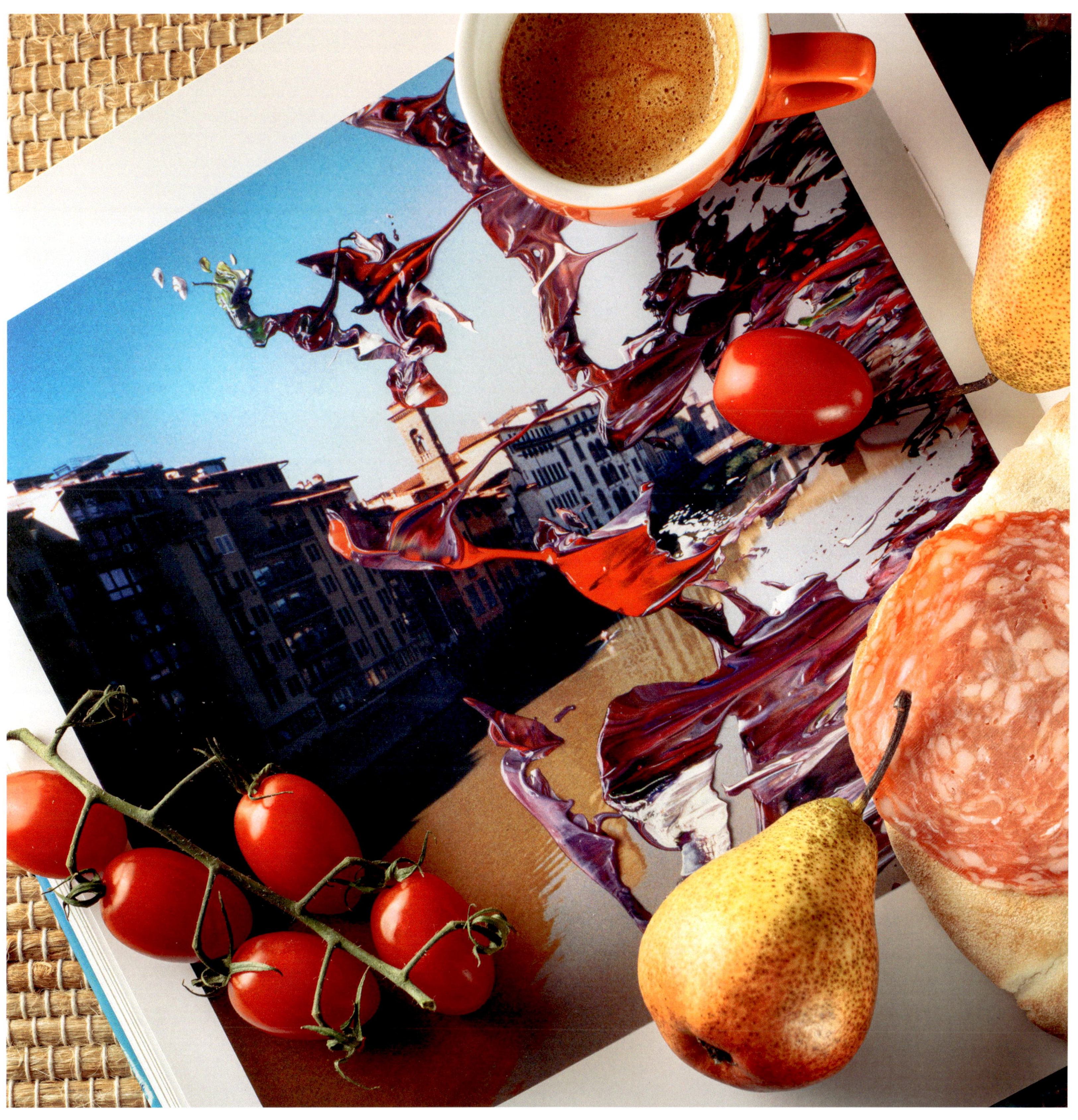

Breakfast with Gerhard Richter 2000, 2024

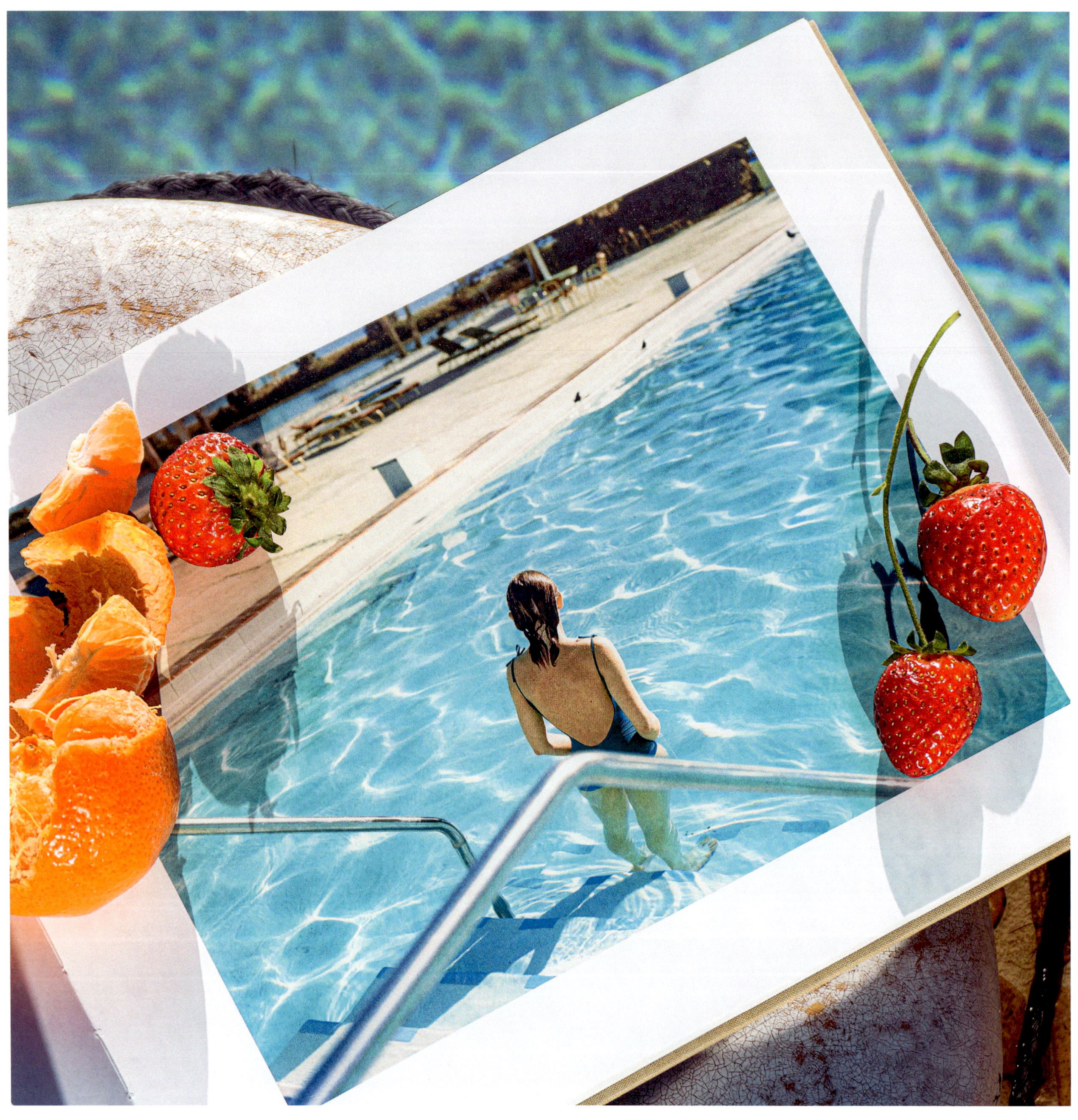

Breakfast with Stephen Shore 1977, 2018

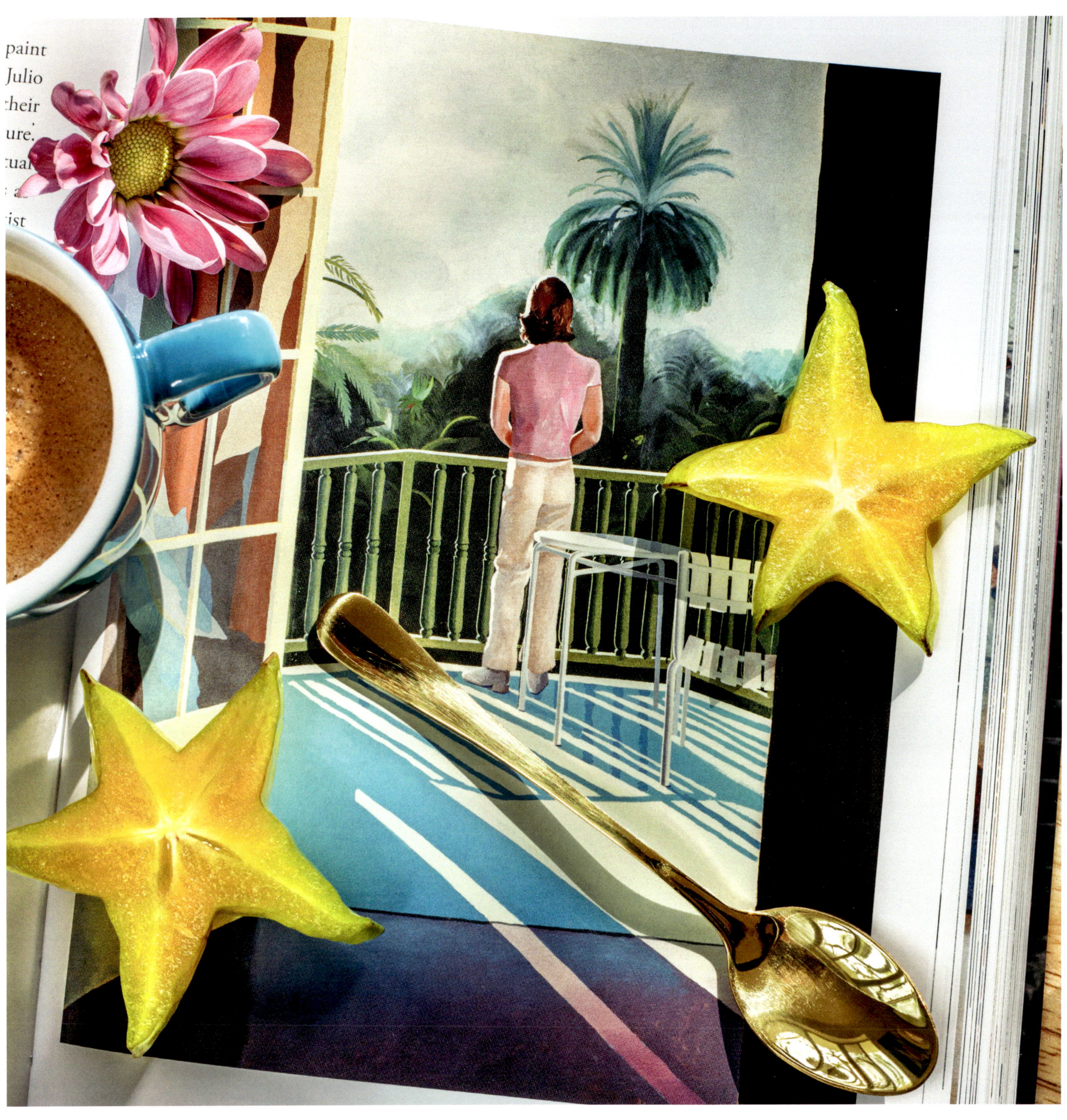

Breakfast with David Hockney 1971, 2024

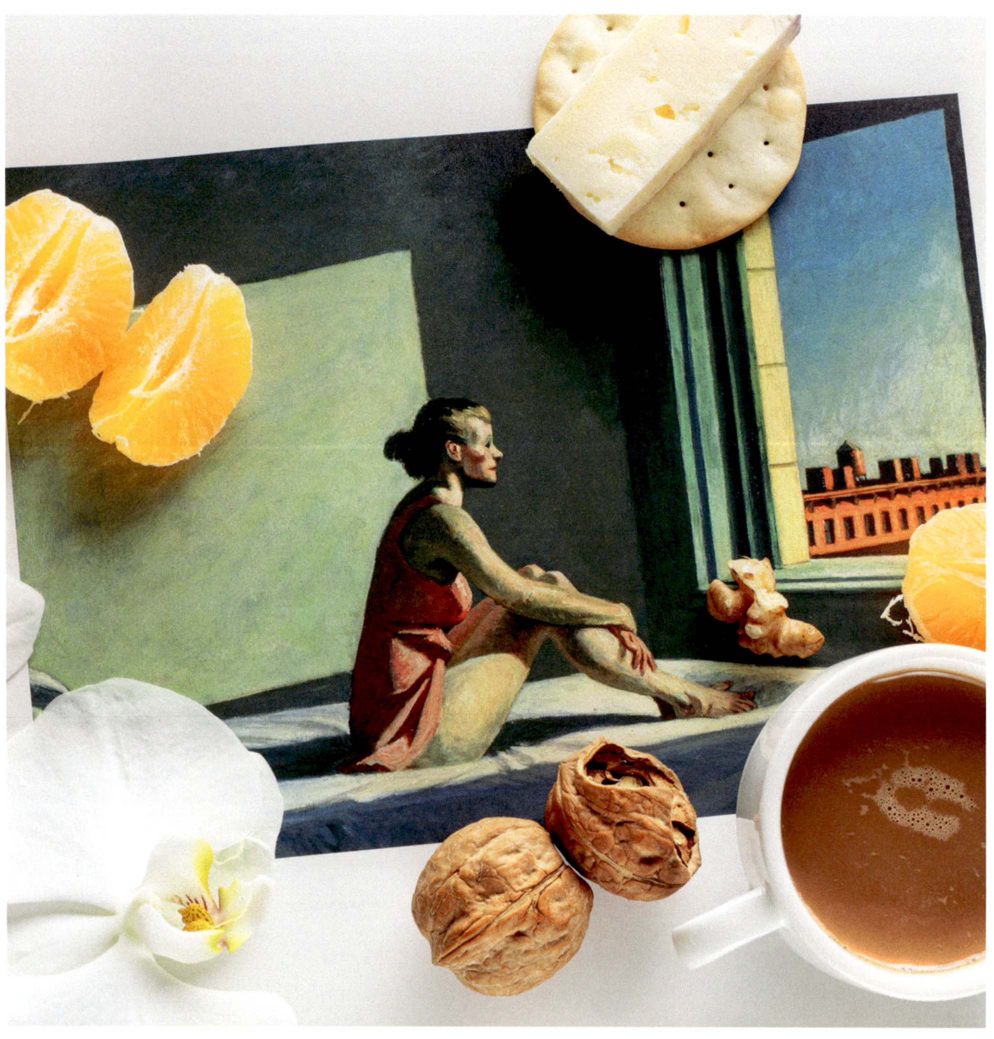

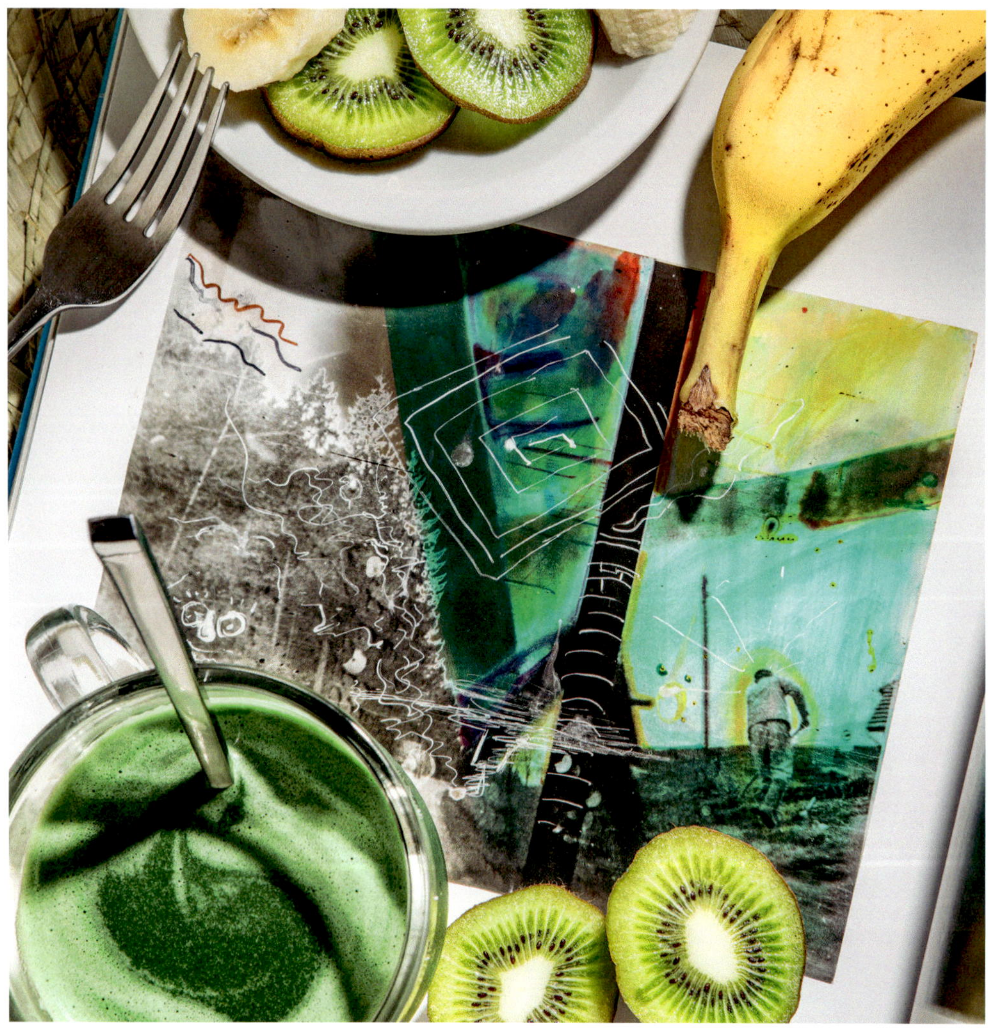

^ Breakfast with Edward Hopper 1952, 2024
⌄ Breakfast with Sigmar Polke 1975, 2017

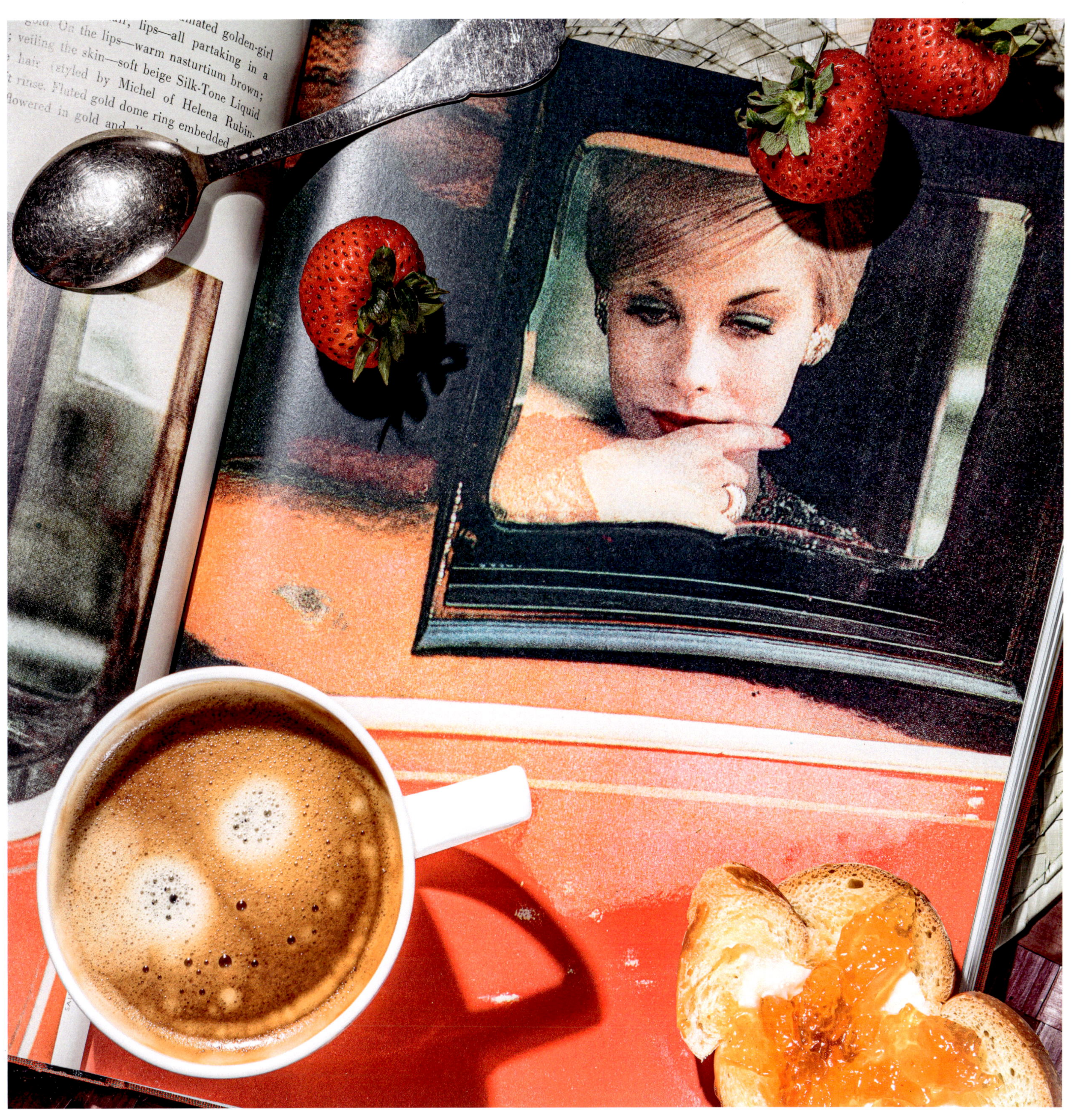

Breakfast with Saul Leiter 1959, 2017

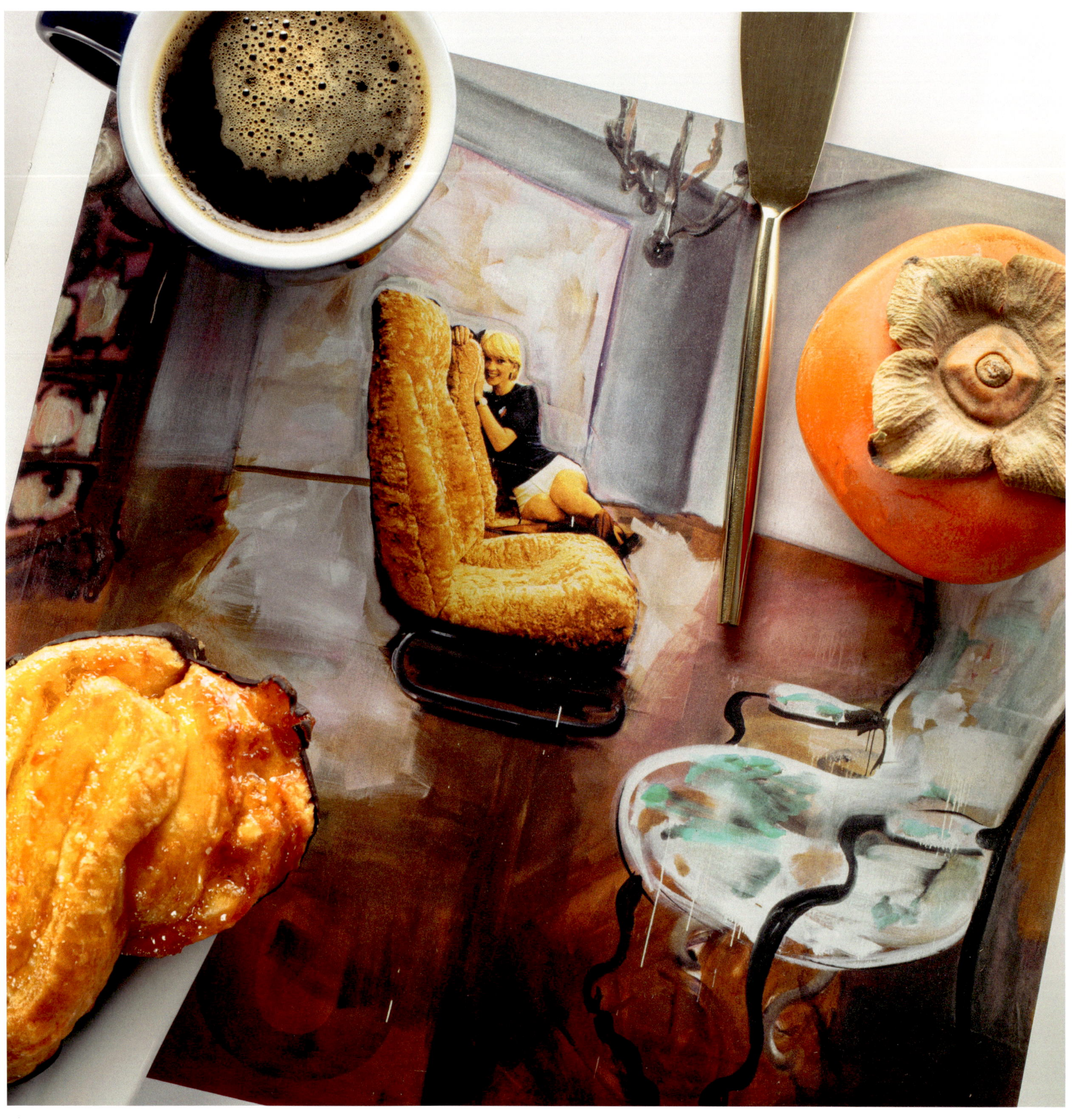

Breakfast with Albert Oehlen 2004, 2024

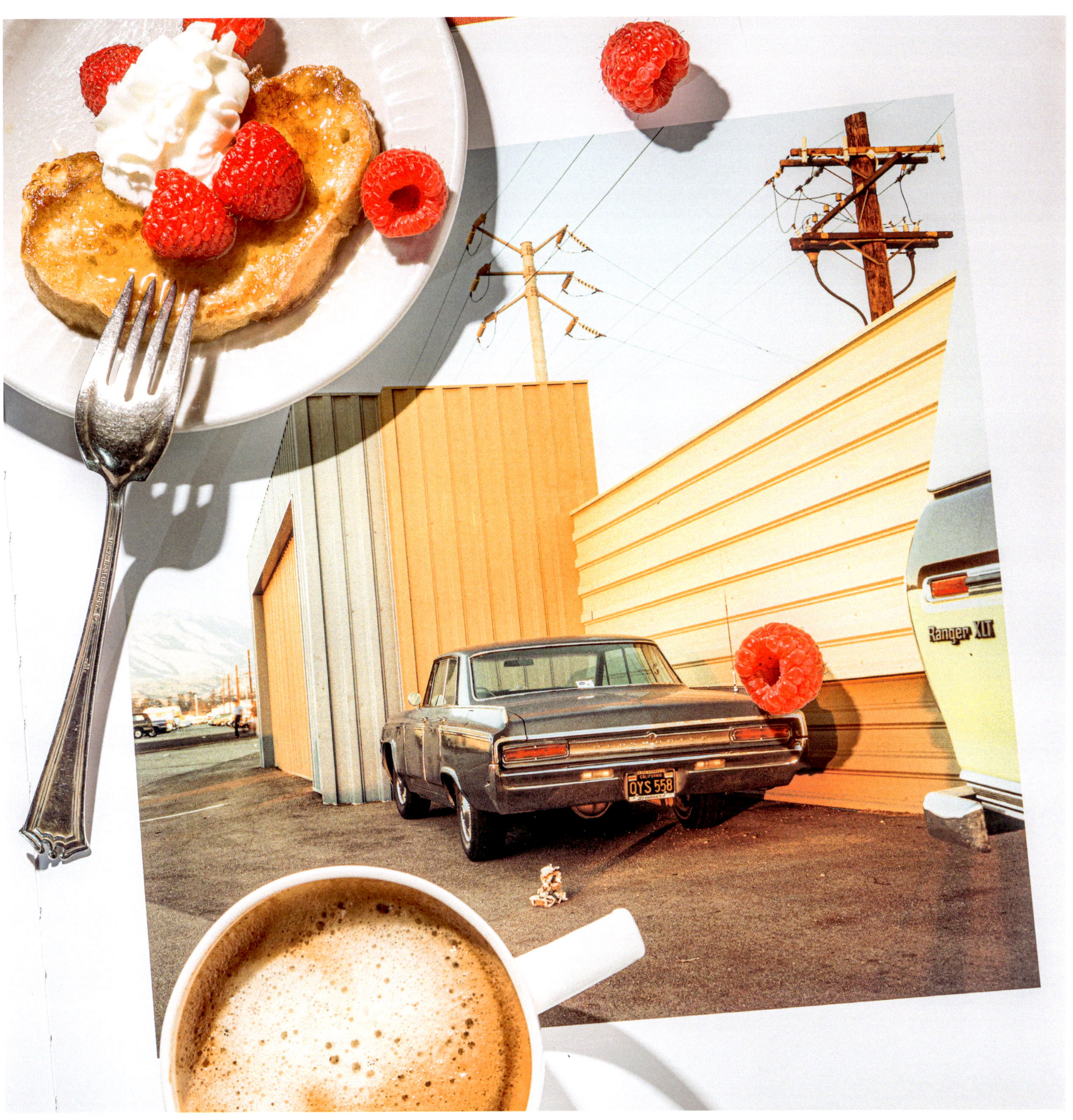

Breakfast with William Eggleston 1976, 2017

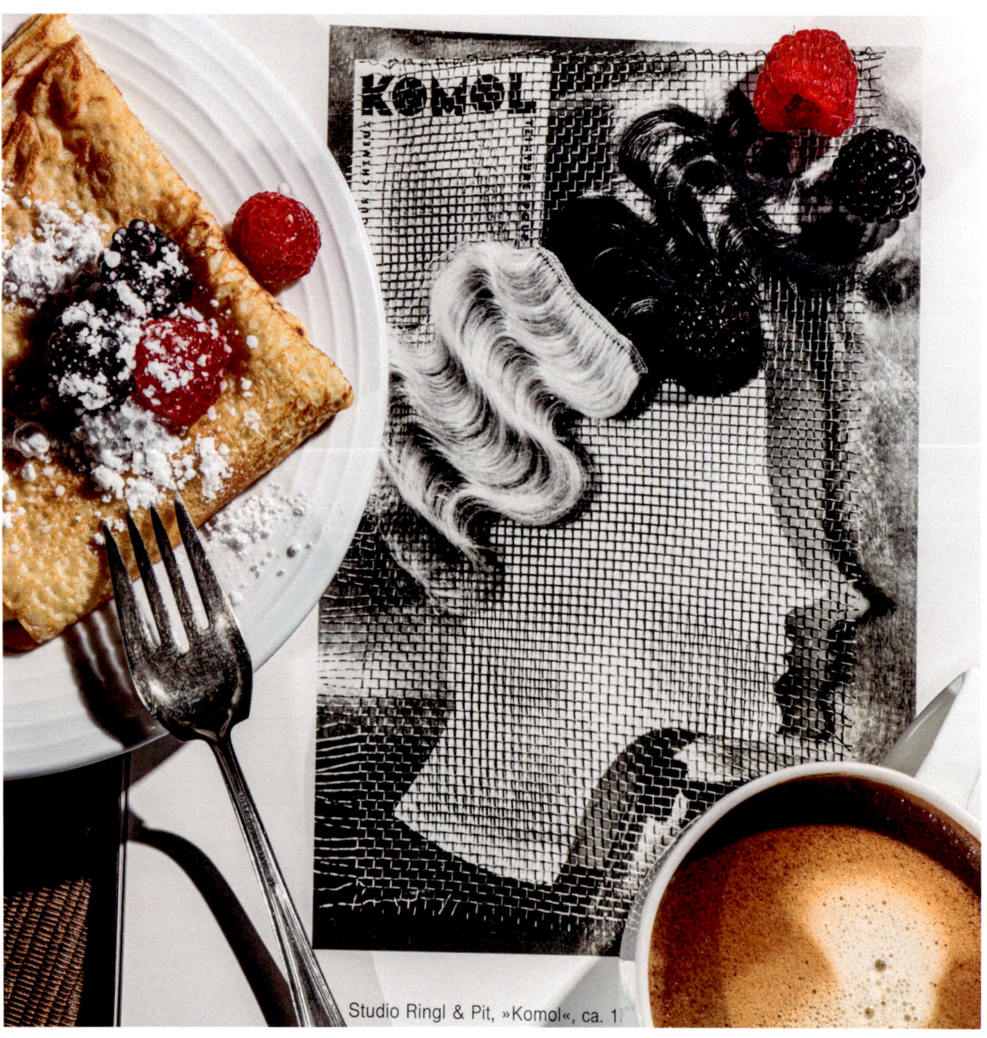

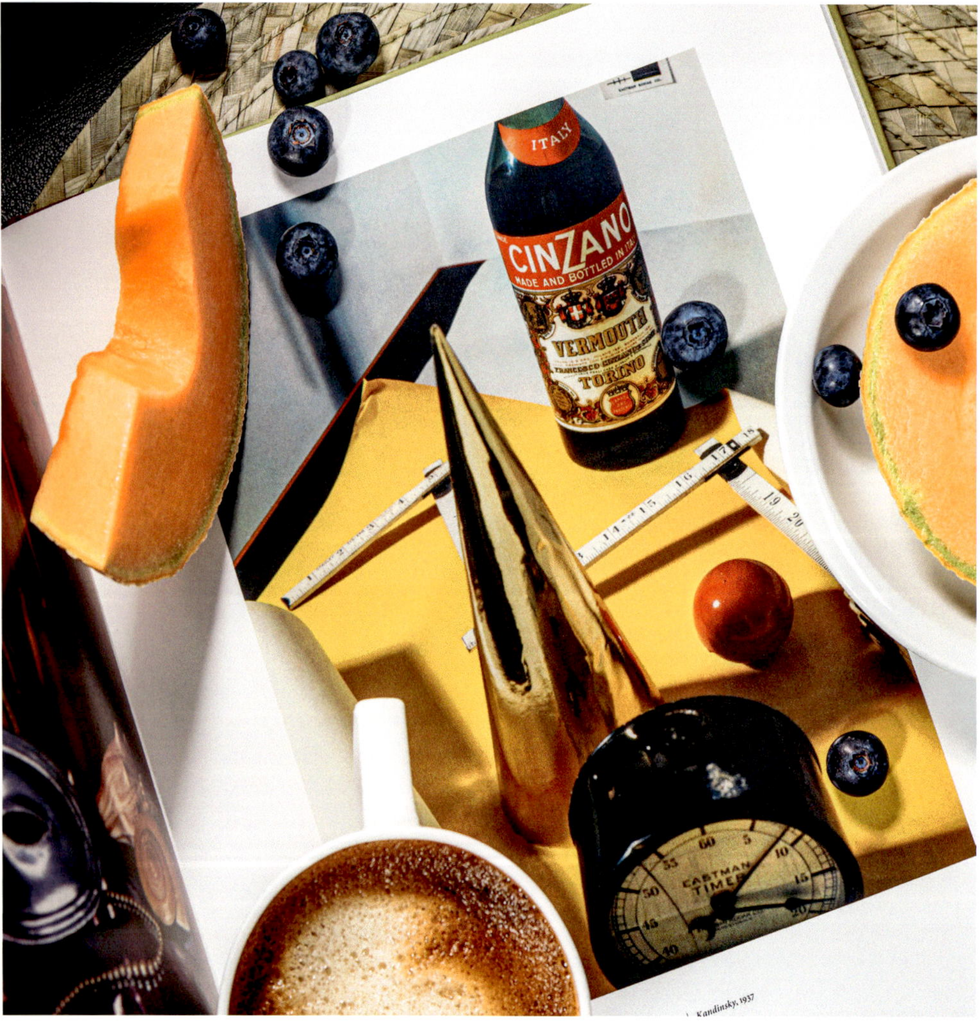

^ Breakfast with Studio Ringl and Pit 1932, 2017

ˇ Breakfast with Paul Outerbridge 1937, 2017

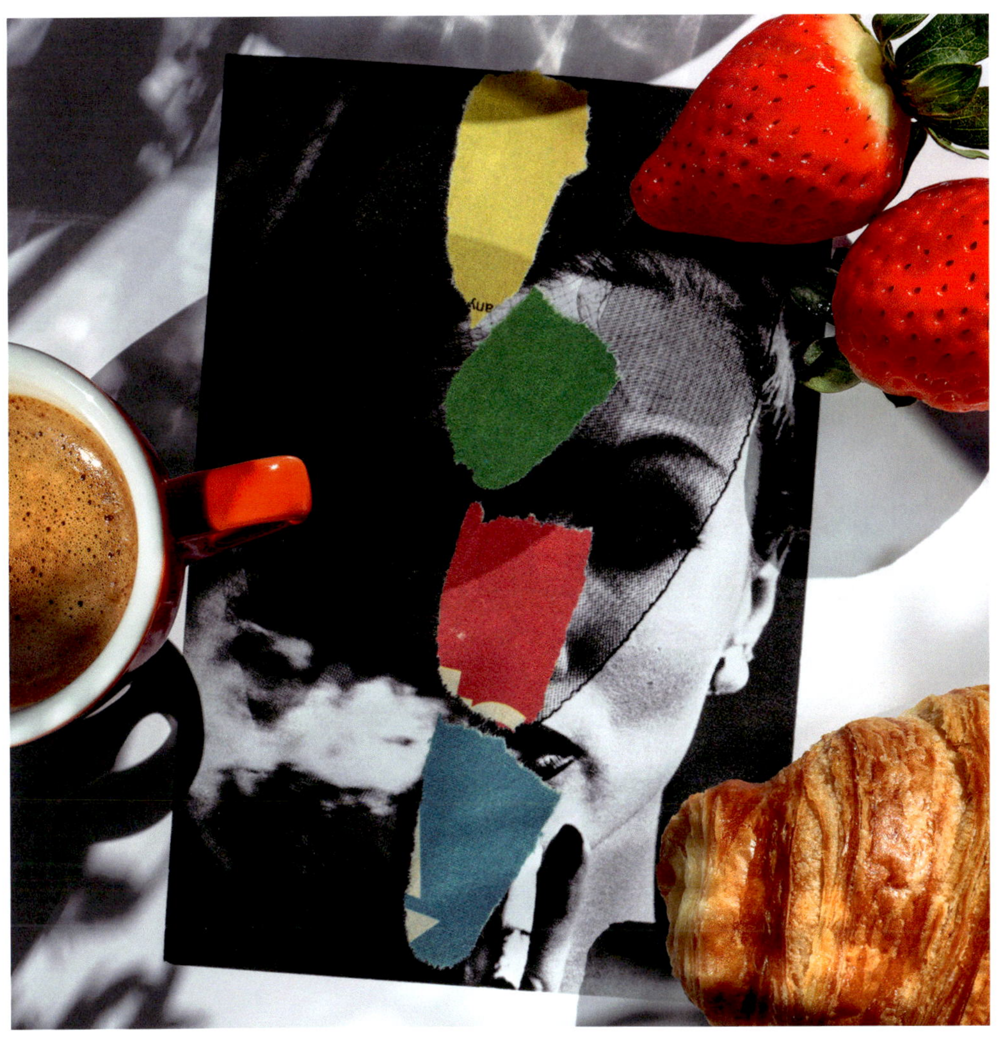

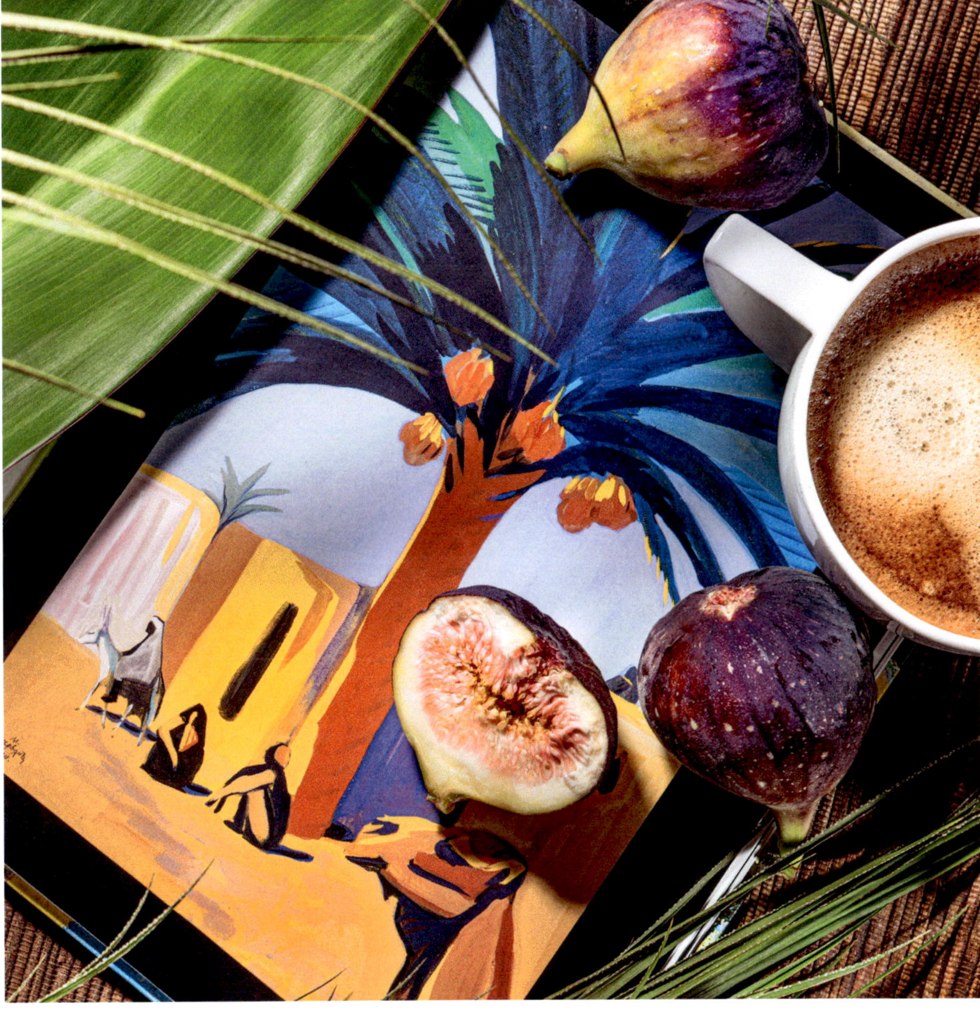

⌃ Breakfast with Ellsworth Kelly (and William Klein) 1985, 2024
⌄ Breakfast with Martiros Saryan 1911, 2017

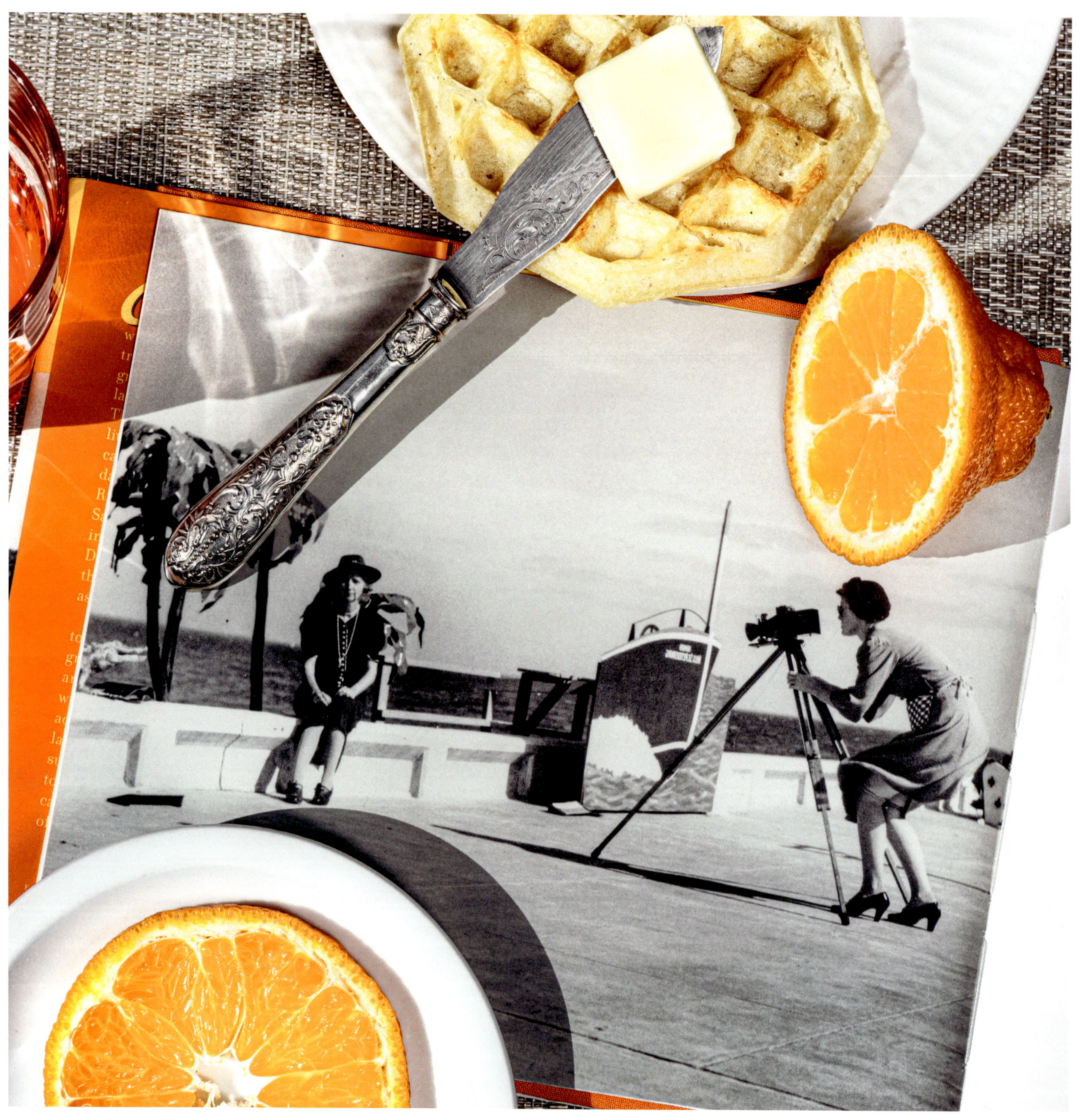

Breakfast with Walker Evans 1941, 2020

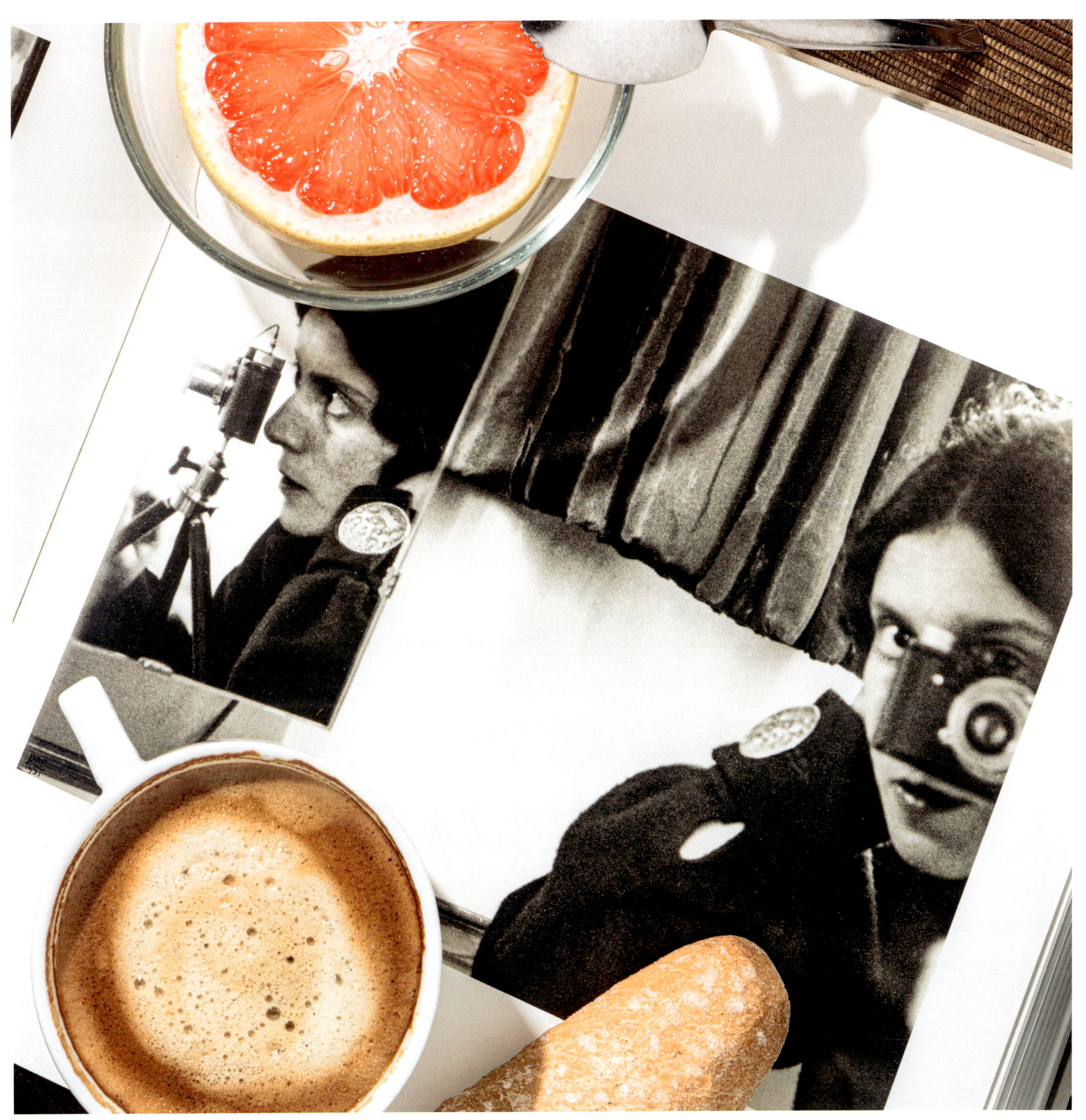

Breakfast with Ilse Bing 1931, 2018

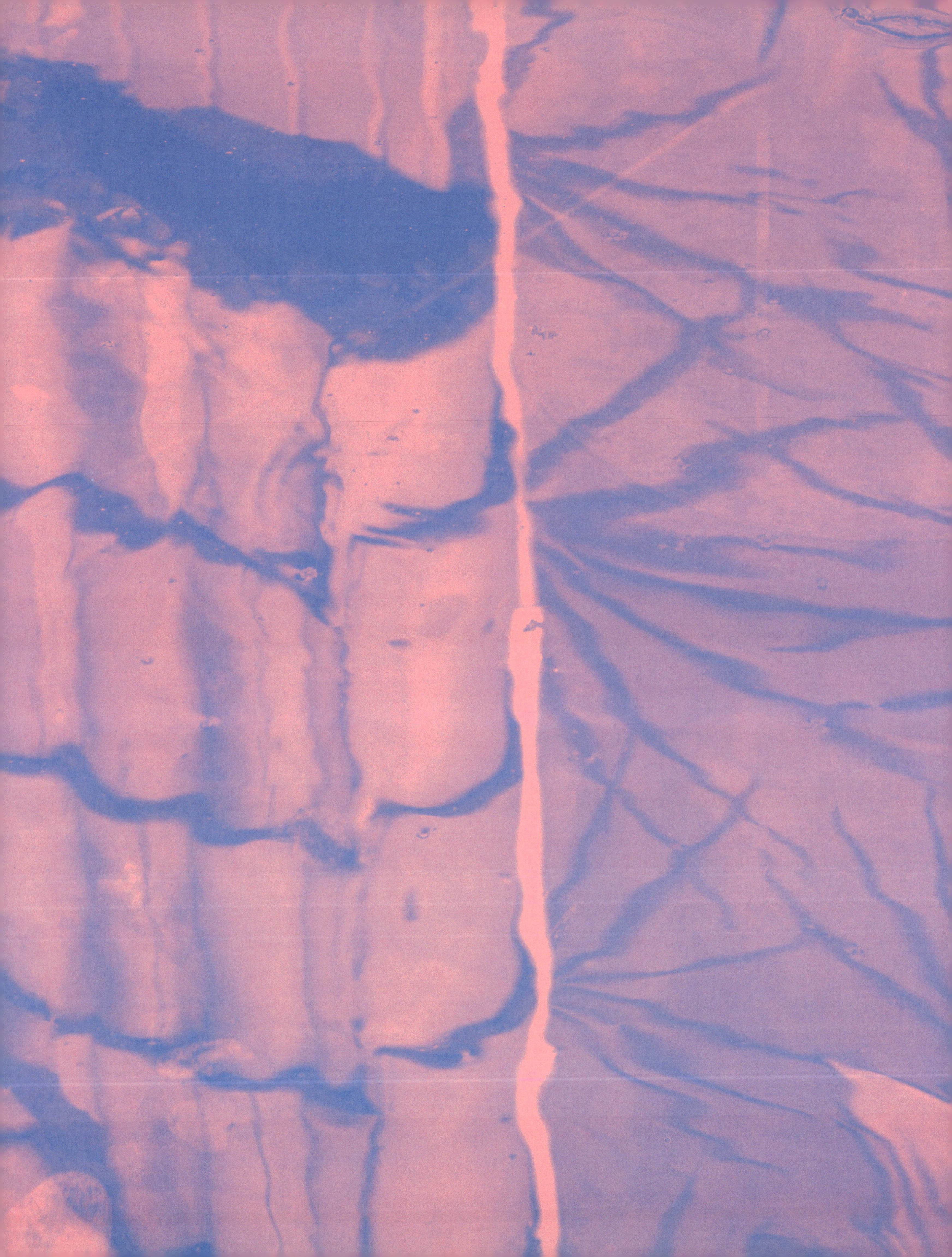

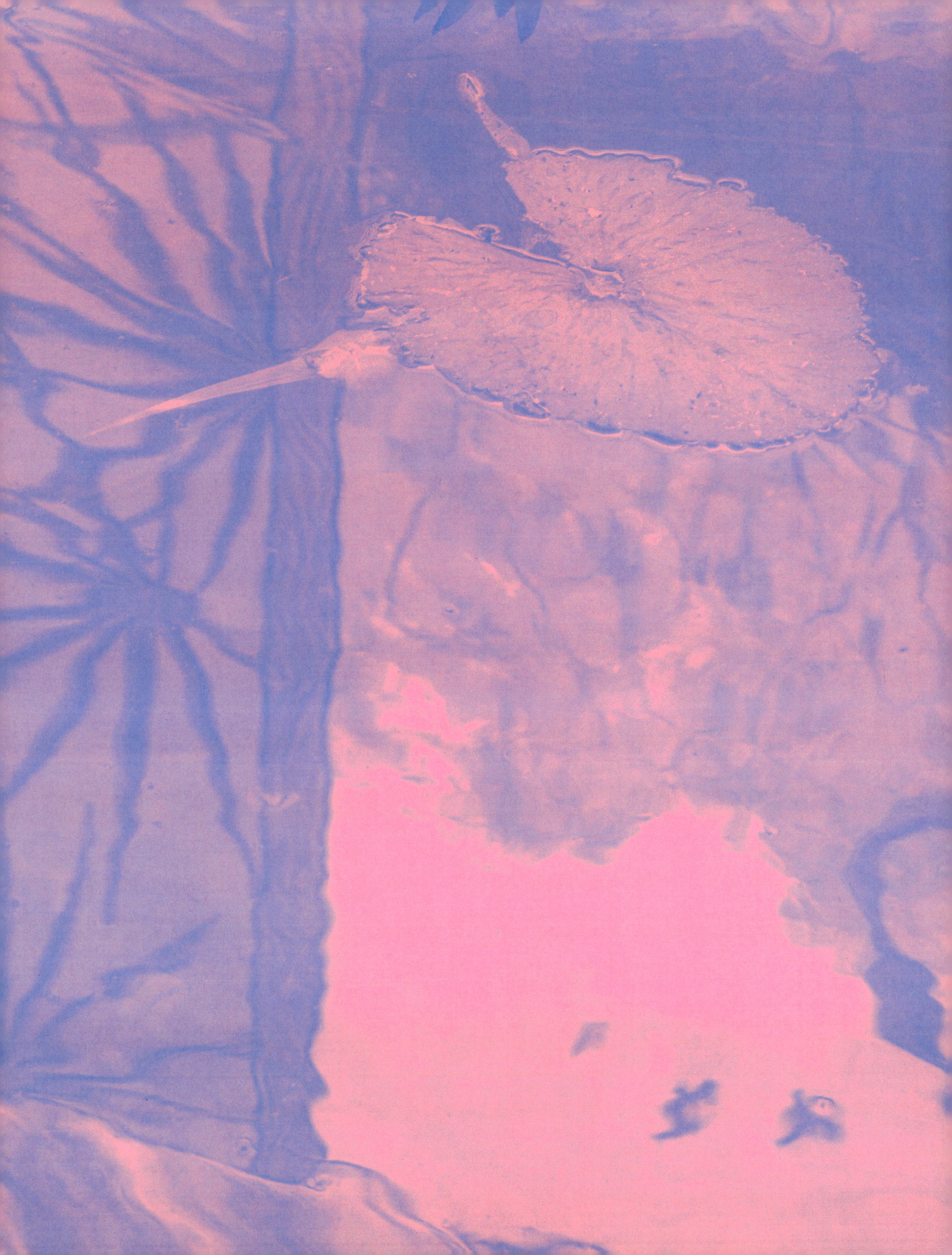

For a long time, Florida has been seen by the USA and the wider world as a caricature, home to the nation's extremes, which are acted out for public display and ridicule. Political differences, wealth and poverty, presumed shallowness and selfishness, racial divisions and the obsession with image over substance are not the whole story, but Donald Trump's presidency intensified the problem. Given the sheer weight of Florida's stereotypes, could an open and nuanced visual response be made? And if it could, how might it be received? It was an artistic risk.

Samoylova covered every corner of Florida, from the Keys in the south to the Forgotten Coast of the northwest. Dozens of road trips were researched and planned, although most of her pictures came from wandering in small towns. Aesthetically, there is an overlap with the *FloodZone* series, but the photographs are often simpler and more direct, with a deeper sense of history.

Over time, Samoylova found her approach was close to that of Walker Evans (1903–75), whose empathetic but wary eye led him to observe Florida with a cool wit and layered irony. Now and then, Samoylova was making images that could almost be mistaken for his, particularly her black-and-white photographs of unchanged places. For the *Floridas* book (2022), the bold decision was made to bring together the work of Samoylova and Evans. This led to an exhibition of photographs, paintings and collages by both artists at New York's Metropolitan Museum of Art in 2024.

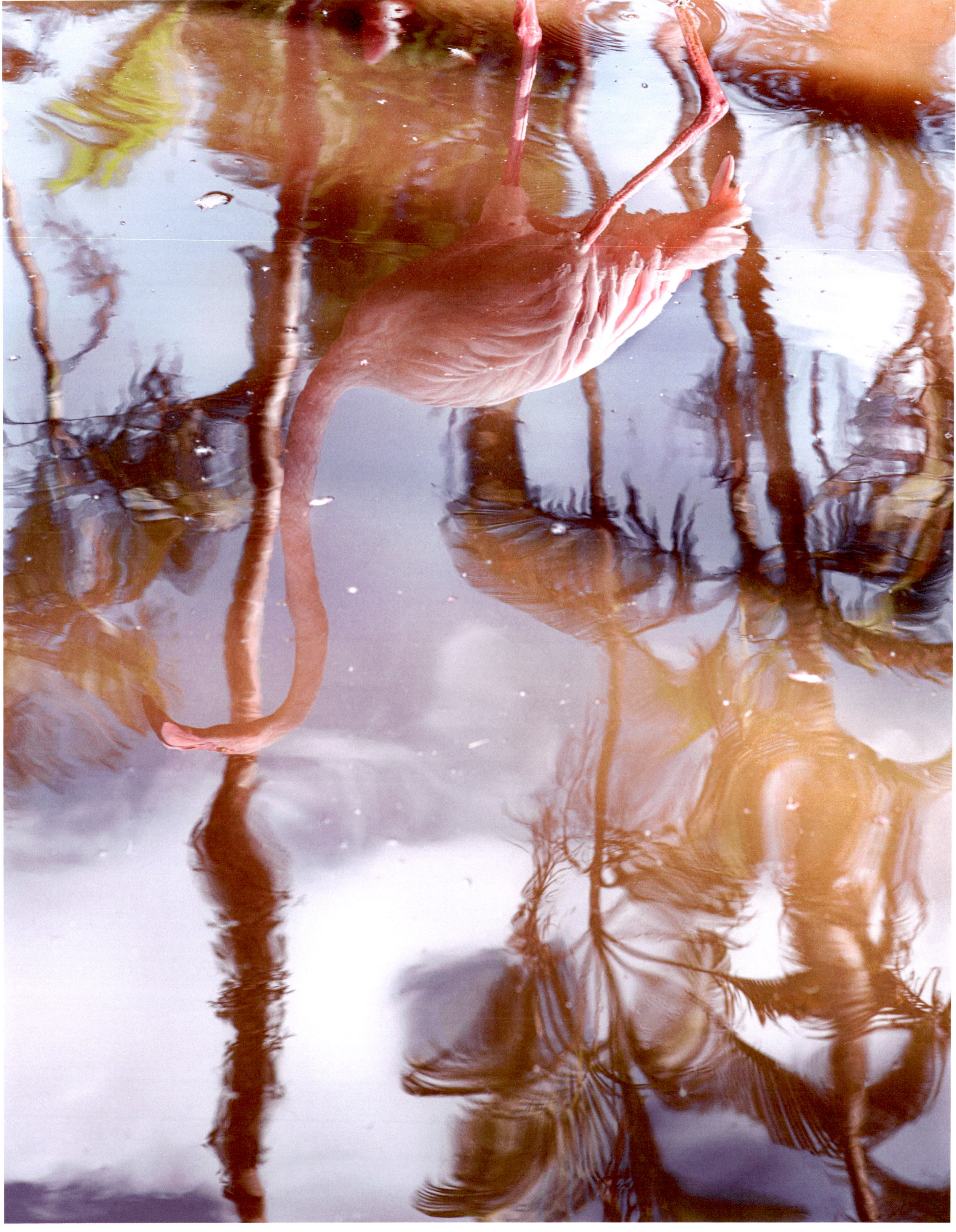

Flamingo Reflection, 2018

» New Condominium, Bonita Springs, 2021

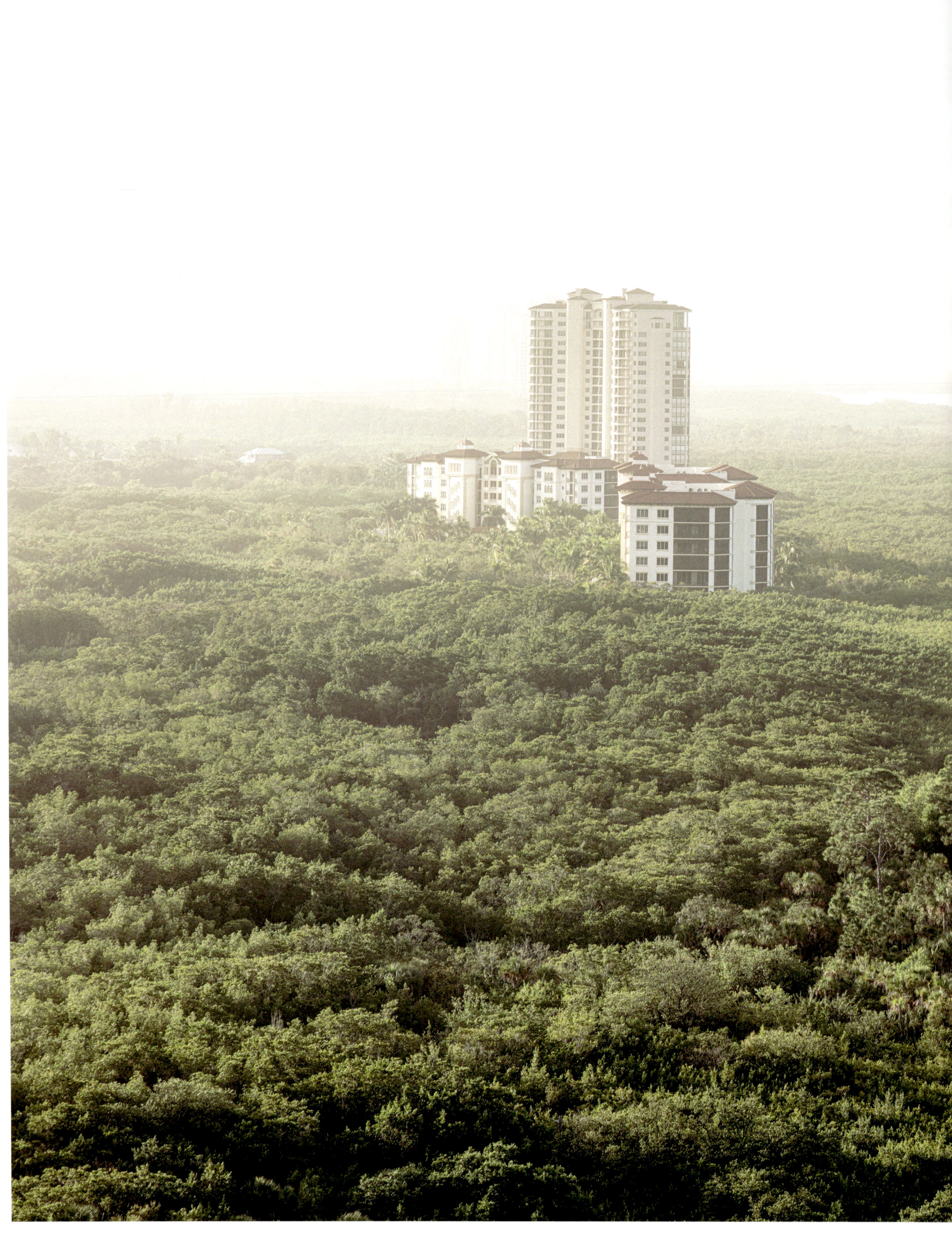

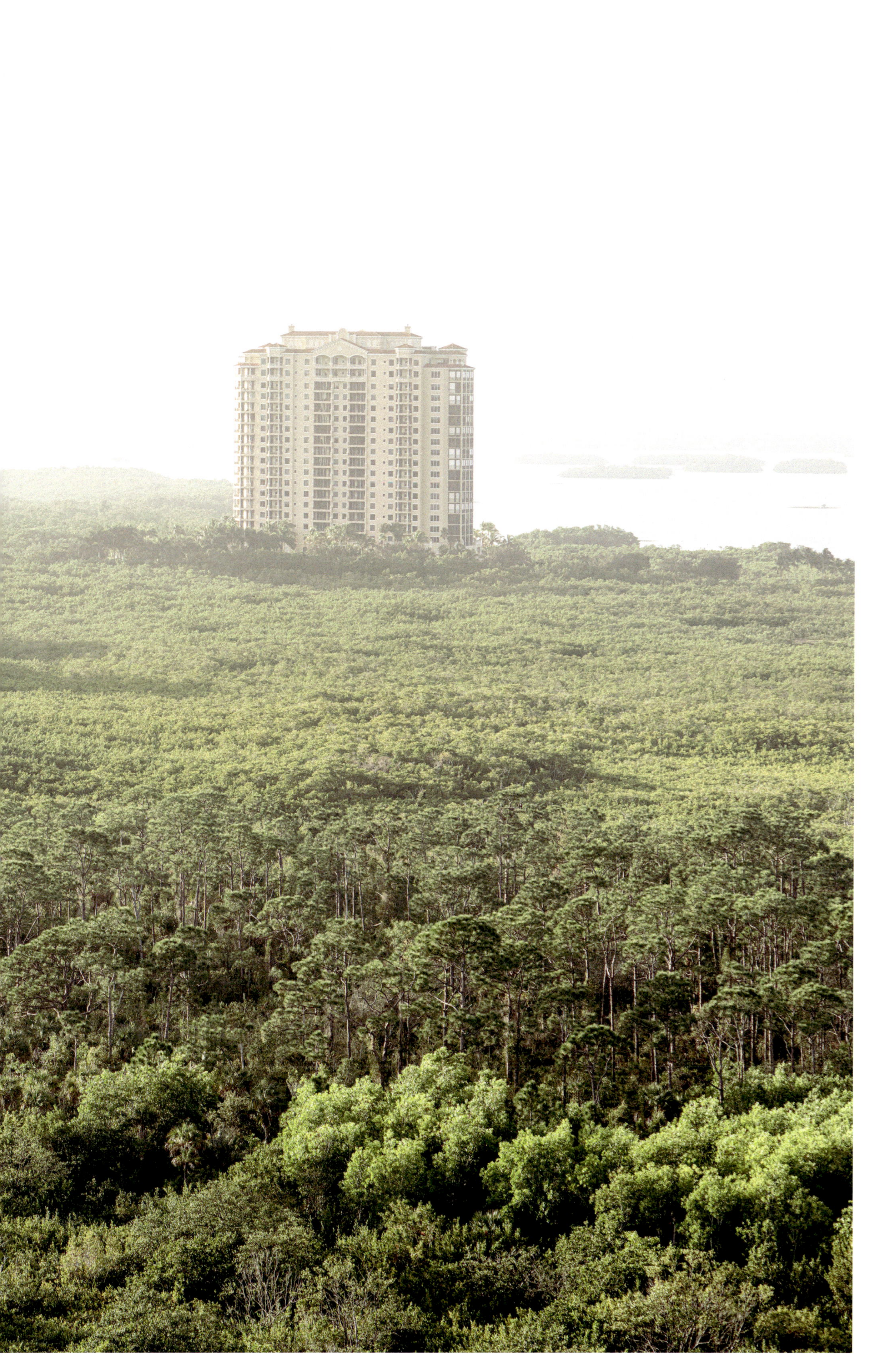

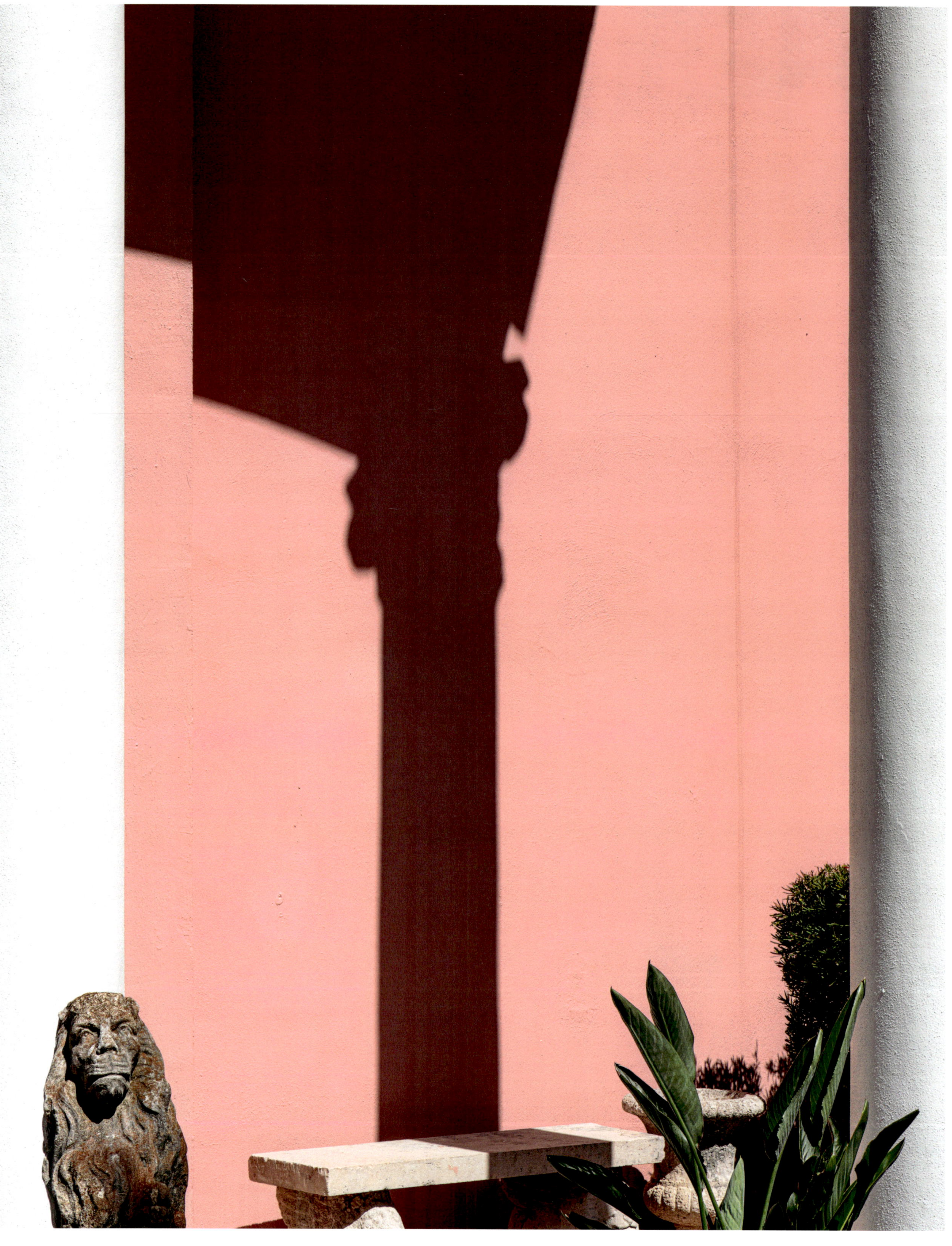

Lion, Sarasota, 2020

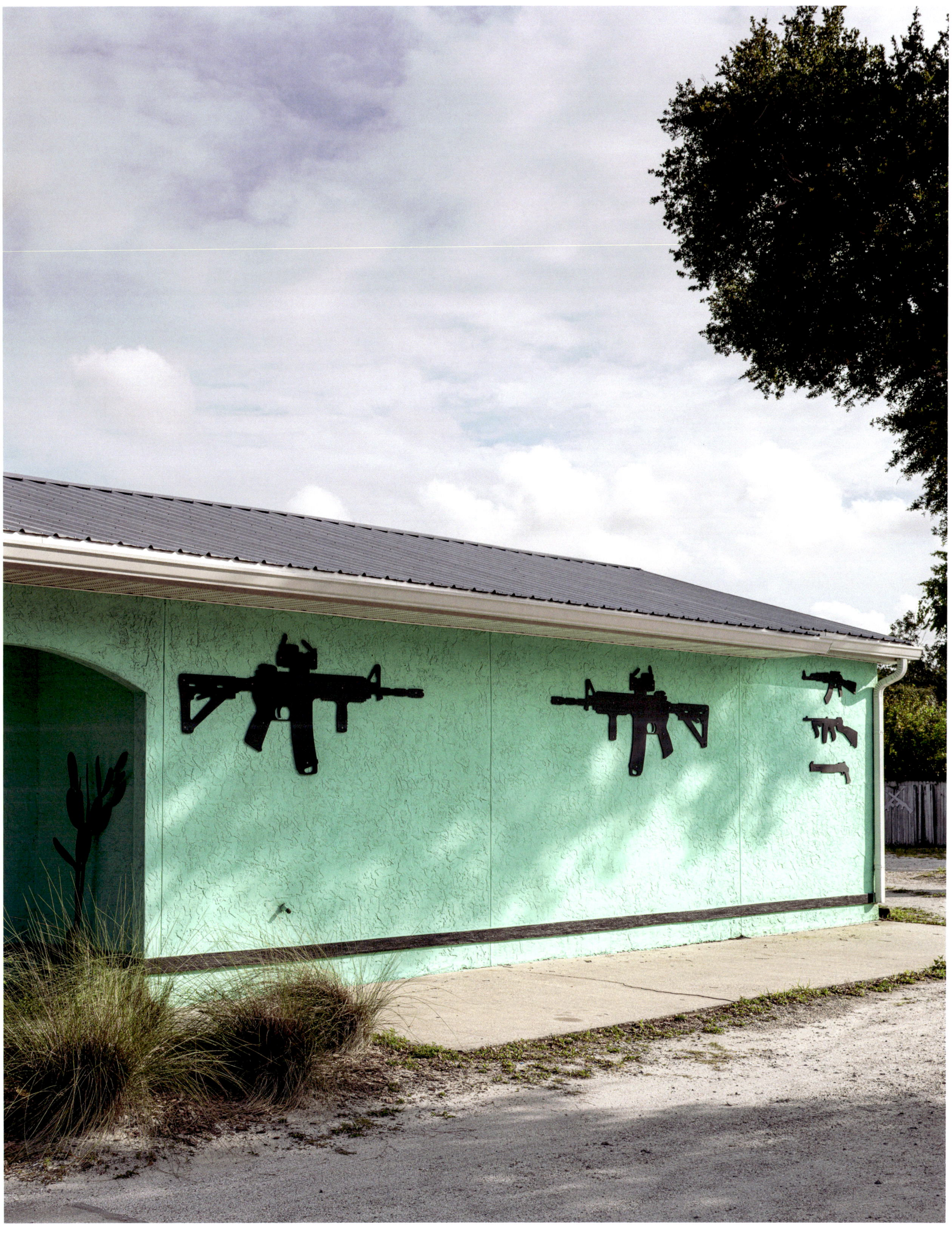

Gun Shop, Port Orange, 2019

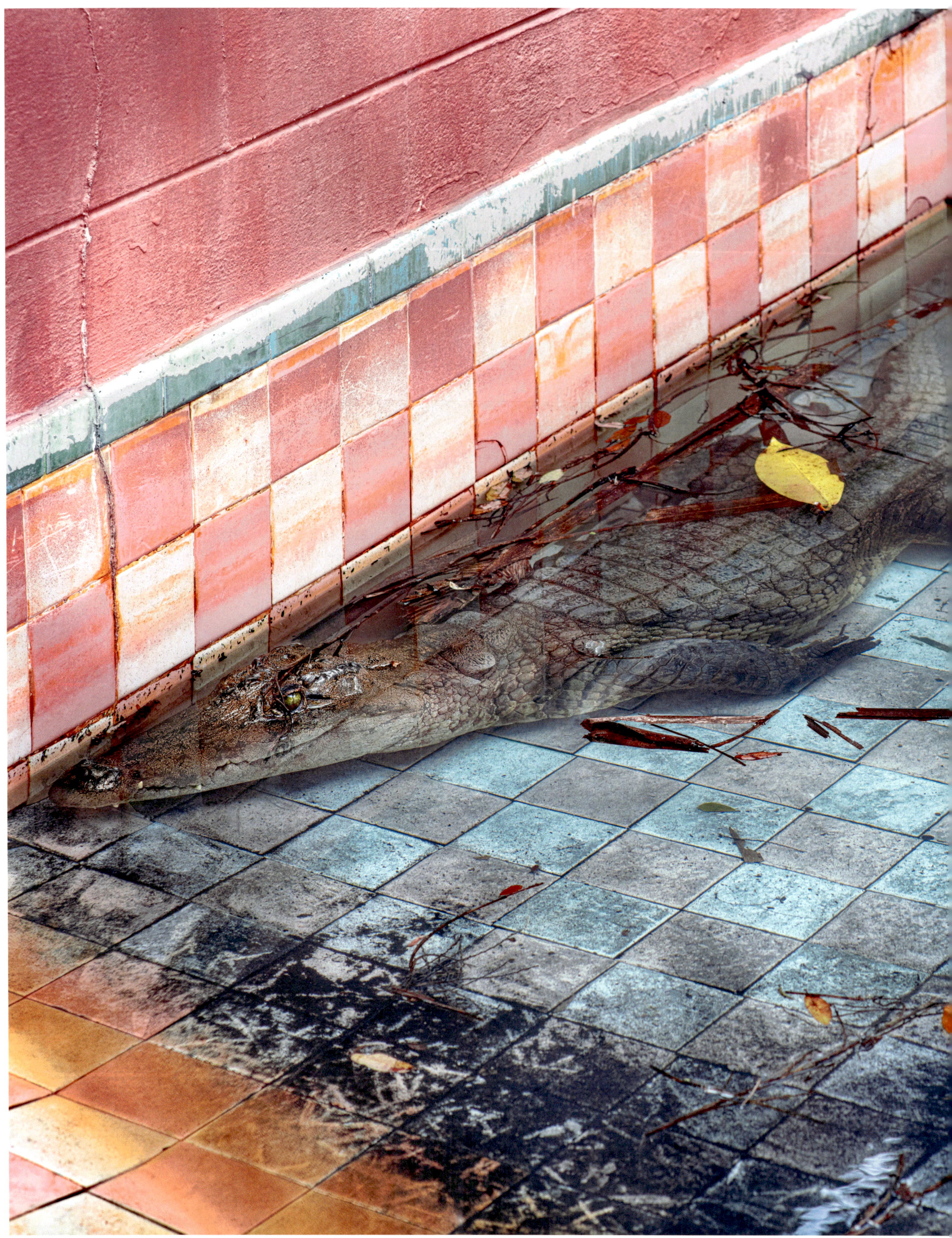

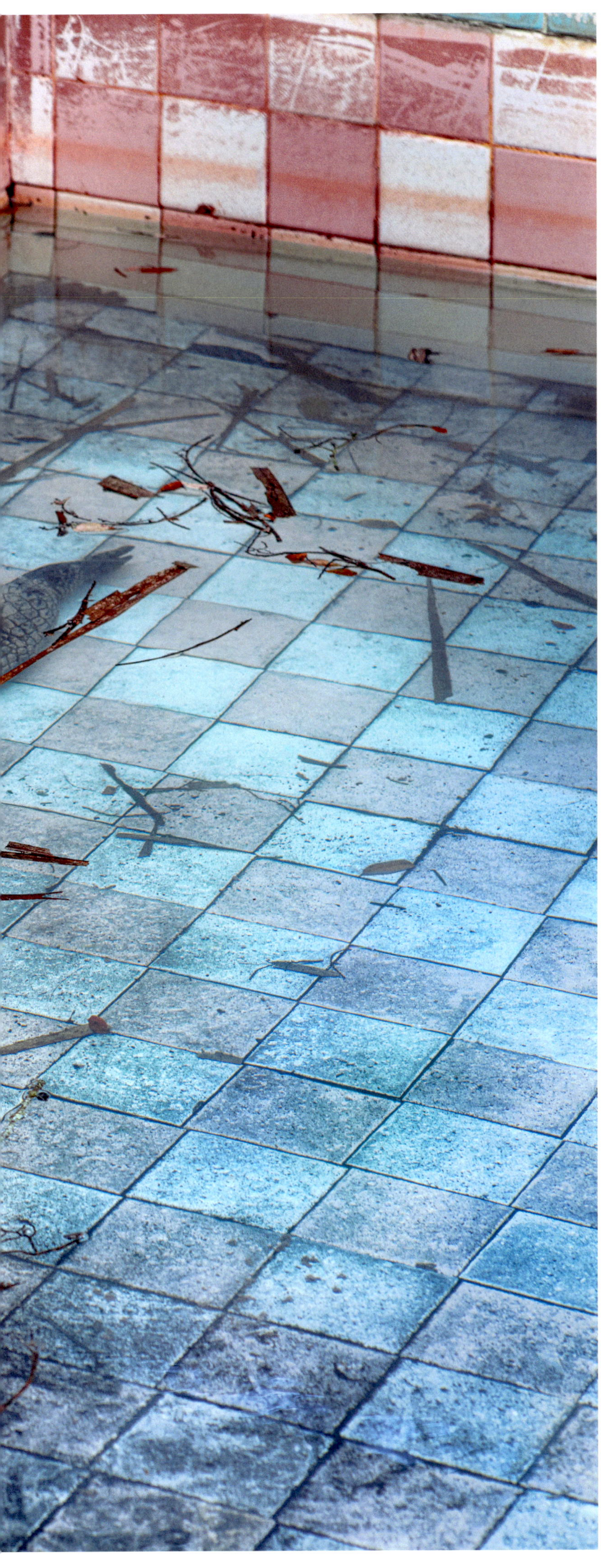

Pink Pool, Palmdale, 2020

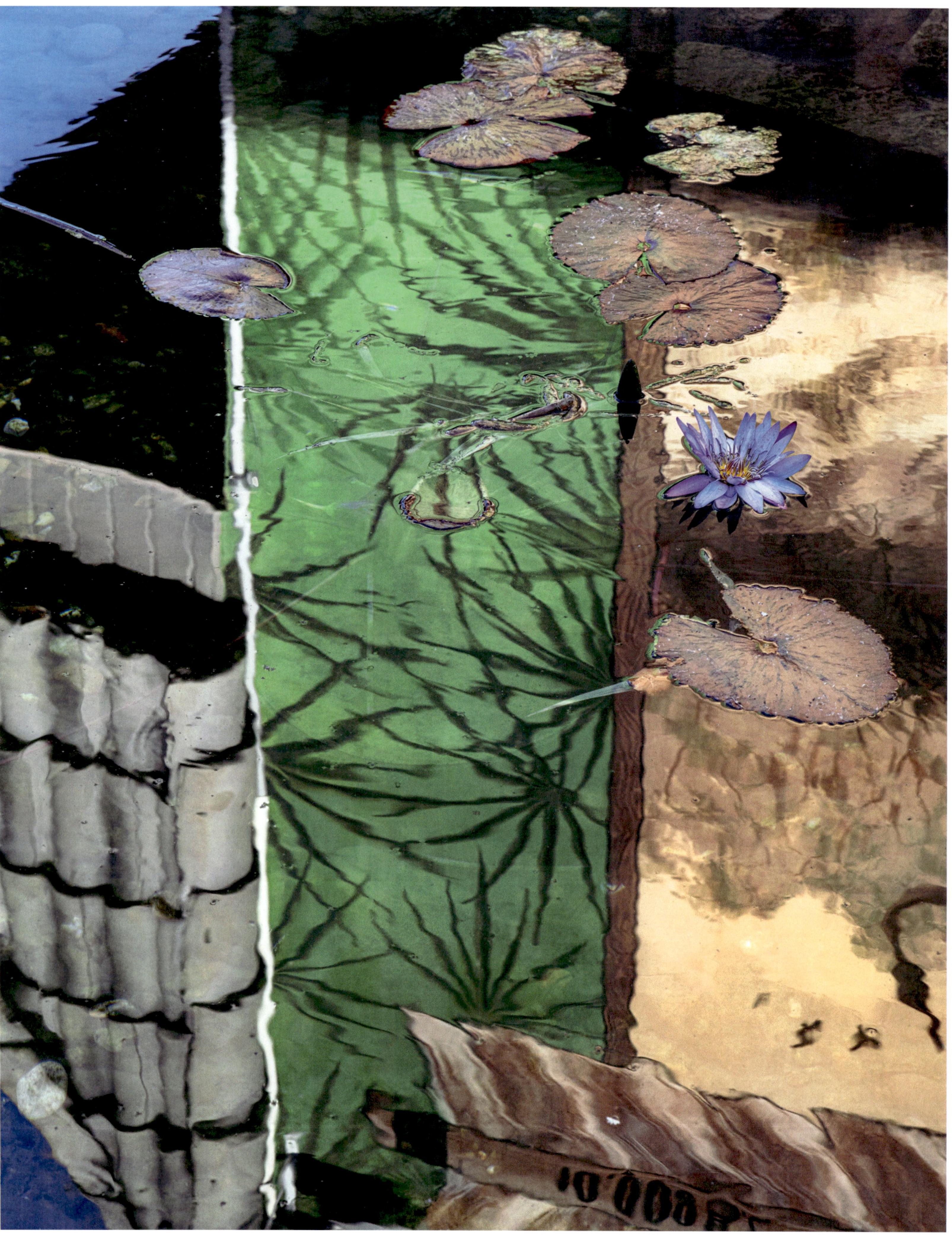

Reflection, Lake Placid, 2020

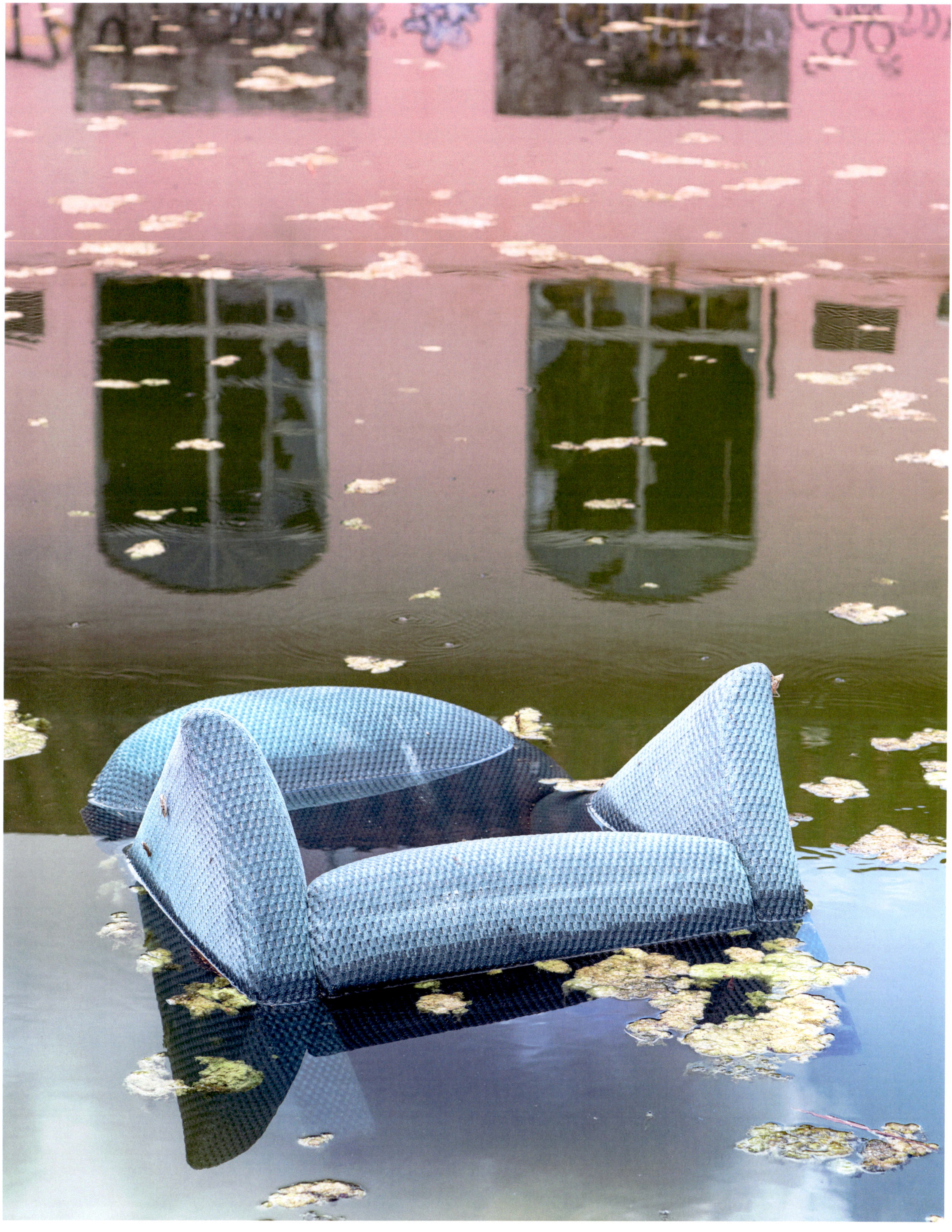

Blue Velvet Chair, 2020

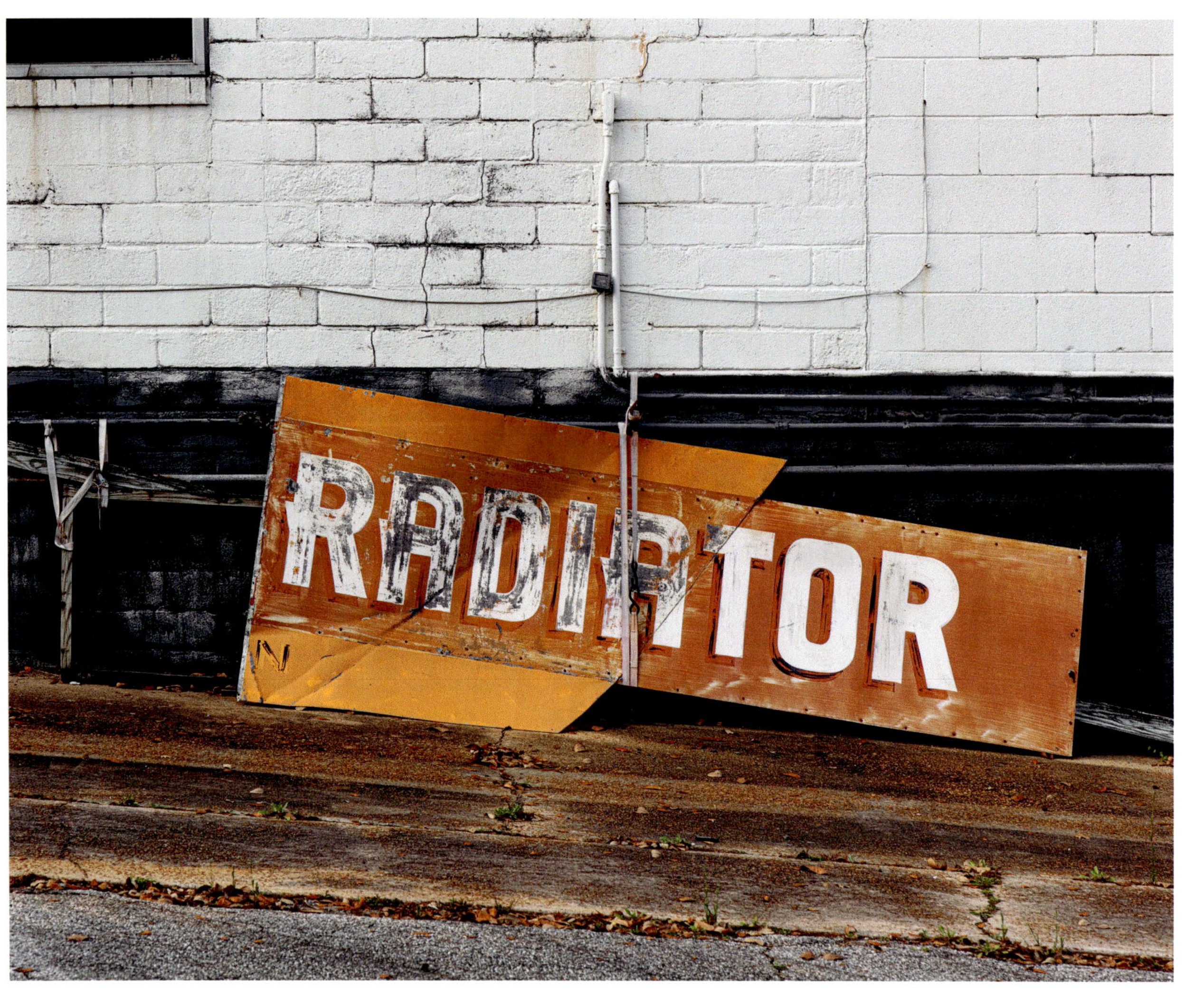

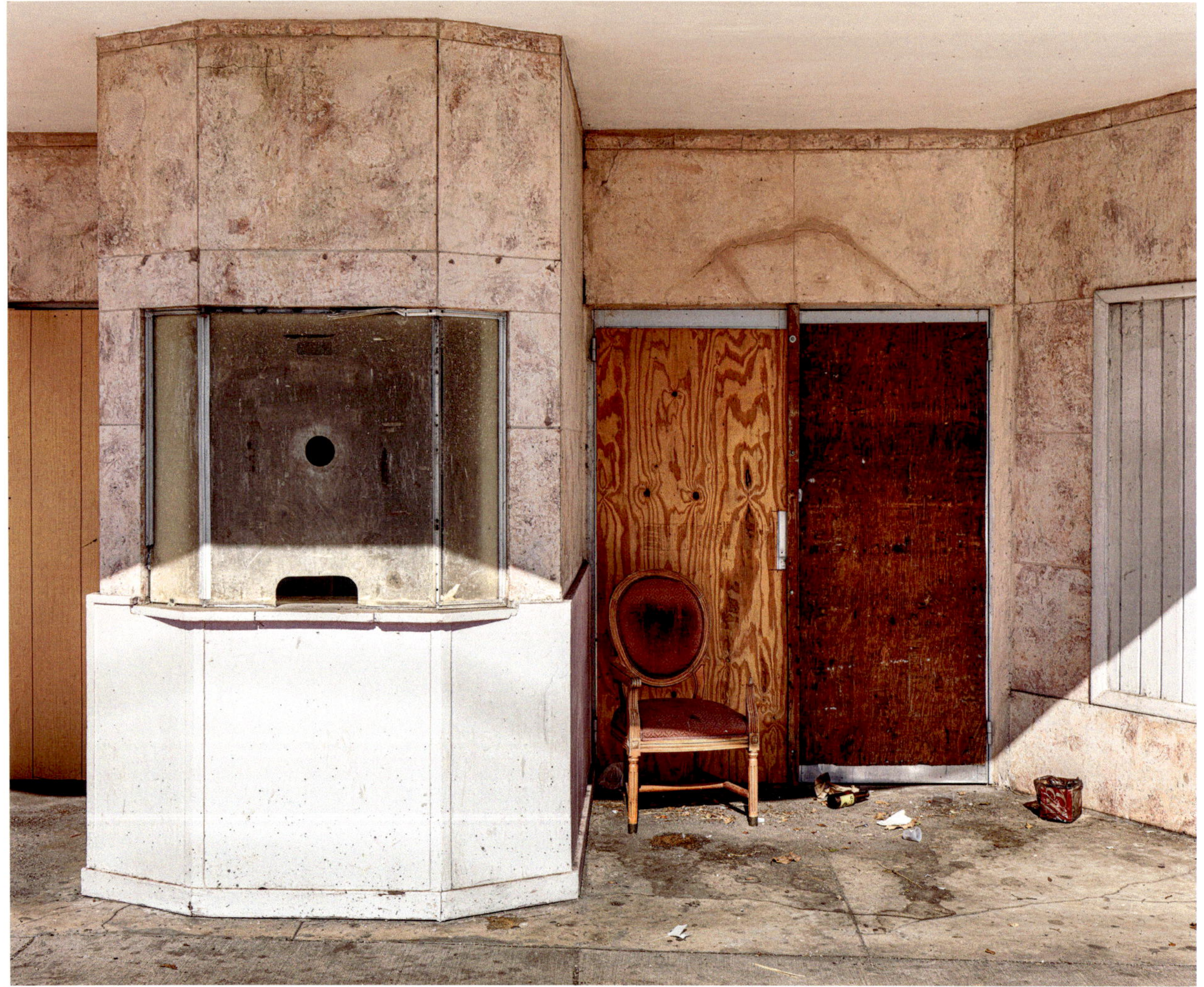

⌃ Shop Sign, Tallahassee, 2021 ⌄ Movie Theater, Pahokee, 2018

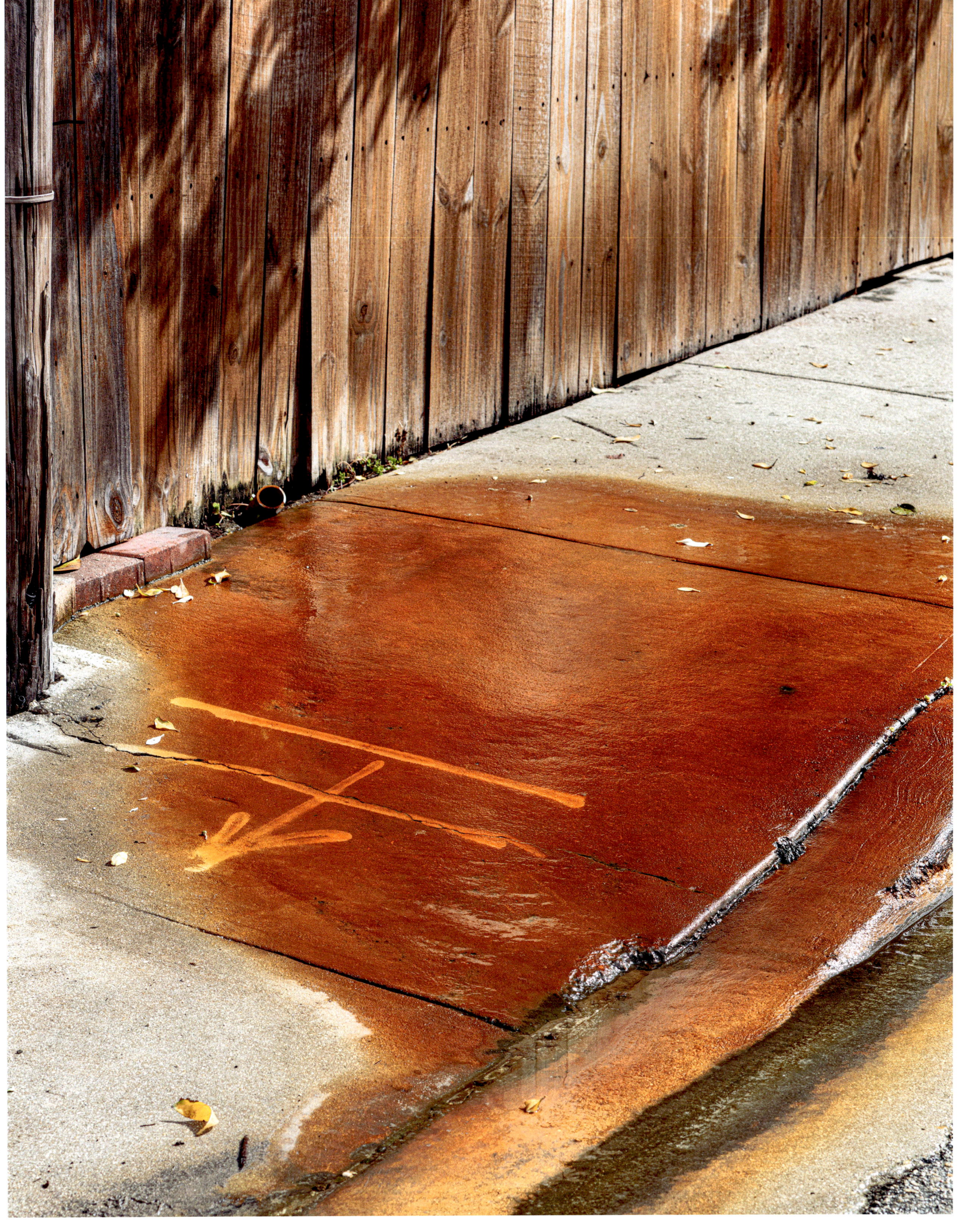

Rust, Hollywood, 2019

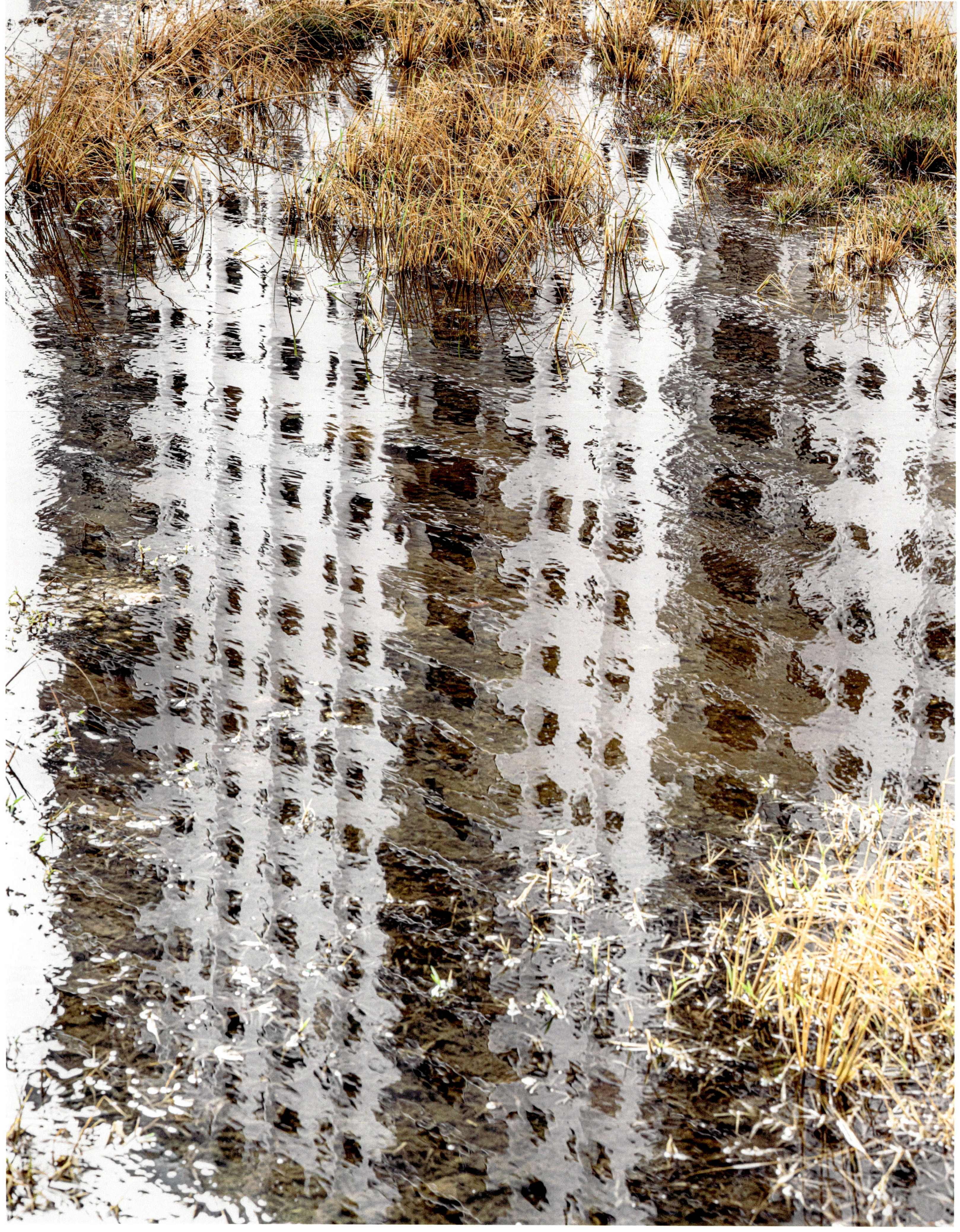

Condo Reflection at King Tide, Hollywood, 2019

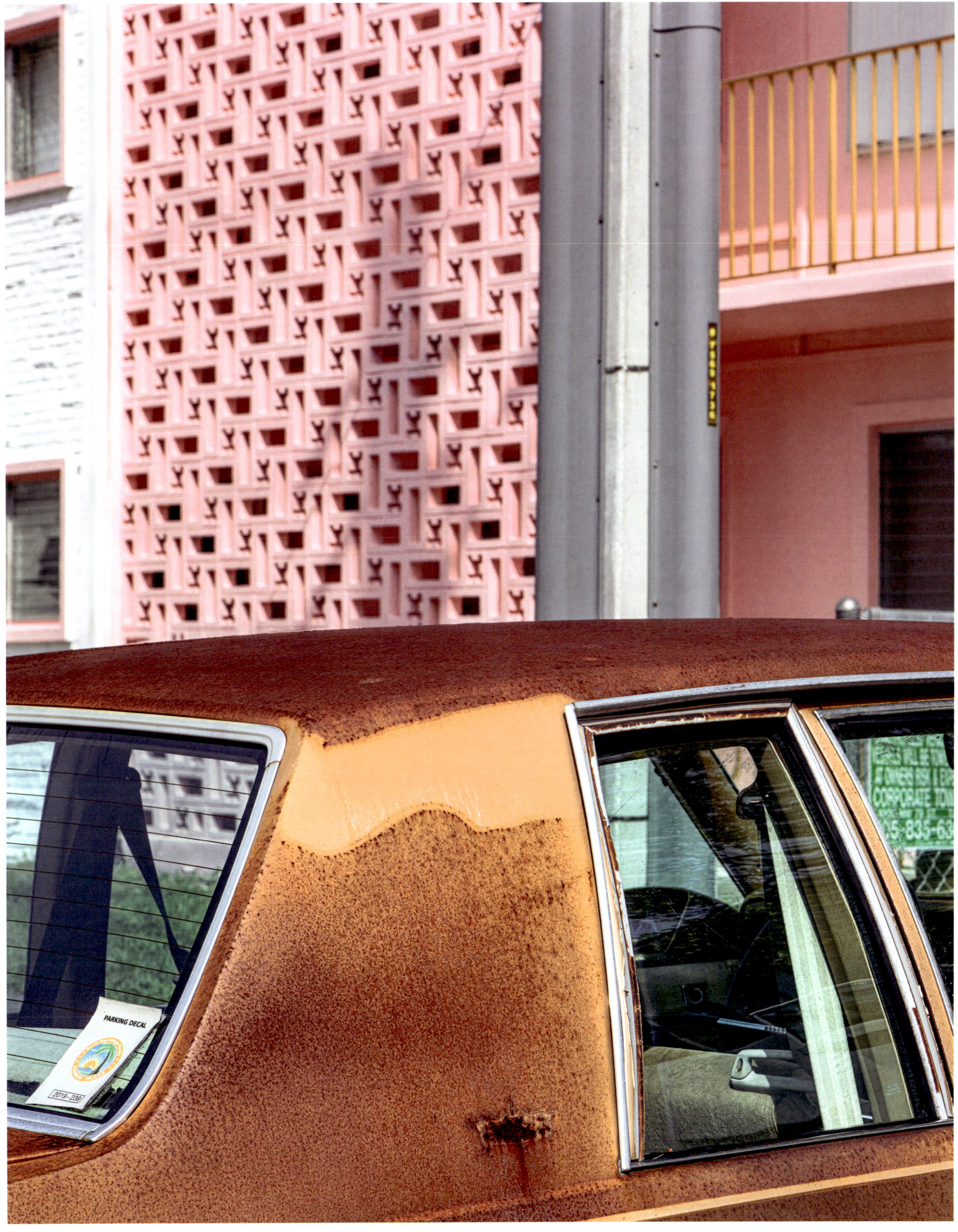

Rust, Hollywood, 2019

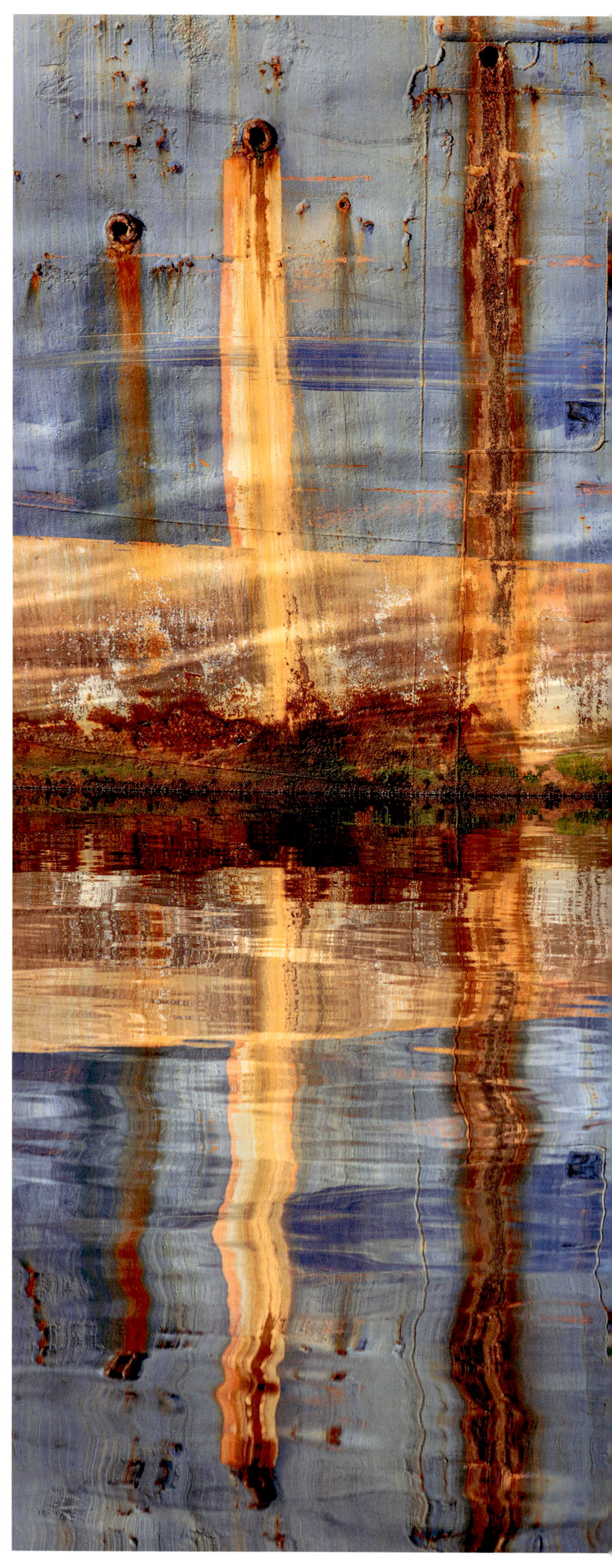

Barge, Miami River, 2021

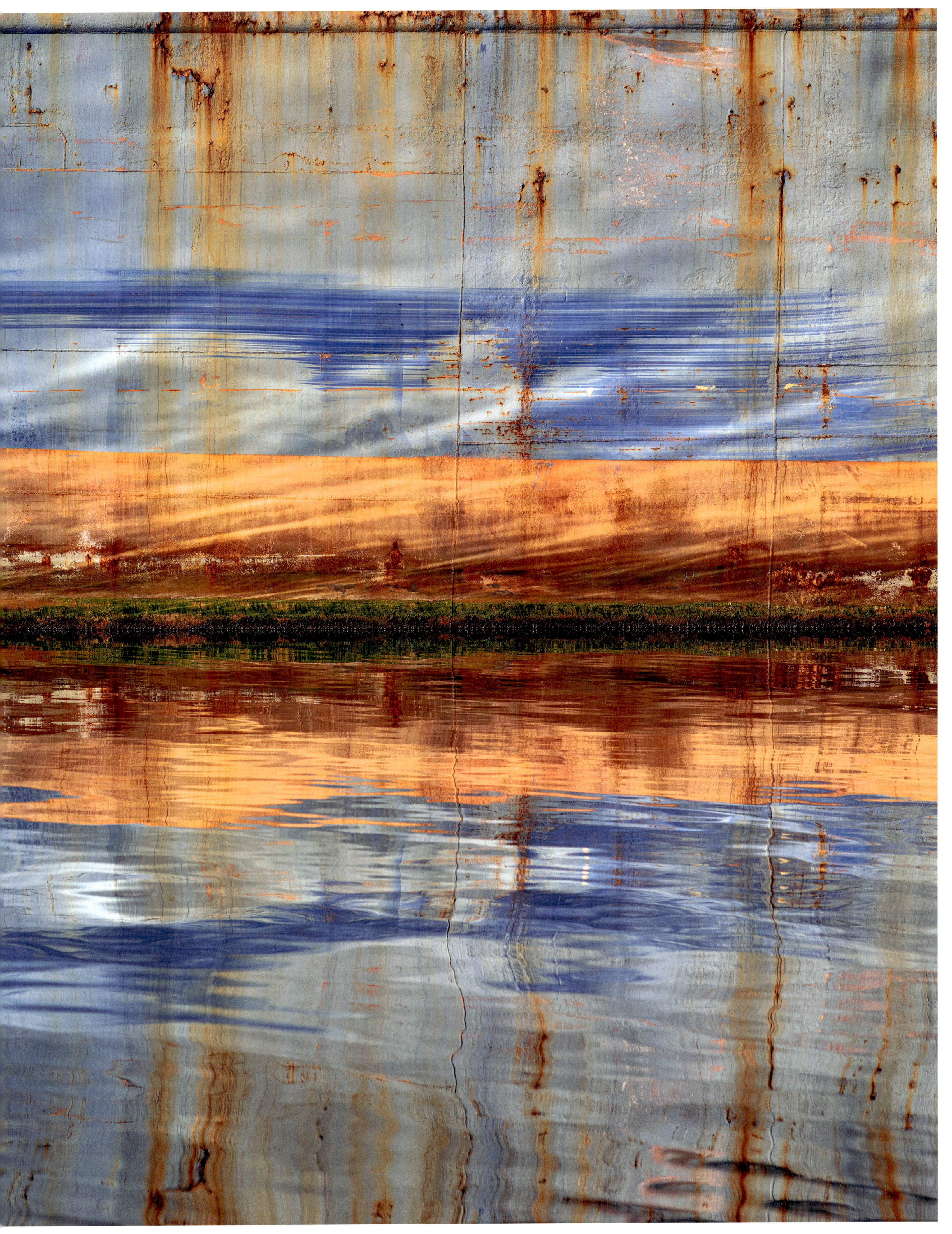

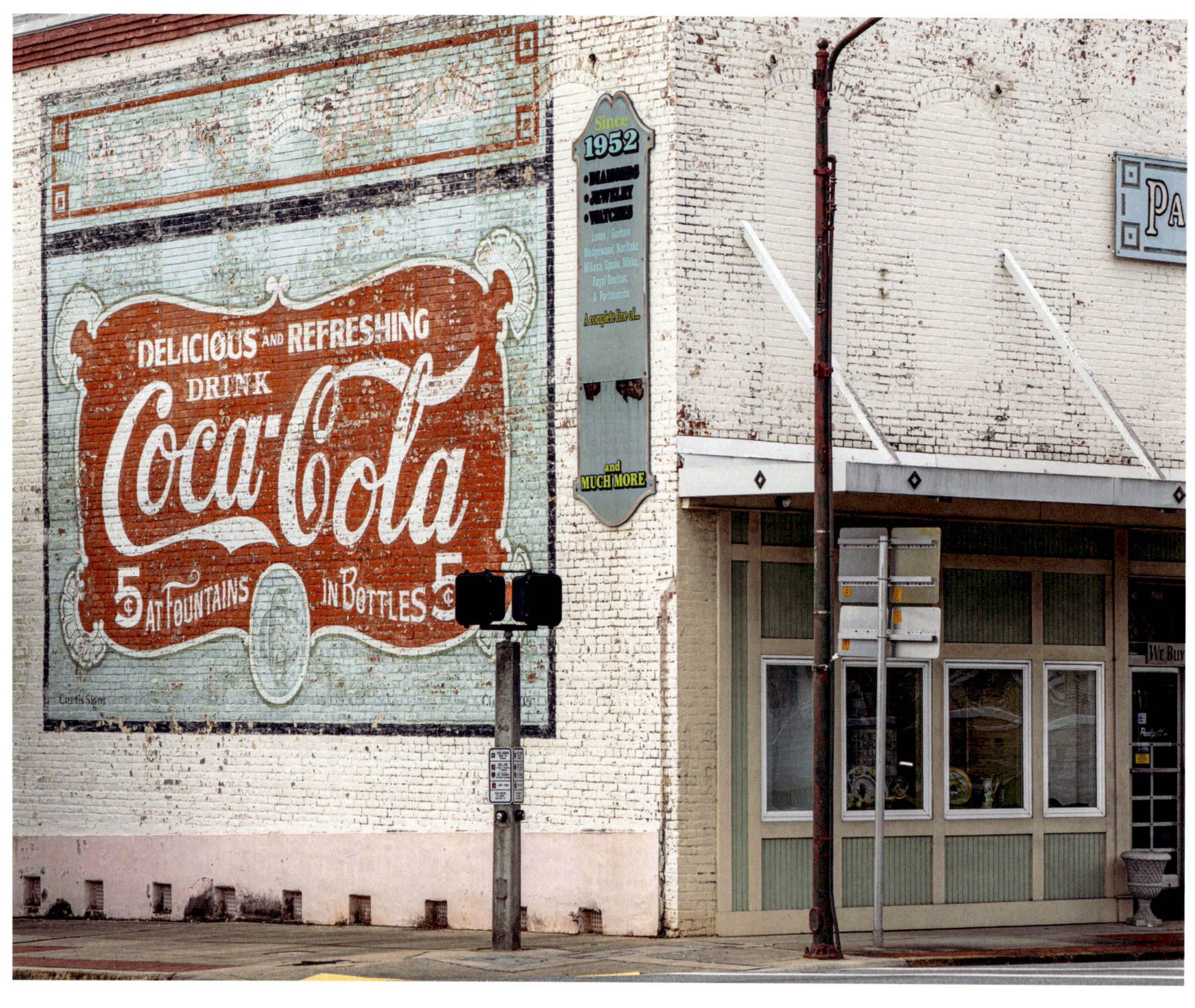

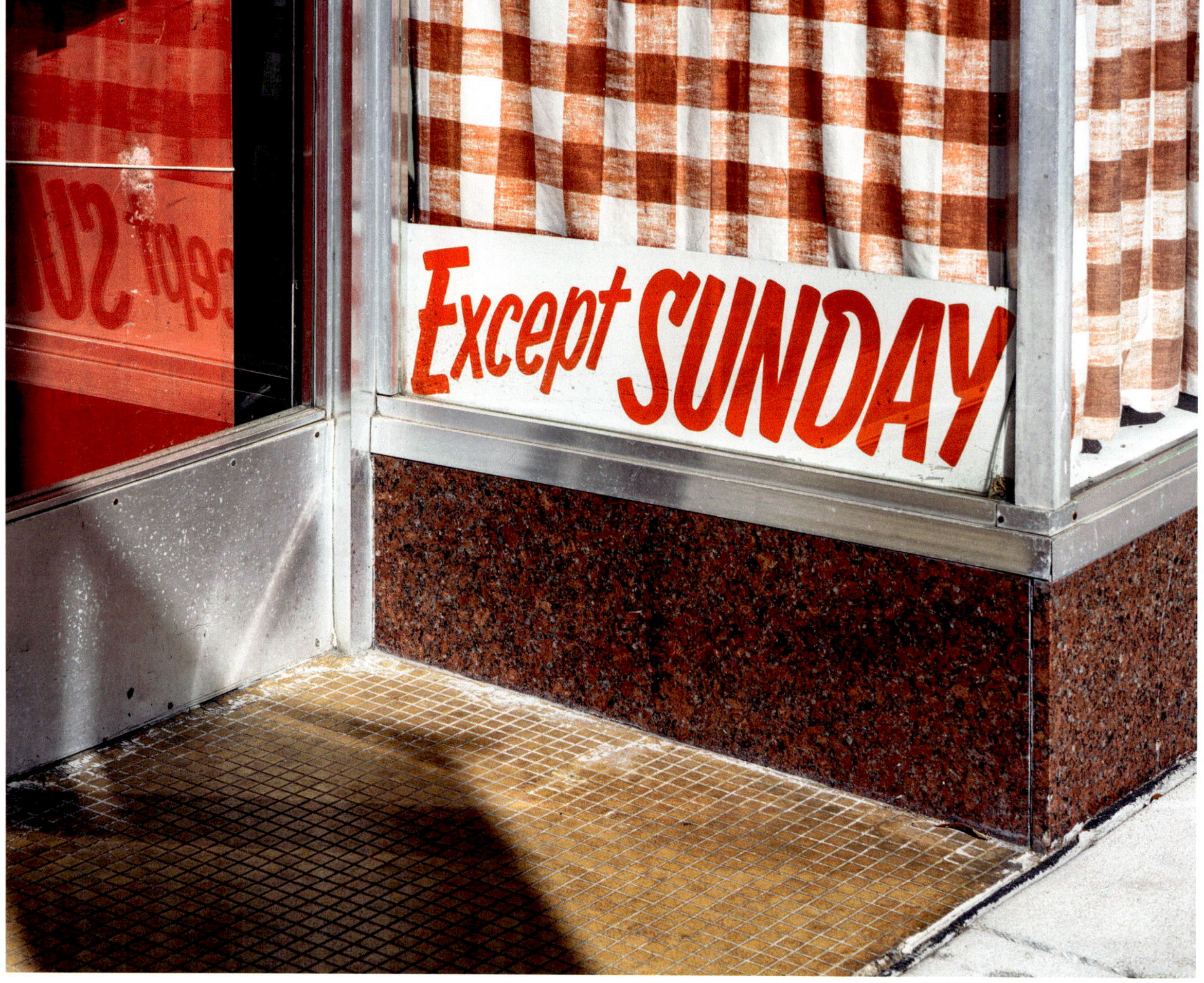

^ Coca-Cola Mural, Quincy, 2020 ⌄ Except Sunday, Panama City Beach, Florida, 2000

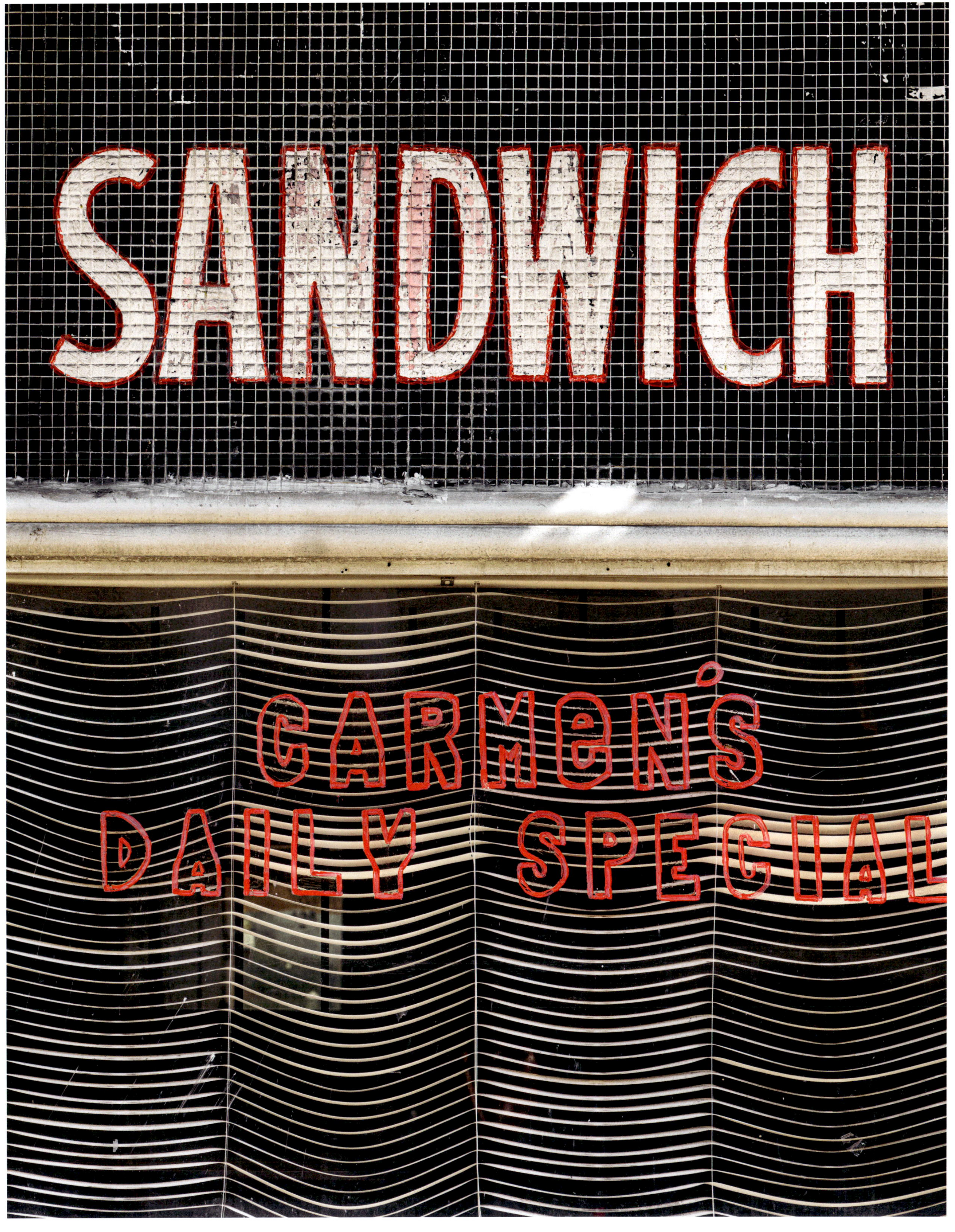

Sandwich Shop, Tampa, 2020

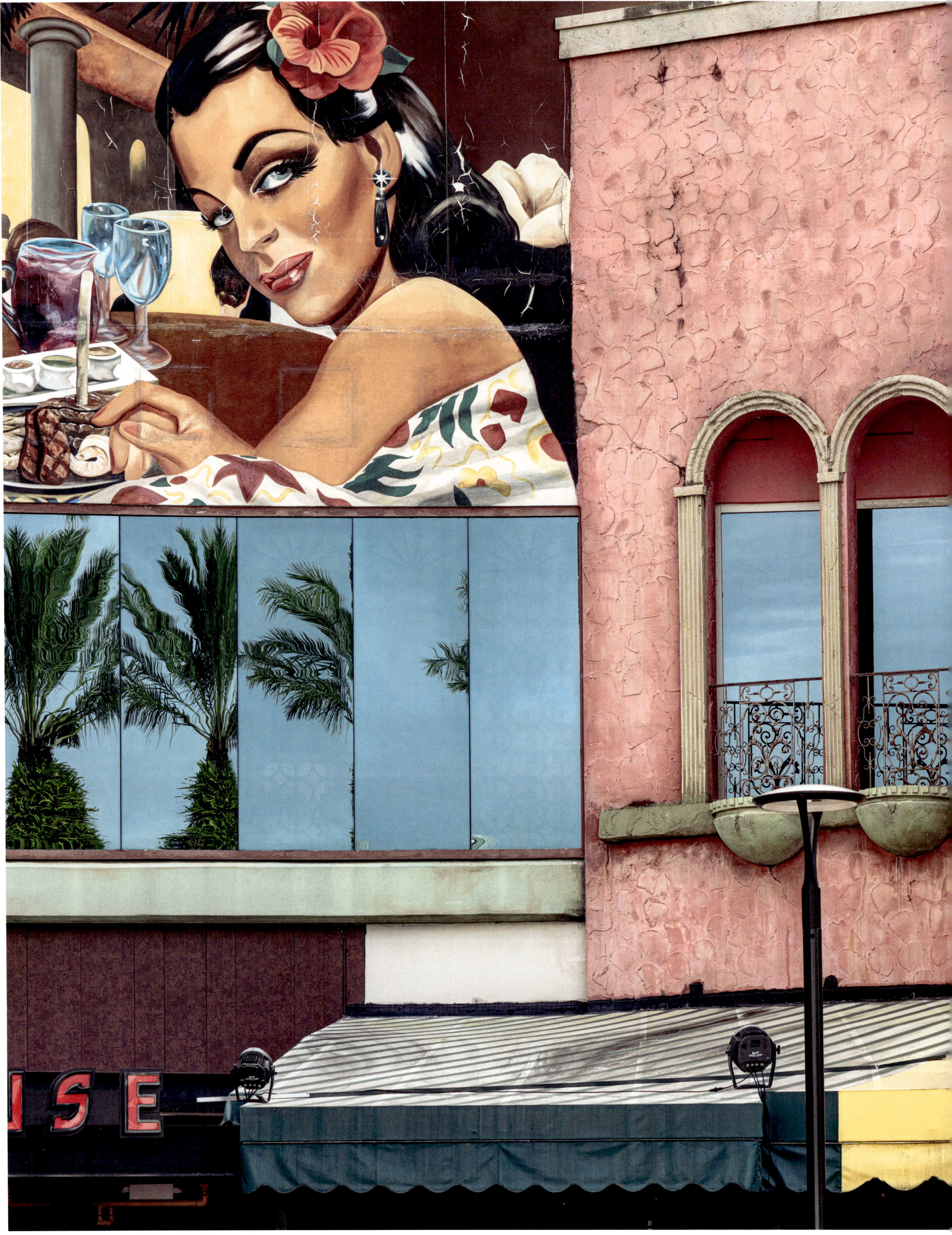
SE

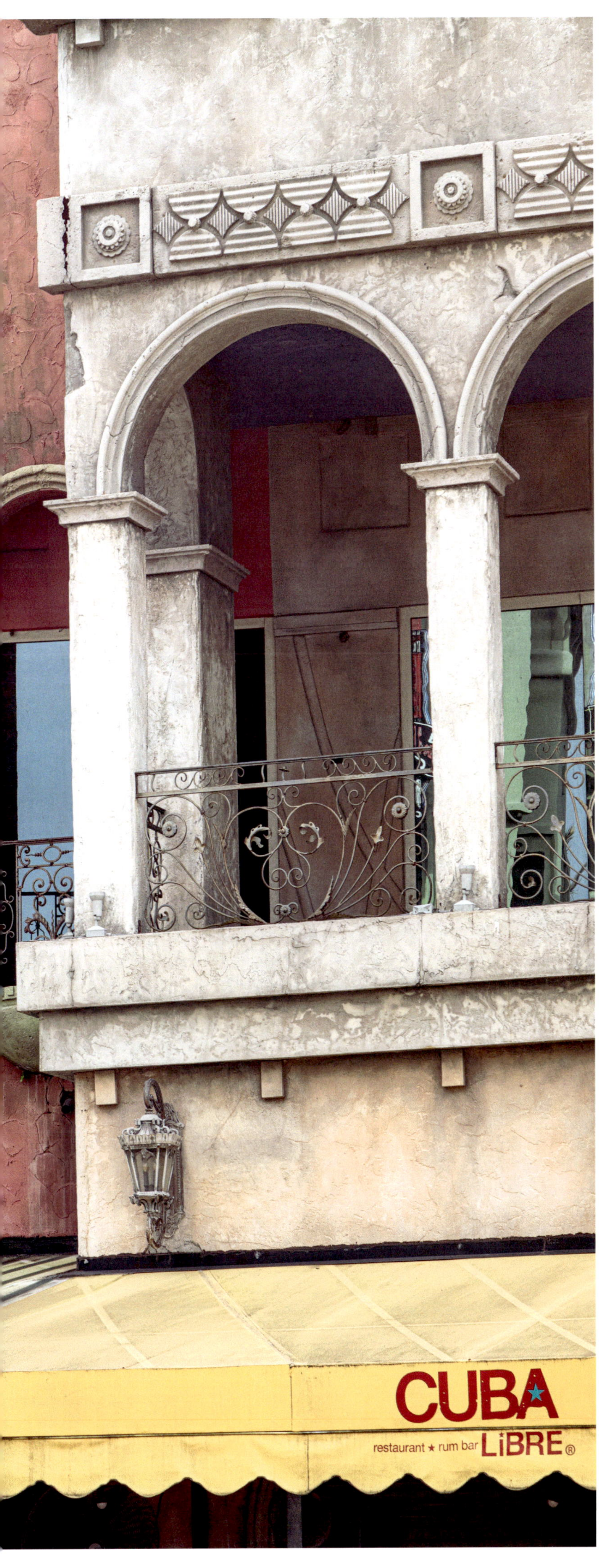

Pointe Mall, Orlando, 2020

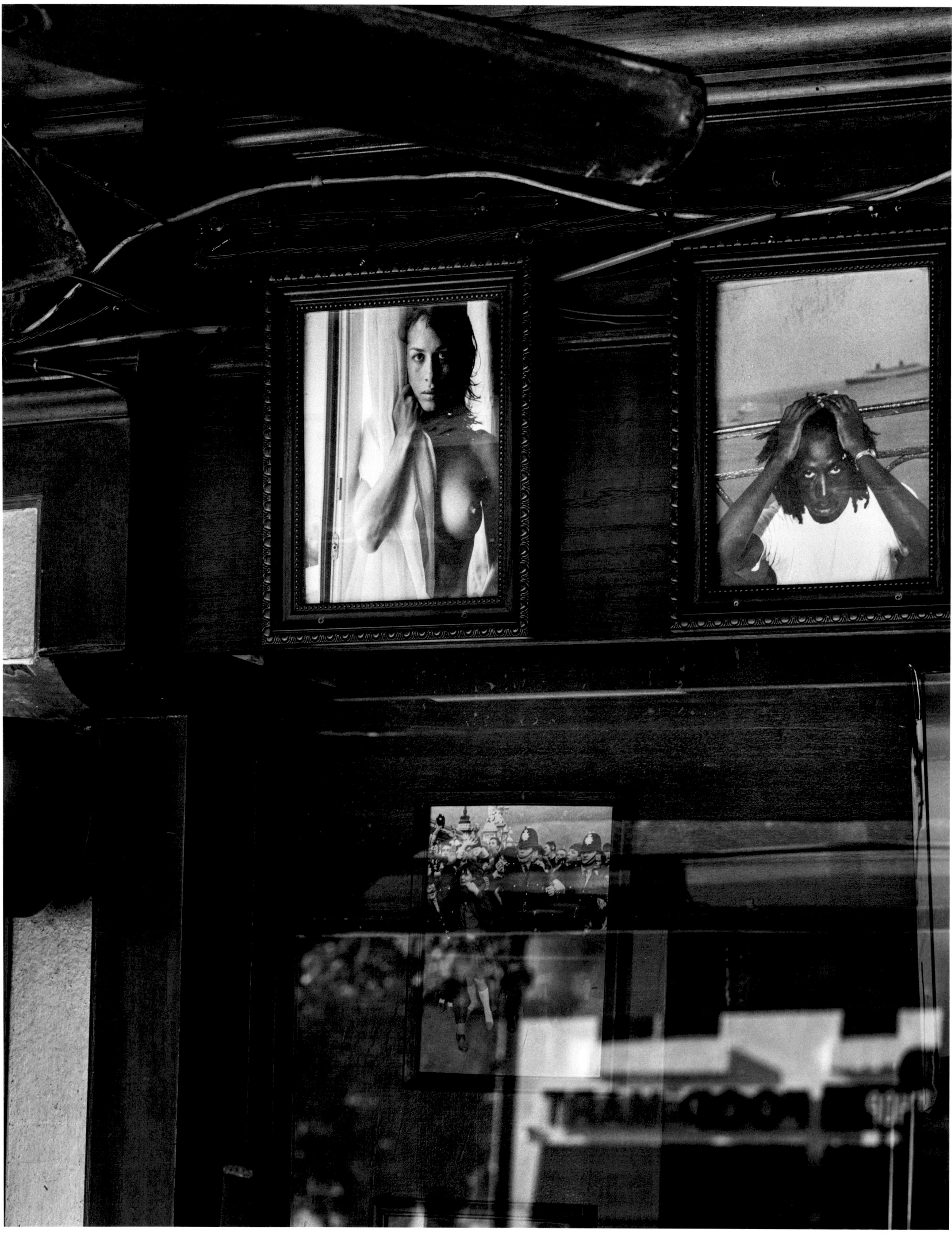

Cafe, Miami Beach, 2019

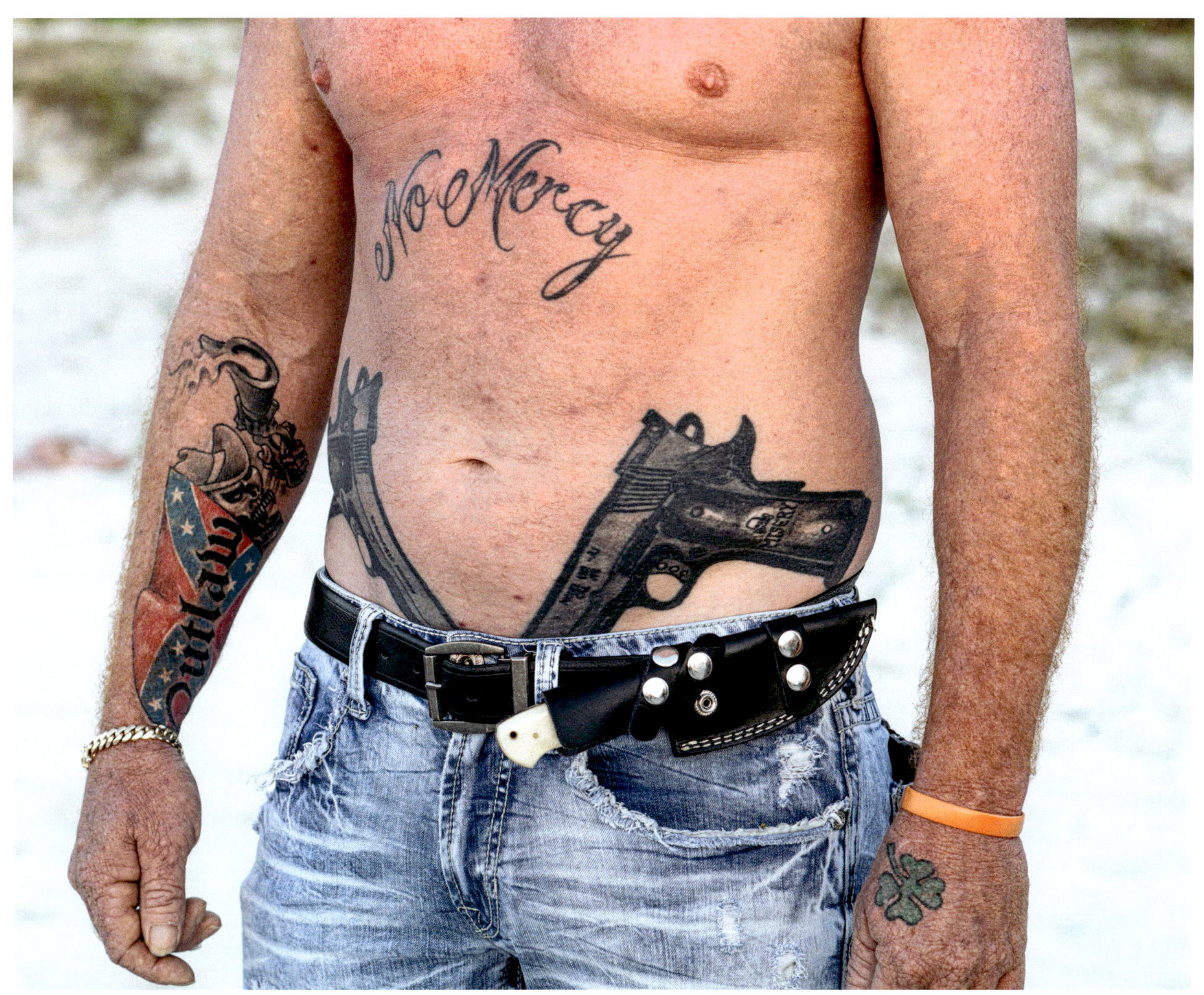

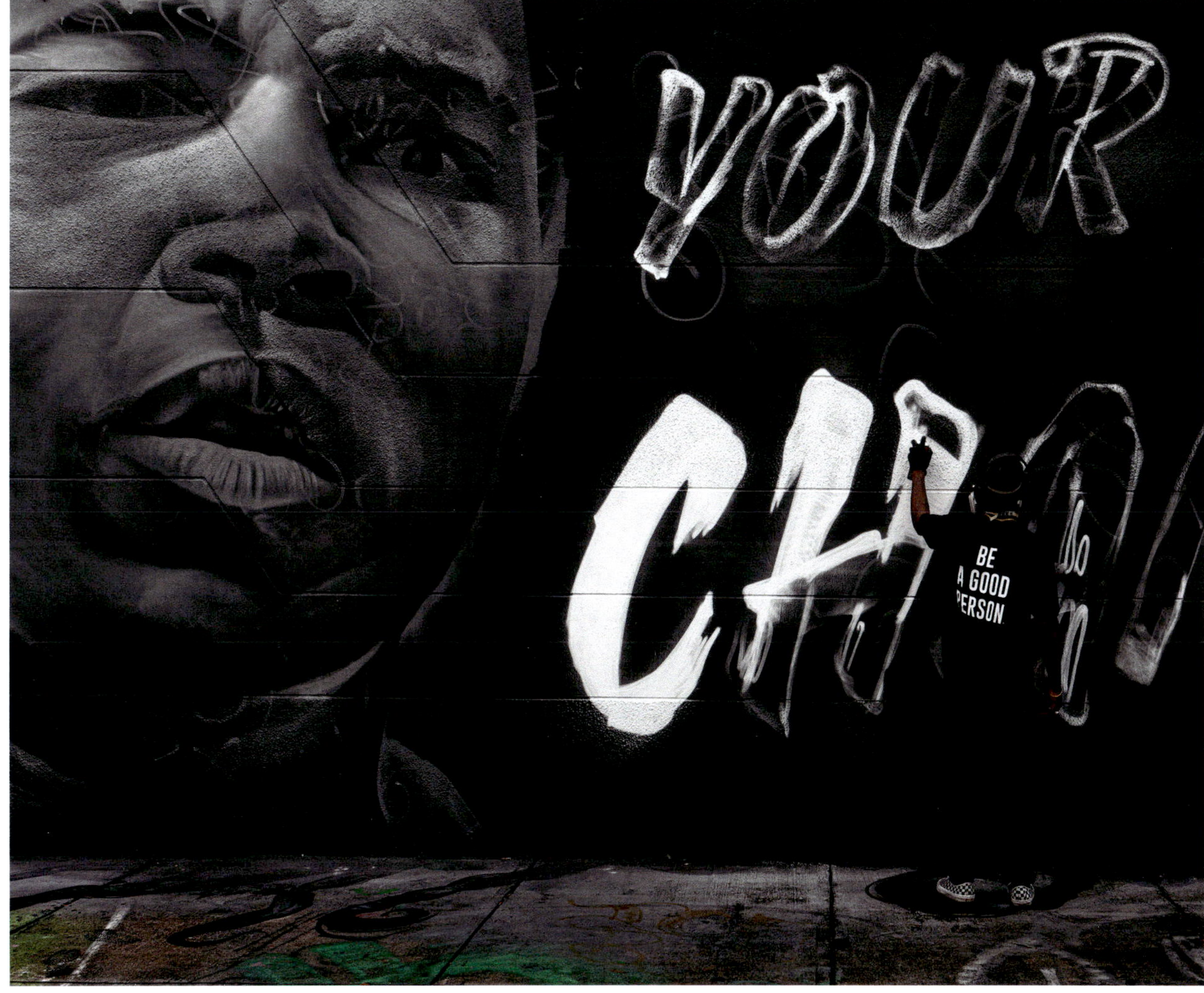

^ Beachgoer, Naples, 2021 ˇ Mural Painter, Miami, 2020

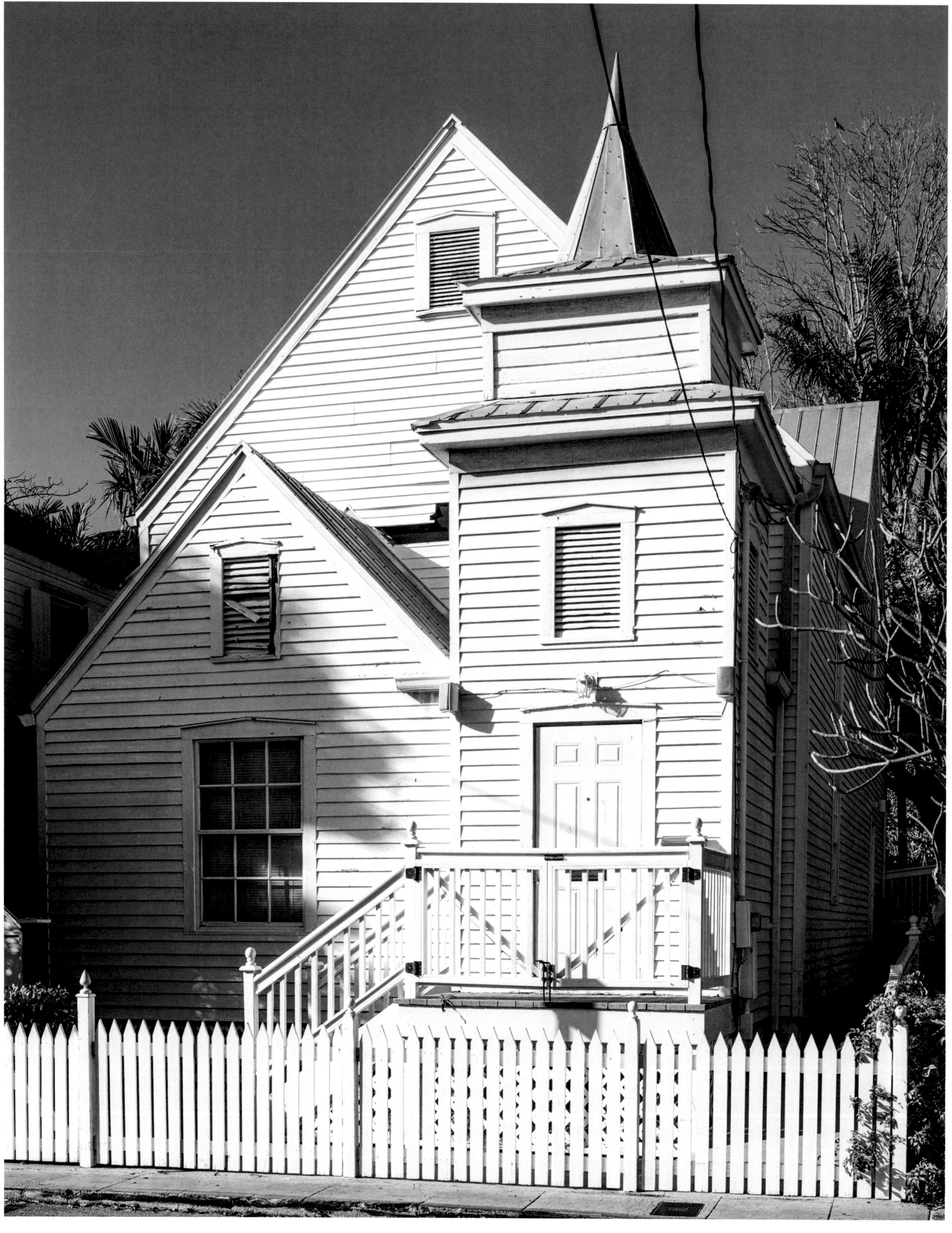

White Church, Key West, 2021

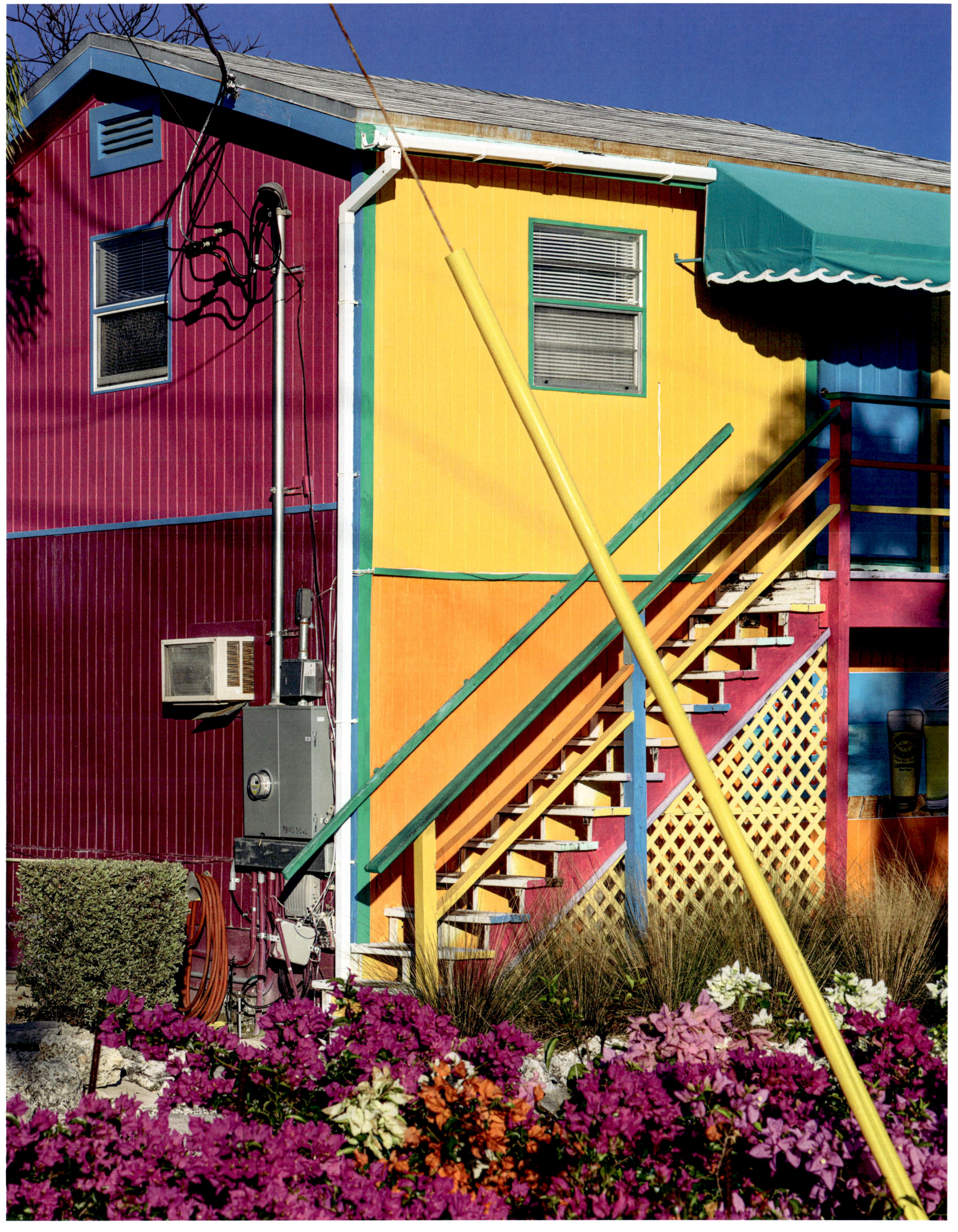

Bar, Key Largo, 2020

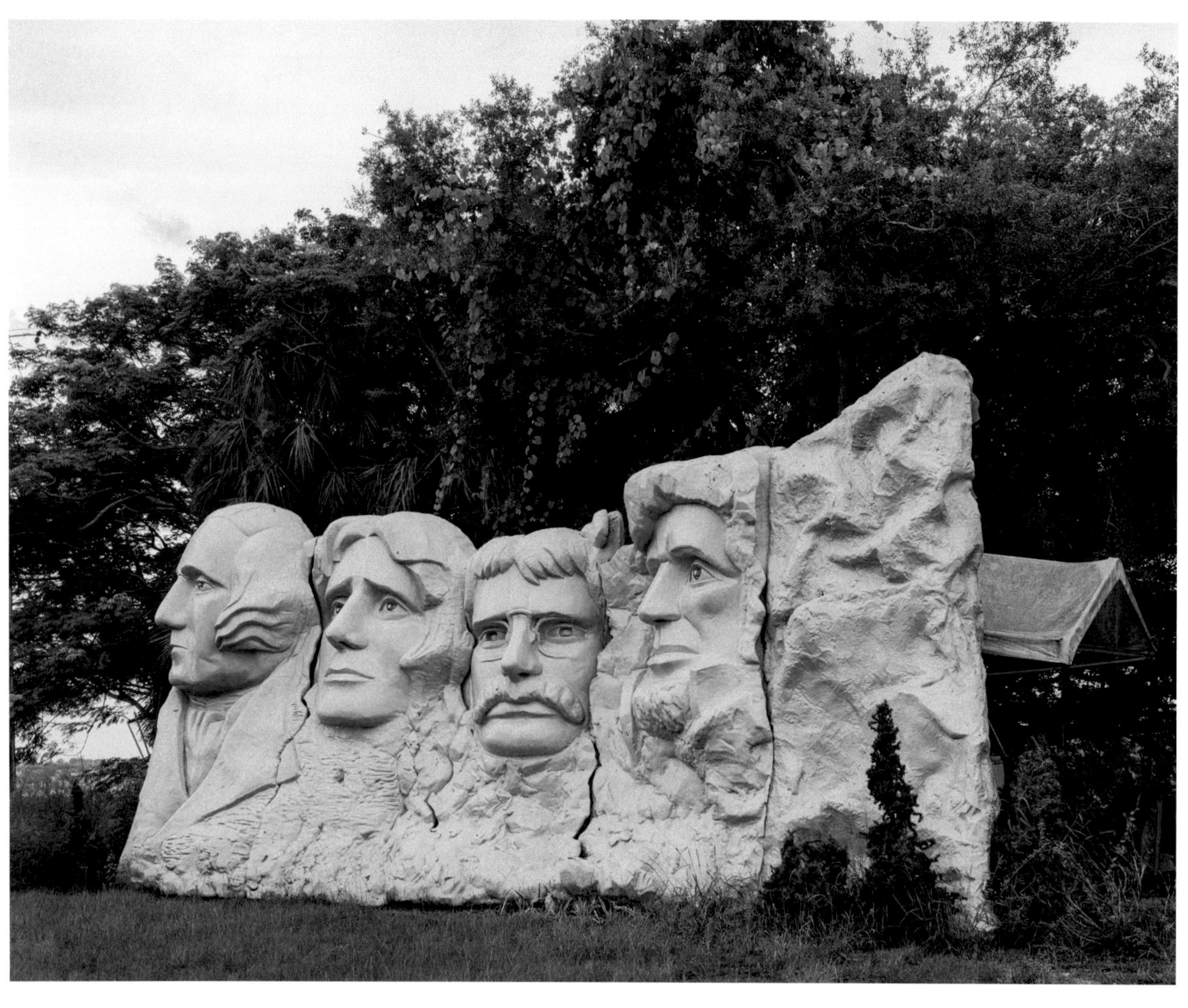

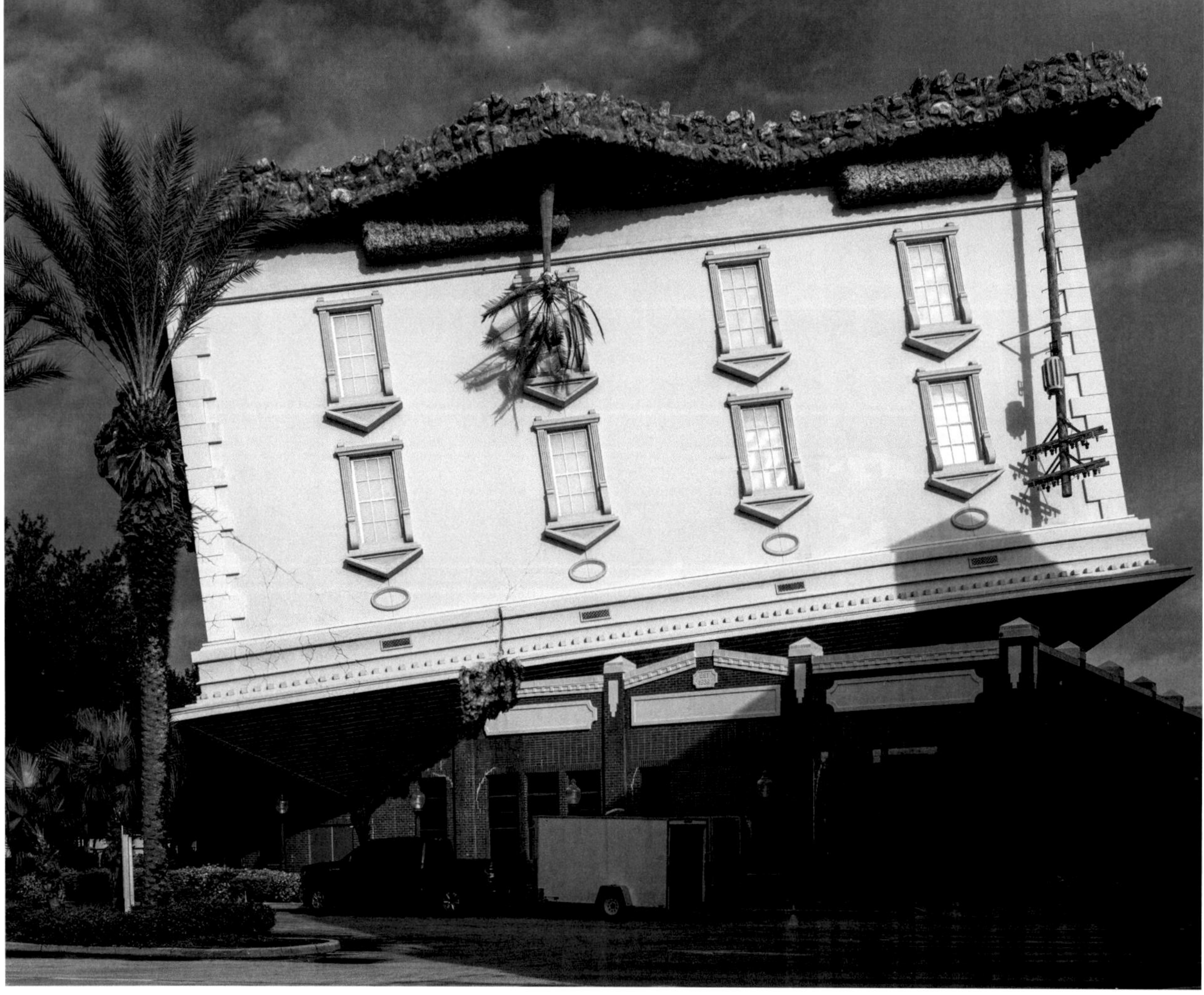

^ Presidents Hall of Fame, Clermont, 2020 ˅ Tourist Attraction, Orlando, 2020

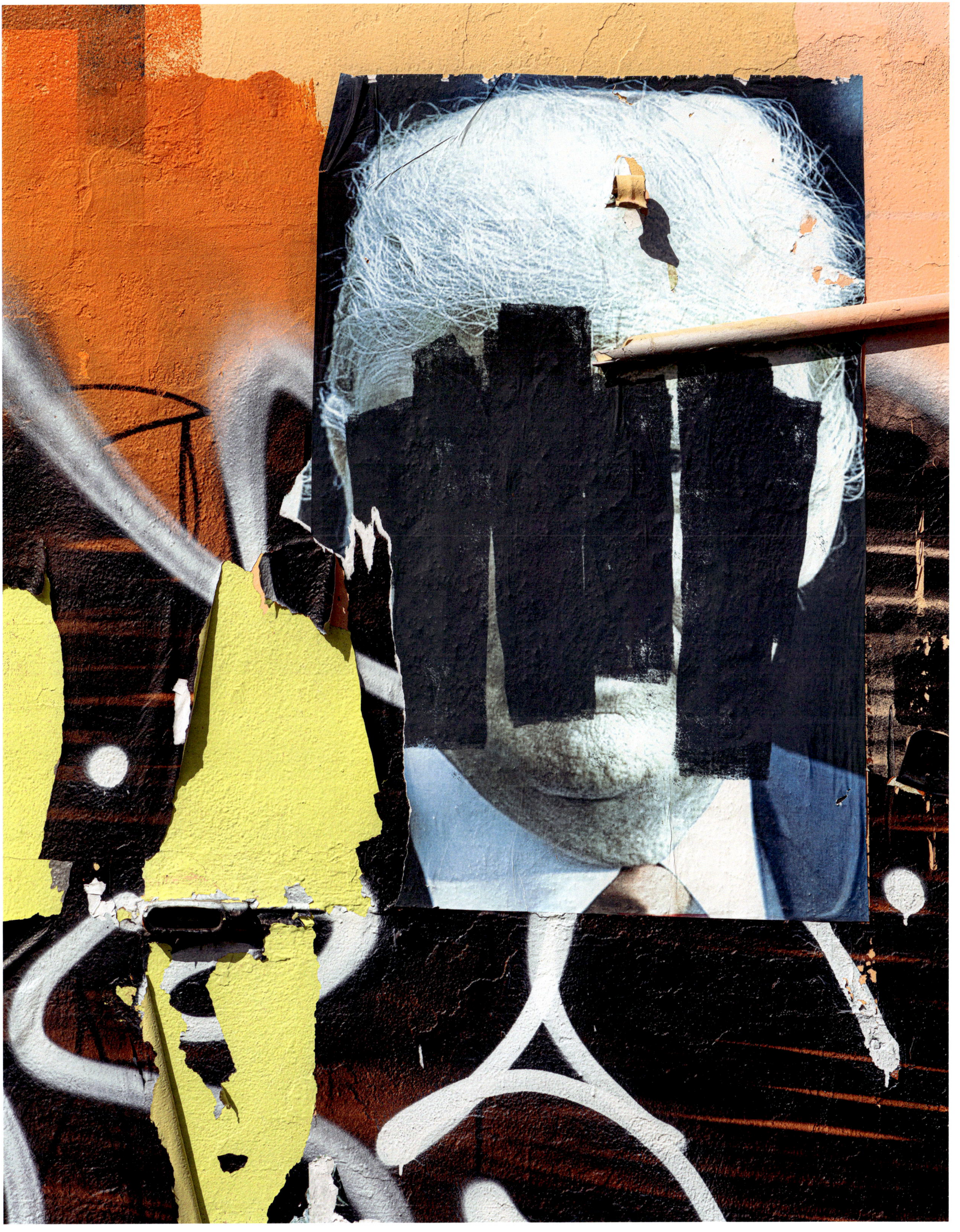

Overpainted Poster, Miami, 2020

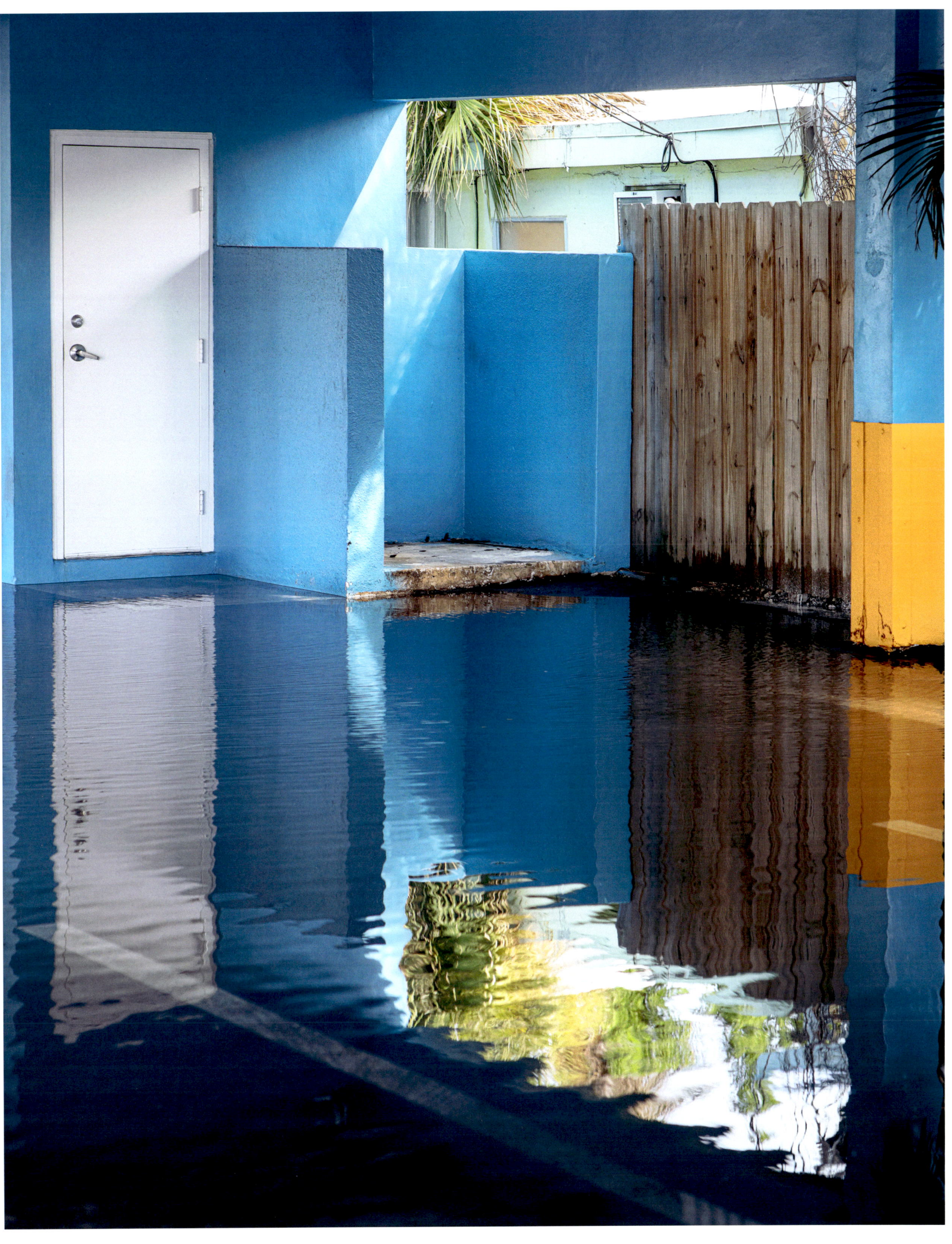

Blue Courtyard, Hollywood, 2019

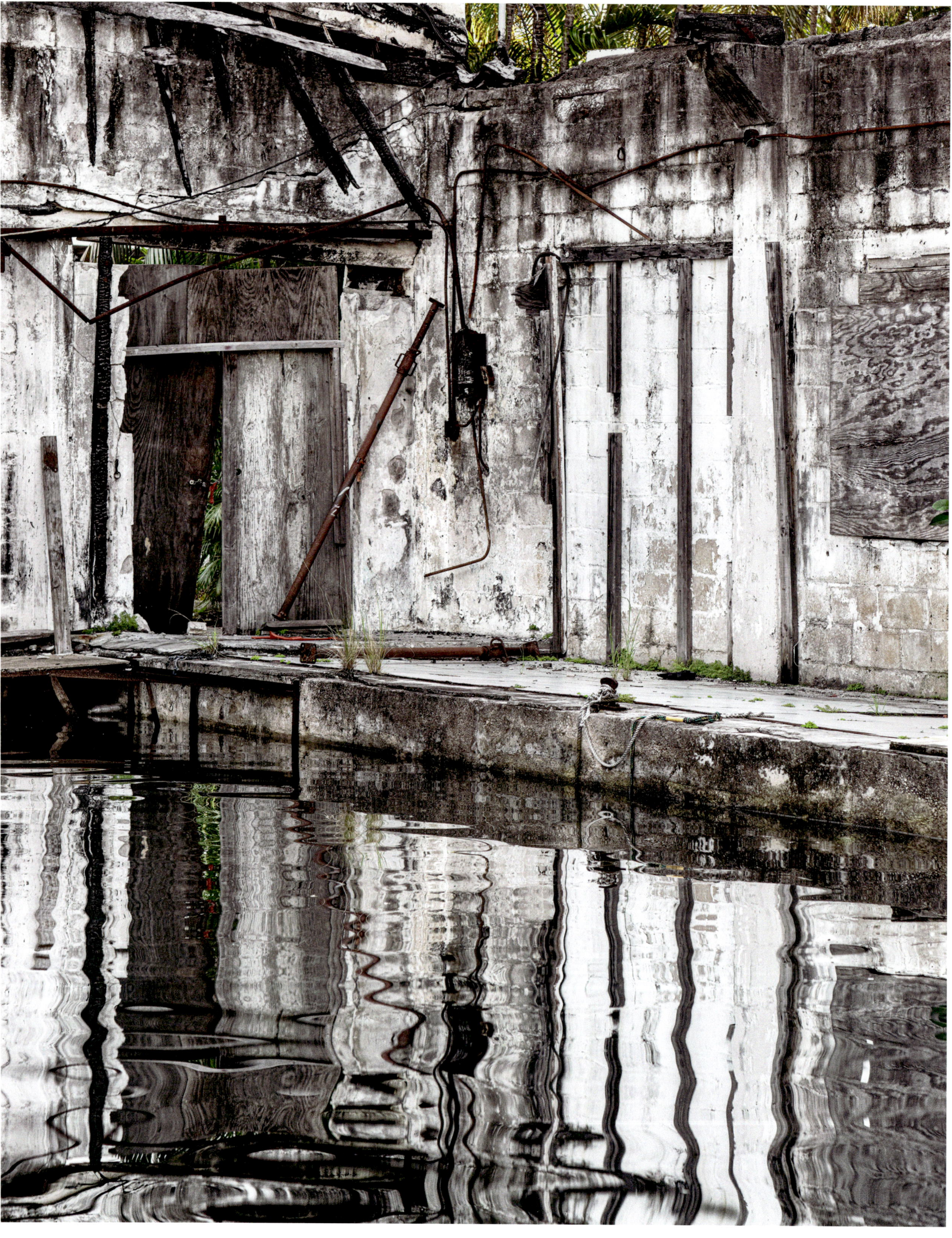

Abandoned Building on Miami River, 2021

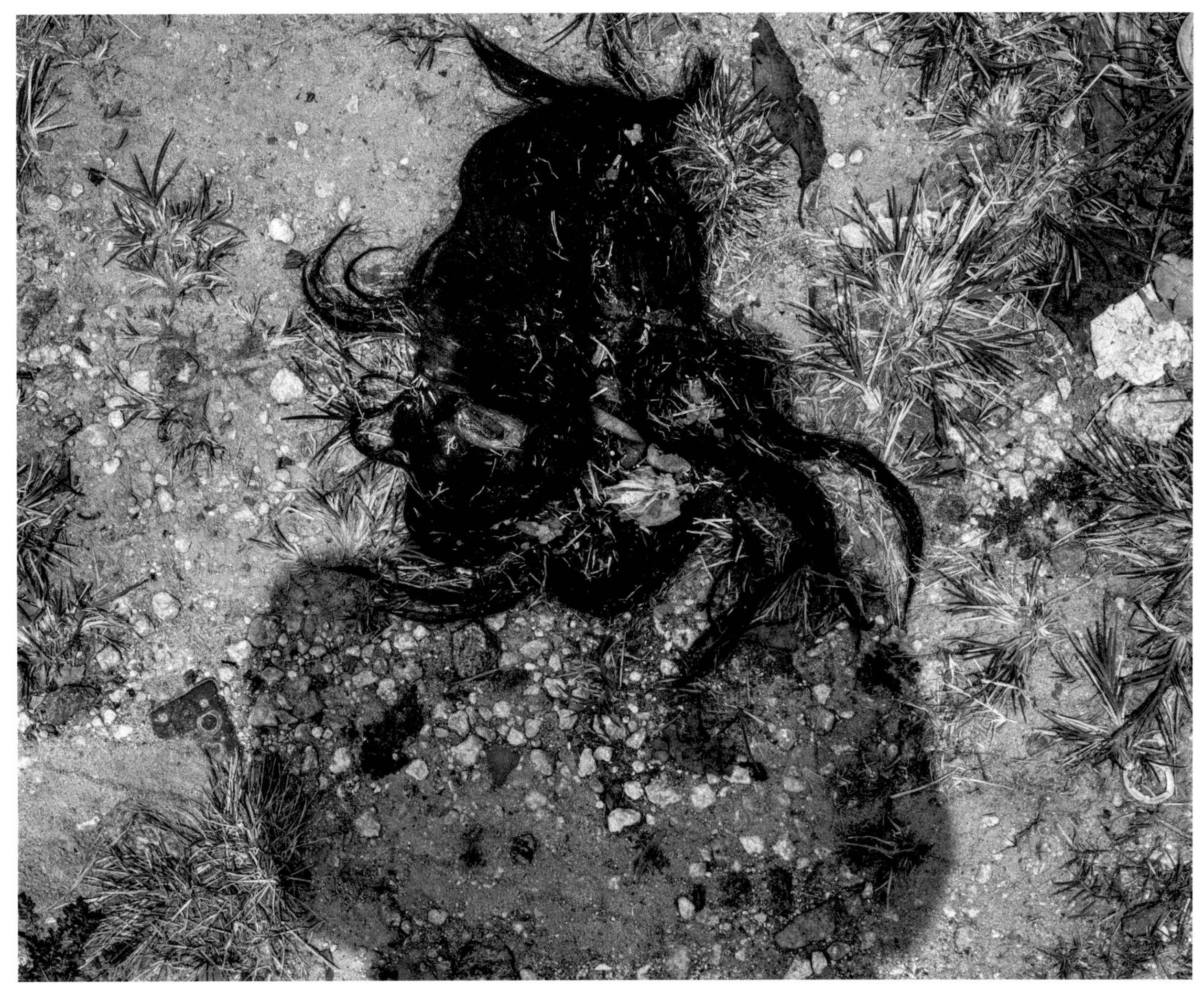

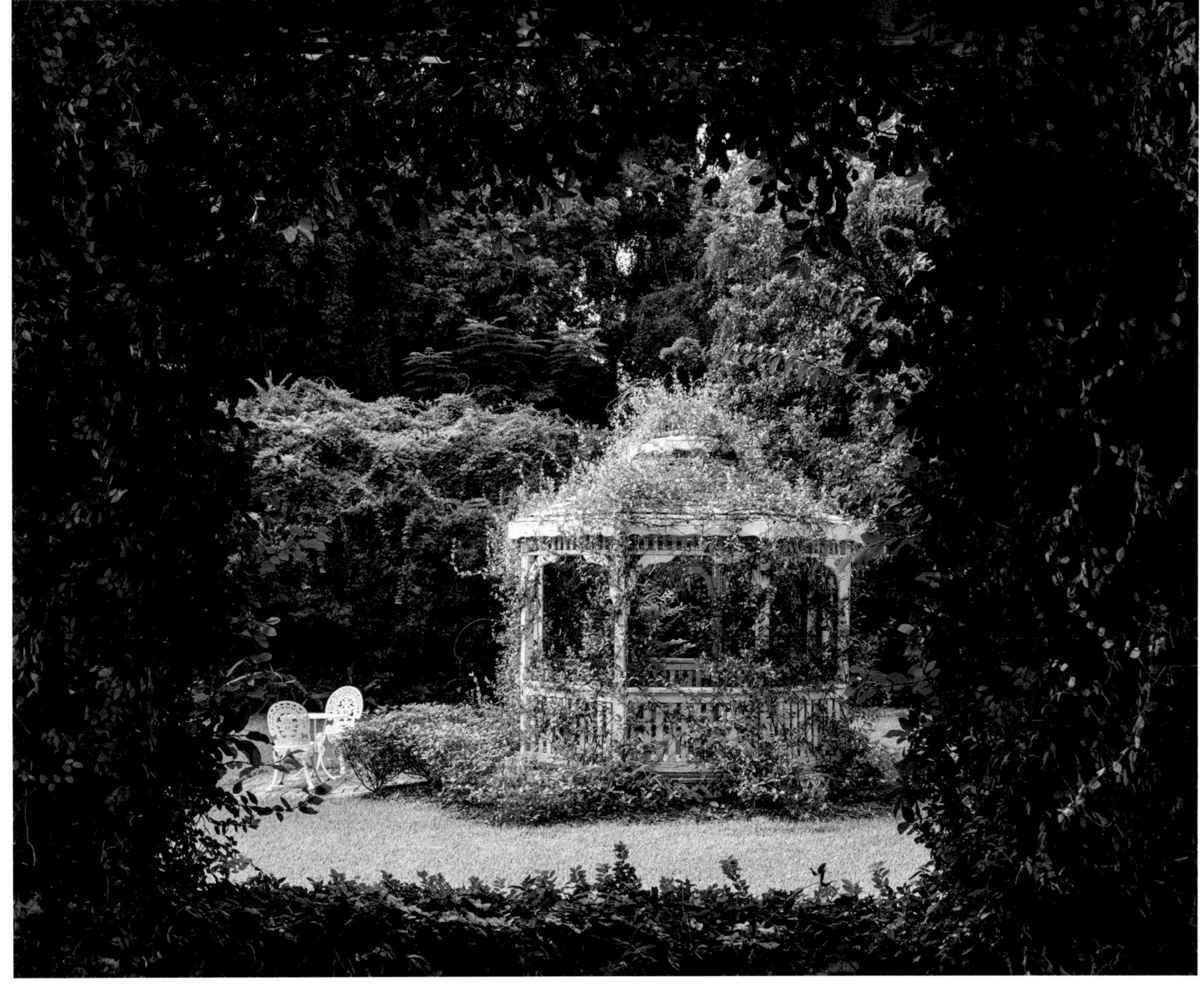

⌃ Lost Wig, 2017 ⌄ Garden, Micanopy, 2020

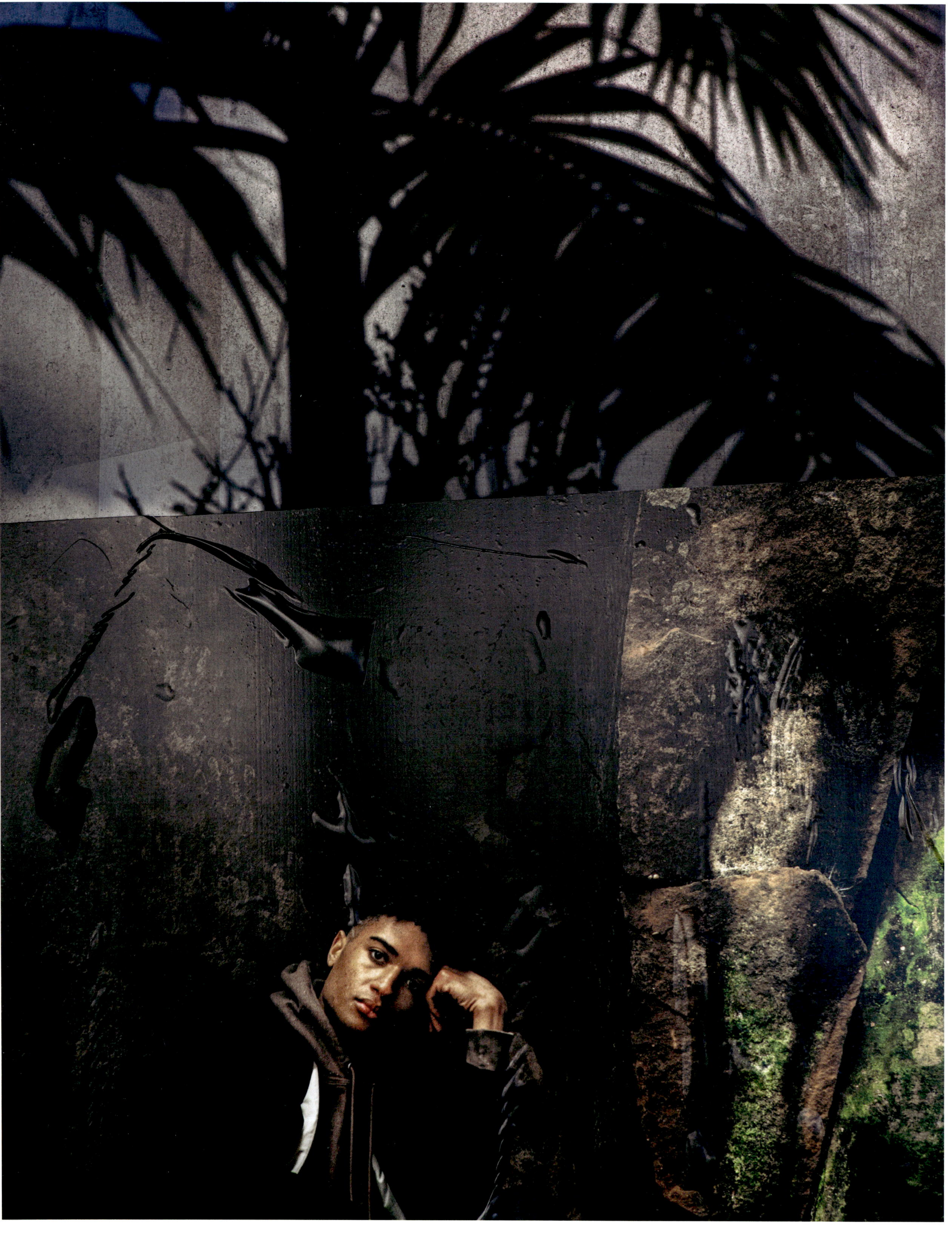

Outdoor Advertisement, Miami, 2021

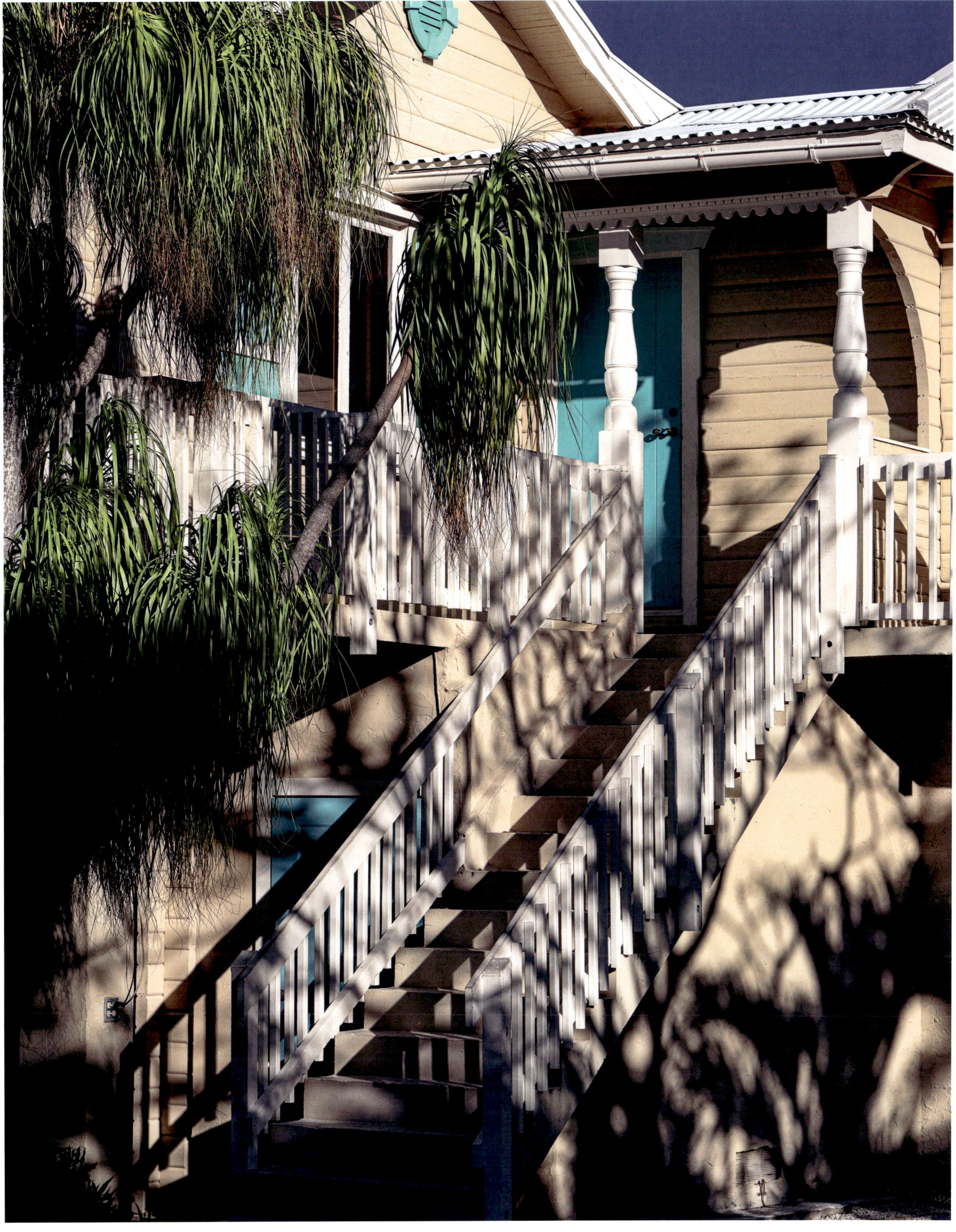

Porch, Key Largo, 2020

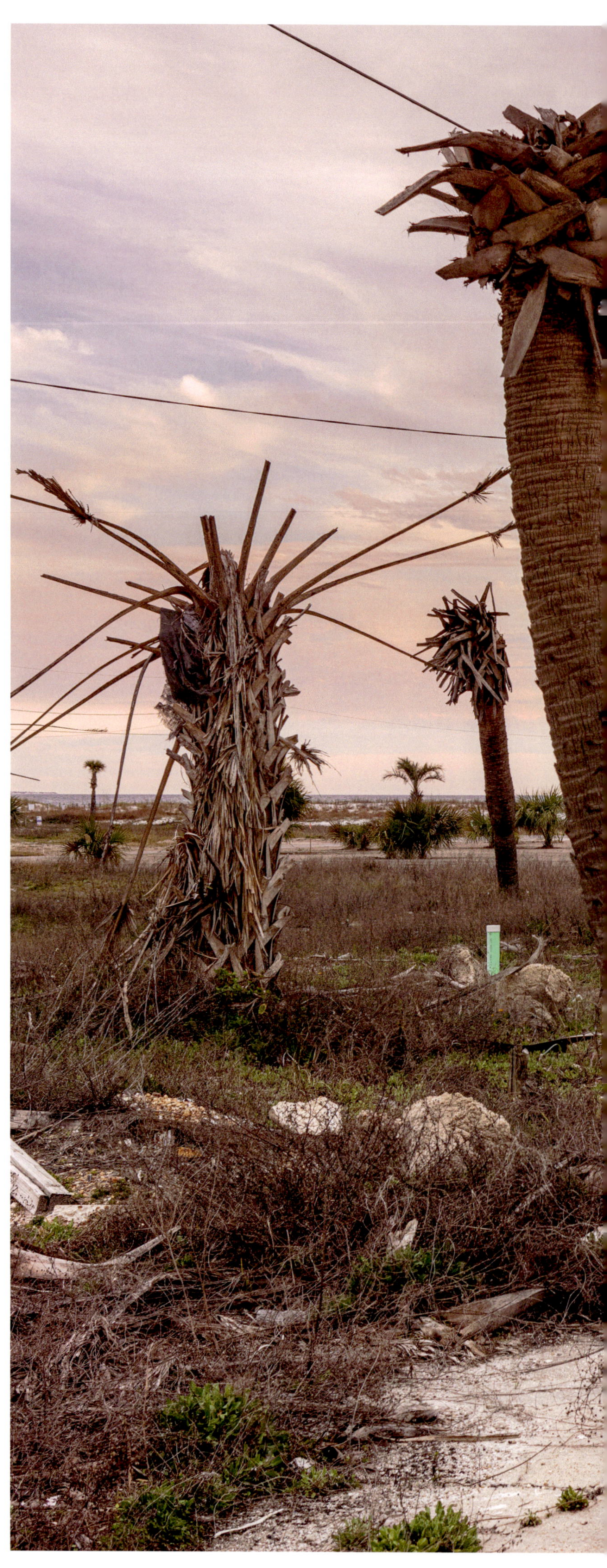

Empty Lots, Mexico Beach, 2021

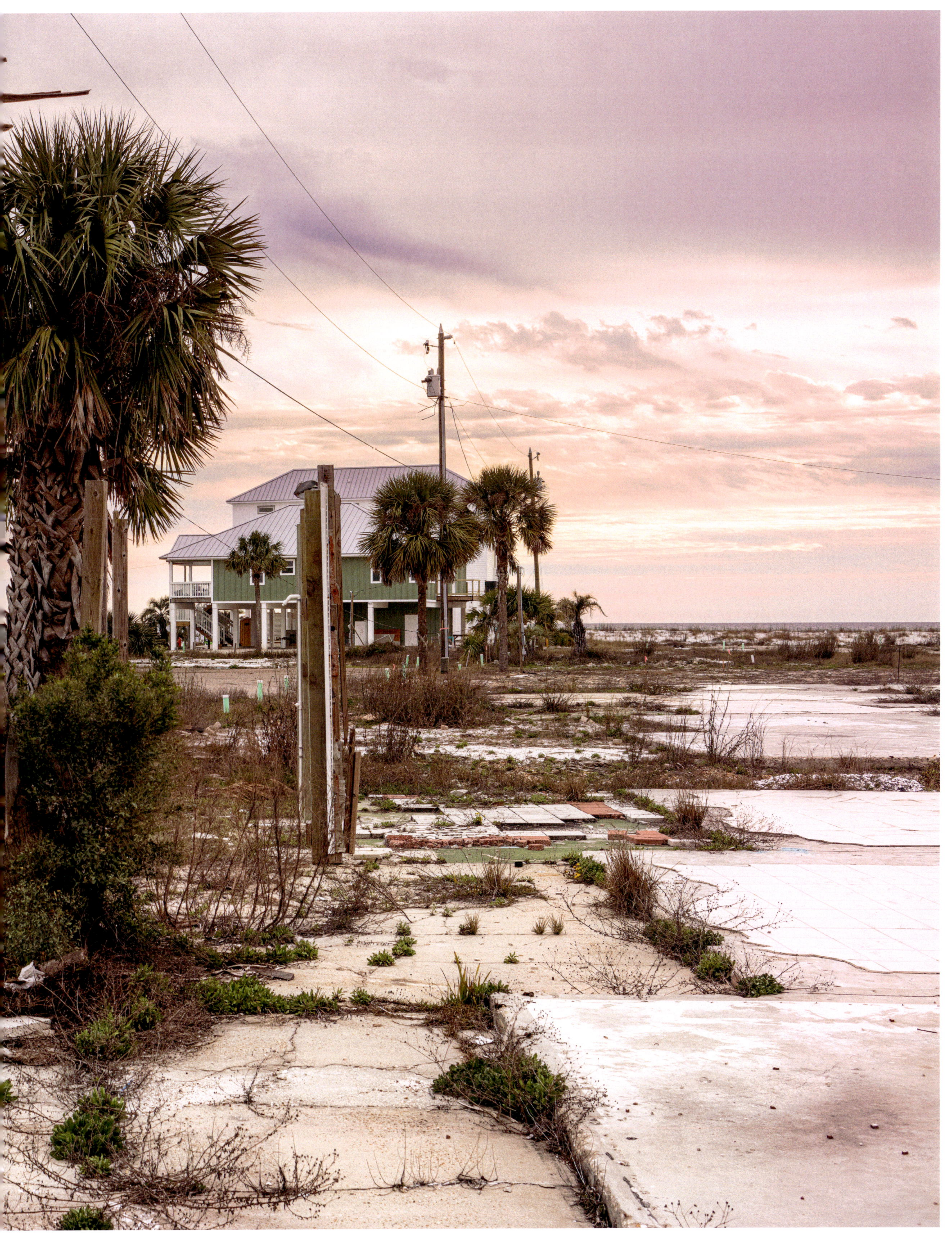

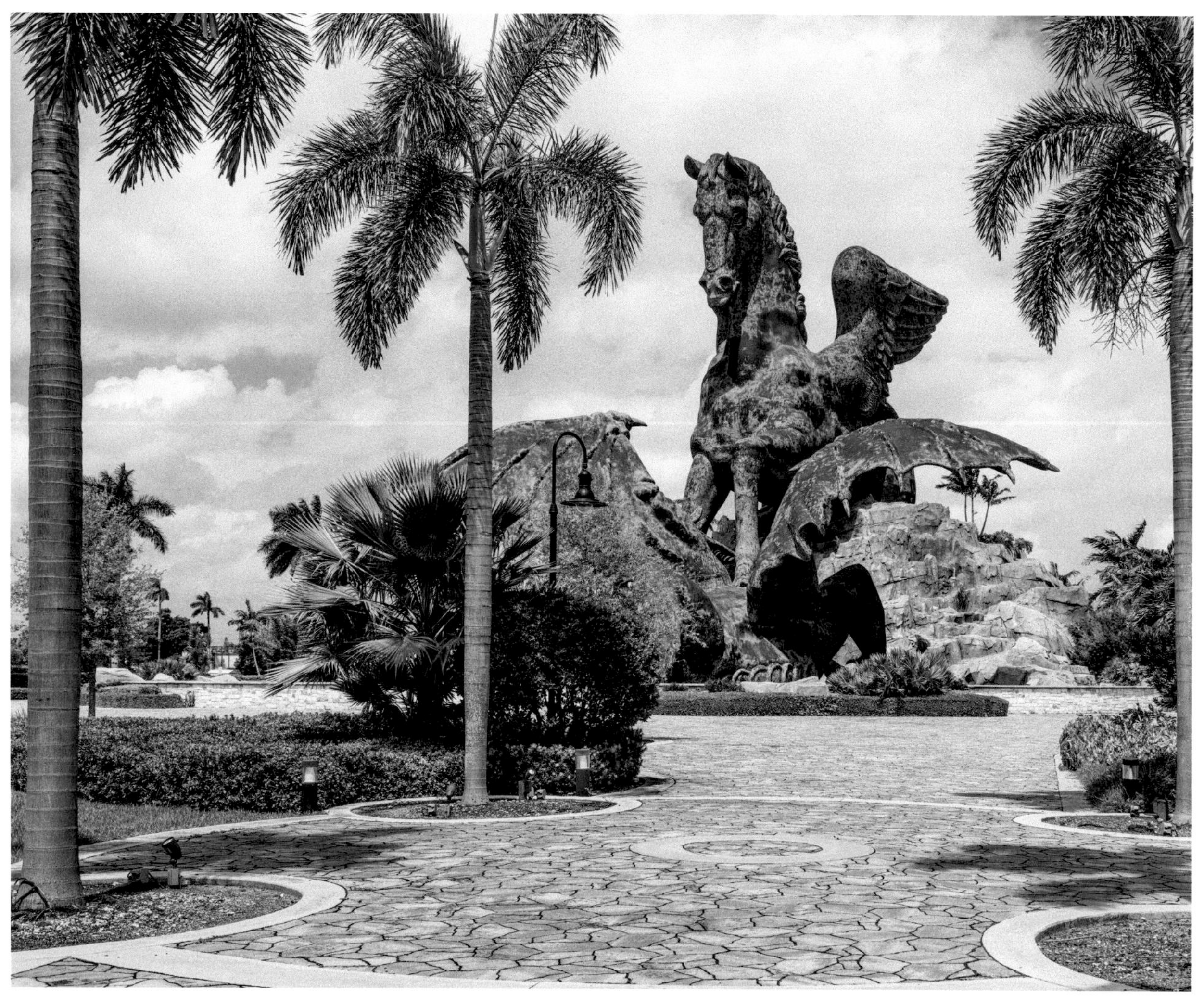

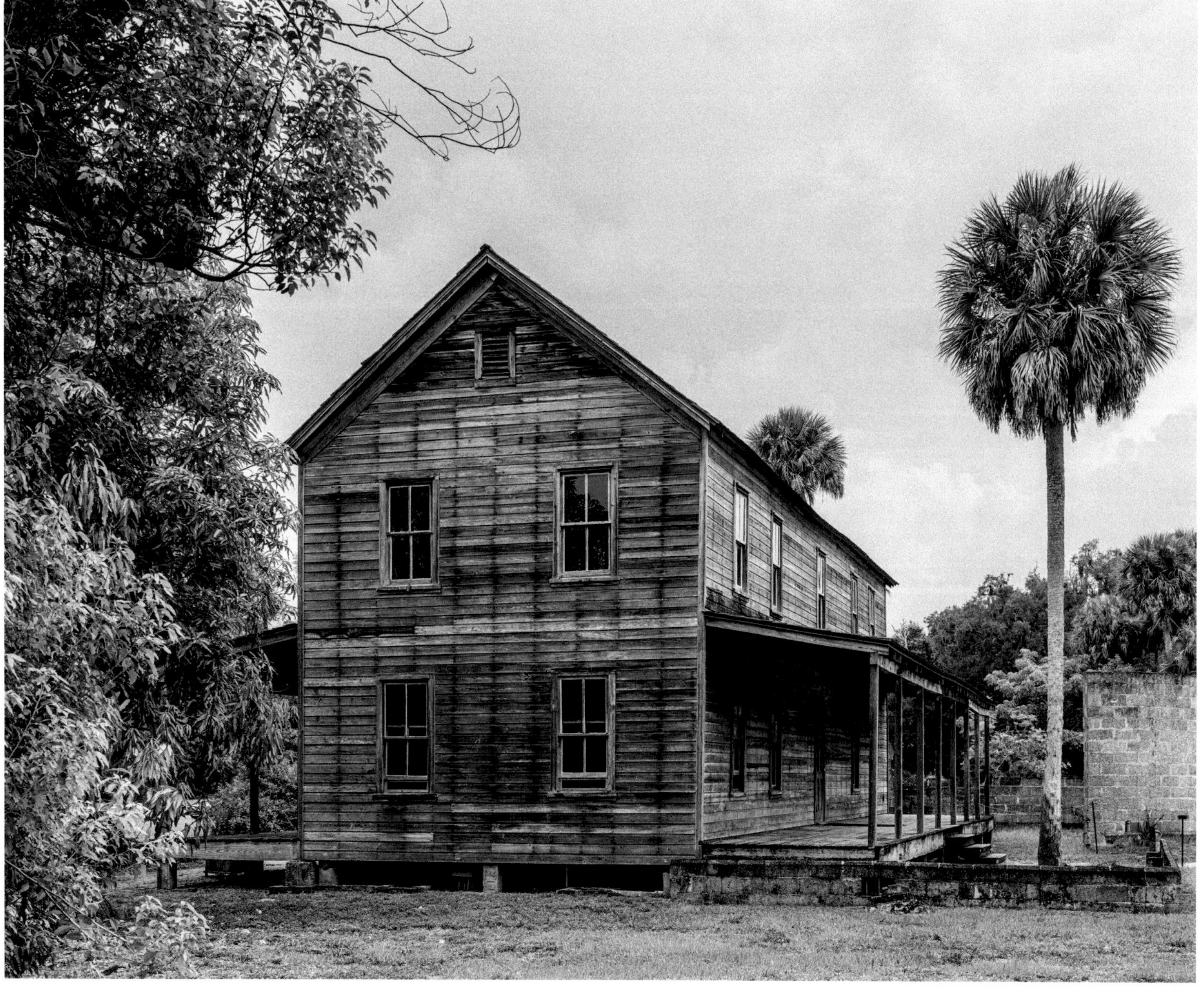

^ Pegasus and Dragon, Hallandale, 2020 ˇ Koreshan Unity Settlement, Estero, 2020

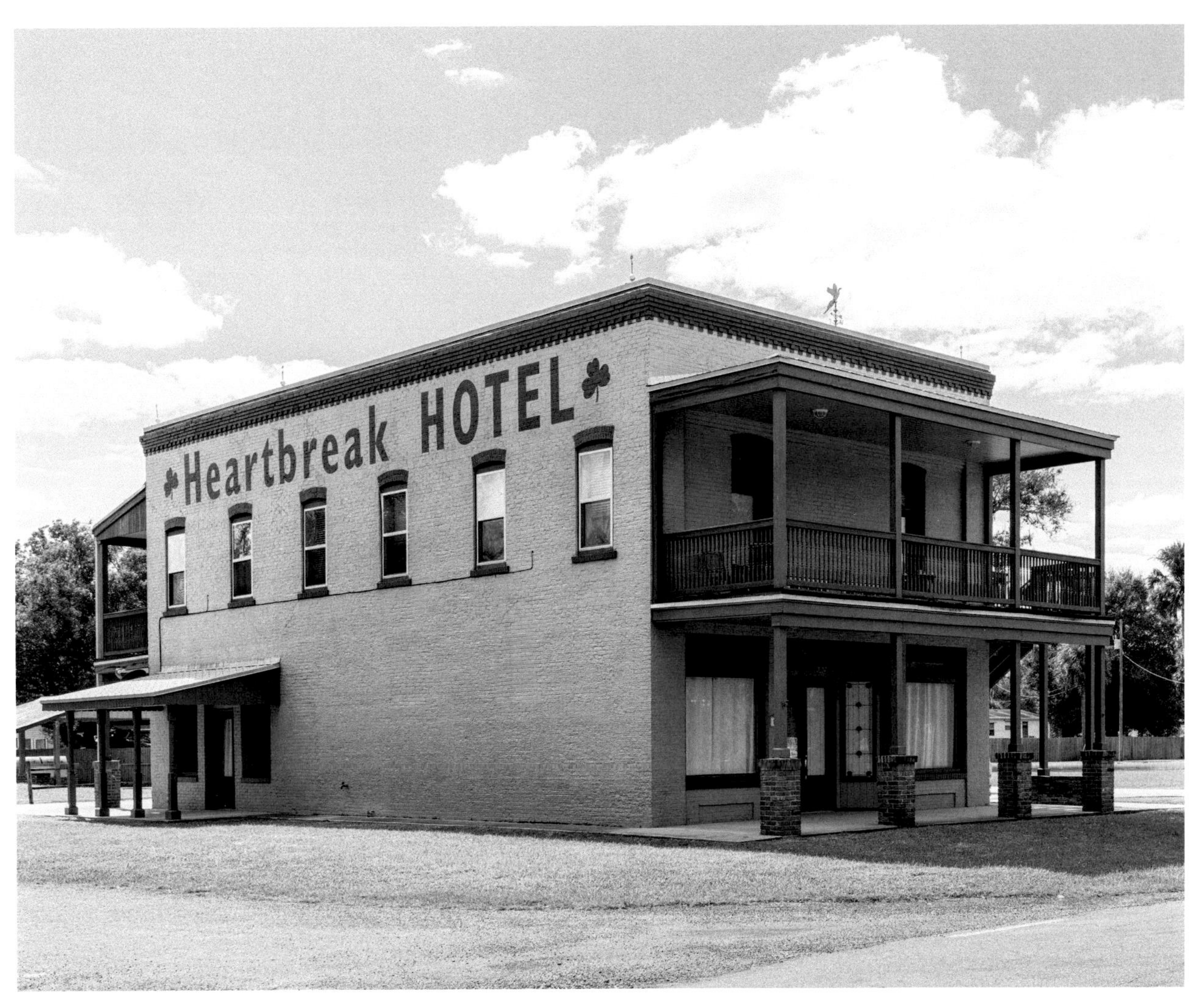

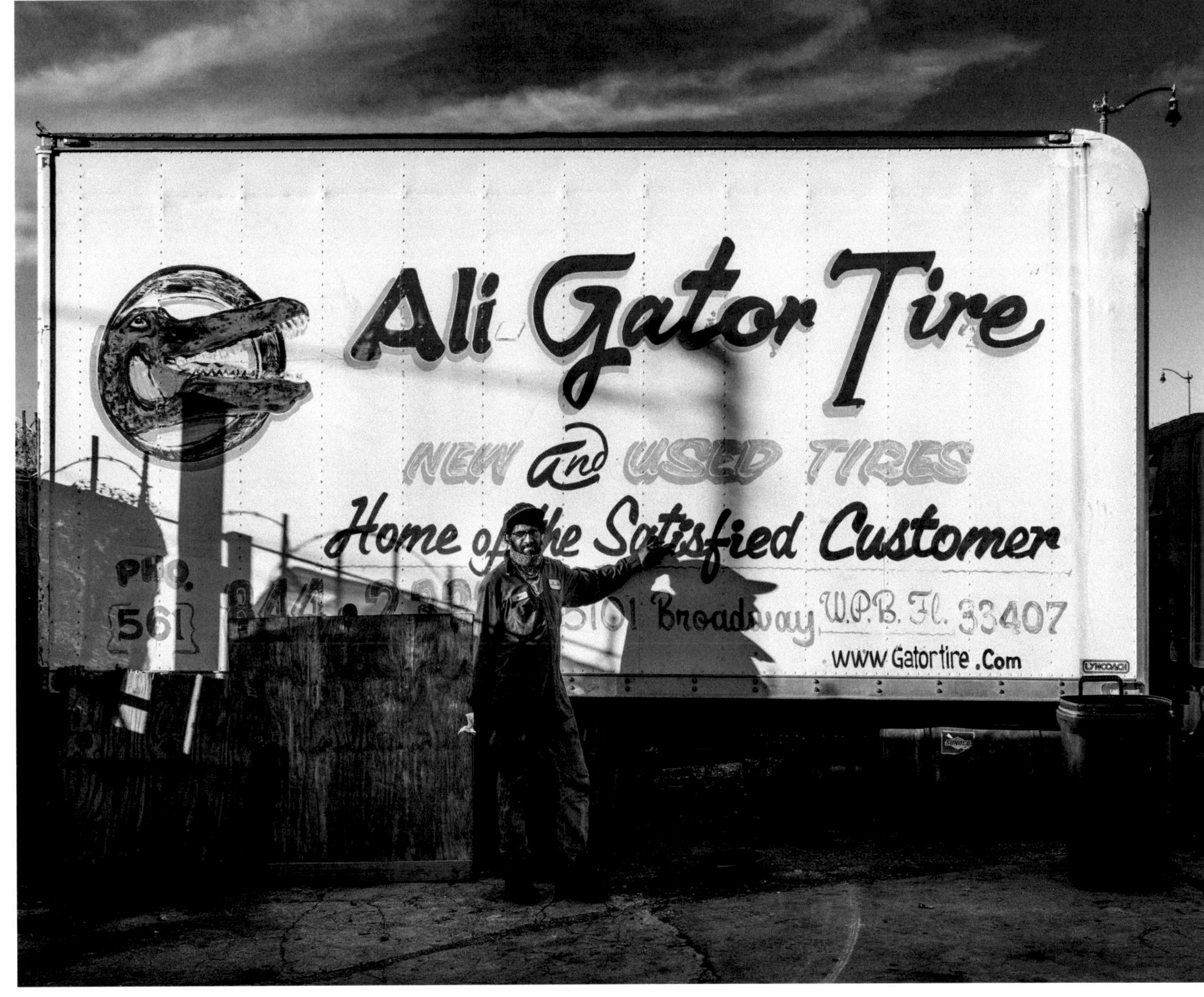

^ Heartbreak Hotel, Kenansville, 2020 ˇ Ali Gator Tire, West Palm Beach, 2021

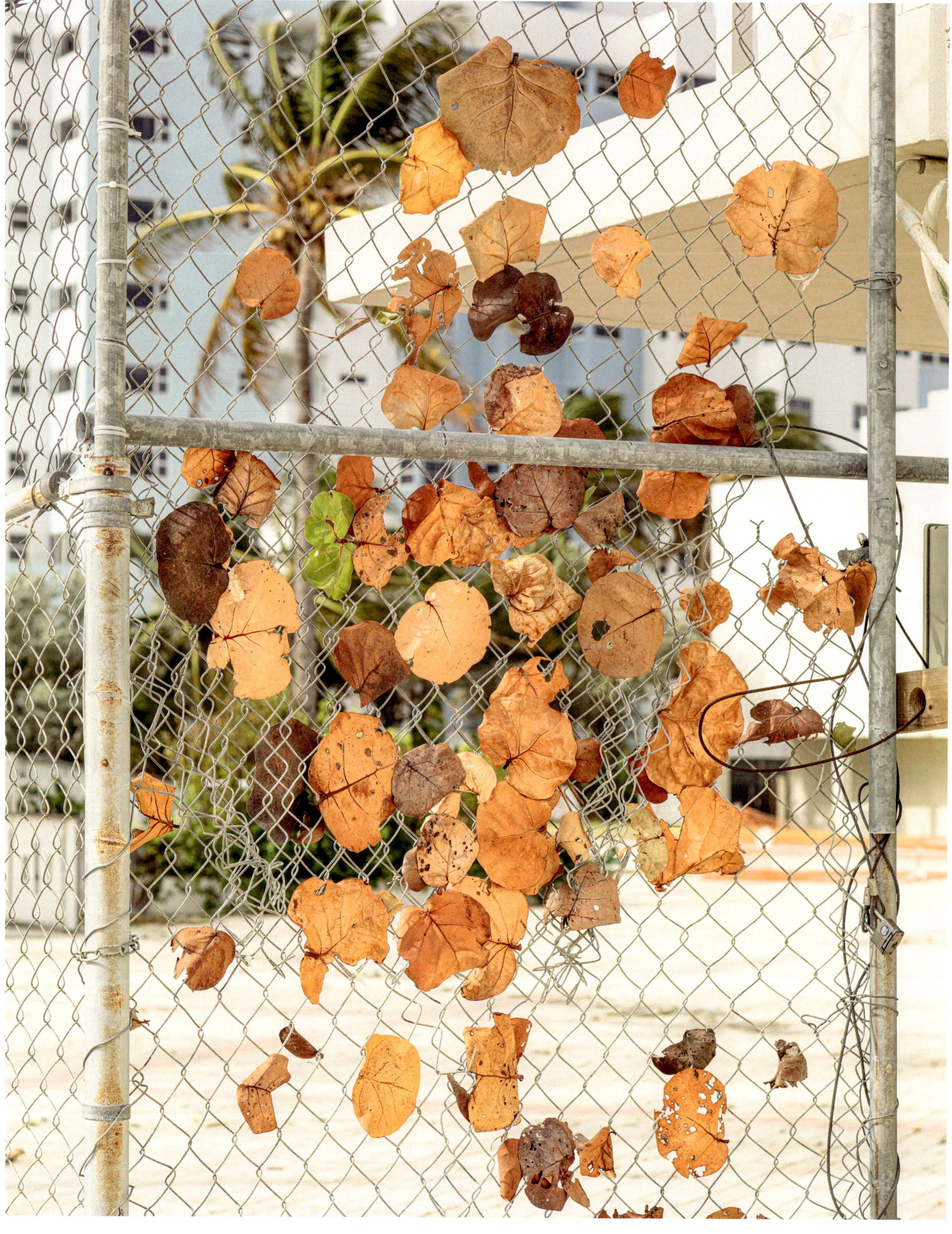

Wind, Miami Beach, 2020

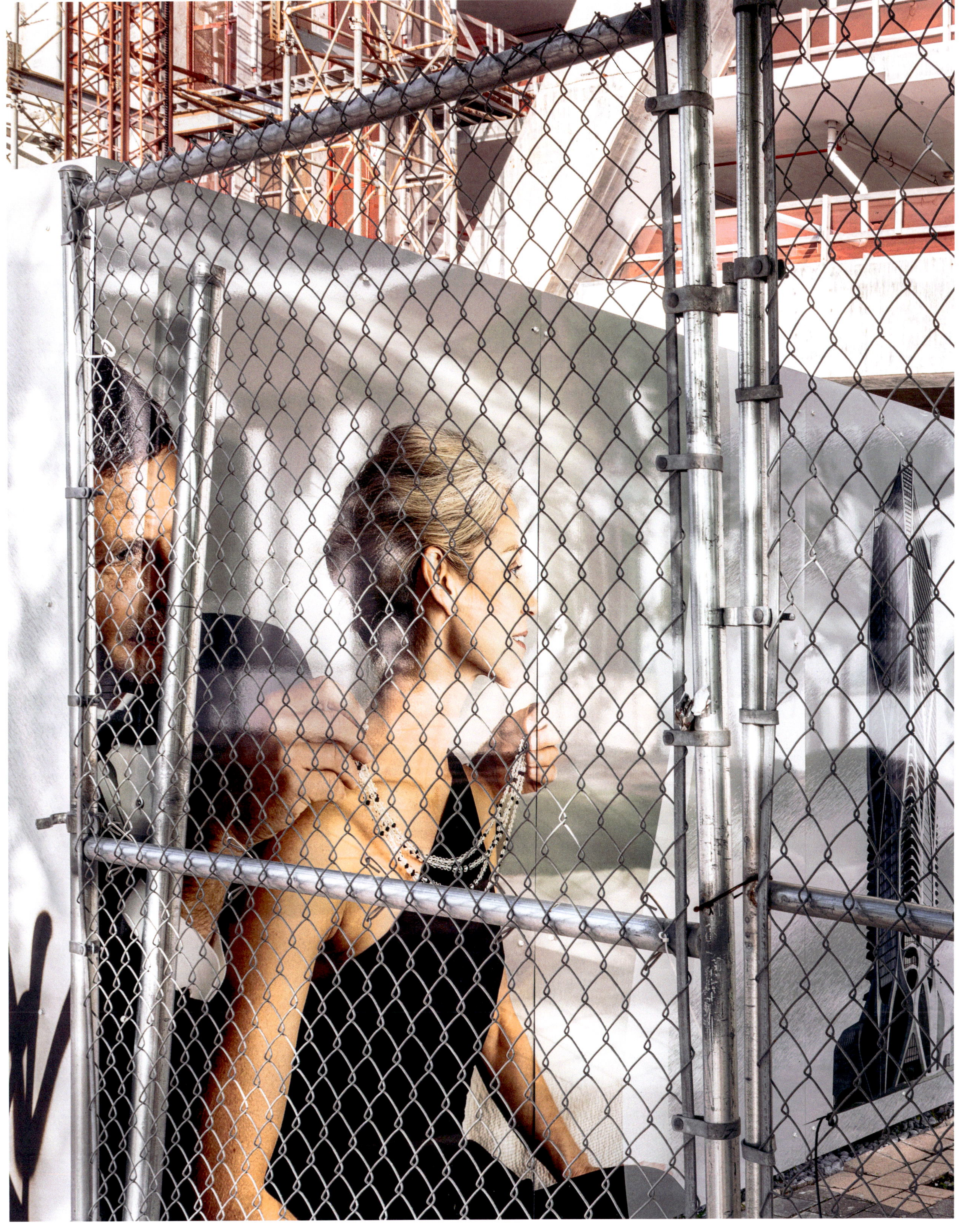

Chain Link Fence, Miami, 2018

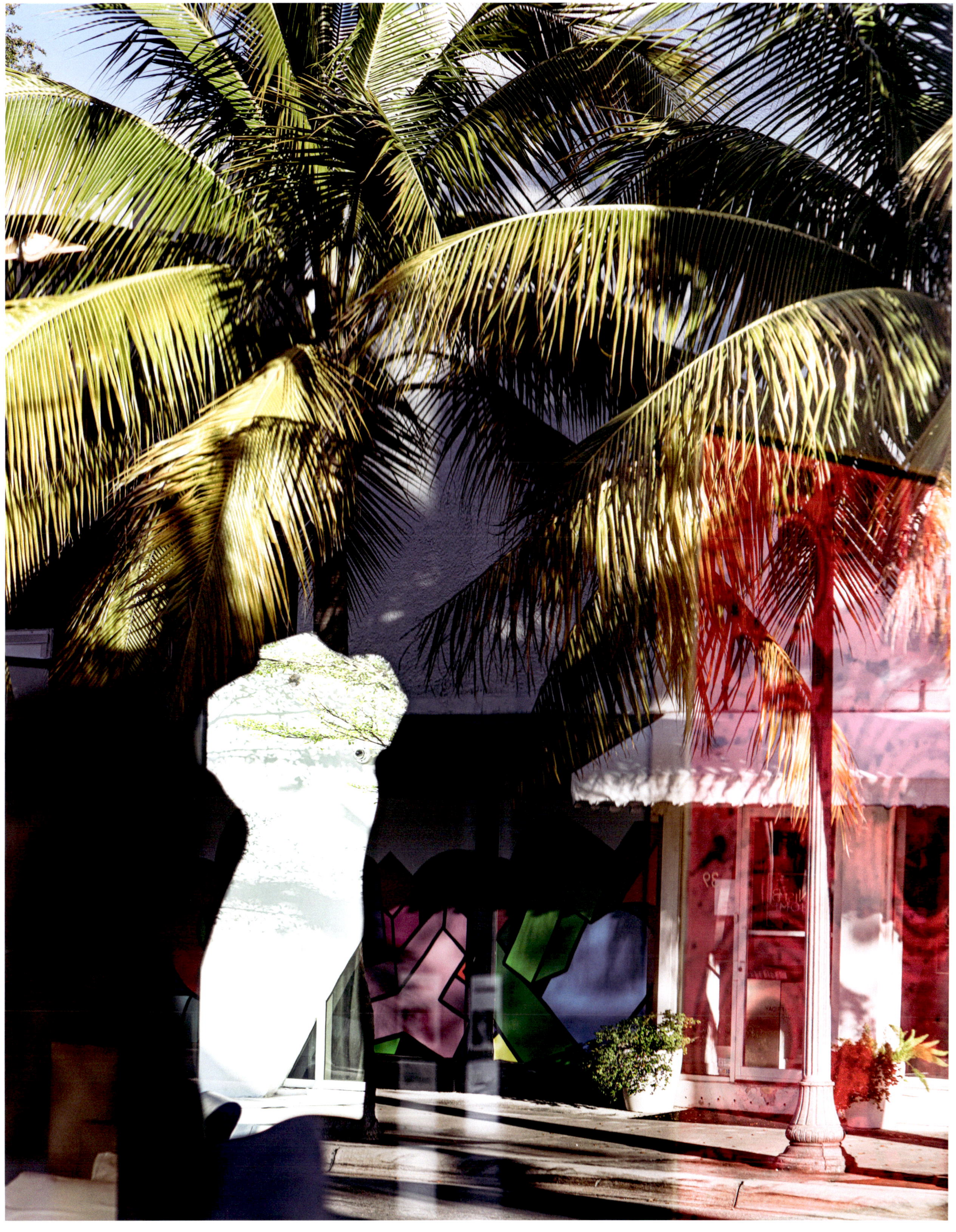

Venus Mirror, Miami, 2020

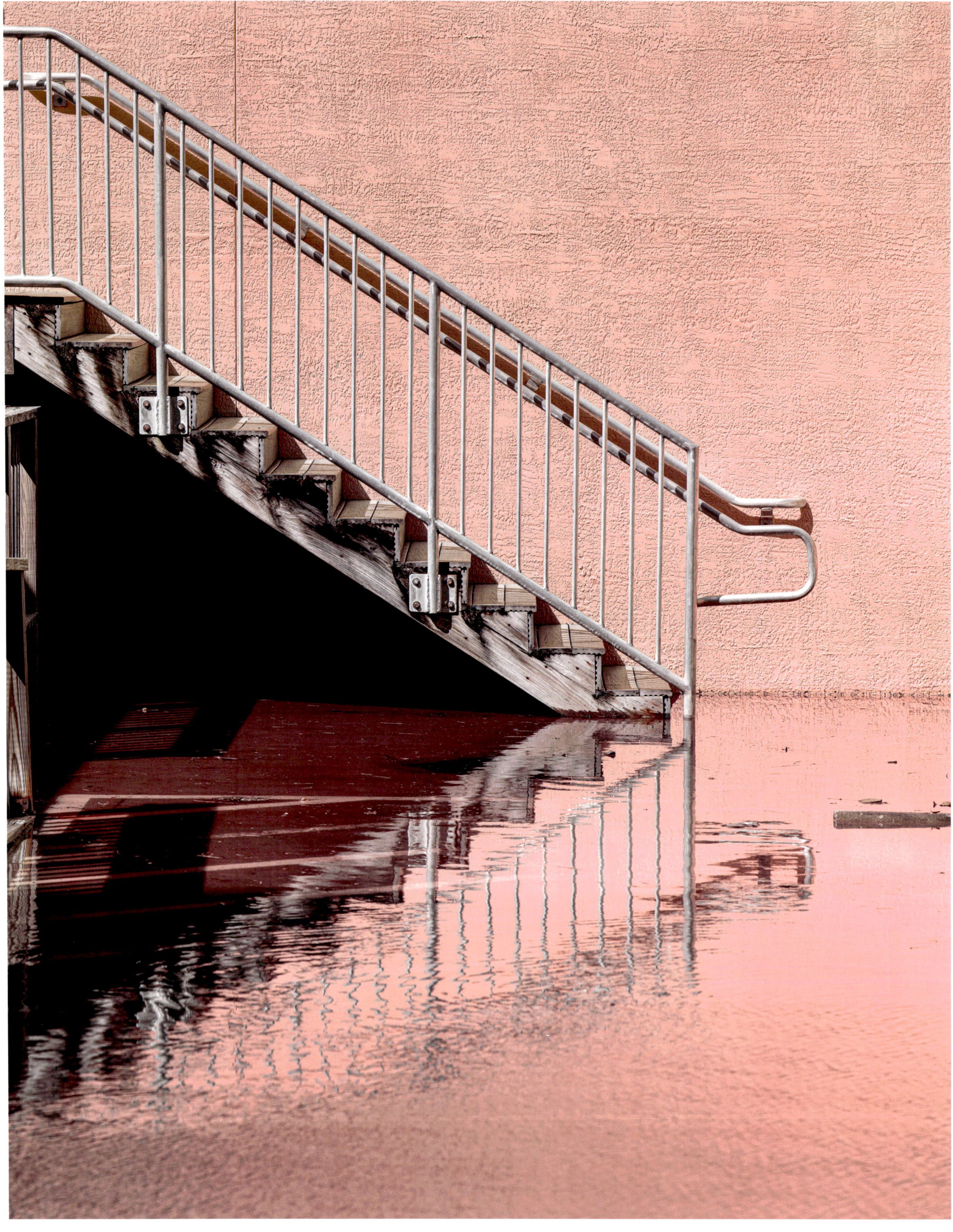

Staircase at King Tide, Hollywood, 2019

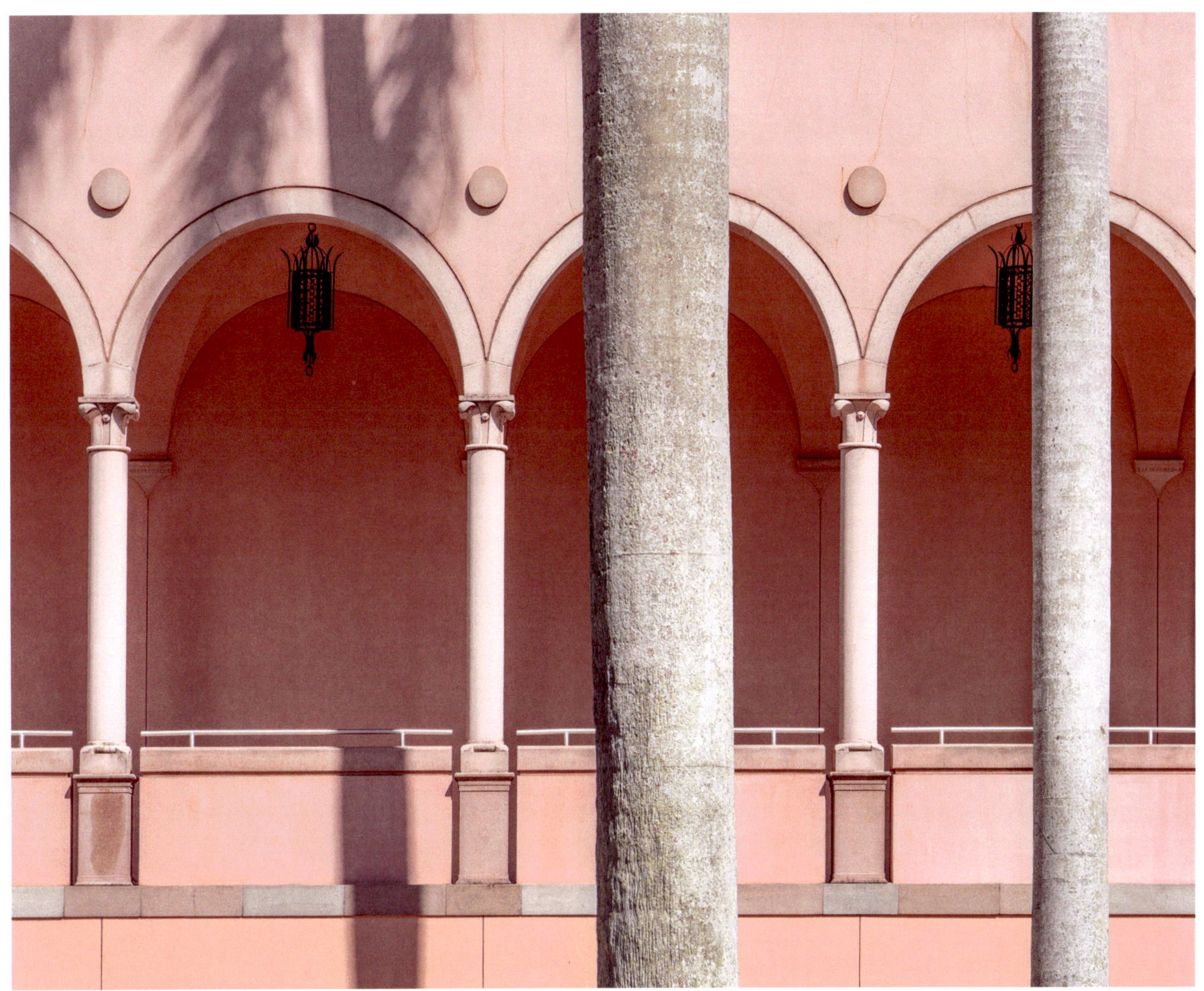

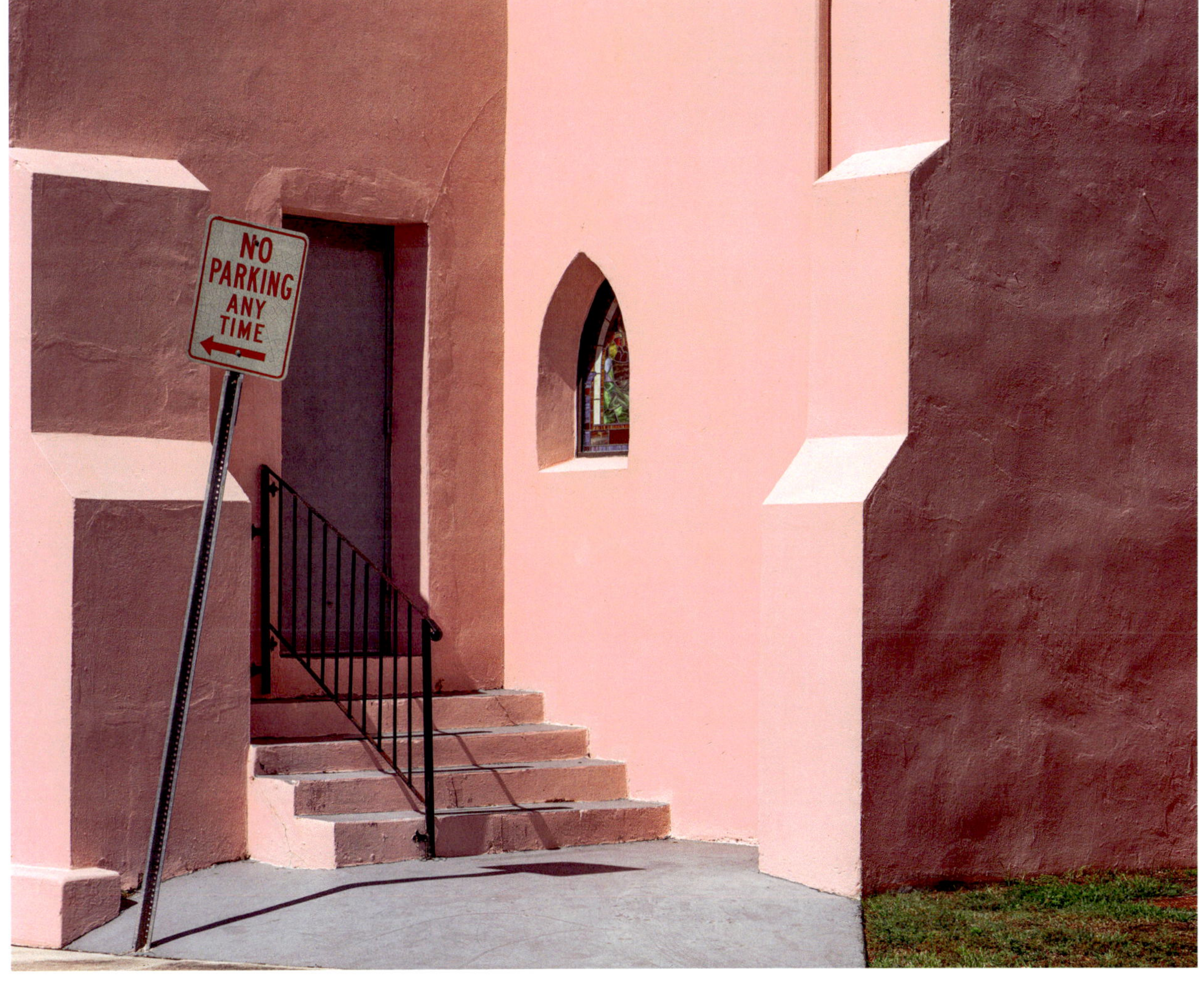

⌃ Arcade, Sarasota, 2020 ⌄ Church, Miami, 2020

» Road Destroyed by Hurricanes, Alligator Point, 2021

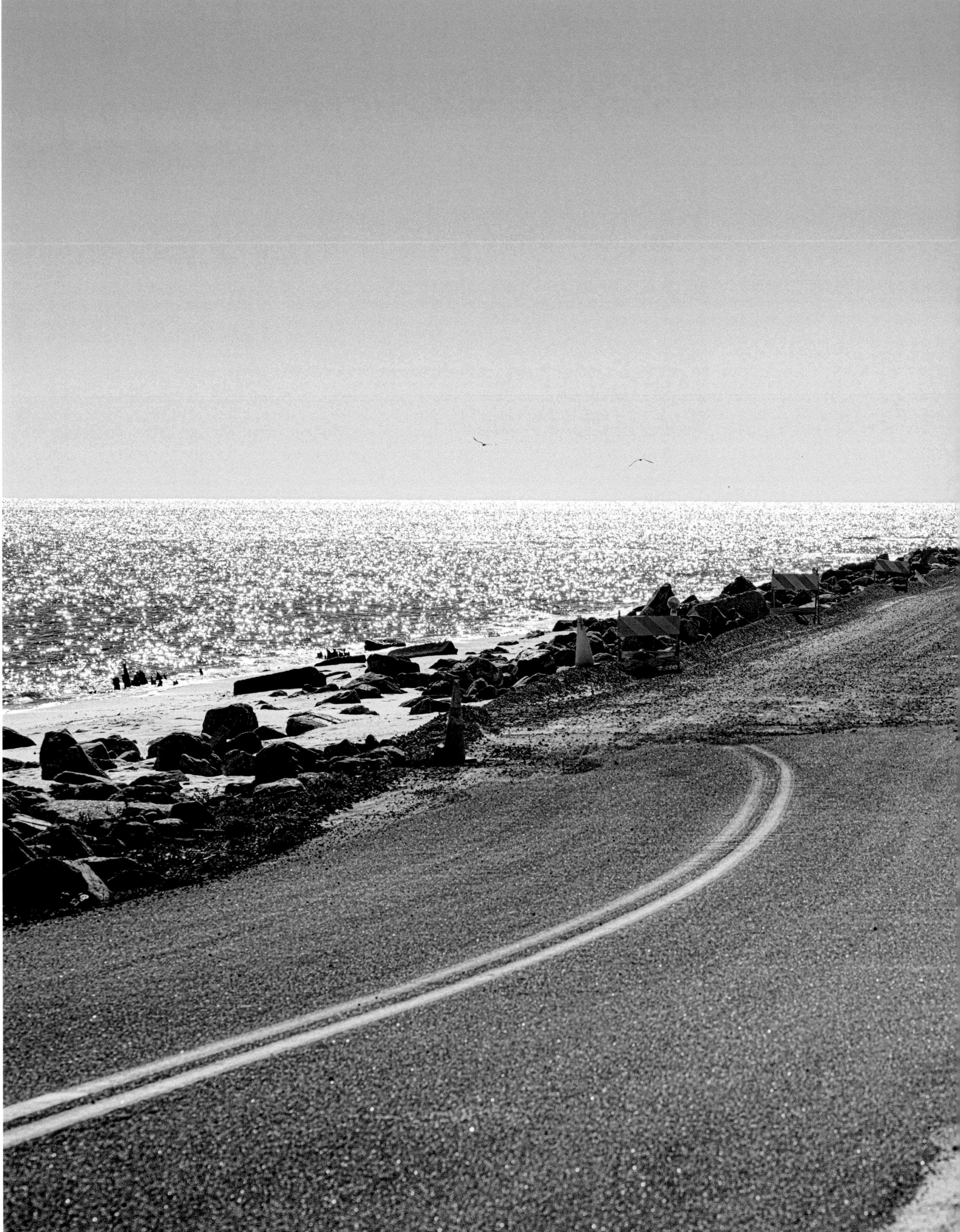

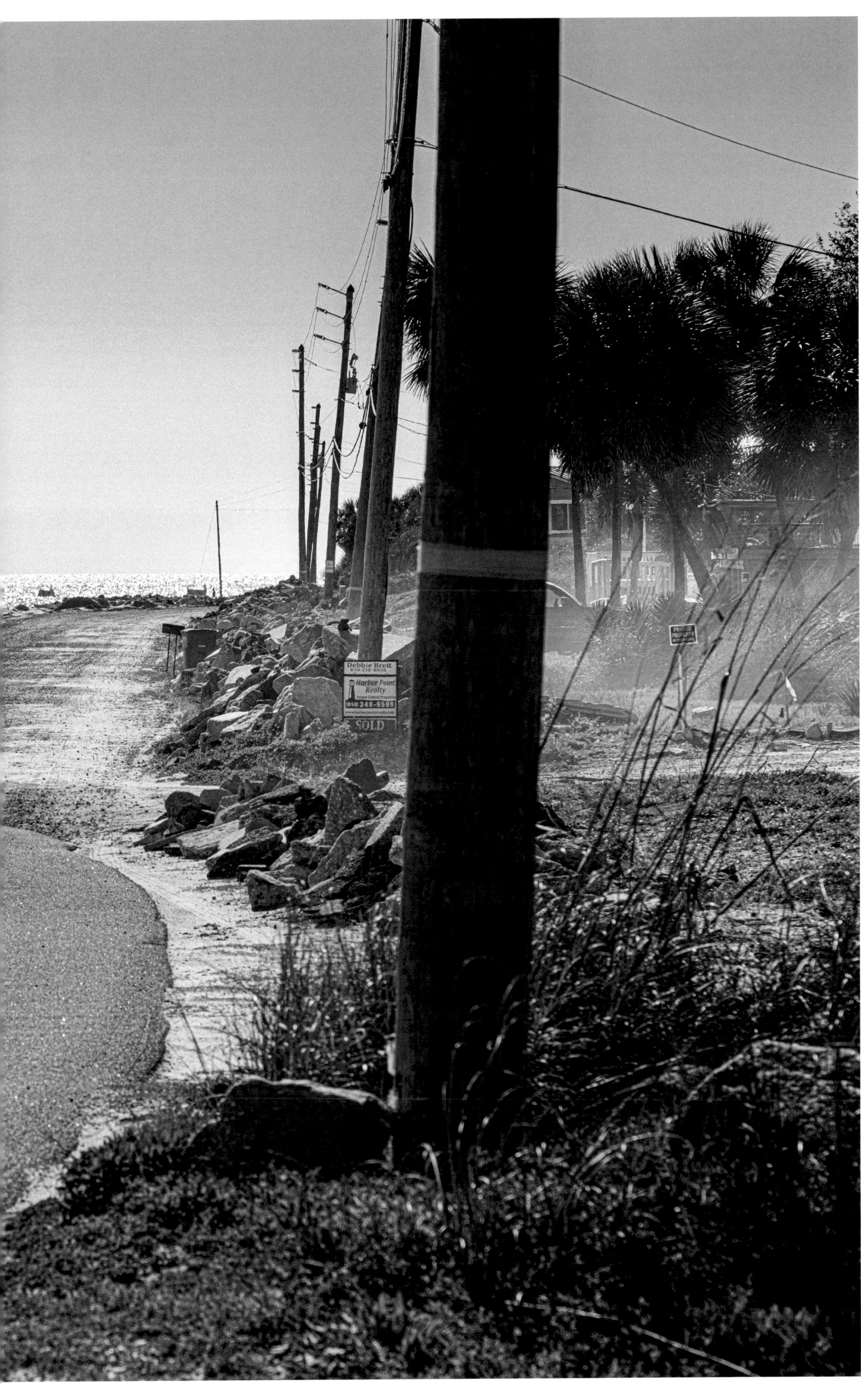
Debbie Brett
850-210-8936
Harbor Point Realty
(850) 349-9599
SOLD

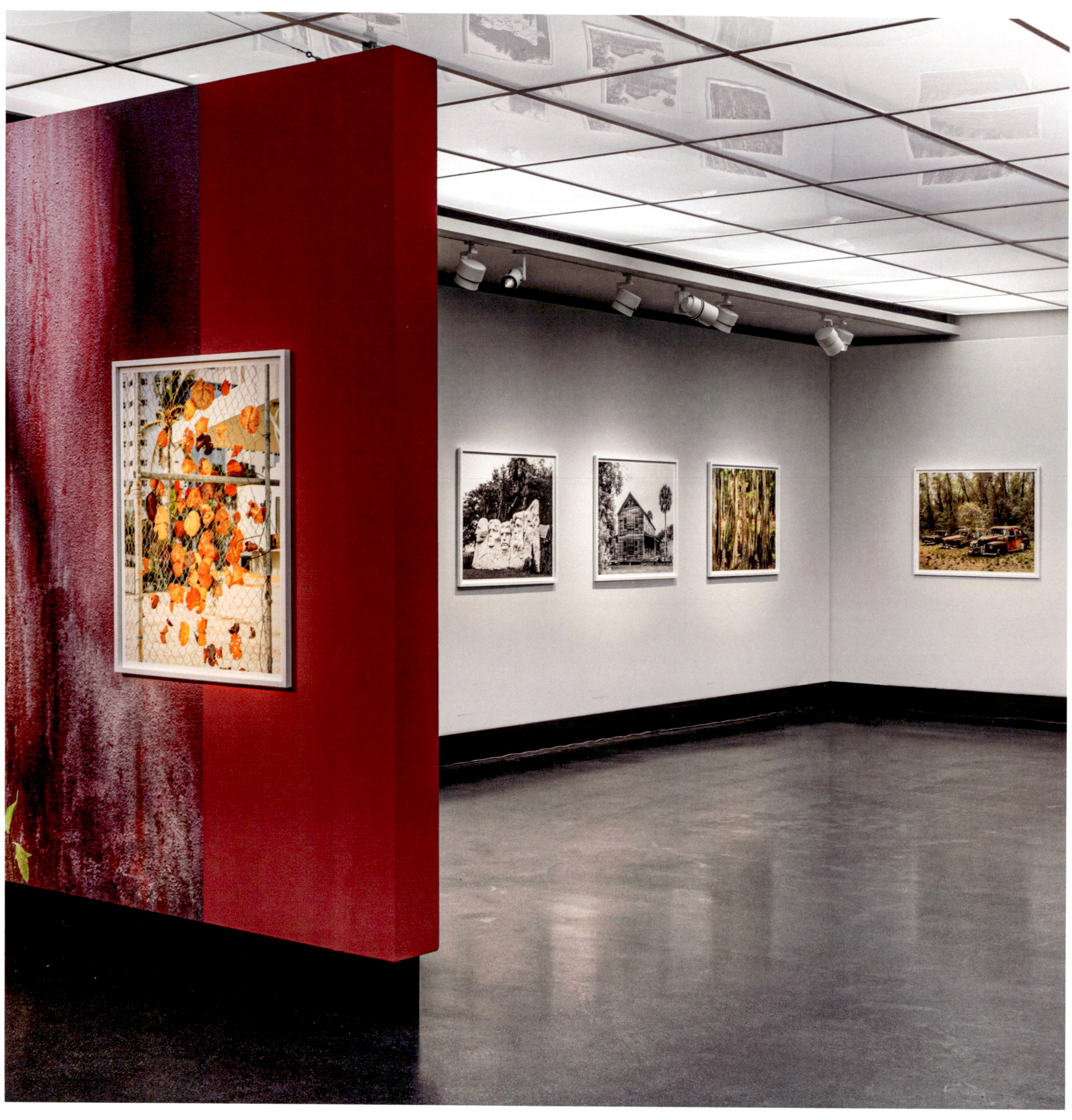

Floridas exhibition, C/O Berlin, 2023

STATE OF THE STATE

MIA FINEMAN

Anastasia Samoylova's *Floridas* is a nuanced portrait of a strange place during strange times. She began work on the project in 2017, soon after Donald J. Trump took office as president of the United States. The last photographs were made in 2021, in the dramatic aftermath of Trump's failed bid for re-election and the 6 January attacks on the Capitol. Formerly a pivotal swing state, Florida over the past two decades has become the epicentre of the Republican universe, a political testing ground for every flavour of right-wing extremism, a MAGA mecca. Trump's Palm Beach estate, Mar-a-Lago, metamorphosed into the 'Winter White House', providing an opulent backdrop for foreign dignitaries' visits, fundraiser photo ops, and bankers boxes stuffed with classified documents. Governor Ron DeSantis, backed by a Republican supermajority in the state legislature, zealously pursued an ultraconservative agenda of anti-'woke' policies, signing a plethora of laws banning books, restricting abortion rights and targeting immigrants, women, LGBTQ individuals and Black Americans. His ill-fated campaign for the 2024 Republican presidential nomination broadcast a portentous vision for the future: 'Make America Florida.'

This is not to say that Samoylova's *Floridas* is a chronicle of the Trump era or a political diatribe. The project offers a visually innovative interpretation of the state's idiosyncratic cultural, economic and ecological conditions: real-estate development and rising sea levels, the lushness of the natural landscape and the fragility of the built environment, the discrepancies between the public image of the Sunshine State as a tourist paradise and the realities of gentrification and climate change. The state's politics create an unusual sense of incongruence in the many Floridas Samoylova explores with her camera: a place both hostile and vulnerable, both hypermodern and primitive, a state often politicized against its own will.

Samoylova is no stranger to political volatility. Born in 1984 in the southern Russian region of Stavropol Krai, where Mikhail Gorbachev began his political career, she relocated with her family to the larger and more politically progressive city of Moscow at the age of five. She came of age as part of Russia's first post-Soviet generation during a time of intense political upheaval and economic uncertainty, when the ideals and the reality of democratic capitalism failed to align. Those early experiences left her with an astute scepticism regarding the truth of media images and a lifelong preoccupation with the kaleidoscopic complexities of visual culture. A naturalized US citizen since 2021, Samoylova has lived in the States for most of her adult life. Straddling the line between insider and outsider, she wields a dual perspective that enriches her artistic vision and drives her passionate interest in exploring place: how a region's values, ideologies and ecologies change and challenge each other over time.

Samoylova began the *Floridas* project as a series of road trips, a quest 'to understand the place on a deeper level and to see whether there were signs in its past that foretold present events'. From her home base in Miami, she crisscrossed the state by car, travelling from the southernmost Keys to the state borders with Alabama and Georgia, and up and down the Gulf Coast. Her excursions were inspired, in part, by the American photographer Berenice Abbott, one of the few women of her era to create a body of work in the traditionally male-dominated genre of American road-trip photography. In 1954, a year before Robert Frank embarked on the cross-country tour that would lead to his landmark photobook, *The Americans*, Abbott travelled with two companions up and down America's first national highway, US Route 1, which runs along the Atlantic seaboard from Maine to the Florida Keys. Driving along Florida's Atlantic coast, she was particularly captivated by the state's abundance of tourist kitsch, its novelty motels and trailers, its billboards and county fairs.

What struck Abbott most powerfully on her journey, however, were the changes wrought by the automobile on the American landscape – an encroaching sameness that effaced the regional specificity that distinguished one place from another. In a prospectus for a never-published book of her US Route 1 photographs, Abbott wrote: 'Particularly noticeable is the absence of people. One never seems to see the people walking on the roads; they are always on wheels. One only sees people going into stores or coming out of stores. But people have left their tracks behind them – in tourist homes, tourist cabins, hotels, motels, trailer camps, motor courts, gasoline stations, "EAT" signs, traffic signs, historical markers, religious "ads", billboards. Thus has the automobile changed the American scene. The "mechanized magic carpet" has freed people, but it has also destroyed the old face of America.'

A lifelong advocate of descriptive realism in photography, Abbott sought to record the look and feel of the American landscape at that particular historical moment, and her project is inextricably tied to Cold War politics and the expansion of the military–industrial complex. In 1956, President Dwight D. Eisenhower, responding to the perceived threat of an atomic war with the Soviet Union, signed legislation funding the US Interstate Highway System, which was designed to allow for easier transport of military resources across the country. By the 1970s, Abbott's beloved US Route 1 had been superseded by the grim monotony of Interstate 95.

What Samoylova shares with Abbott is a careful attentiveness to the particularities of place, an interest in capturing the visual contours of a cultural landscape that will inevitably shift, grow or disappear. Like Walker Evans, another significant influence, she cultivates a quality of detached empiricism that allows commonplace subjects to appear as if seen for the first time. Her photographs are highly structured, visually seductive and inflected with a lightly ironic sensibility. Although Florida's political extremism was but one aspect of Samoylova's quest to comprehend the complexities and contradictions of her adopted state, the political mood of

Trumpism in Florida is inescapable. It permeates the visual landscape, seeping into the pictures like black mould on stucco. 'The question I want to present with my work,' she explains, 'is whether we can try to love a place, and by extension, one another, enough to see beyond the disagreeable leadership. Florida is perfect for this; it is a chameleon. Depending on how you look at it, it can be dystopian or paradisiacal, disturbing or dreamy.'

Most references to politics in Samoylova's photographs are understated. There are no pictures of Mar-a-Lago or MAGA rallies, no portraits of candidates or statehouse reportage. The closest she comes to a literal depiction of Trump is *Overpainted Poster, Miami*, a collage-like photograph of a faded campaign poster on a graffiti-covered brick wall. Broad strokes of black obscure the former president's face, leaving only a bleached-out puff of hair on top, a double chin below and a sliver of eyeball peeking through the blackness, like a child cheating at hide-and-seek. The jagged end of a broken pipe lands strategically in the middle of his forehead. In the tradition of the French *affichiste* Jacques Villeglé, who appropriated torn advertising posters from the streets of Paris and presented them as anonymous works of art, Samoylova's photograph is a collaboration with an unseen vandal. It frames and memorializes a spontaneous gesture of rage, a politicized act of creative disfiguration.

Florida, sometimes known as the 'Gunshine State', has provided a hospitable environment for the radical right's fetishization of firearms. In *Gun Shop, Port Orange*, the sun-dappled facade of a low-slung, seafoam-green building is festooned with silhouettes of automatic rifles. The picturesque curve of a tall tree in the corner of the frame heightens the placid prettiness of the scene, underscoring the dreadful absurdity of America's reigning death cult. More forthright in its portrayal of overtly politicized imagery is *Beachgoer, Naples*, a tightly framed view of a man's bare torso with a pair of trompe-l'oeil pistols inked at his waistline. A sheath knife is clipped to his belt, a Confederate flag on his arm proclaims him an 'Outlaw', and his sternum promises 'No Mercy'. Granted anonymity through judicious cropping, he is a self-created caricature, a vivid incarnation of the undercurrent of violence that buoys the popular appeal of Trumpism.

Reproduced in this book is another photograph documenting an act of political self-expression from across the partisan divide. *Mural Painter, Miami* frames a spray-painted mural featuring a monumental portrait of the boxer and political activist Muhammad Ali. In this case, the historical details of the image exceed its generic caption. Created for the Wynwood Mural Fest in 2020, the painting pays tribute to Ali's association with the Fifth Street Gym in South Beach, where he trained for the famous bout with Sonny Liston that won him the title of World Heavyweight Champion in 1964. The artist, Hiero Veiga, stands with his back to the camera, filling in the white letters of the mural's caption, 'Be Your Own Champion'. Shielded by headphones and a respirator mask, he appears fully absorbed in the act of creation, a quality of absorption that is mirrored by the photographer herself. Printed on the back of his T-shirt, visible to curious passers-by, is a universal imperative that cuts through all political ideologies, an invitation, a challenge, an aspiration: BE A GOOD PERSON.

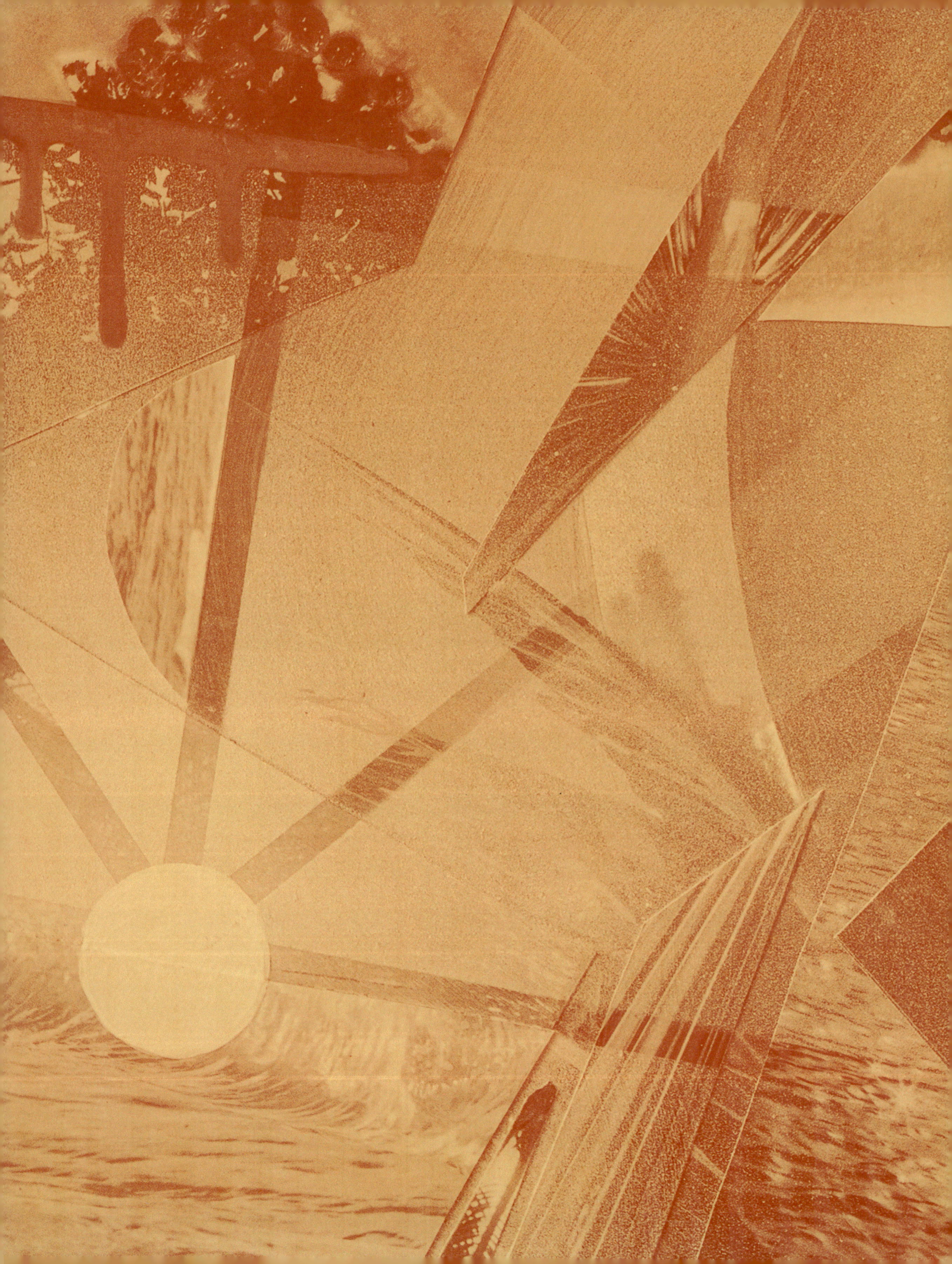

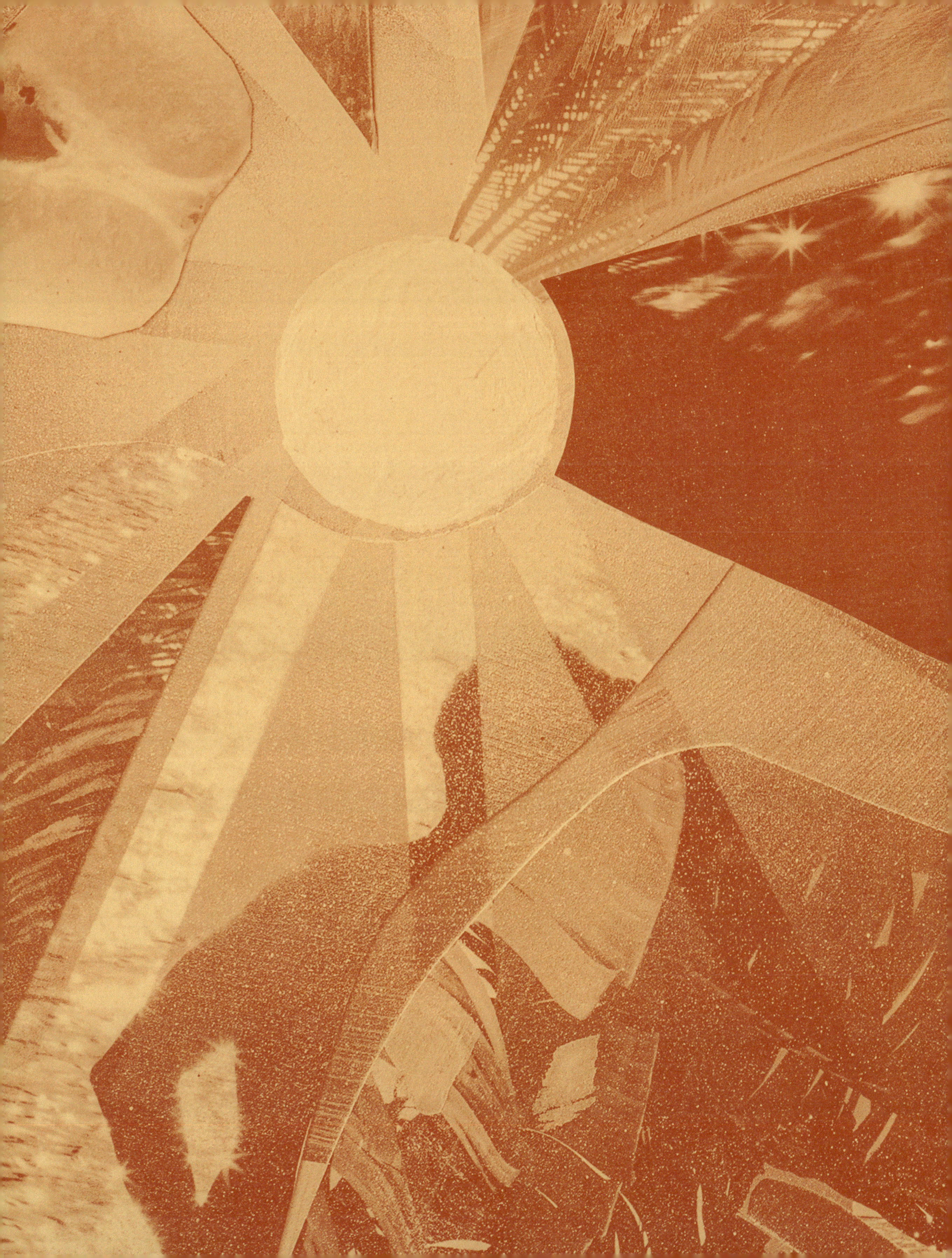

PAINTINGS AND COLLAGES

In much of her work, Samoylova dances nimbly between what may seem like opposites: the abstract and the figurative; the rough and the smooth; surface and depth; the essentially photographic and a mixed-media sensibility. Her collages and paintings grow naturally from her background in drawing, three-dimensional design and architecture. Some of the examples here are from 2016, her first year in Florida, while others are among her most recent works.

Samoylova has an eye for what already feels painterly in the world: the pastel shades of tropical architecture, hand-rendered shop signs, colourful walls mottling and crumbling in humid air. Her compositions and attention to light also echo key movements in modern painting, from the Impressionists to Abstract Expressionism. There are even hints of the Photorealist painting that emerged in the 1960s and '70s. She synthesizes all this into something her own.

Although she is a digital native, having never photographed on film, it is significant that Samoylova rarely collages or 'paints' digitally. For all the hybridity, she keeps a distinction between the photographic and the painterly, with collage as the mediator. Observational photographs are printed in the studio and become elements in new works. Paint extends the realist imagery, then drifts into abstraction, or a photograph is entirely obscured by brush strokes. Motifs and the material of paint drift and swim. The final effect appears to dream outwards from a detail – a palm, a shack, a facade – into something beyond the camera's mechanical eye. Most importantly, these works are where Samoylova's artistic life out in the world and inside her studio come together.

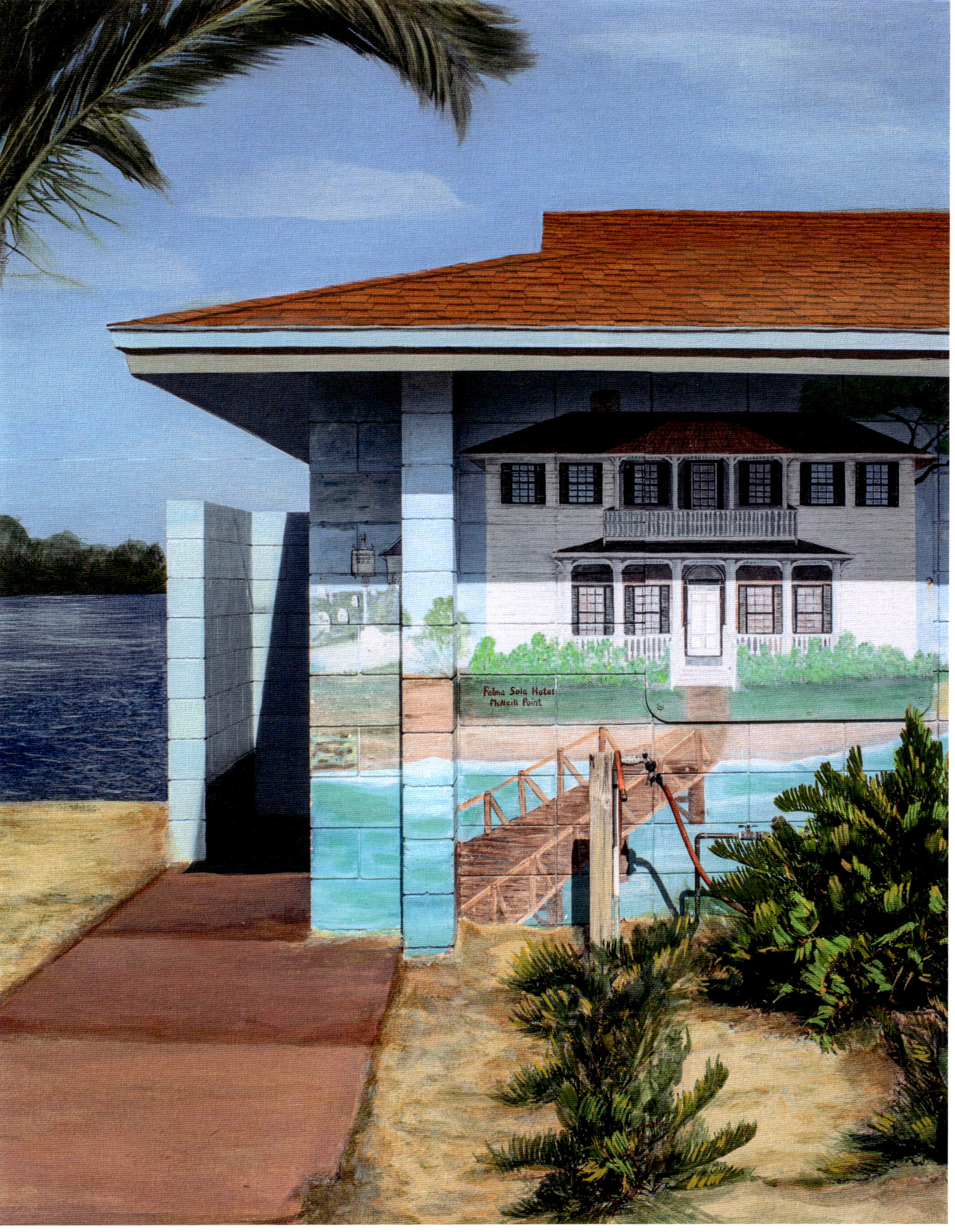

Tile Mural, 2024

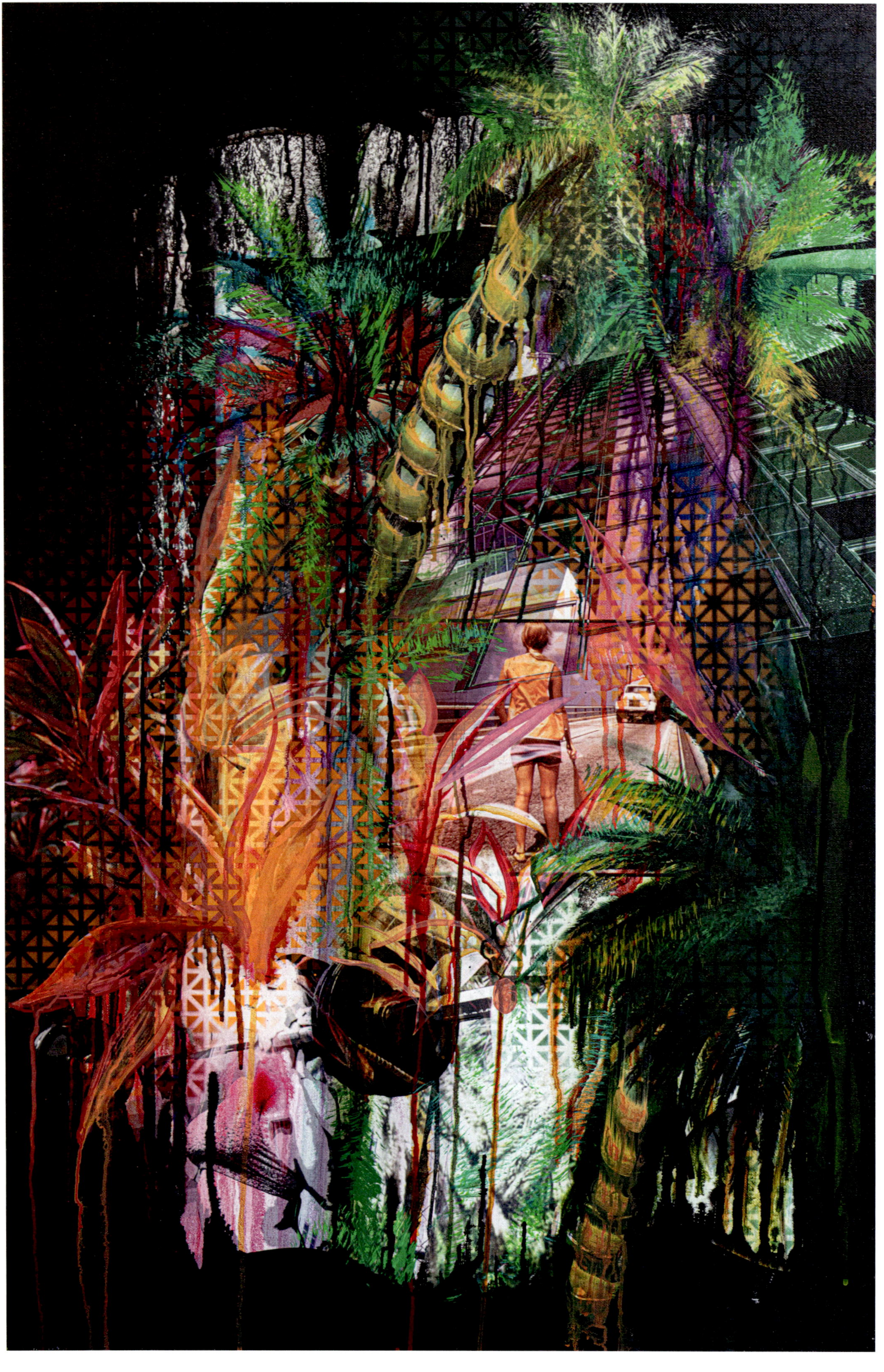

Highway, 2023

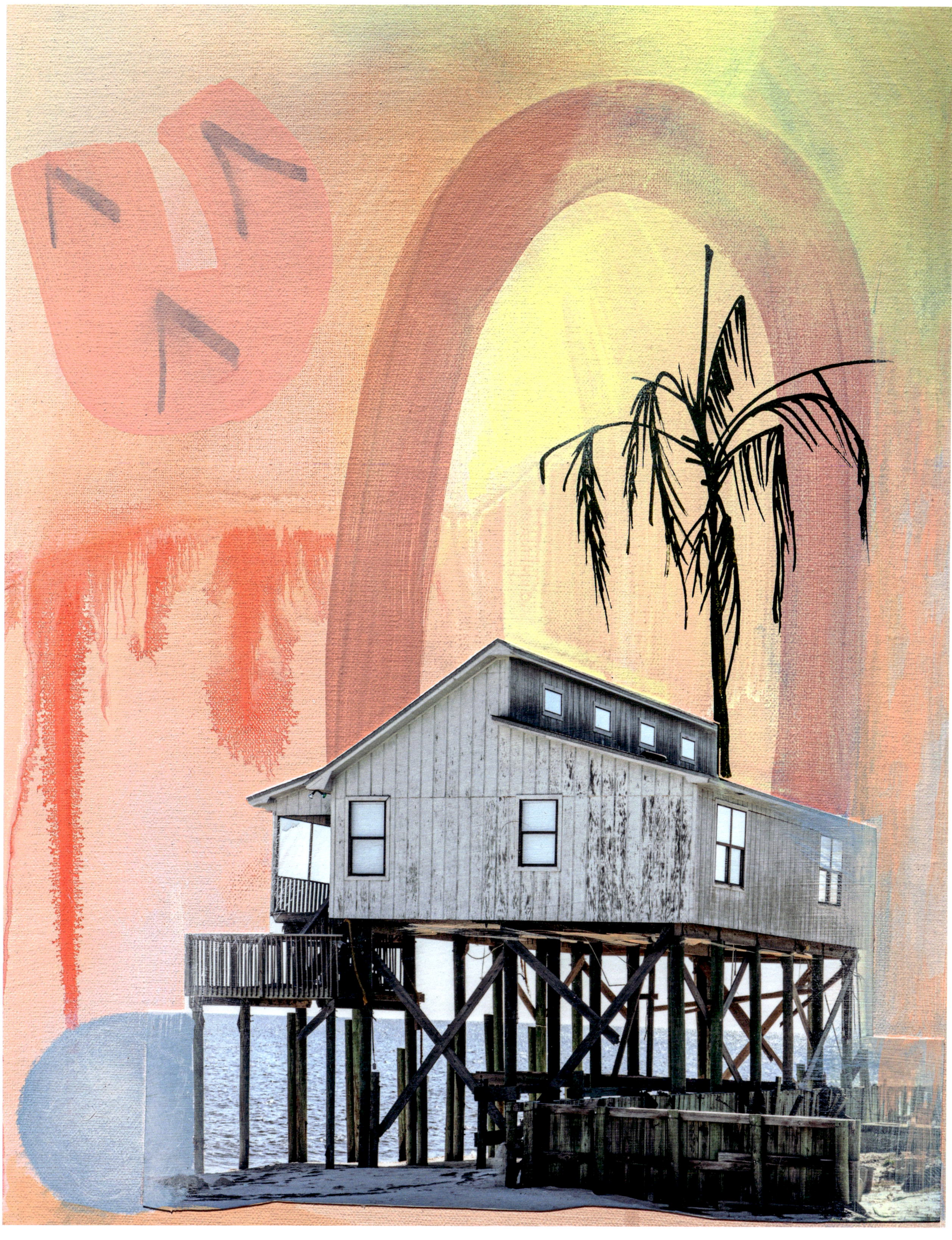

House on Stilts, 2023

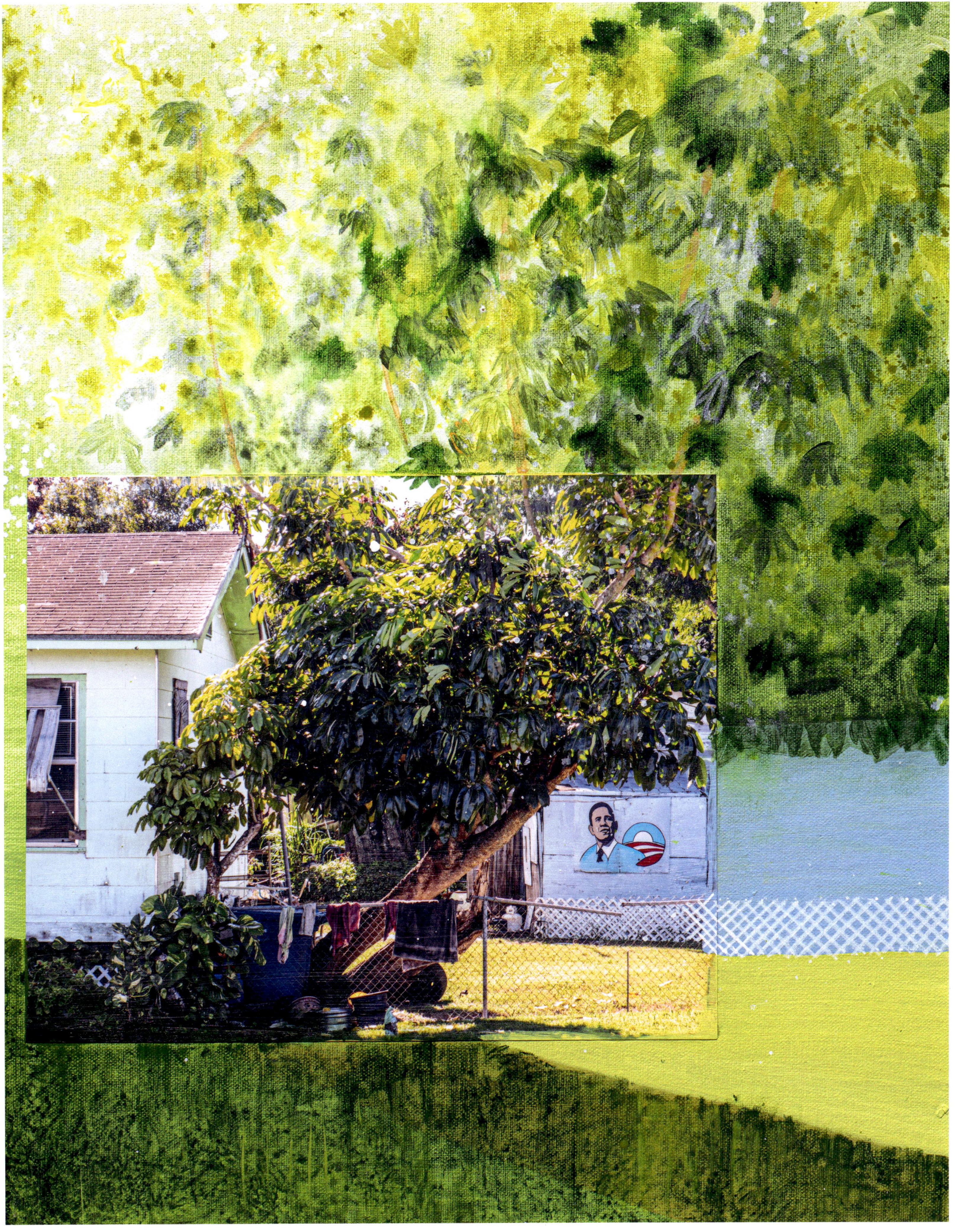

Backyard in Belle Glade, 2023

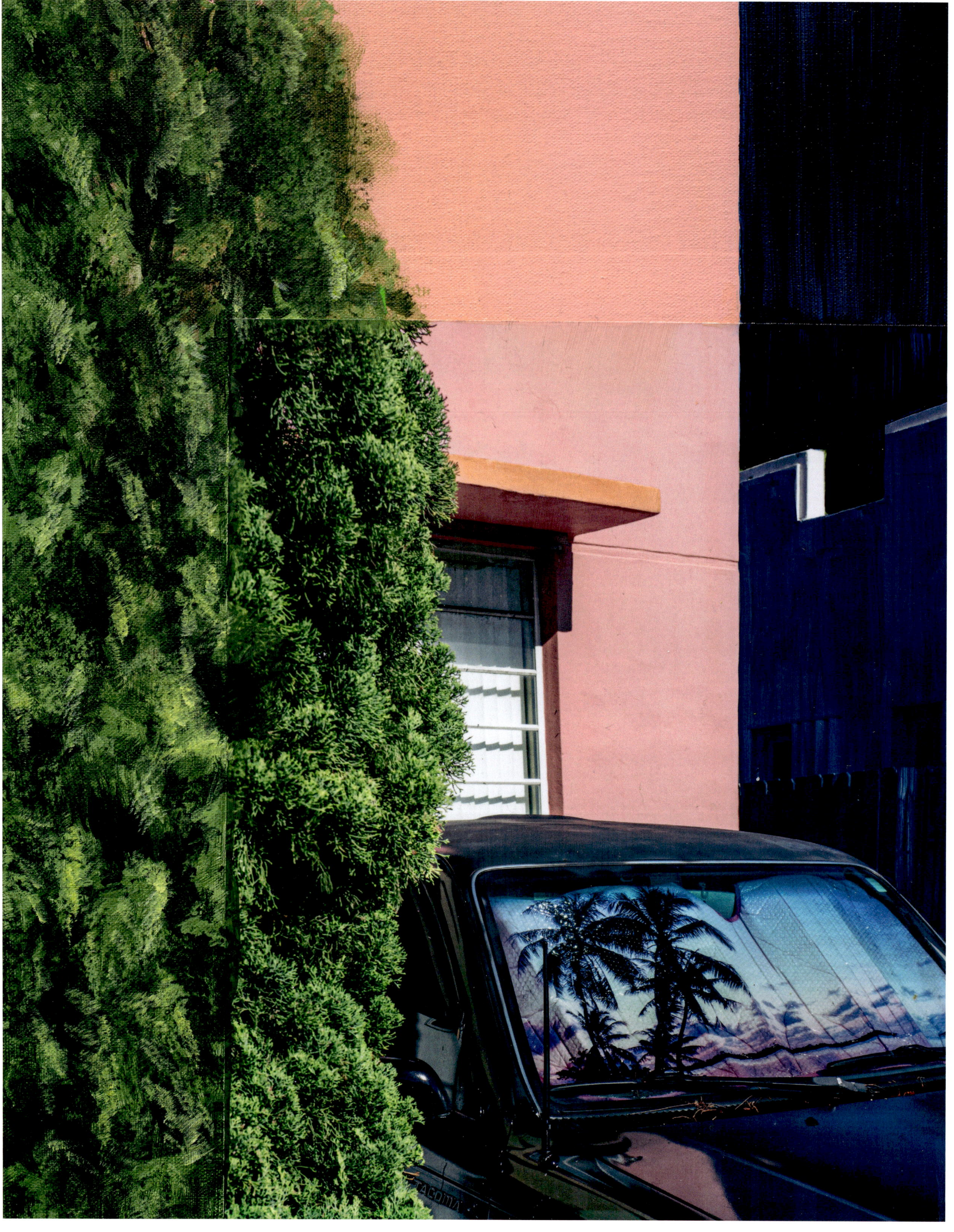

Tacoma, 2023

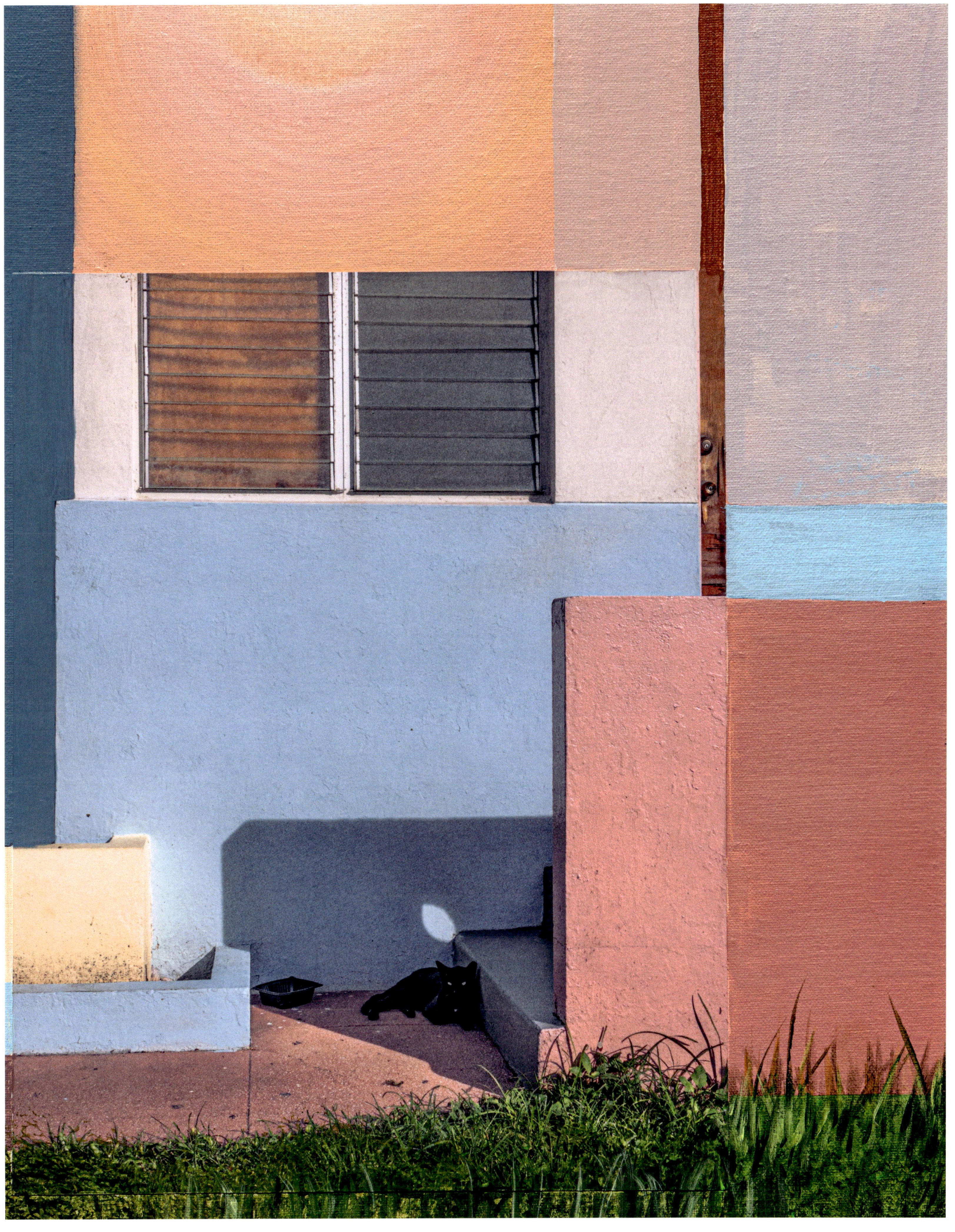

Black Cat, 2023

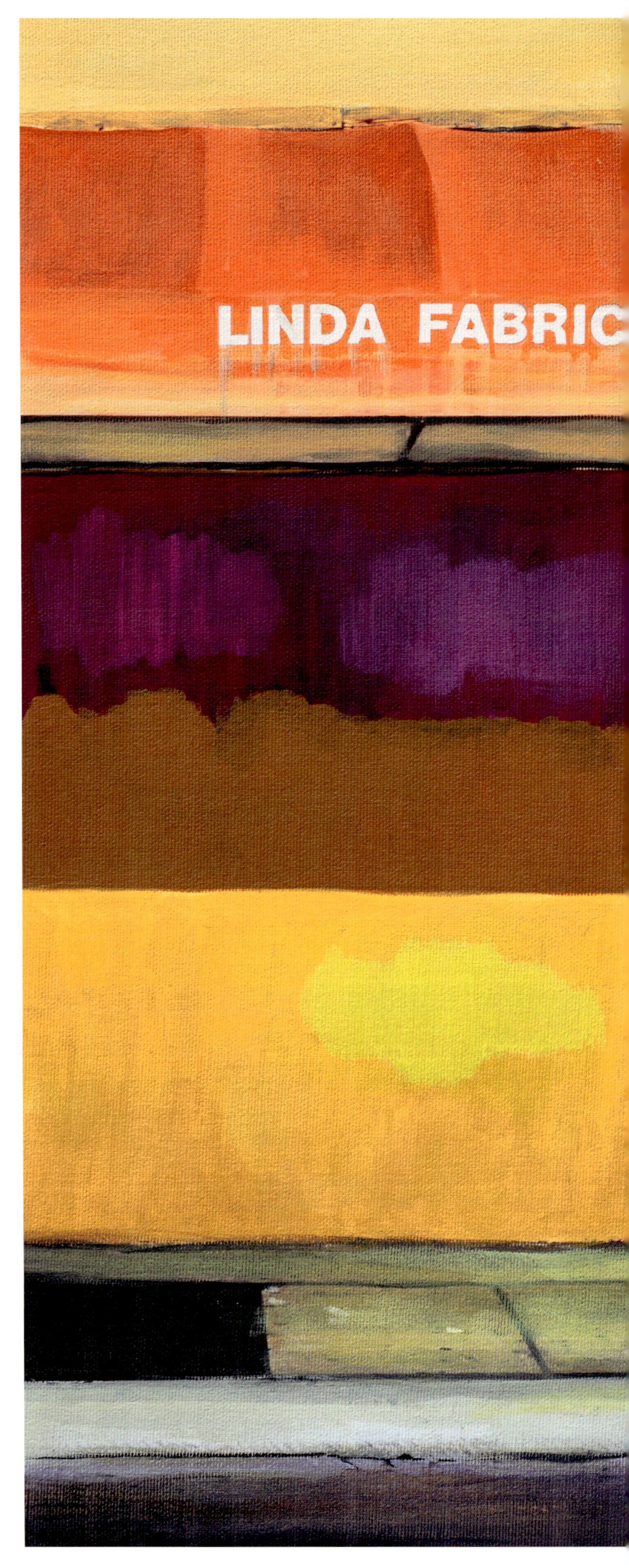

Linda Fabrics, 2024

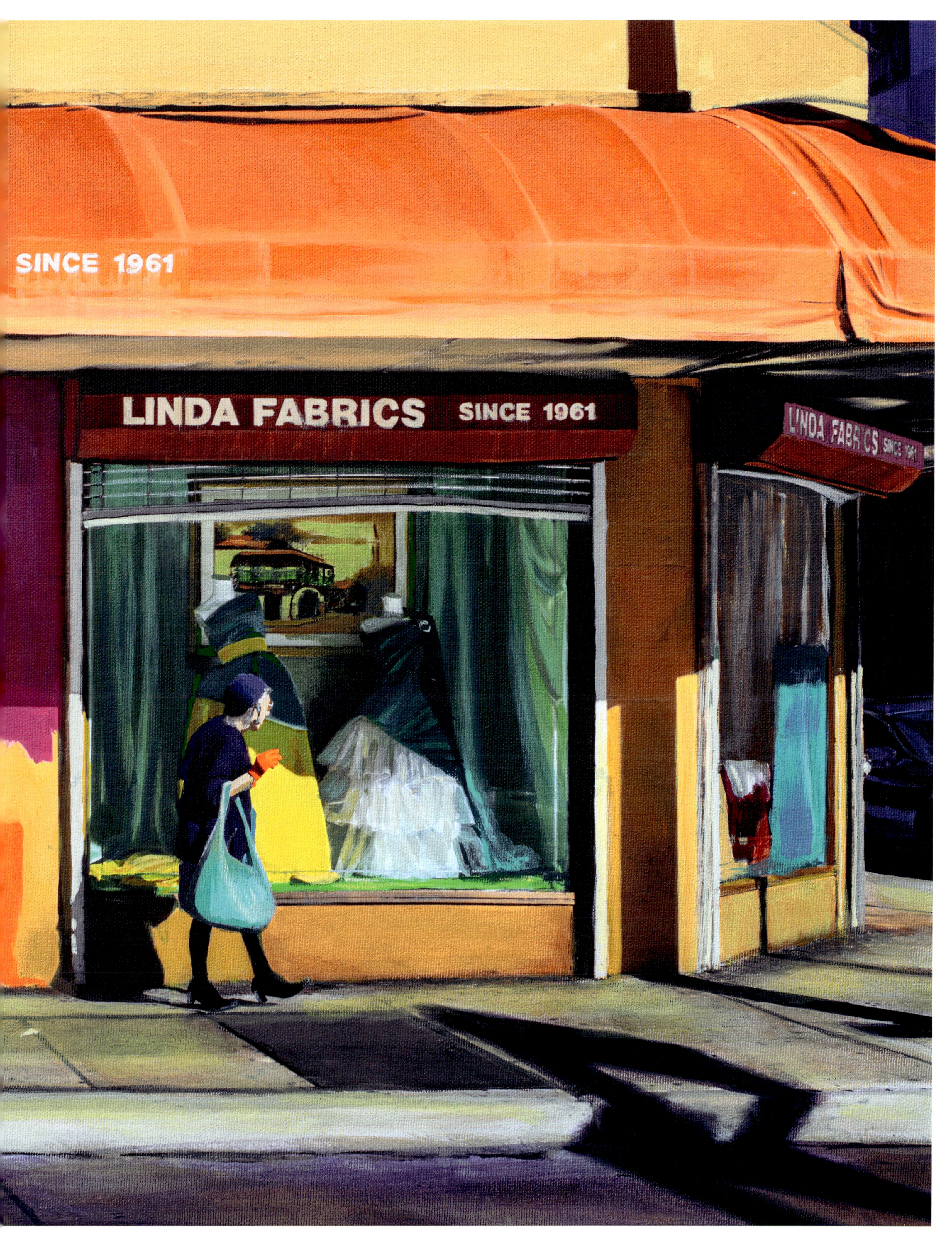
SINCE 1961
LINDA FABRICS
SINCE 1961
LINDA FABRICS

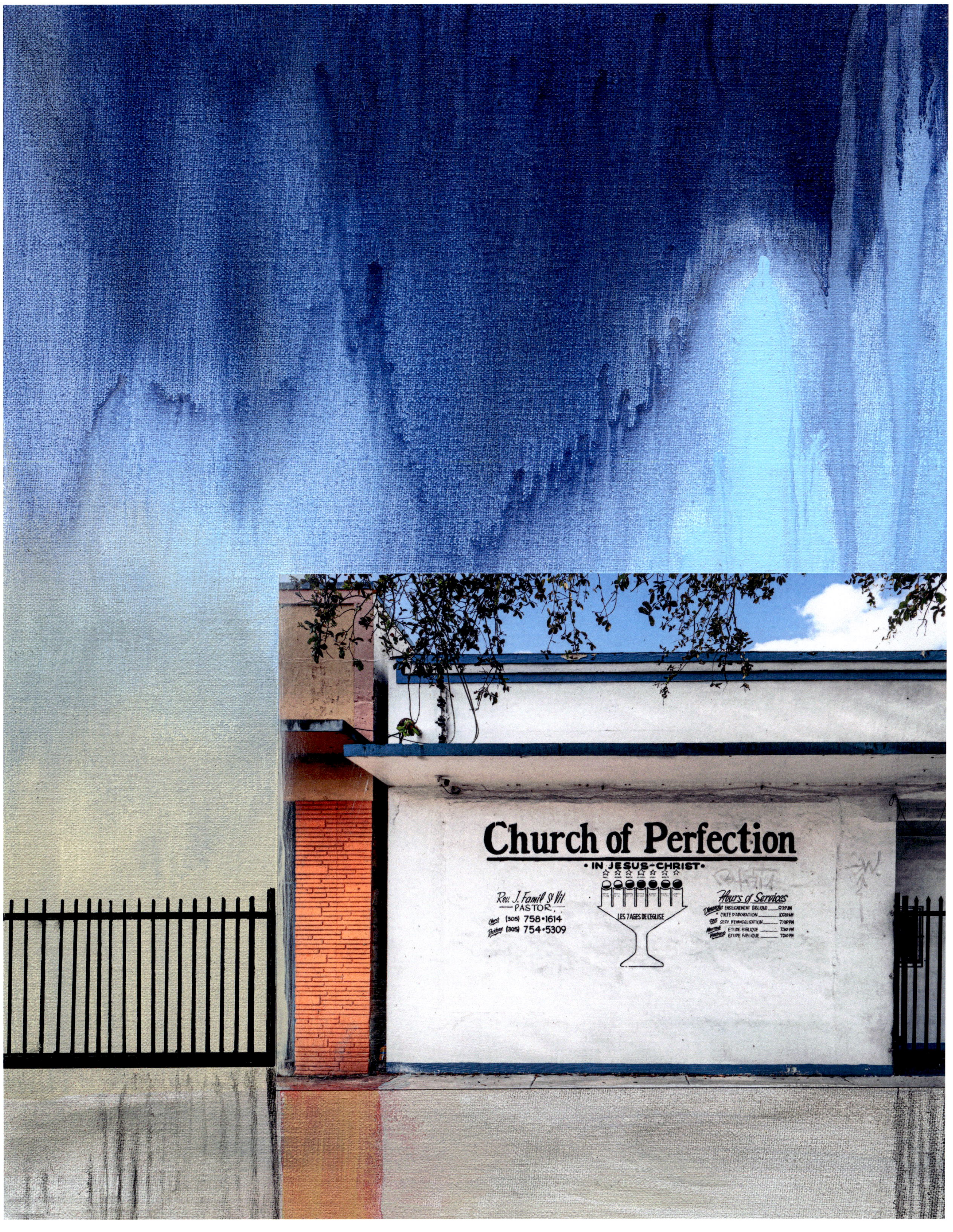

Church of Perfection, 2023

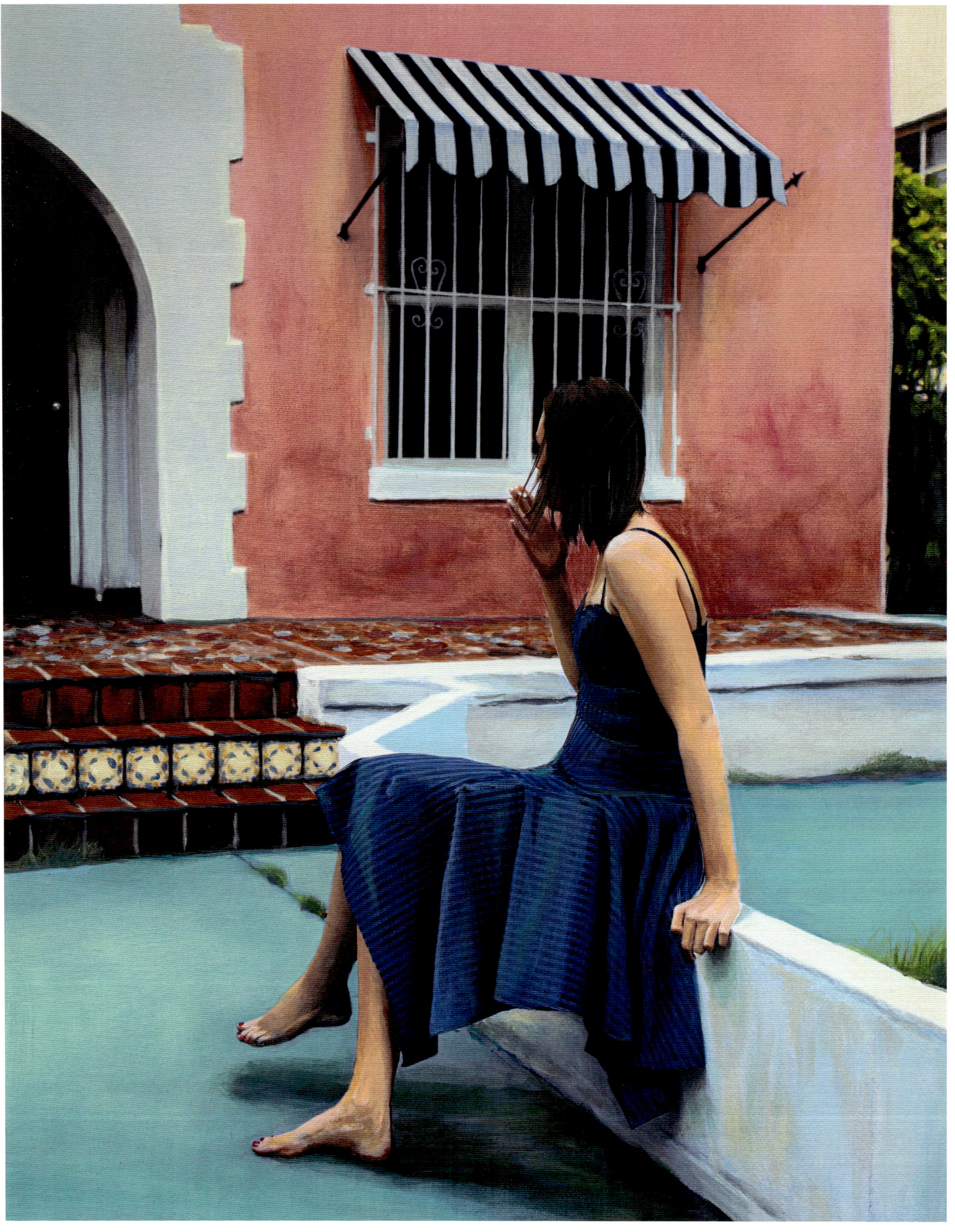

Woman in Blue Dress, 2024

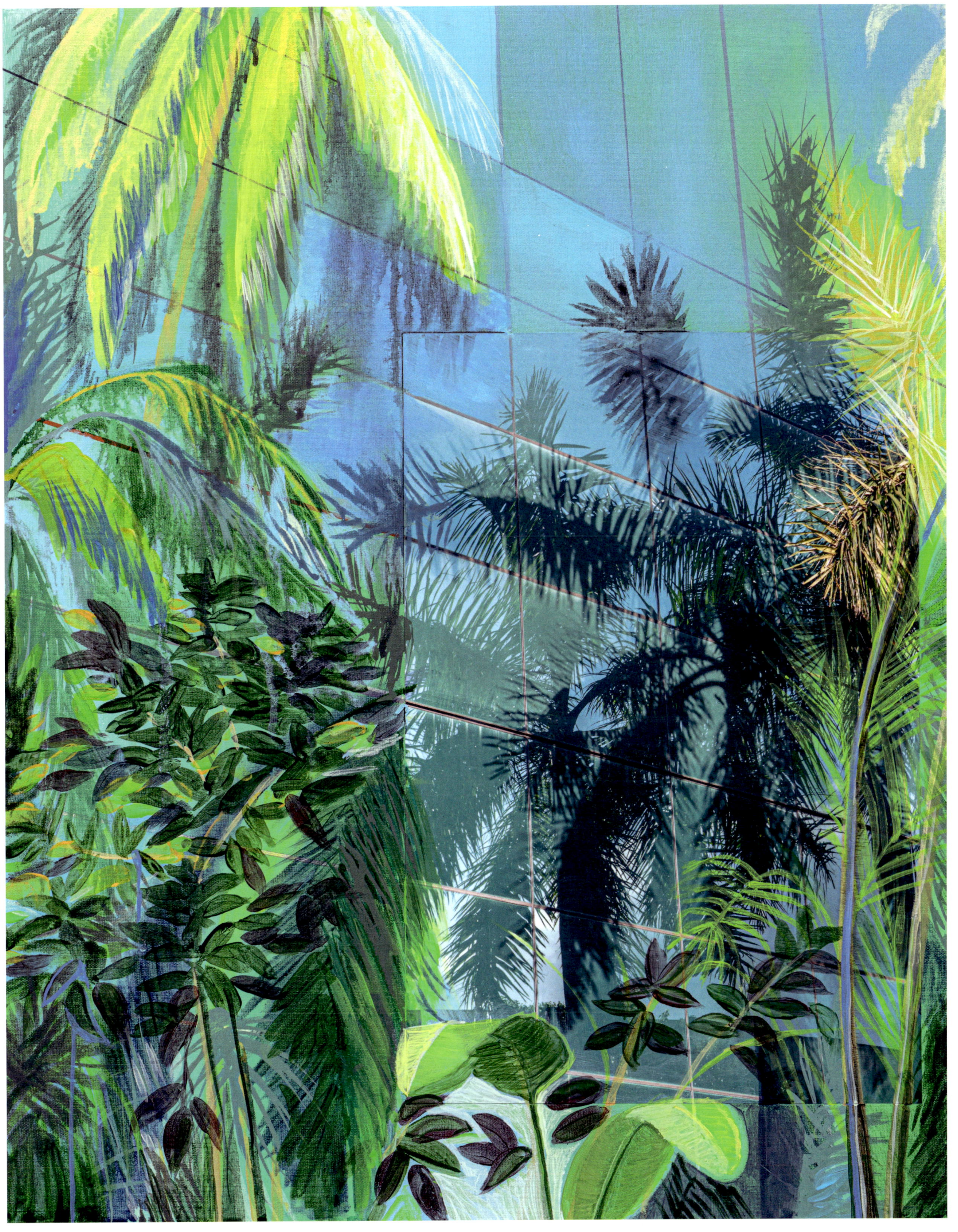

Skyscraper Garden, 2023

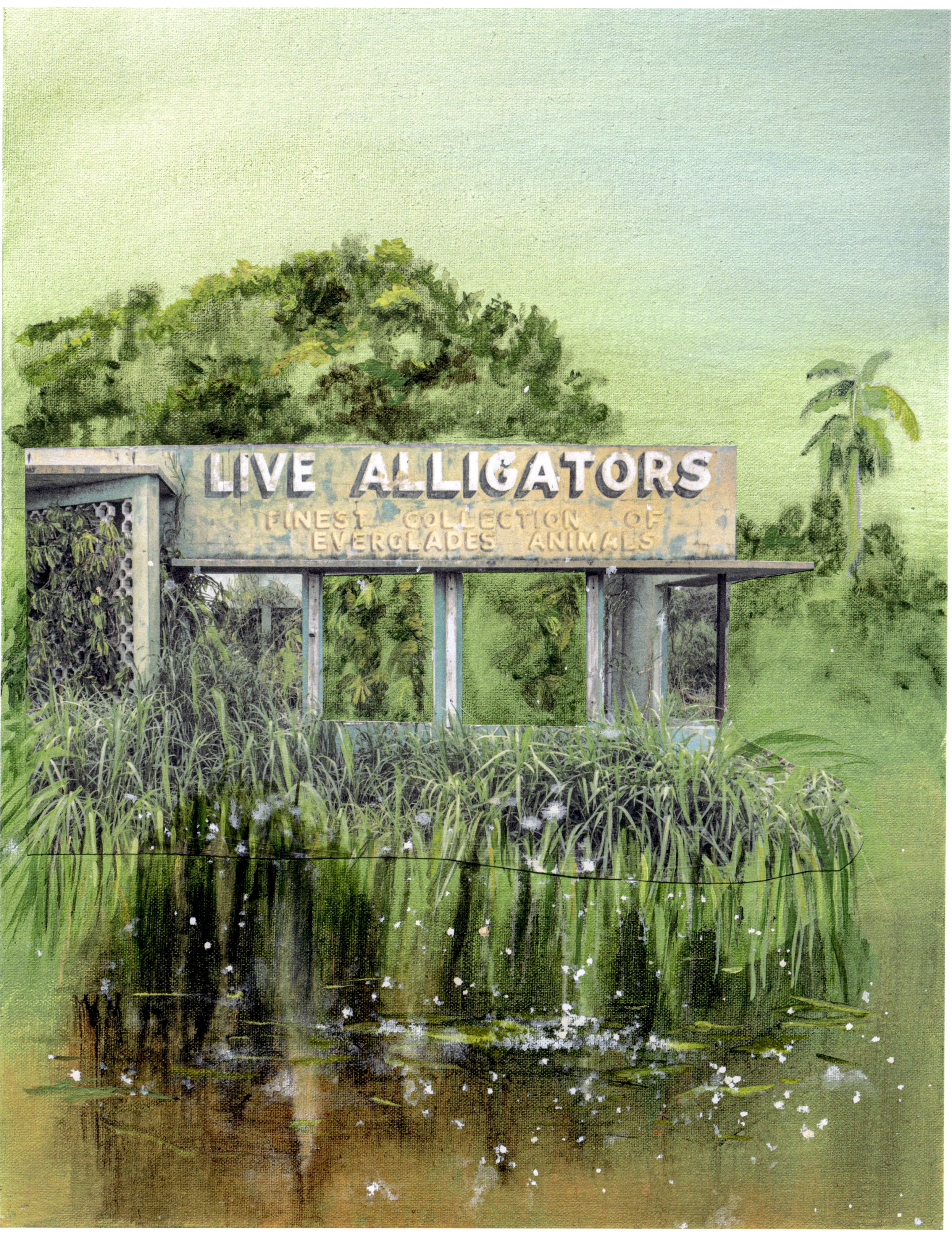

Live Alligators, 2023

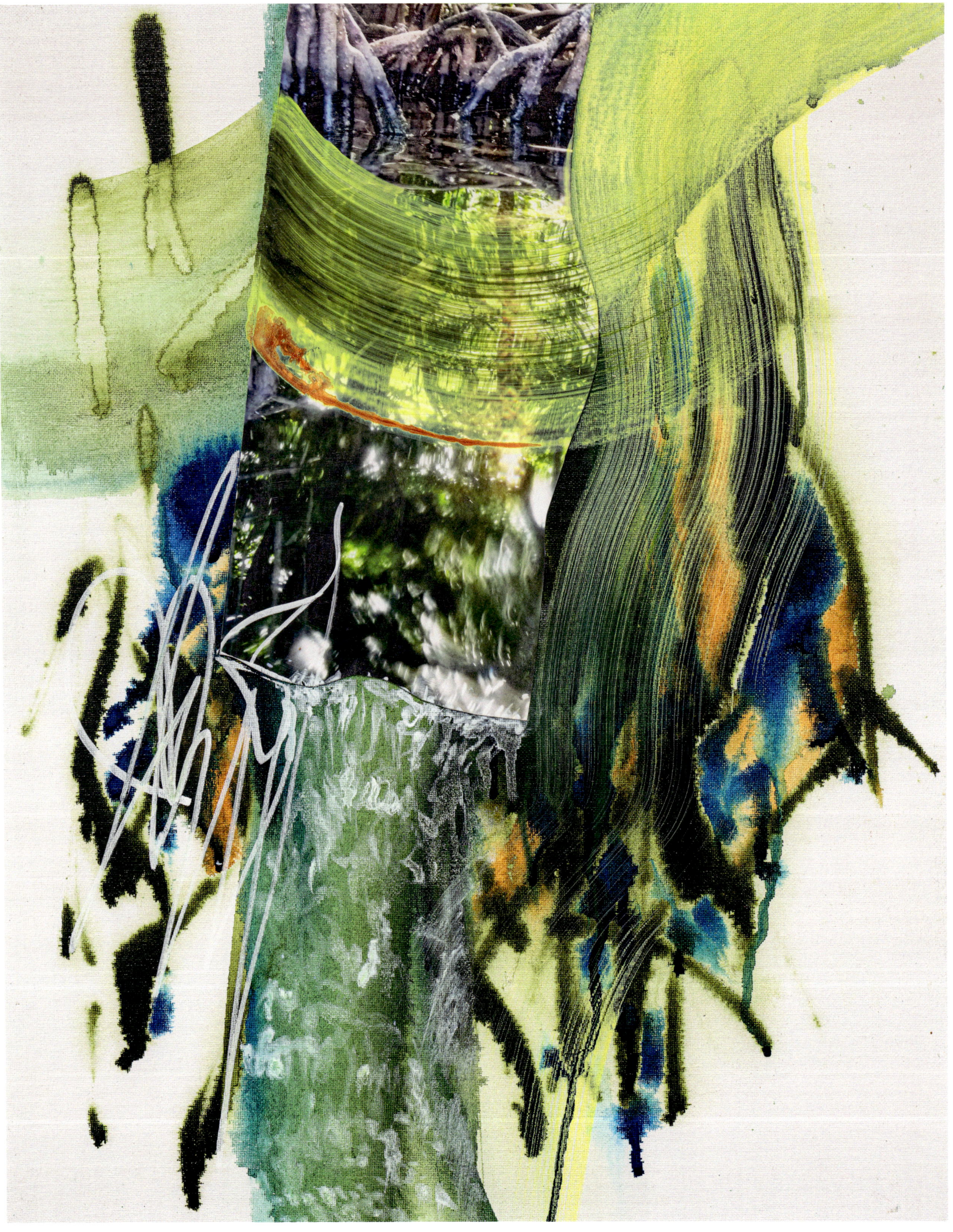

 Mangroves, 2016

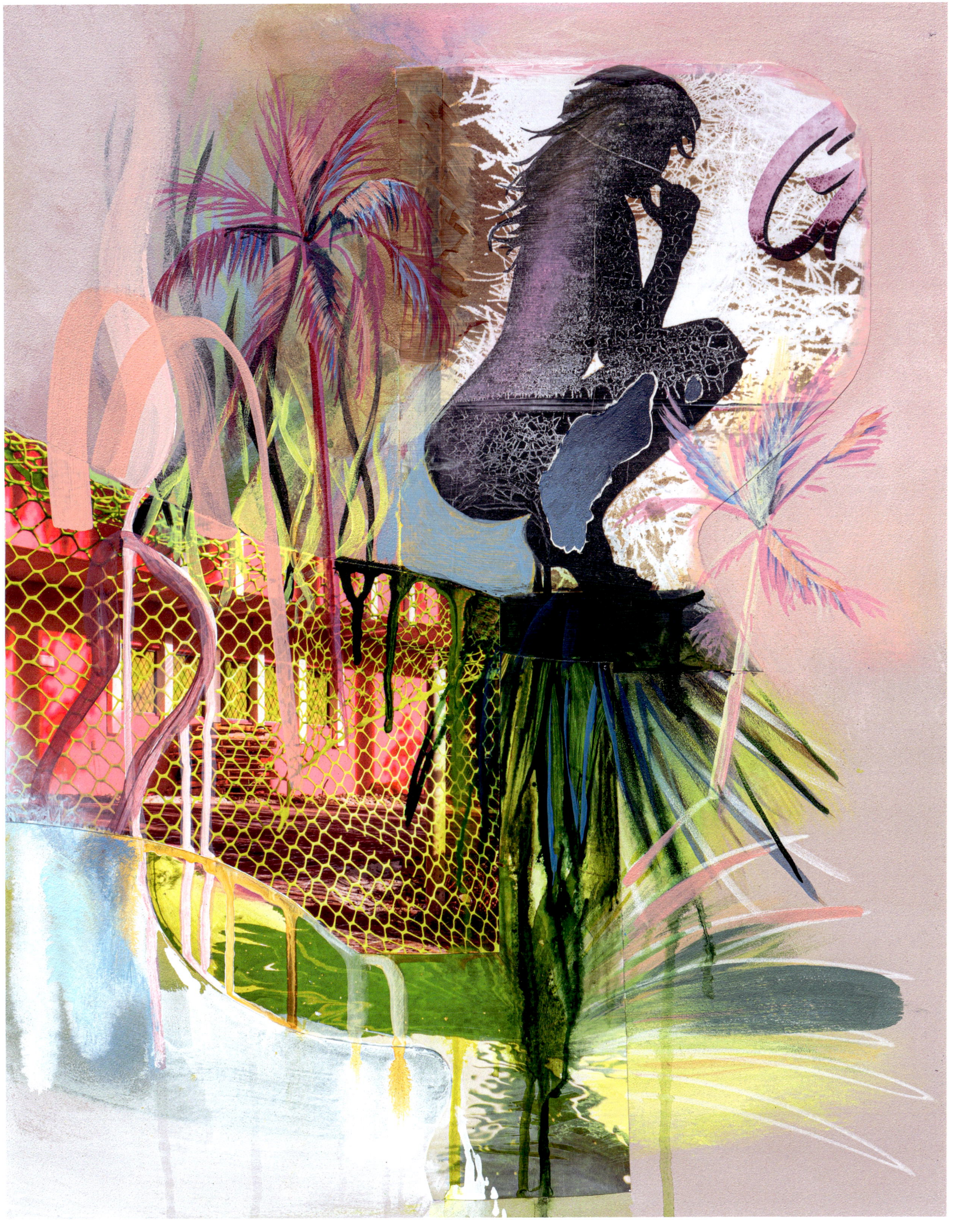

Strip Bar, 2023

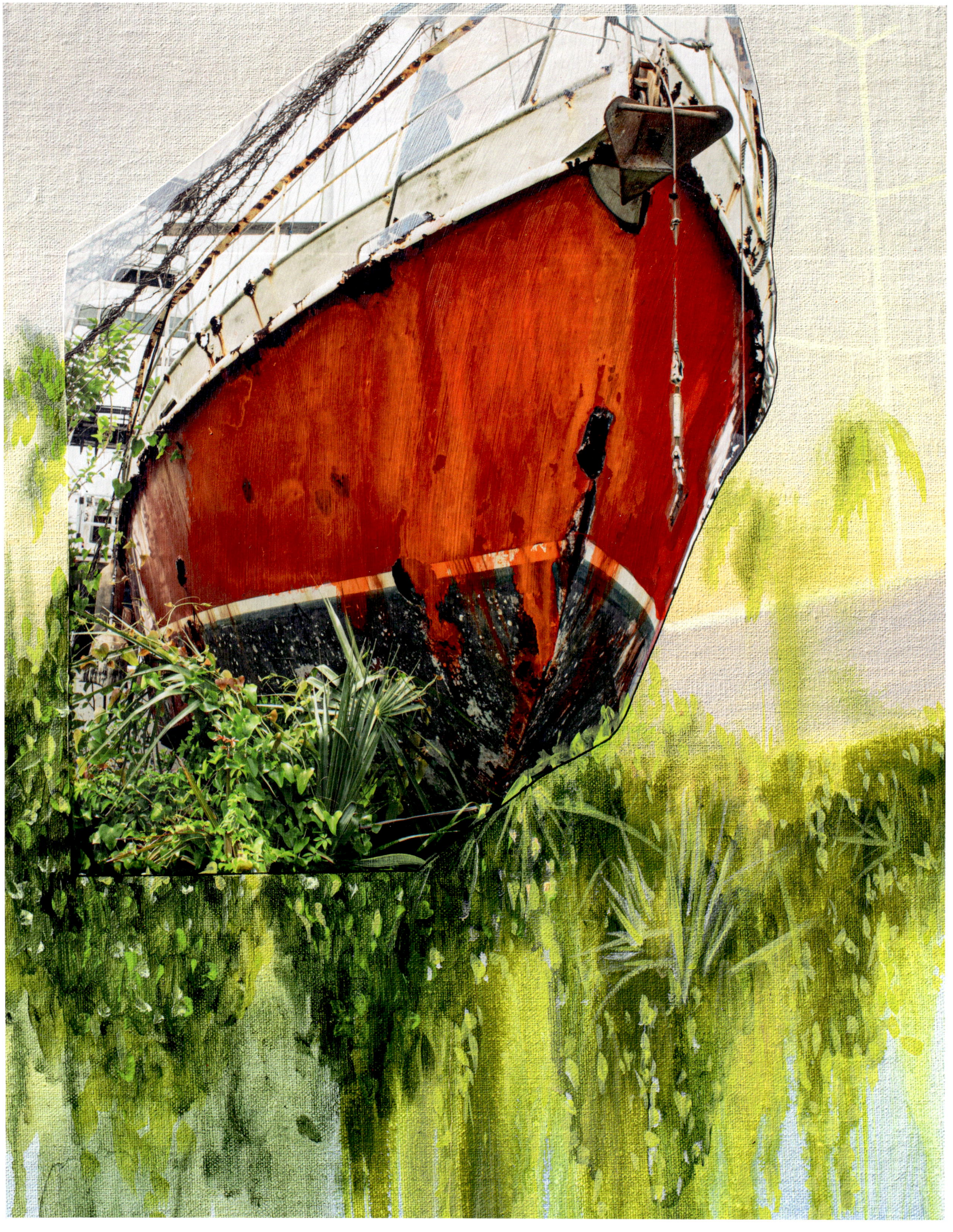

Red Boat, St Augustine, 2024

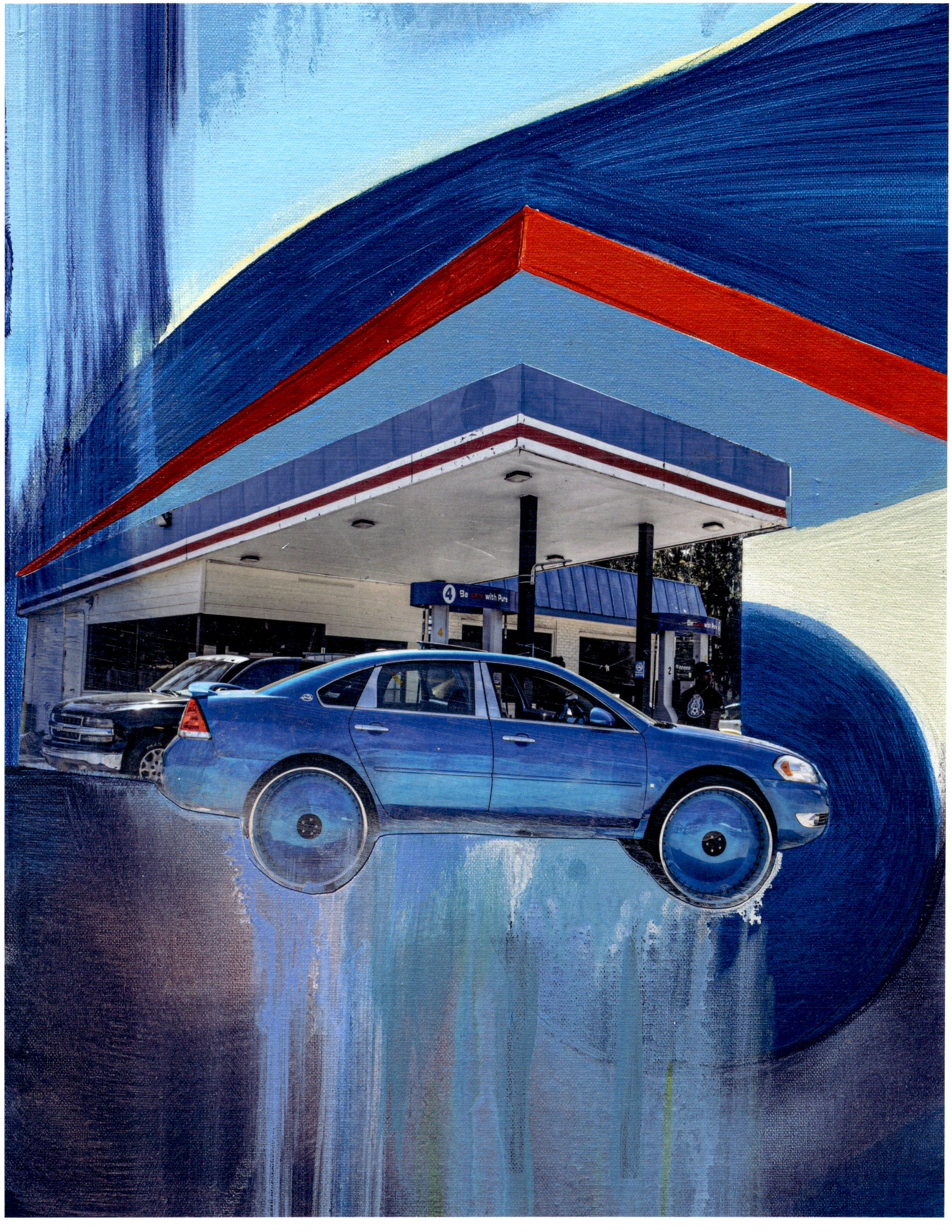

Blue Car, 2023

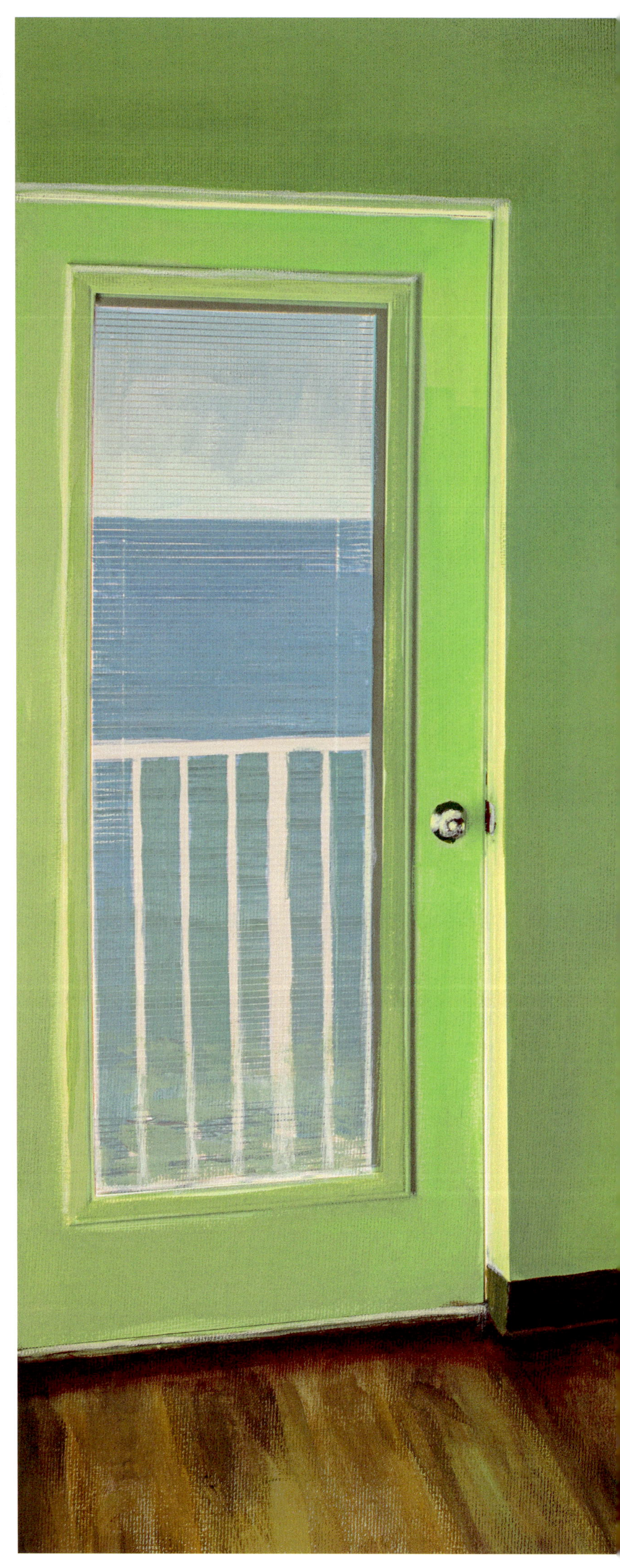

Motel Room, 2024

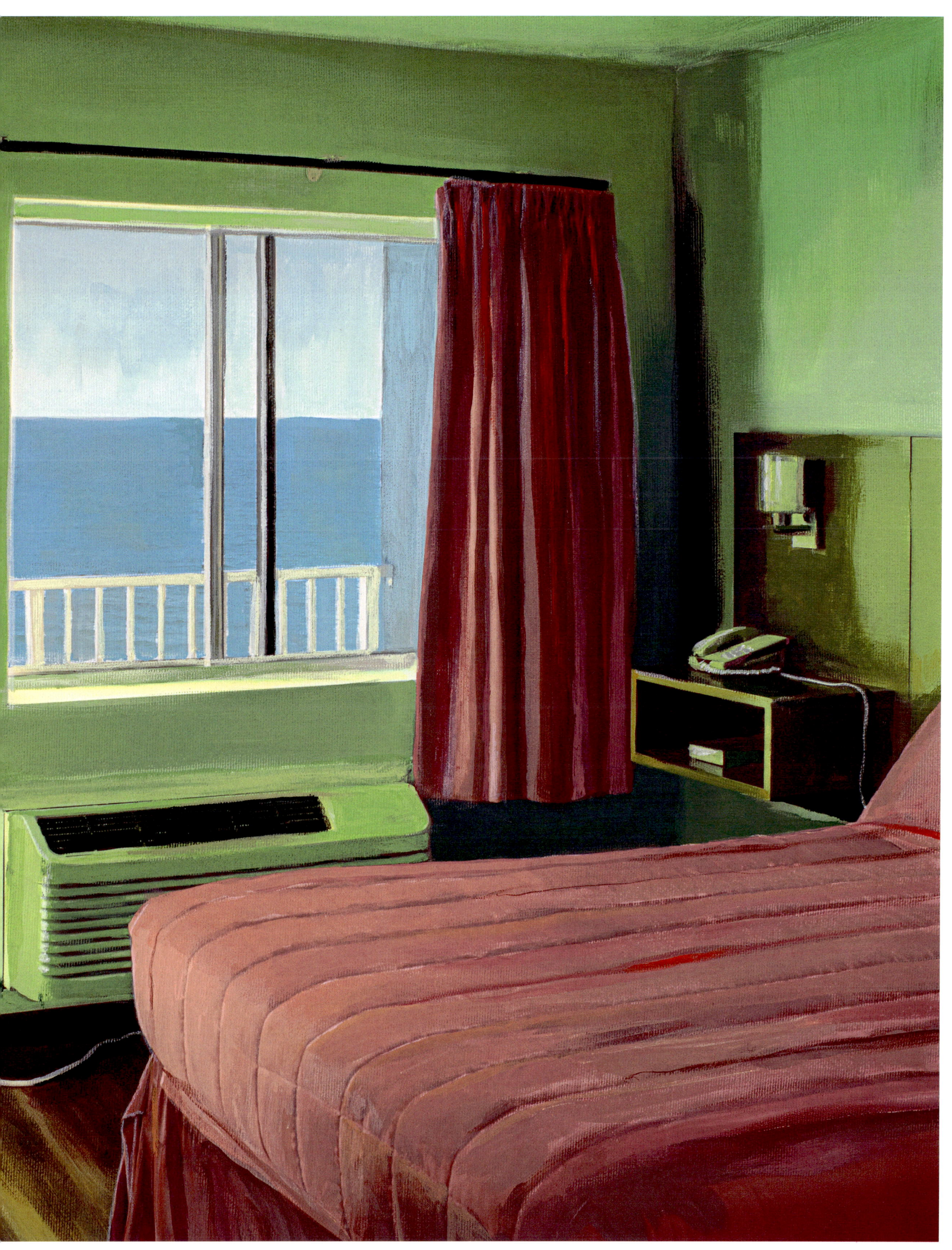

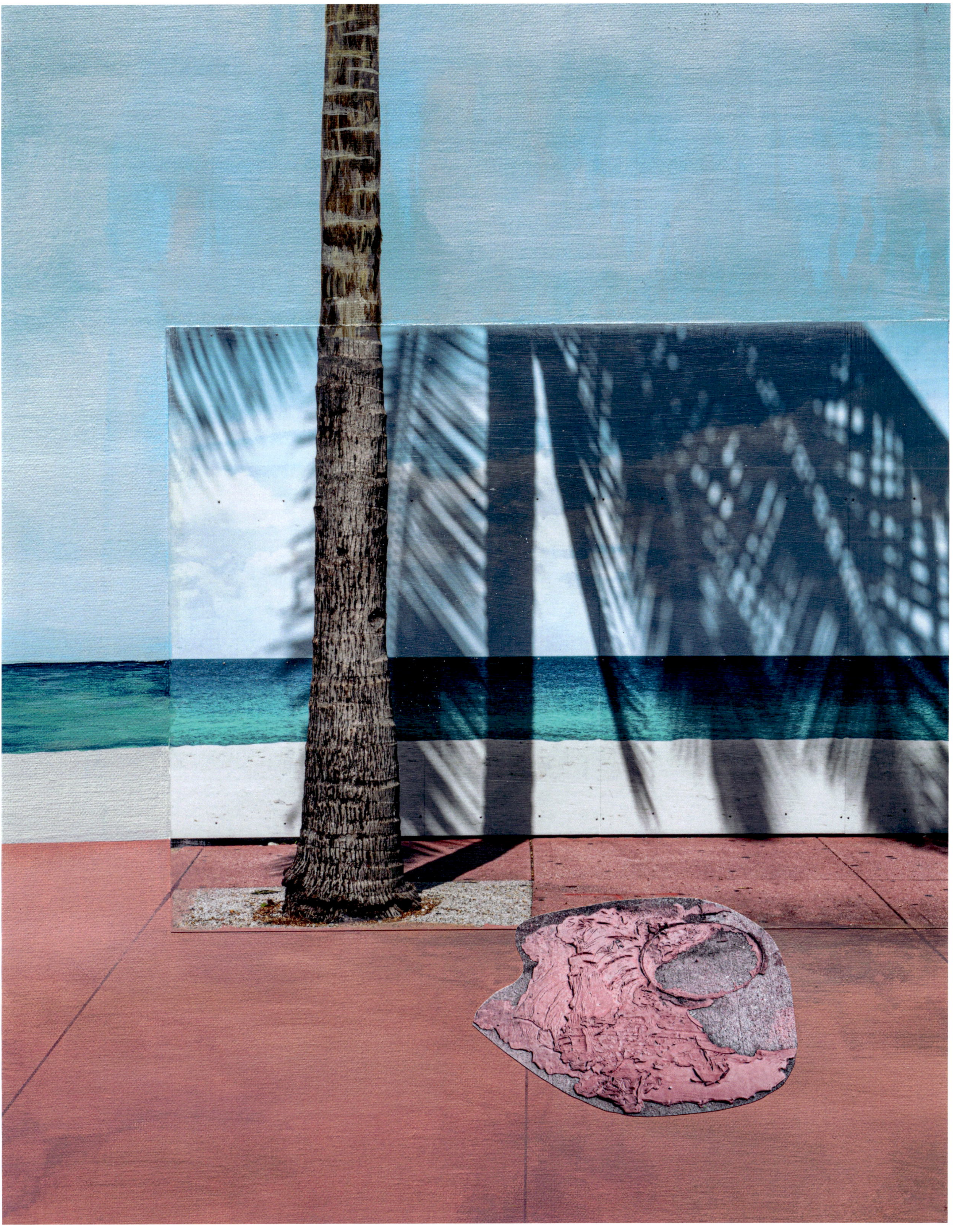

Palm Shadow, 2023

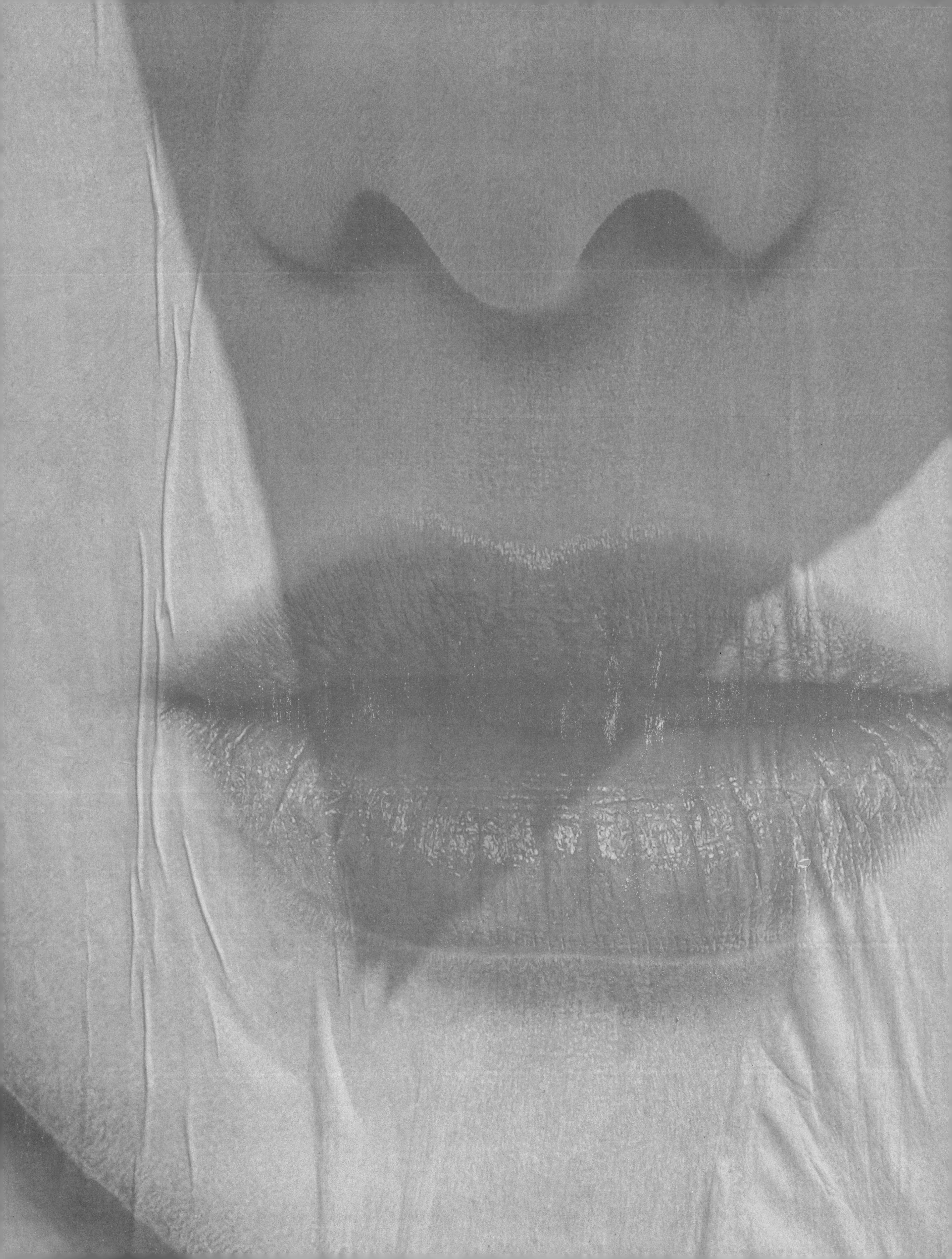

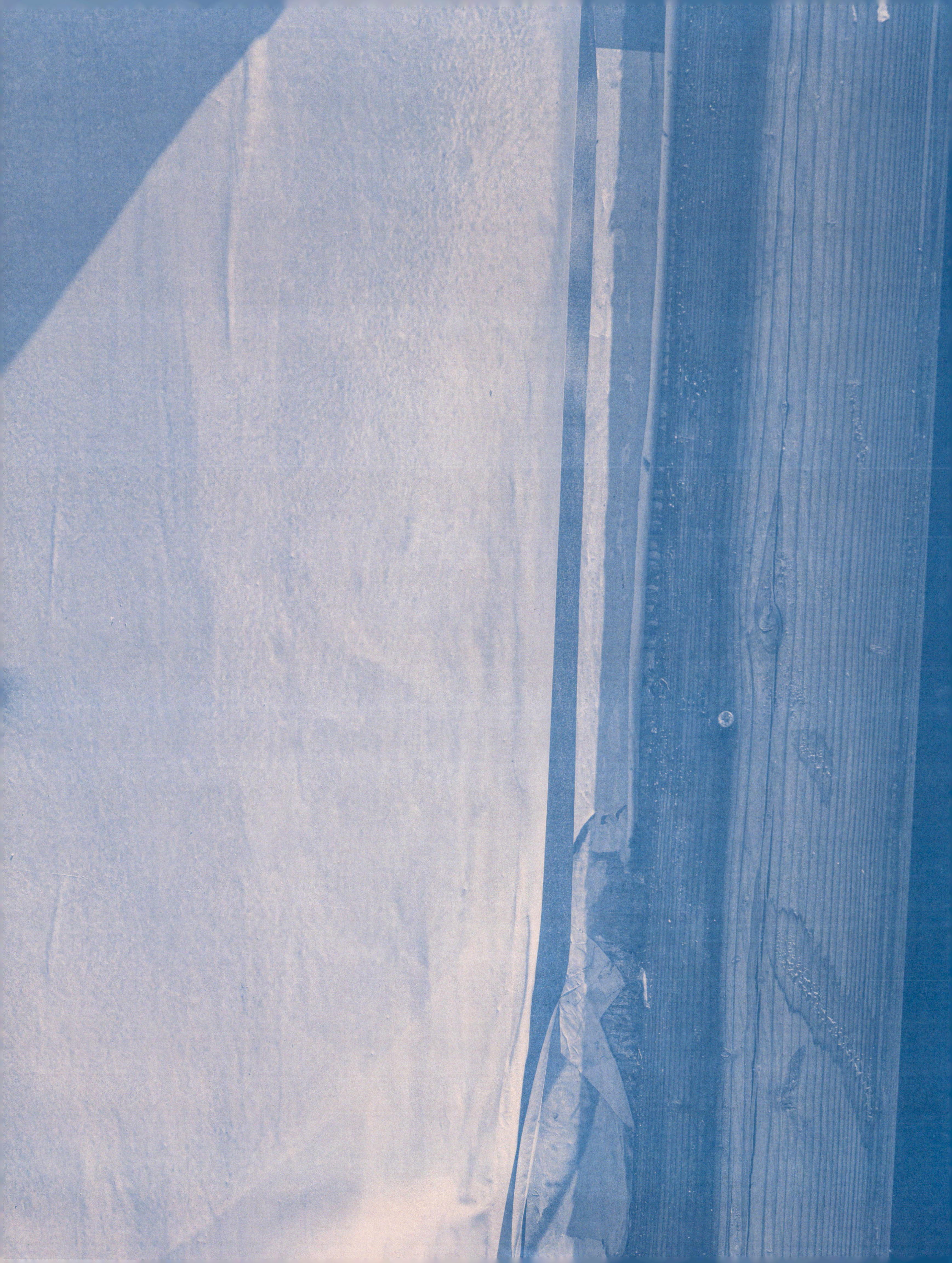

IMAGE CITIES

Shot in just fifteen months (2021–22) and across seventeen locations, *Image Cities* is Samoylova's most wide-reaching project. Moscow, New York City, Zurich, Paris, Mexico City, Frankfurt, Barcelona, London, Vienna, Toronto, Brussels, Madrid, Milan, Amsterdam, Tokyo, Los Angeles and Monaco. The aim was to look at the effects of neoliberal globalization on cities and their image culture. Samoylova had noticed the growing use of large-scale public imagery. Corporate advertising often covers entire facades, and ever-larger electronic displays are integrated into generic architecture. What is local to each city is overrun by a transnational aesthetic and a value system that mirrors the near-borderless flows of money, entertainment and consumer goods.

The choice of cities was informed by a biannual survey published by the Globalization and World Cities Research Network (GaWC). It ranks according to the degree of 'global interconnectedness'. New York and London currently hold the 'Alpha++' rating, followed by Paris, Tokyo, Shanghai, Beijing, Hong Kong, Dubai and Singapore, on 'Alpha+'.

Travelling alone, Samoylova was attuned to the status and image of women in these cities, which have been designed mostly by and for men. Depictions of femininity dominate public visuals, but their meaning is complex. Sometimes they seem no more than spectacle, a shorthand for commodified desire; at other times, they are symbols of the freedoms that may come with financial and social independence.

A telephoto lens helps compress spaces and planes, colliding public image and lived reality. Do cities serve those who live and work in them? Are they becoming little more than manicured stage sets for the promotion of the new economic order? Samoylova made fifteen thousand photographs. The book of the project (2023) has one hundred, while a travelling exhibition has fifty framed prints. A two-channel, twenty-minute digital slideshow brings together around five hundred.

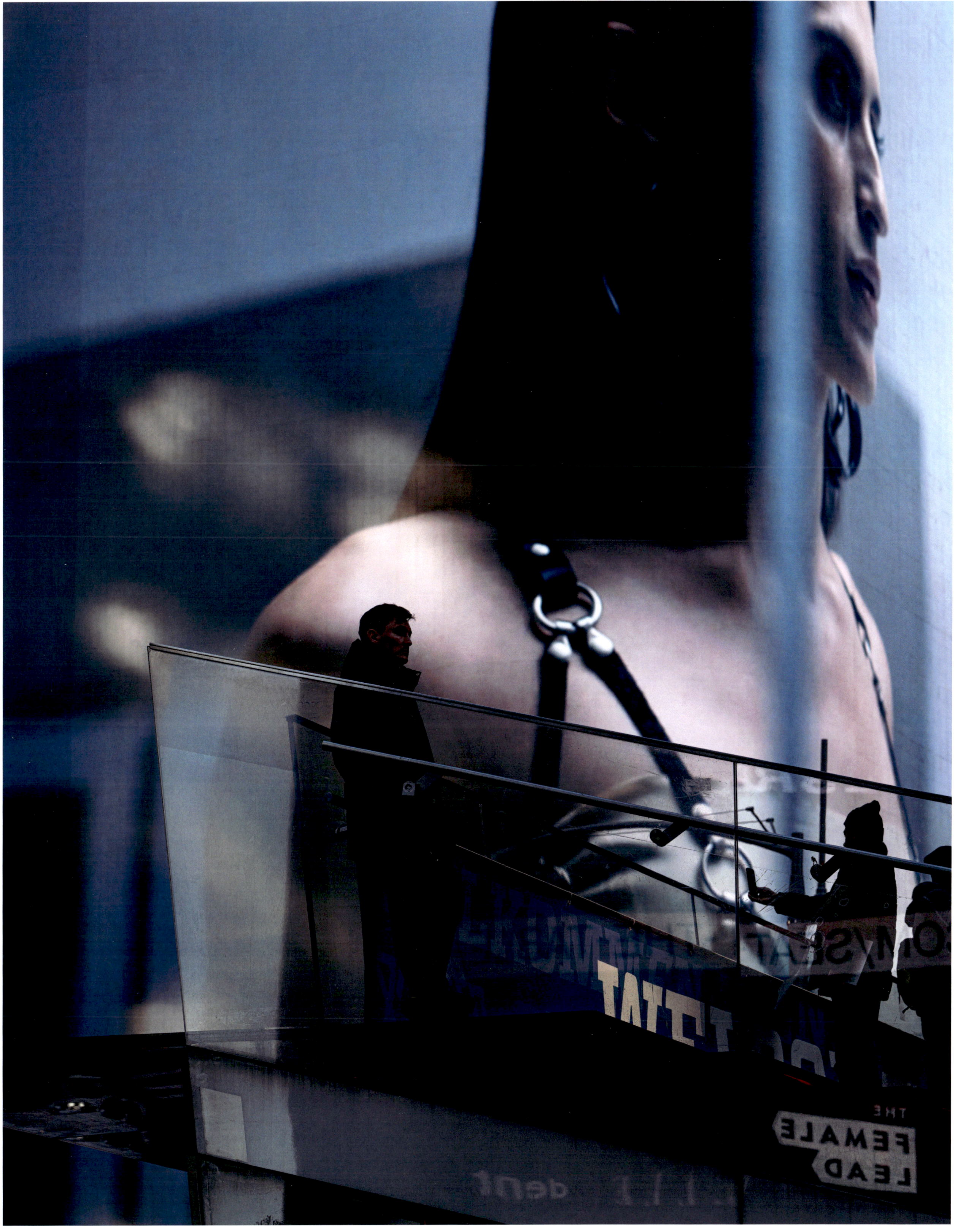

Female Lead, Times Square, 2022

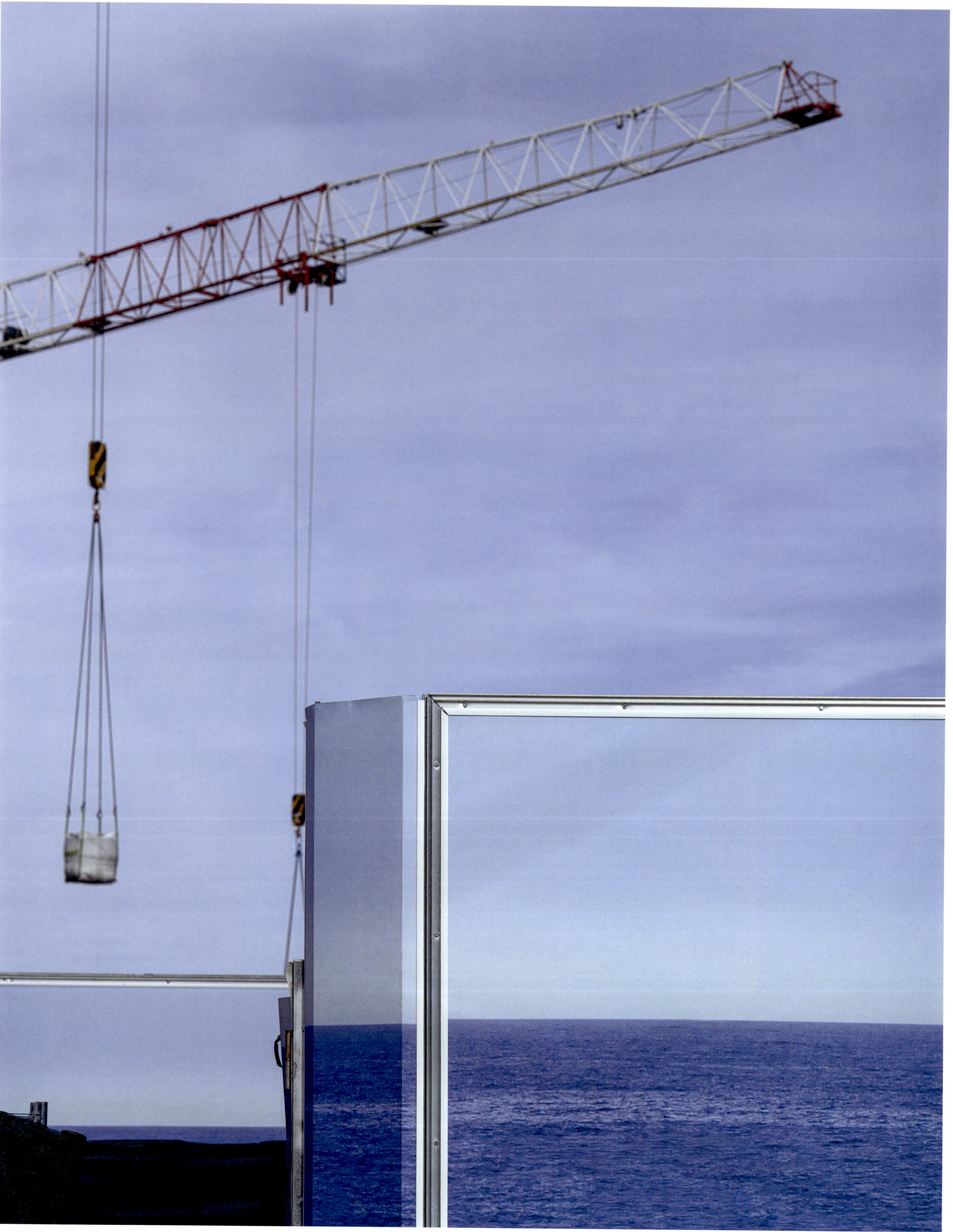

Construction Fence with Sea Image, Monaco, 2022

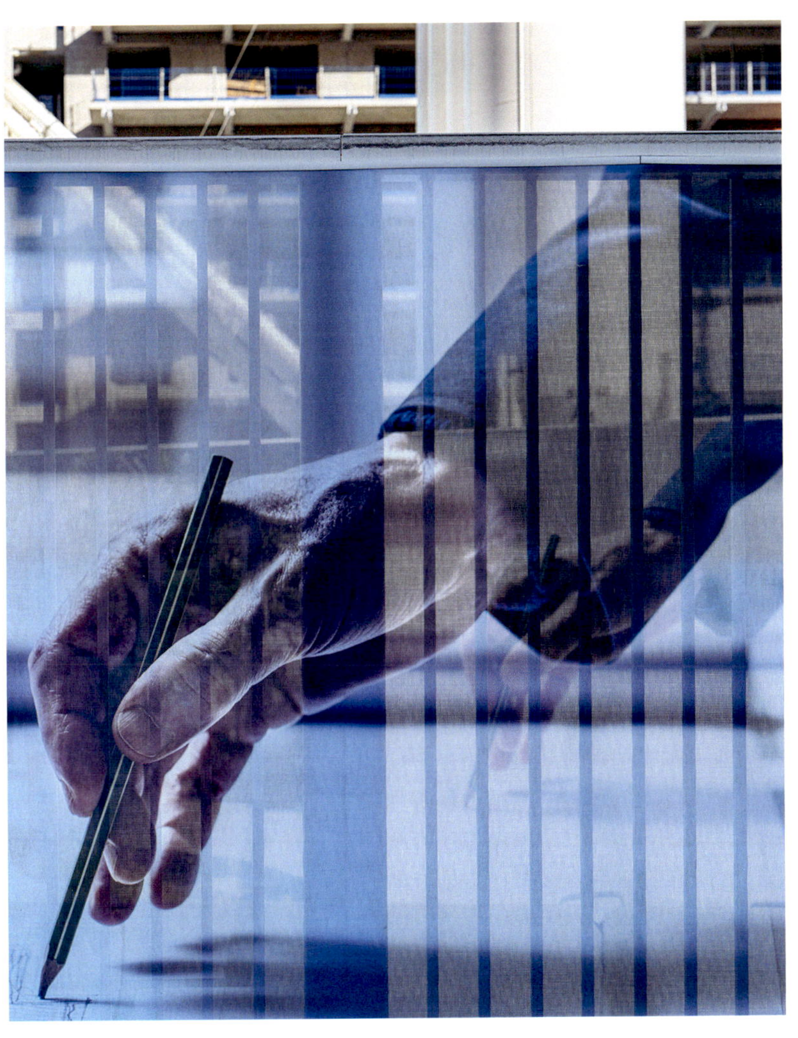

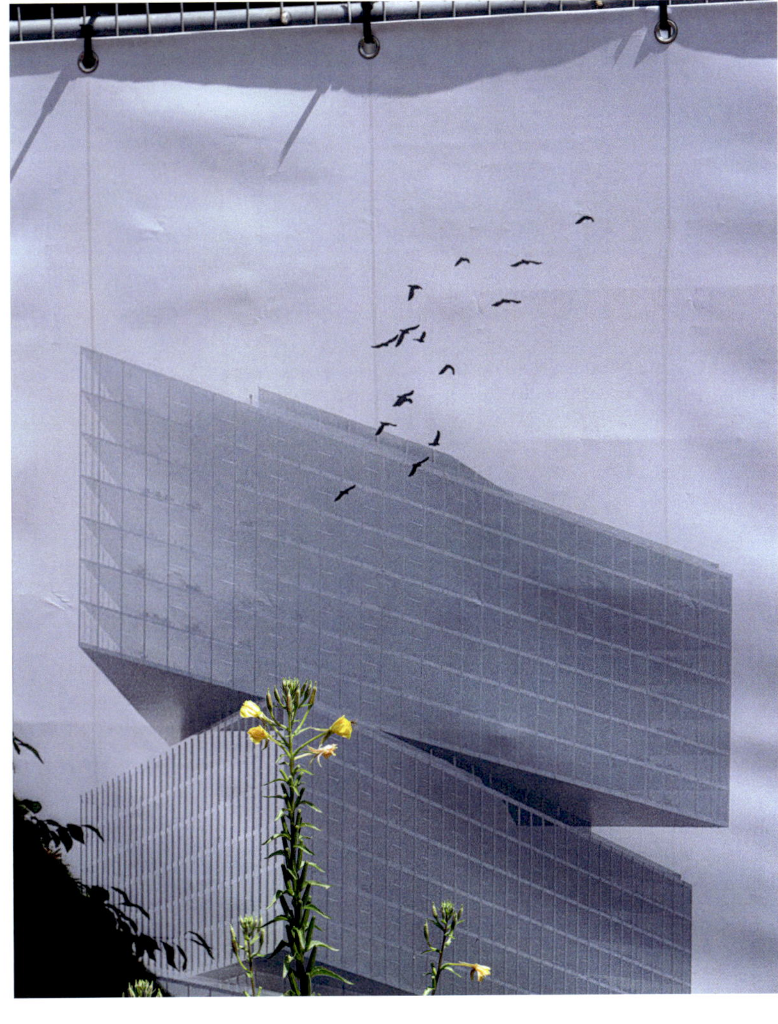

‹ Hand with Pencil, Printed Construction Fence, 2022 › Architectural Rendering with Birds, Amsterdam, 2022

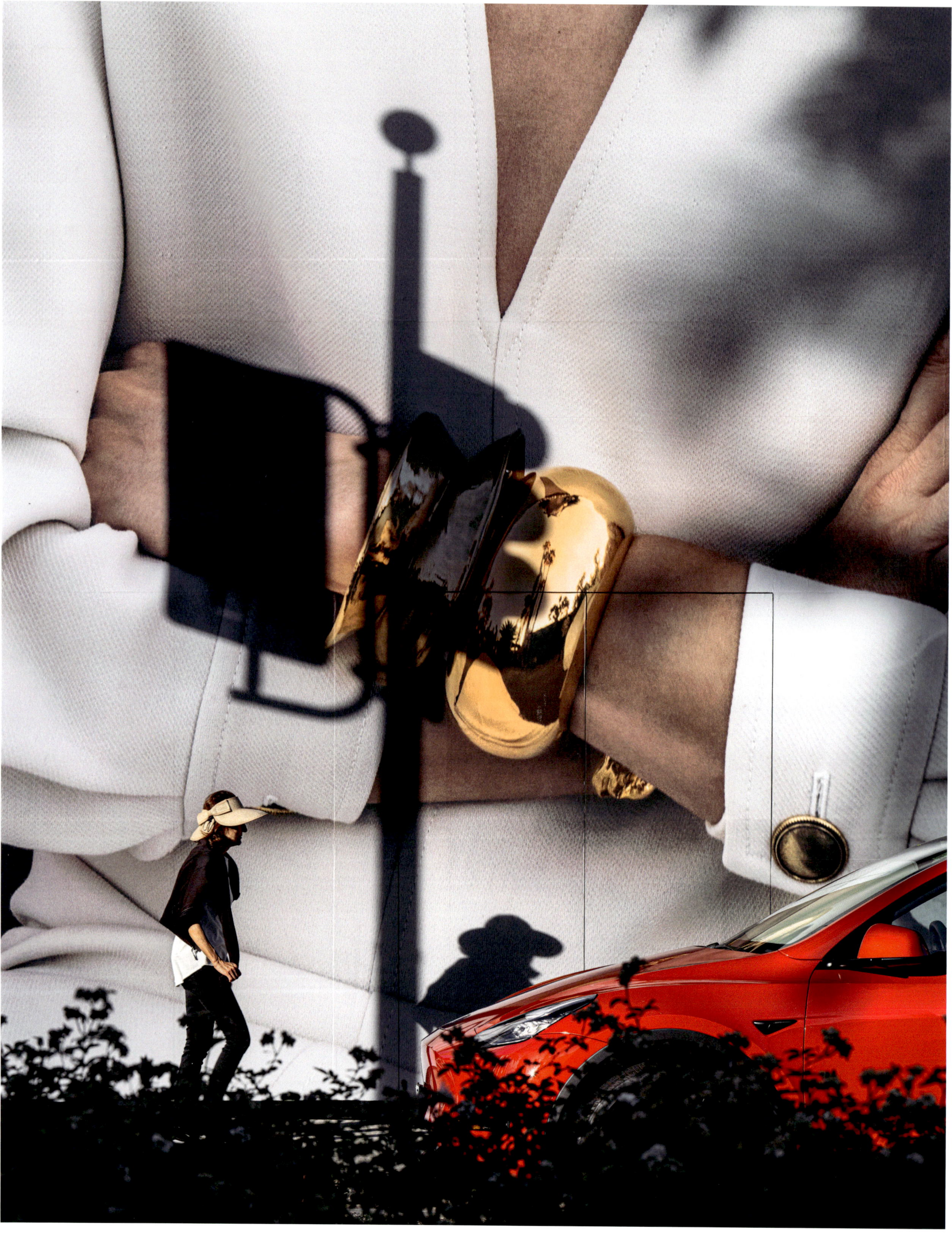

Red Car, Beverly Hills, Los Angeles, 2022

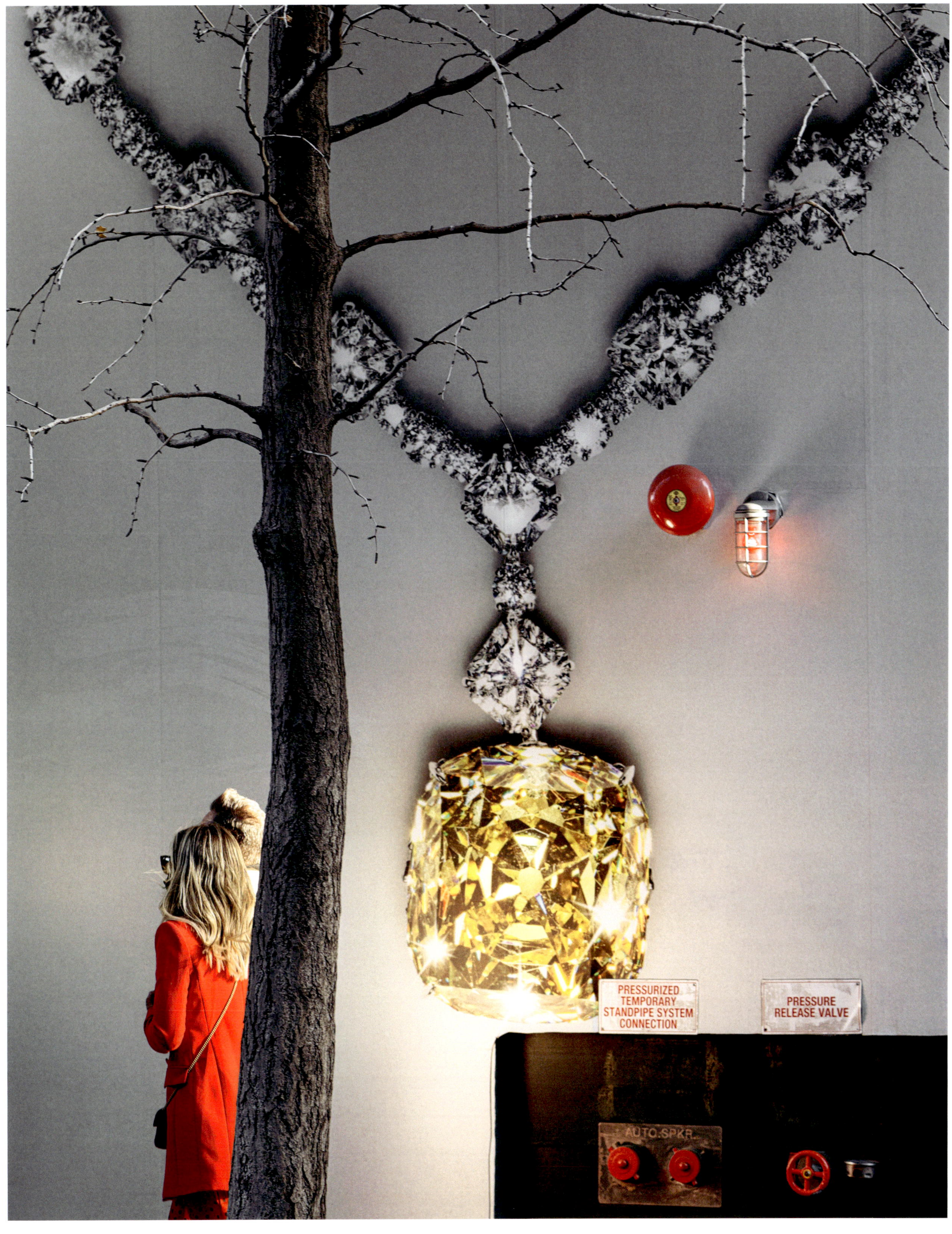

Fifth Avenue, New York, 2021

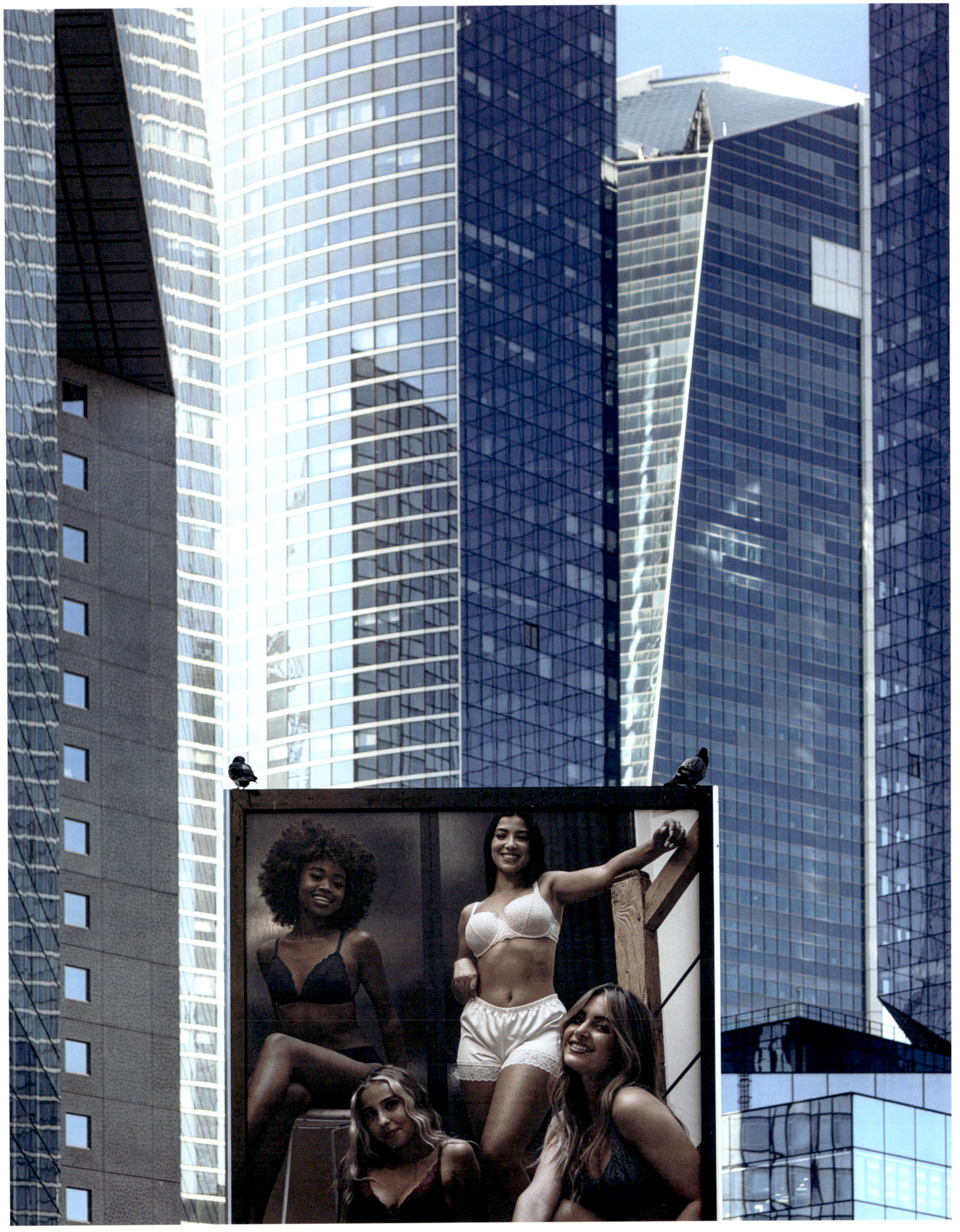

Lingerie Advertisement, Paris, 2021

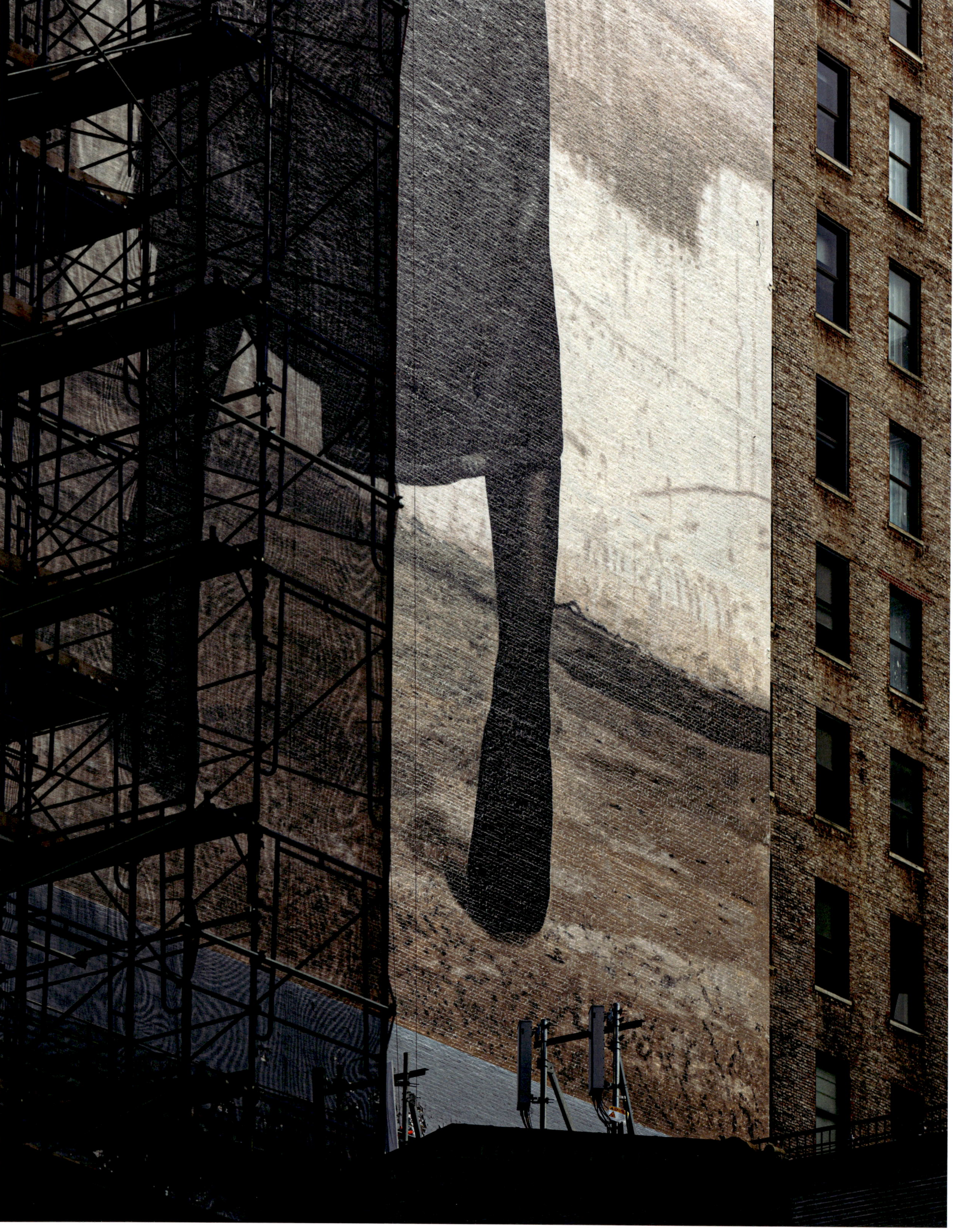

Fashion Advertisement, New York, 2021

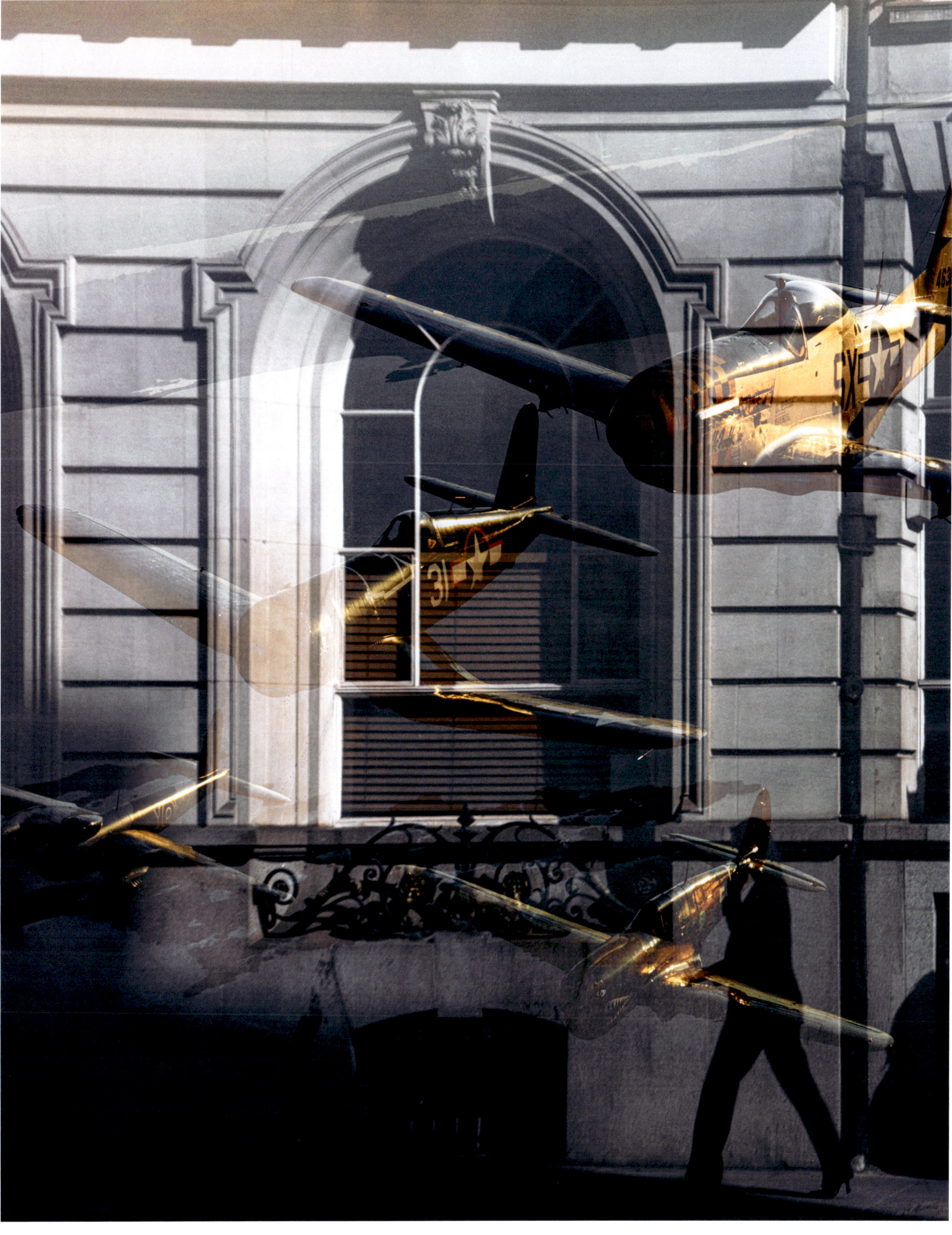

Fighter Planes Reflection, London, 2022

Industrial Building under Printed Cover, Moscow, 2021

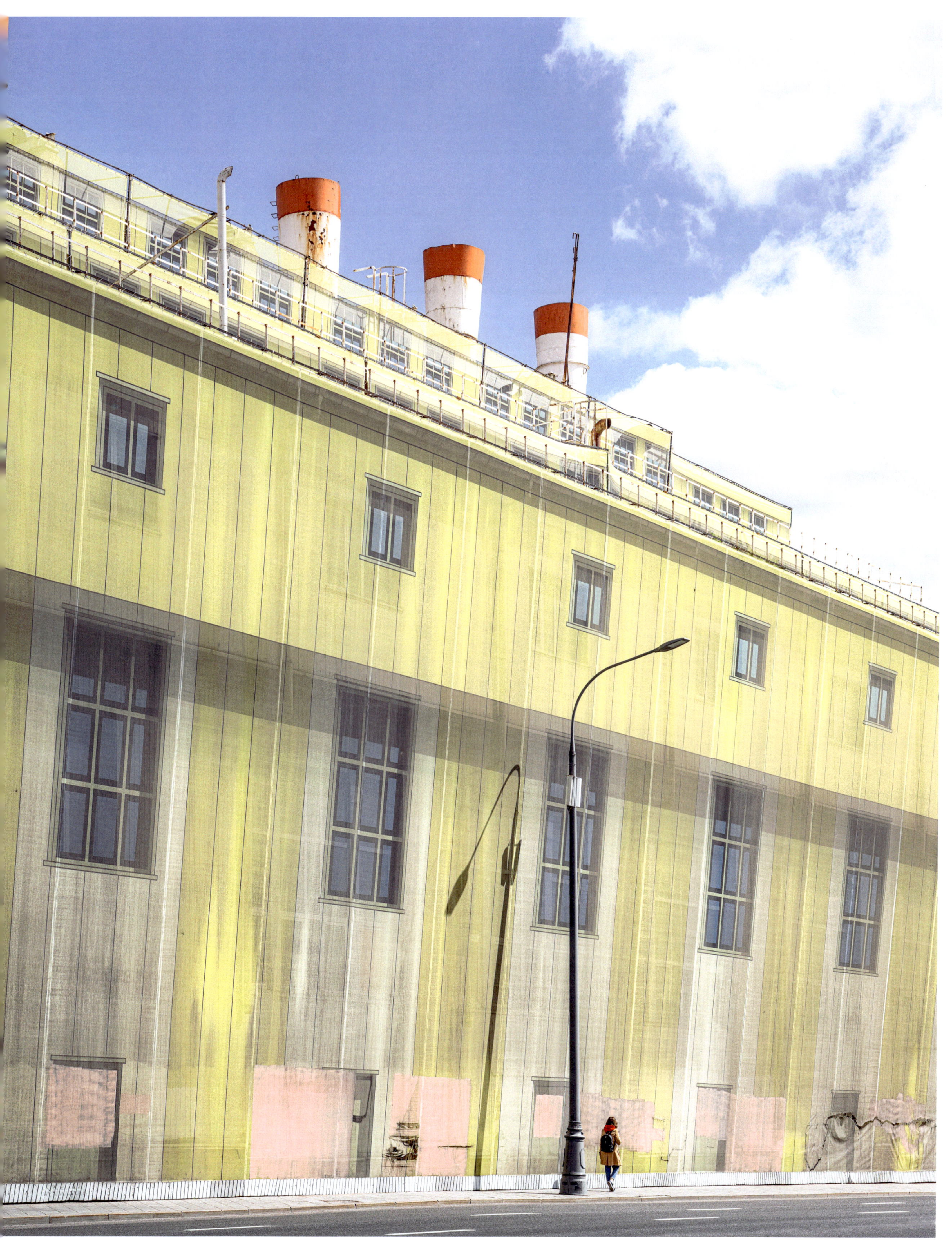

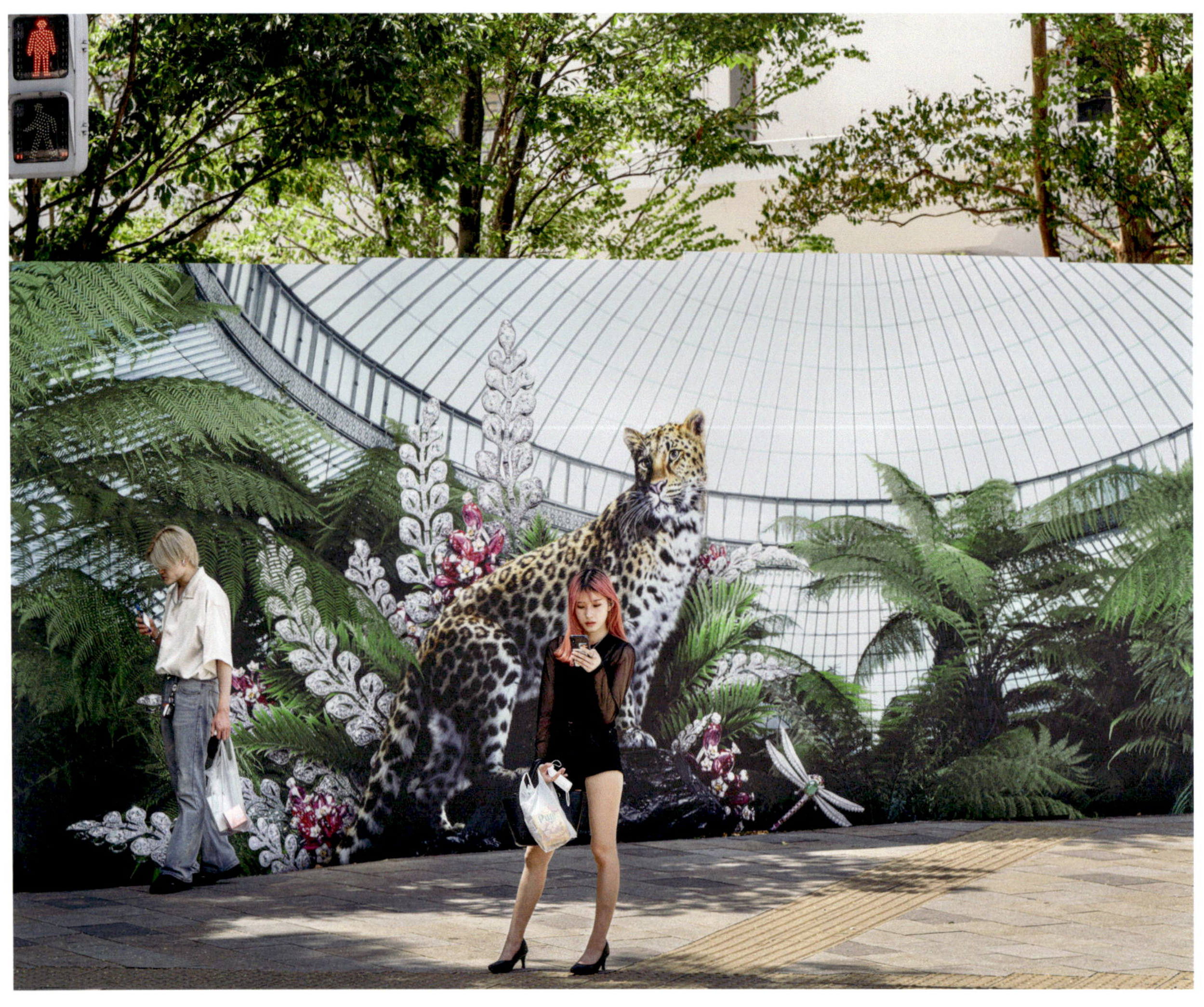

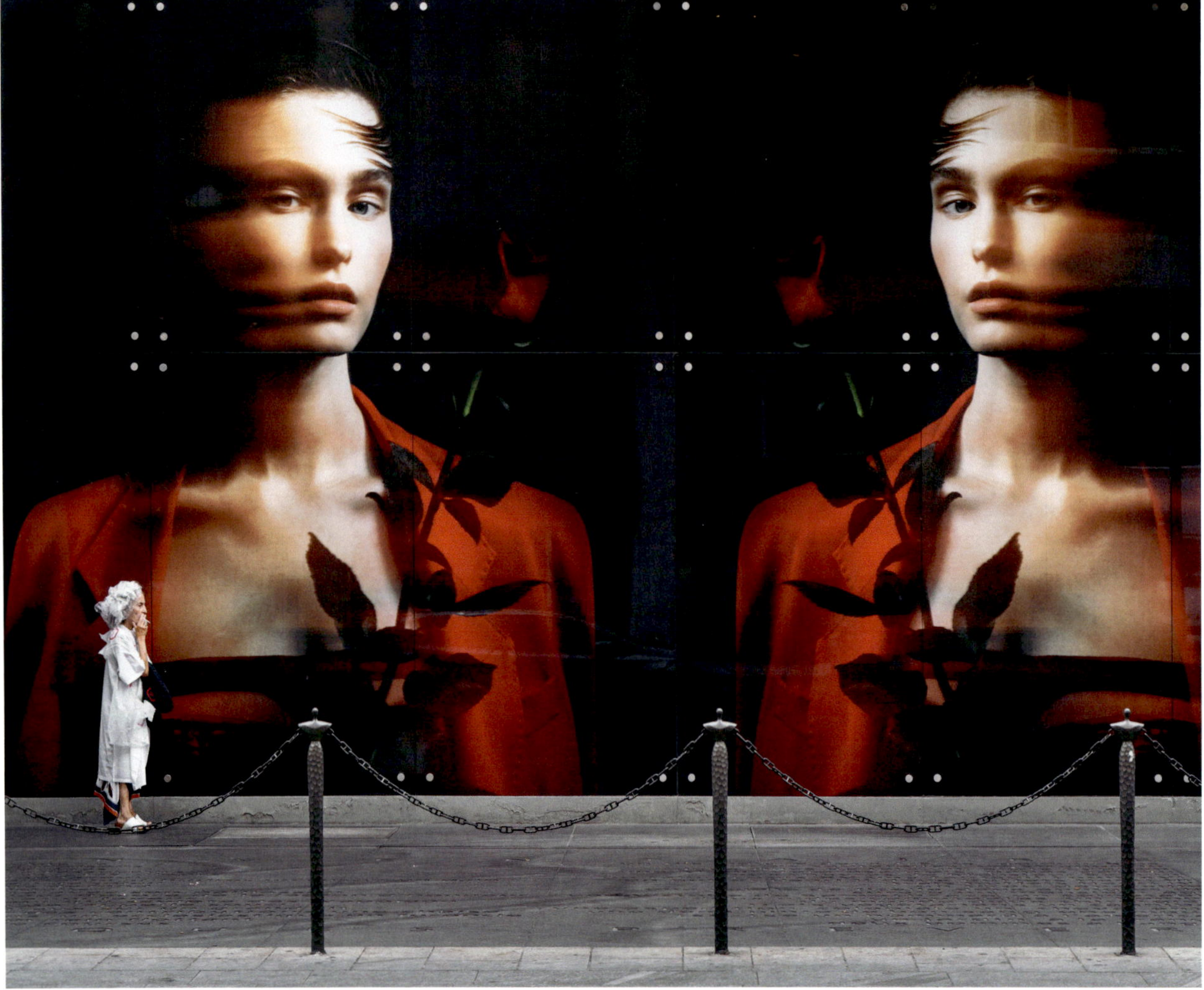

⌃ Jewelry Banner, Tokyo, 2022 ⌄ Beauty Salon, Milan, 2022

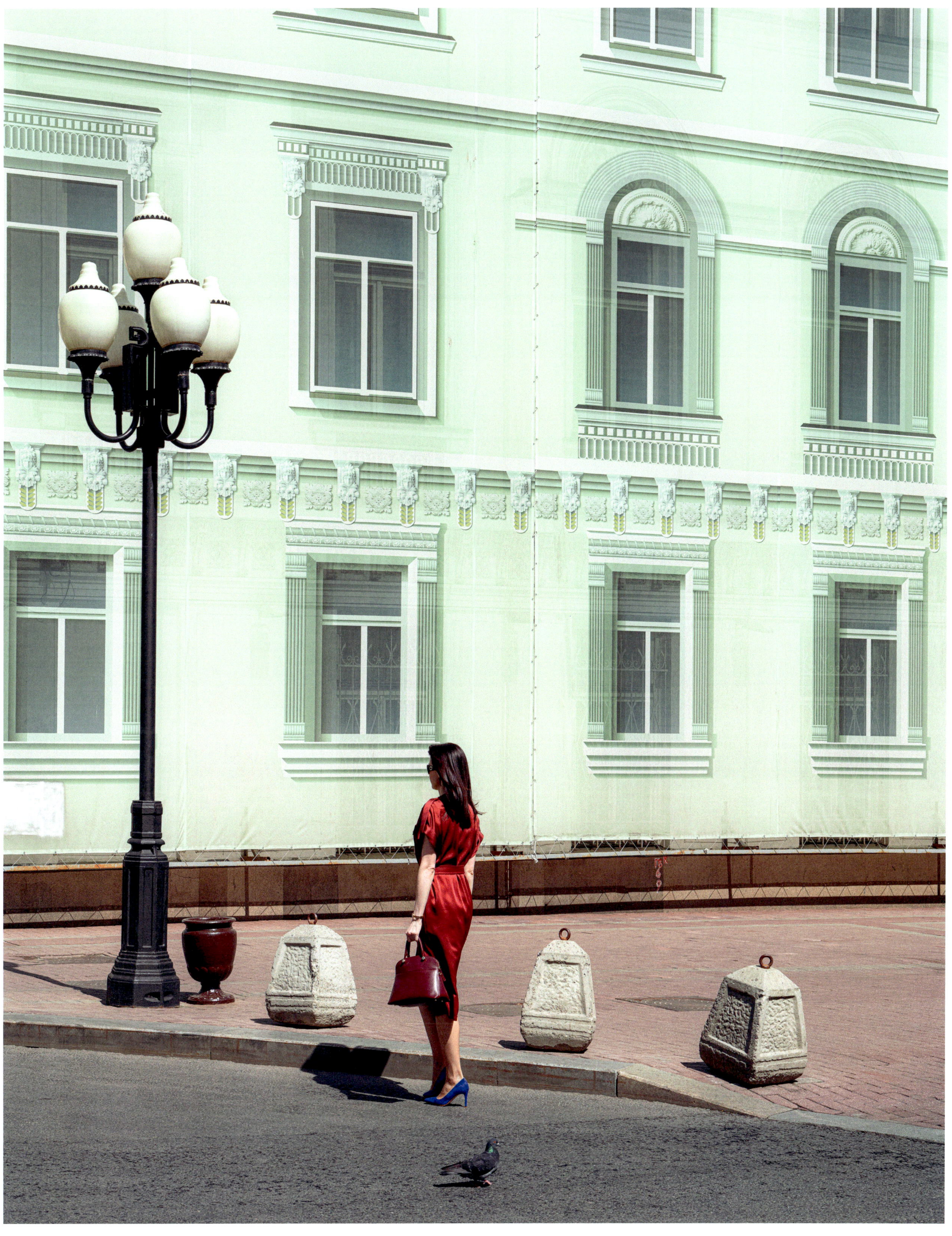

Arbat Street, Moscow, 2021

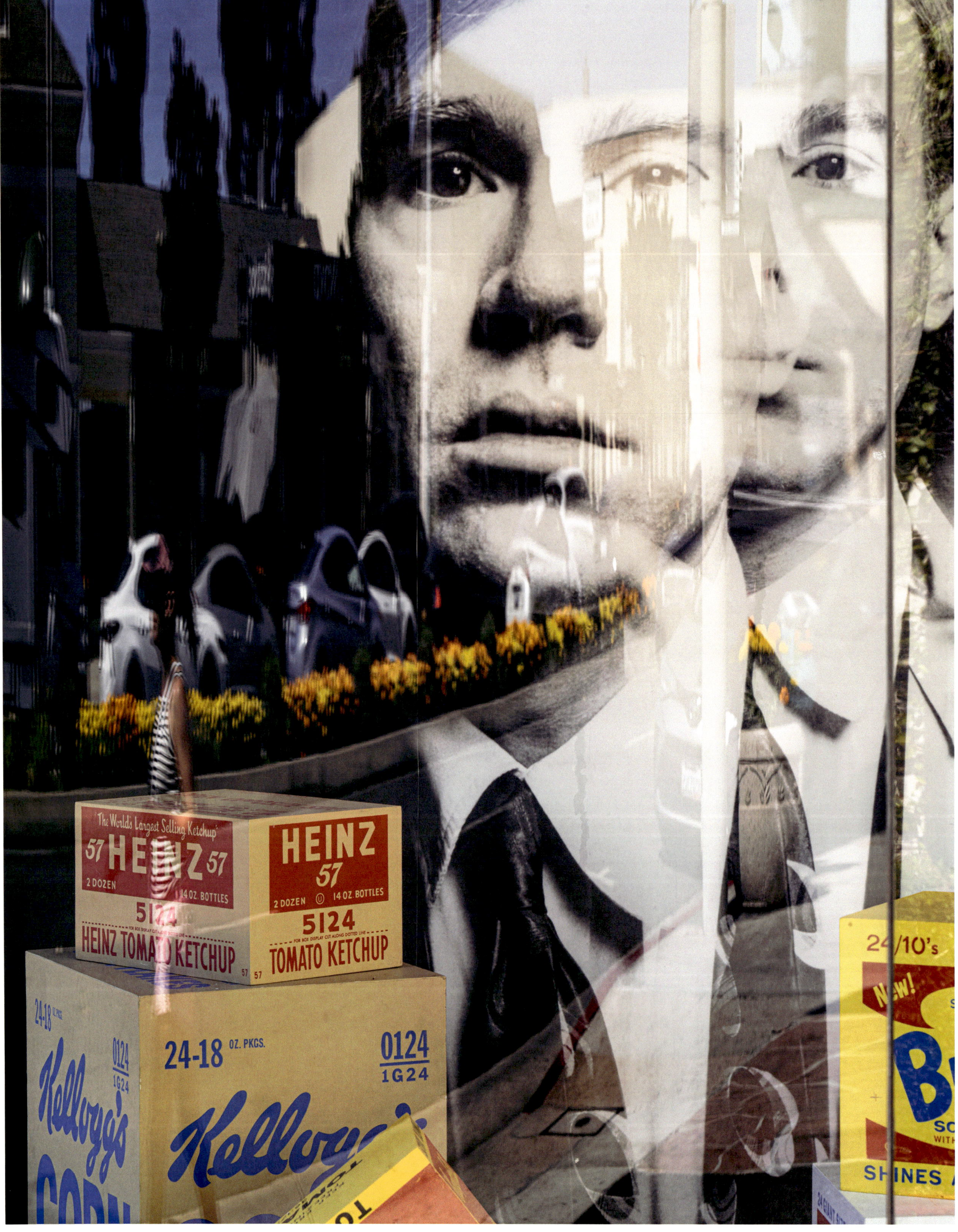

Art Poster (Warhol), Los Angeles, 2022

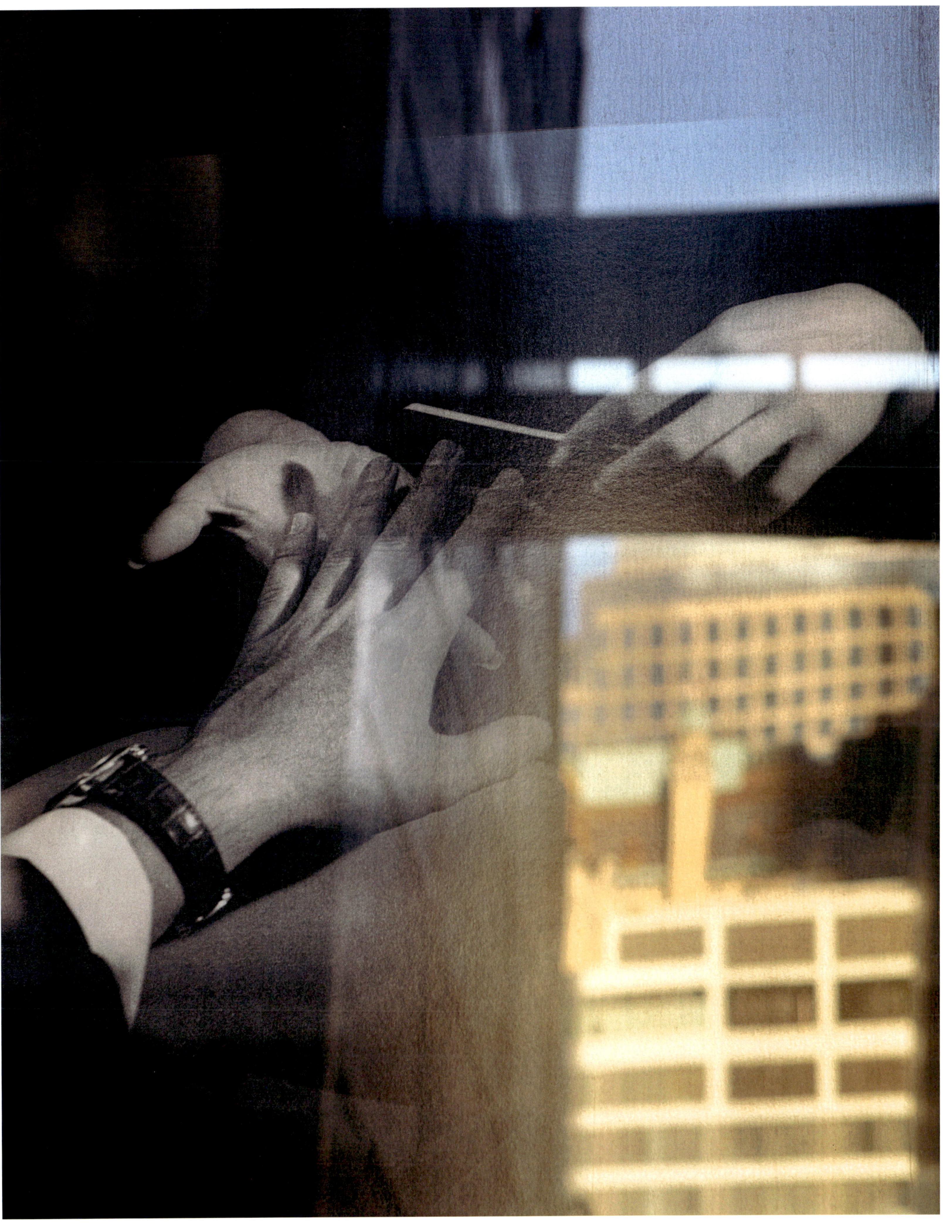

Men's Nail Salon, New York, 2021

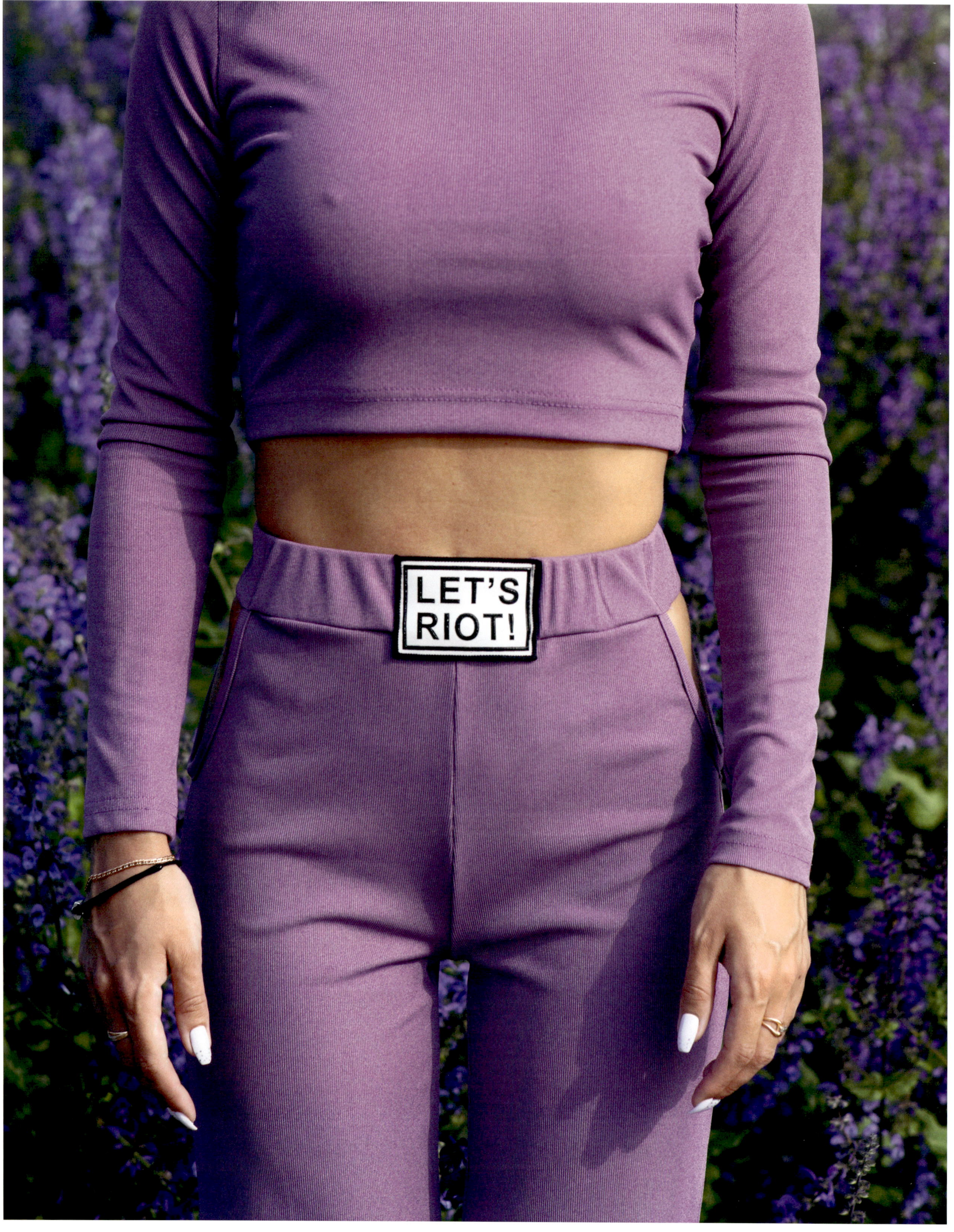

Woman in Lilac Suit (Let's Riot), Moscow, 2021

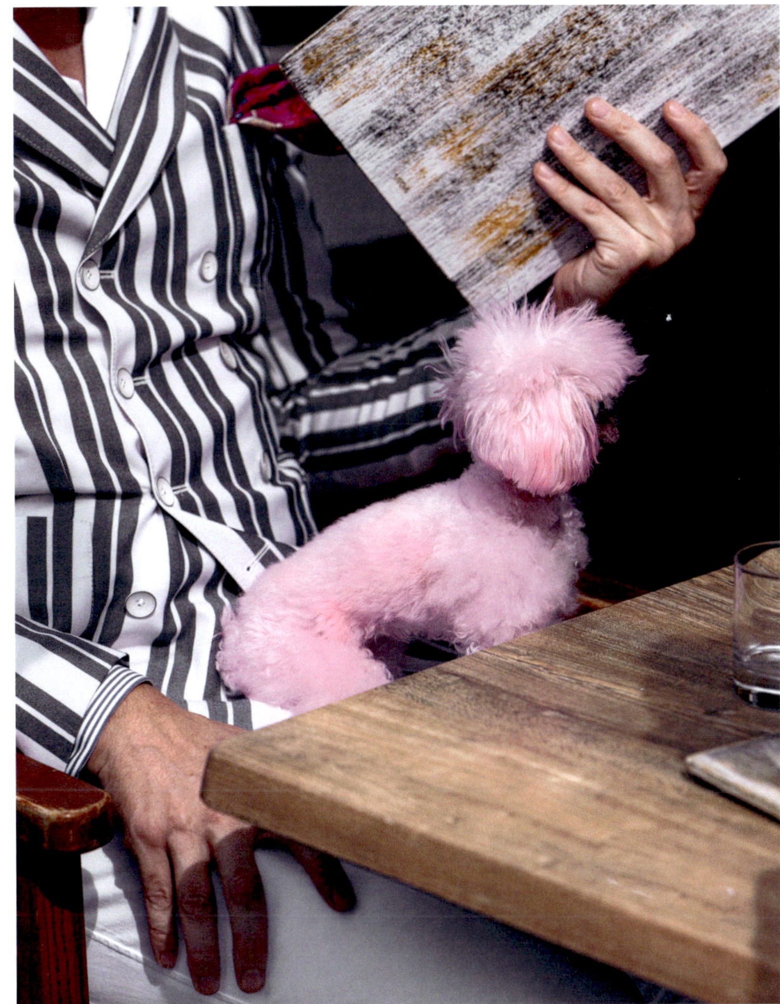

^ Pink Poodle, Monaco, 2022
‹ Glove Under Printed Fence, Paris, 2022
› Discarded Makeup, Los Angeles, 2022

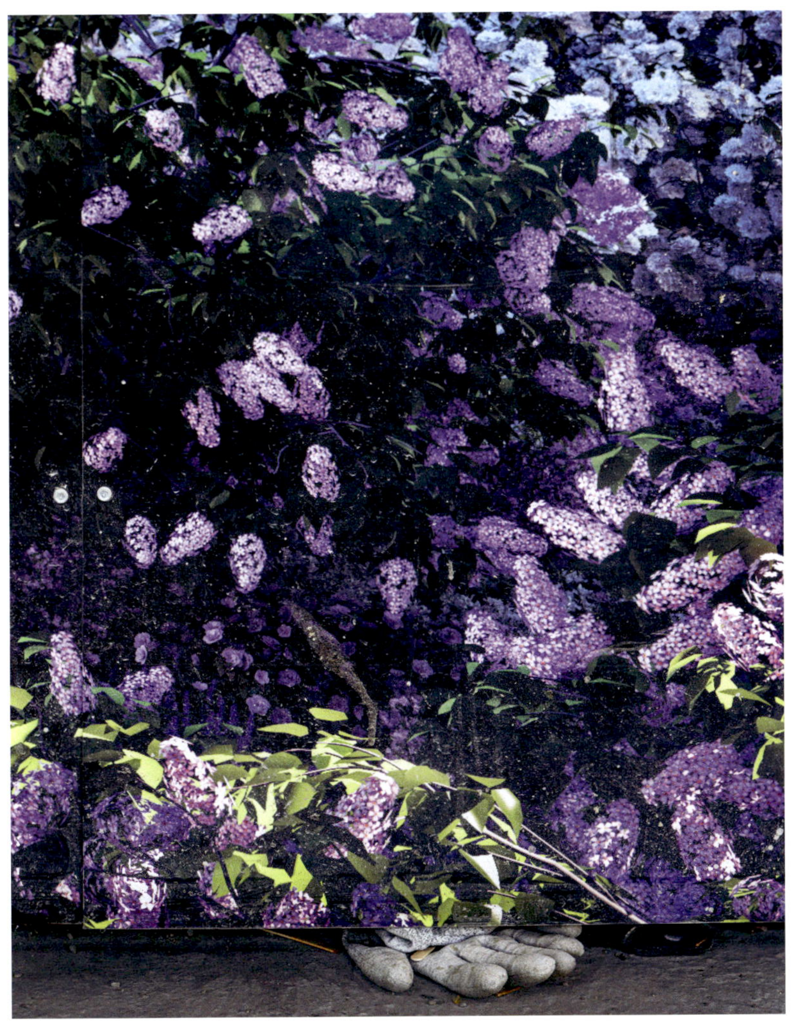

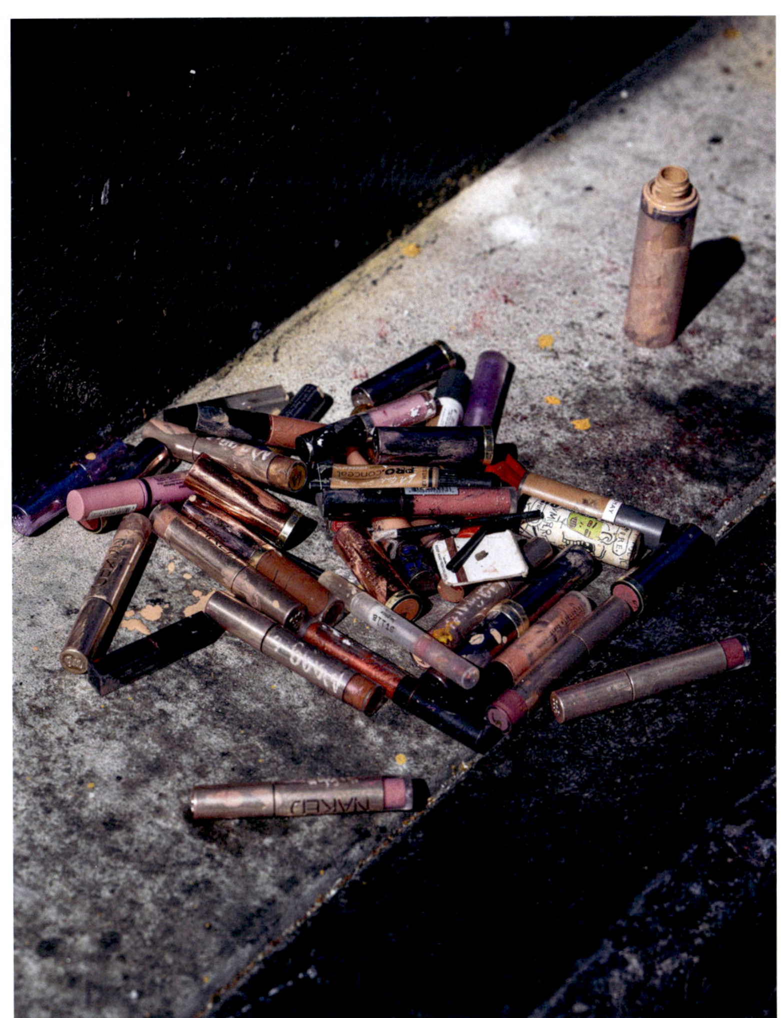

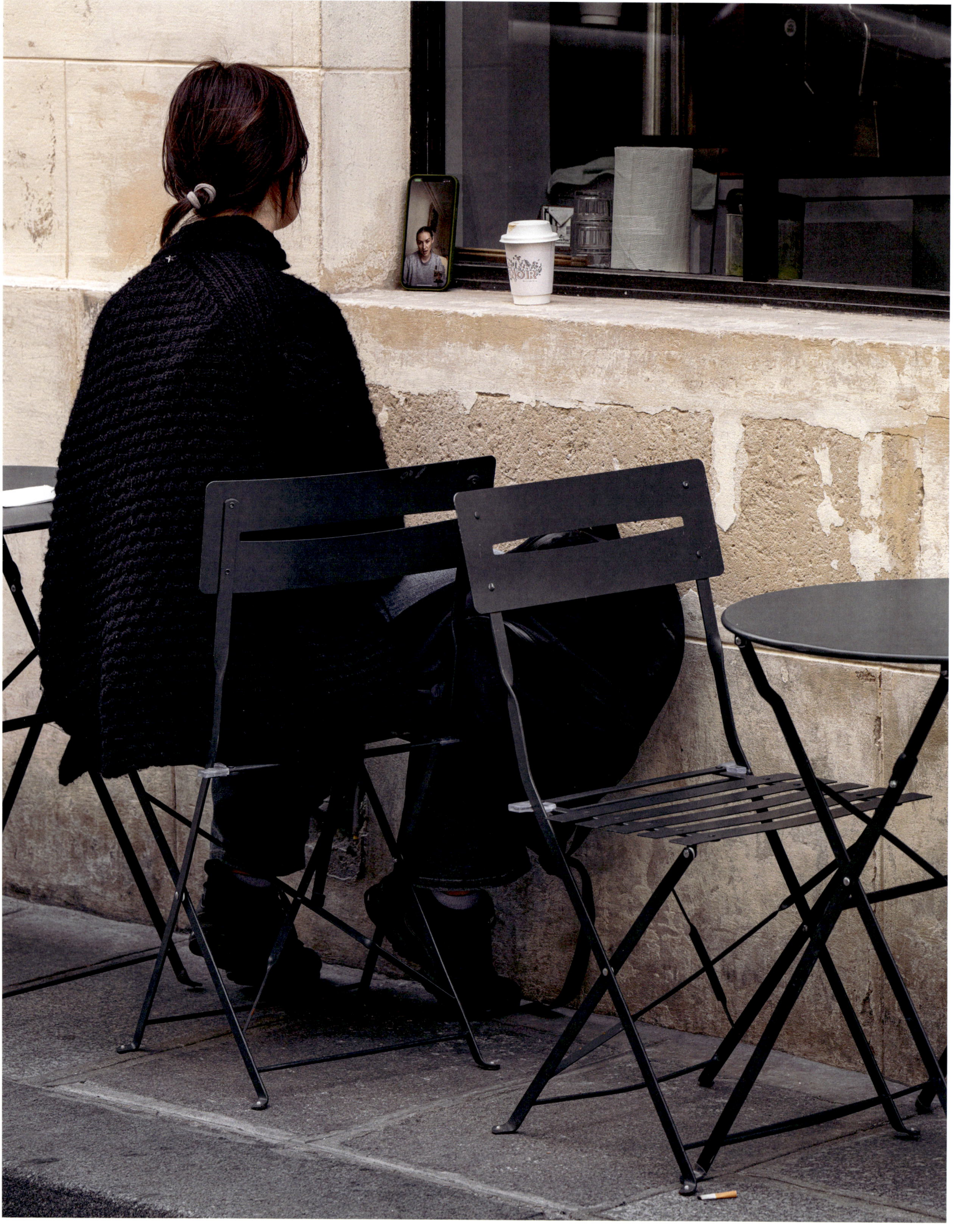

Video Chat, Paris, 2022

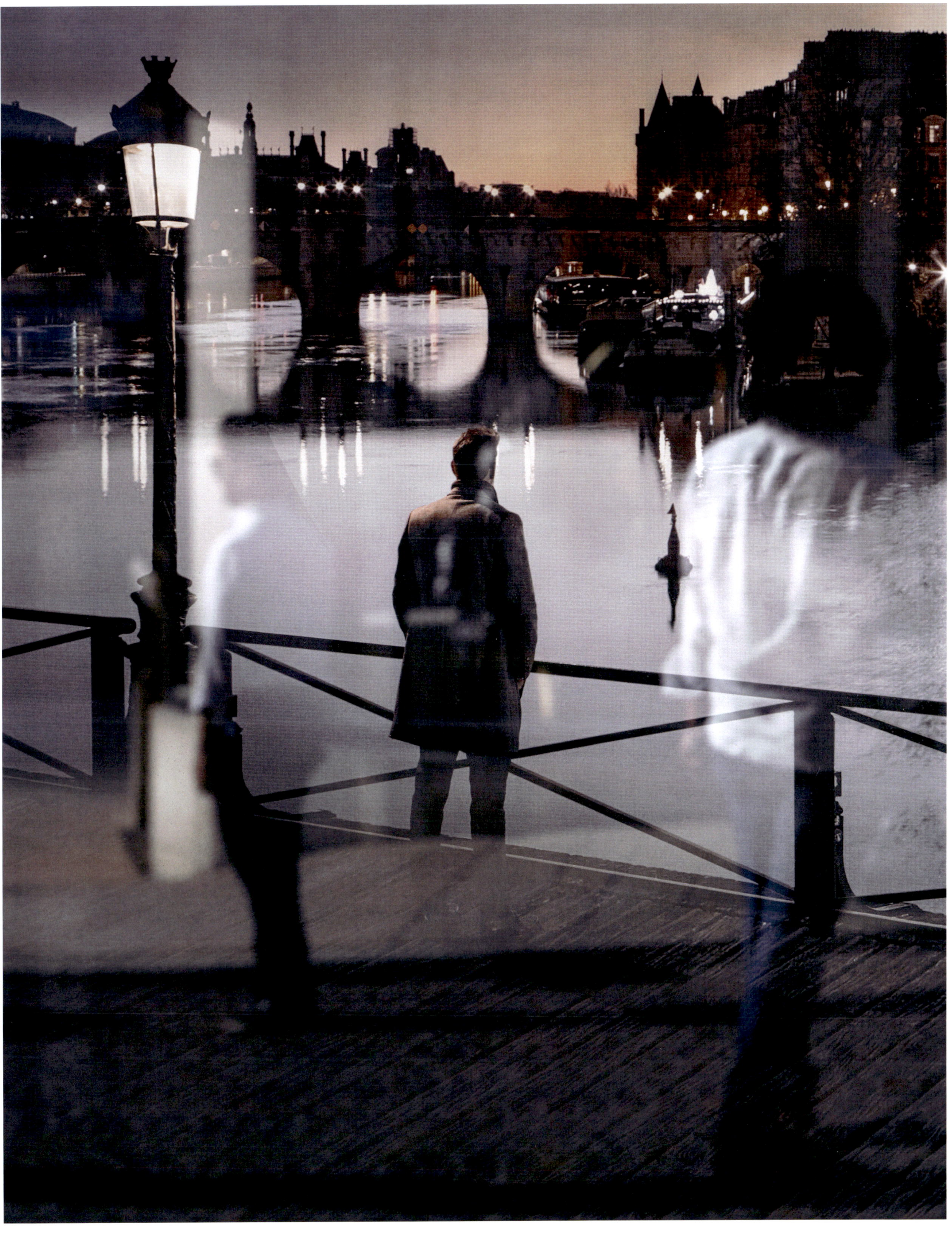

Reflection in Watch Advertisement, Los Angeles, 2022

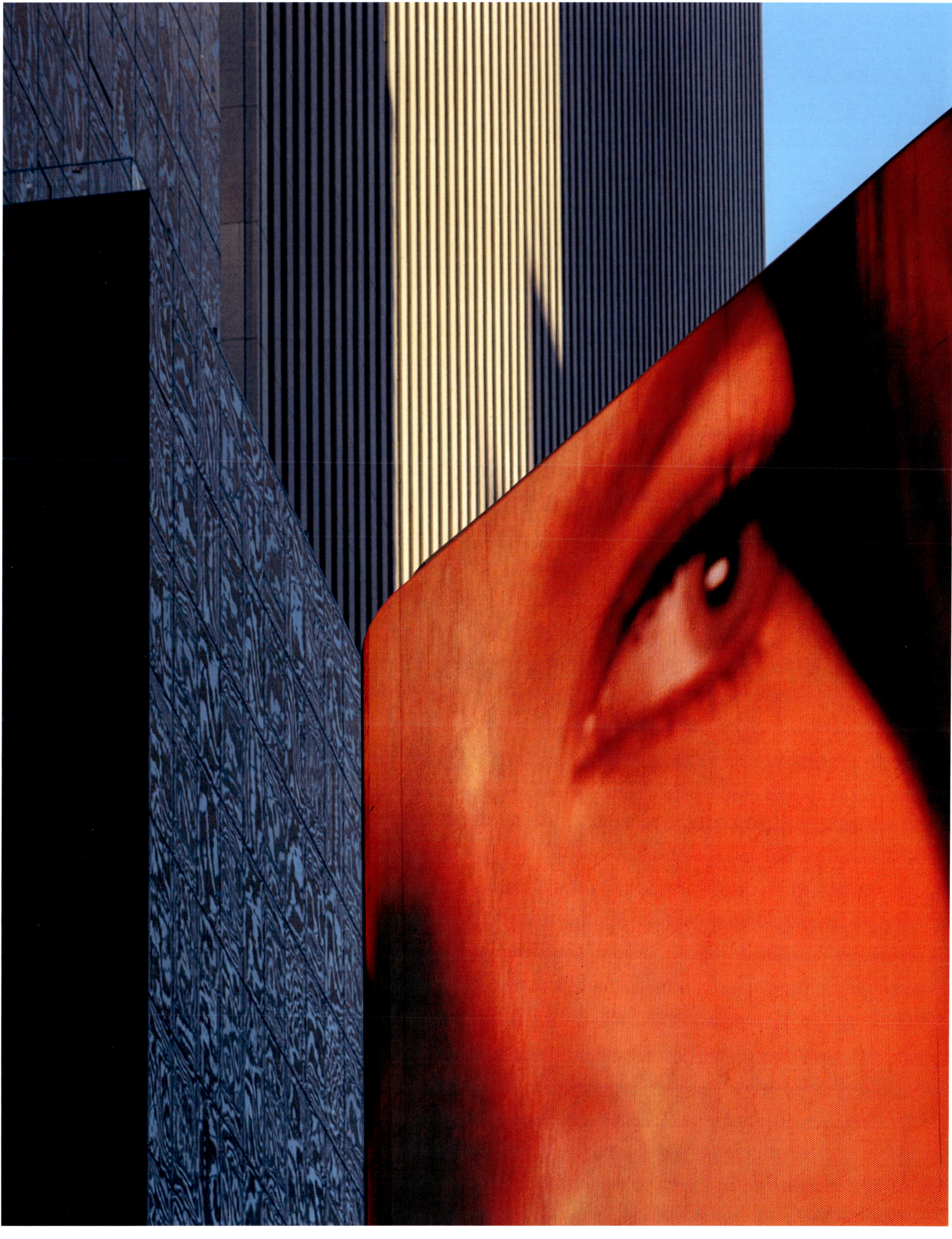

Red Eye, Times Square, New York, 2021

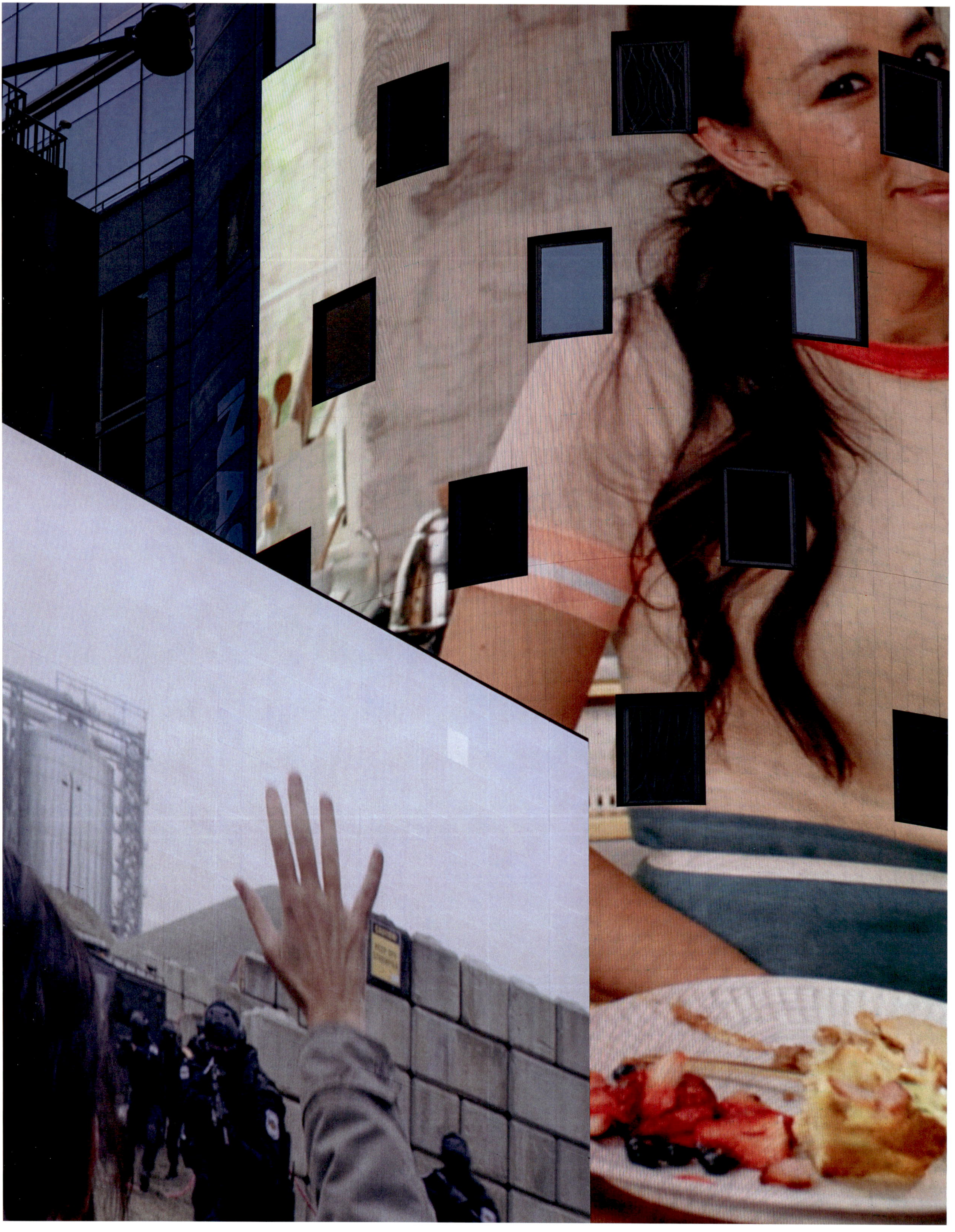

Screens on Buildings, New York, 2021

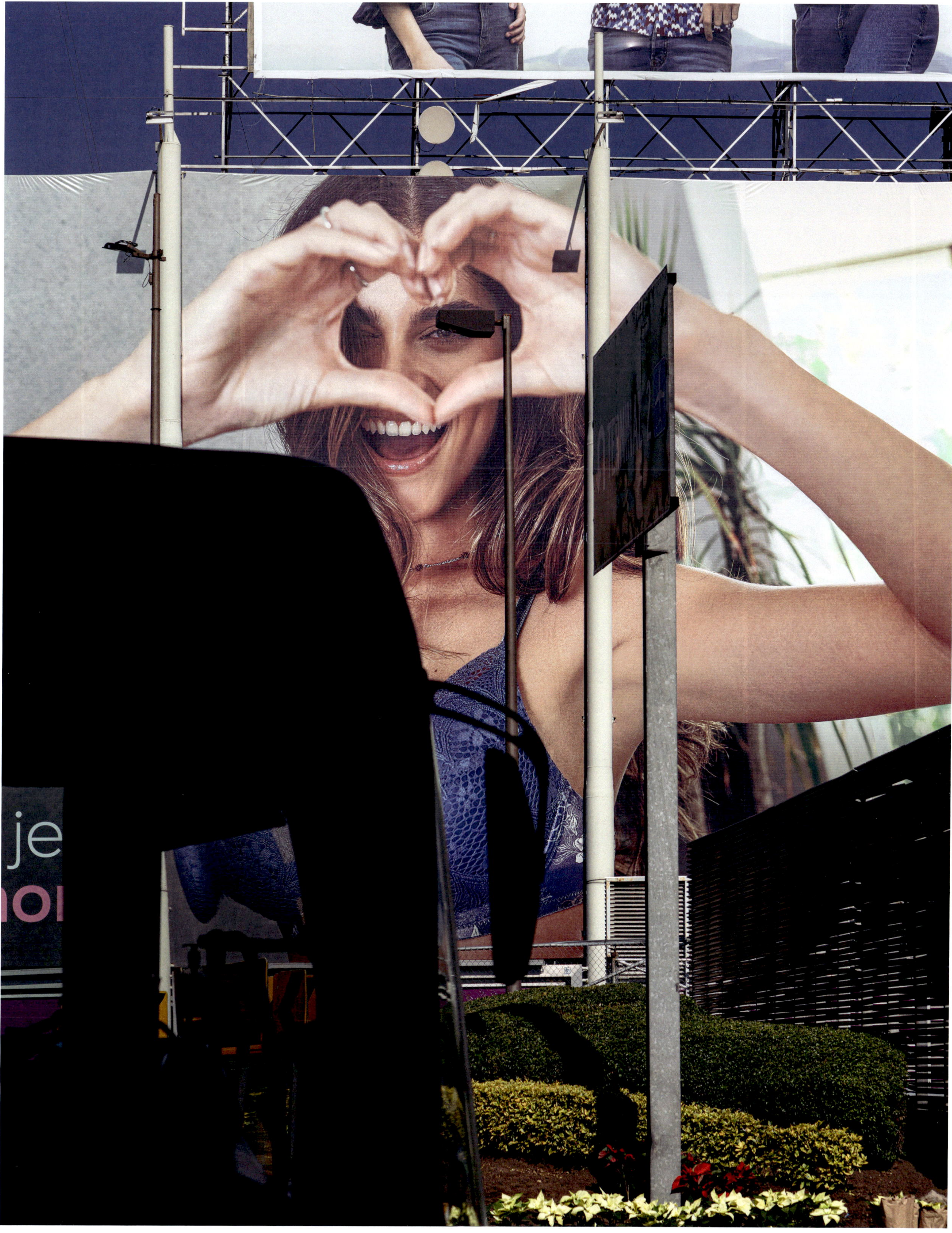

Lingerie Advertisement, Mexico City, 2021

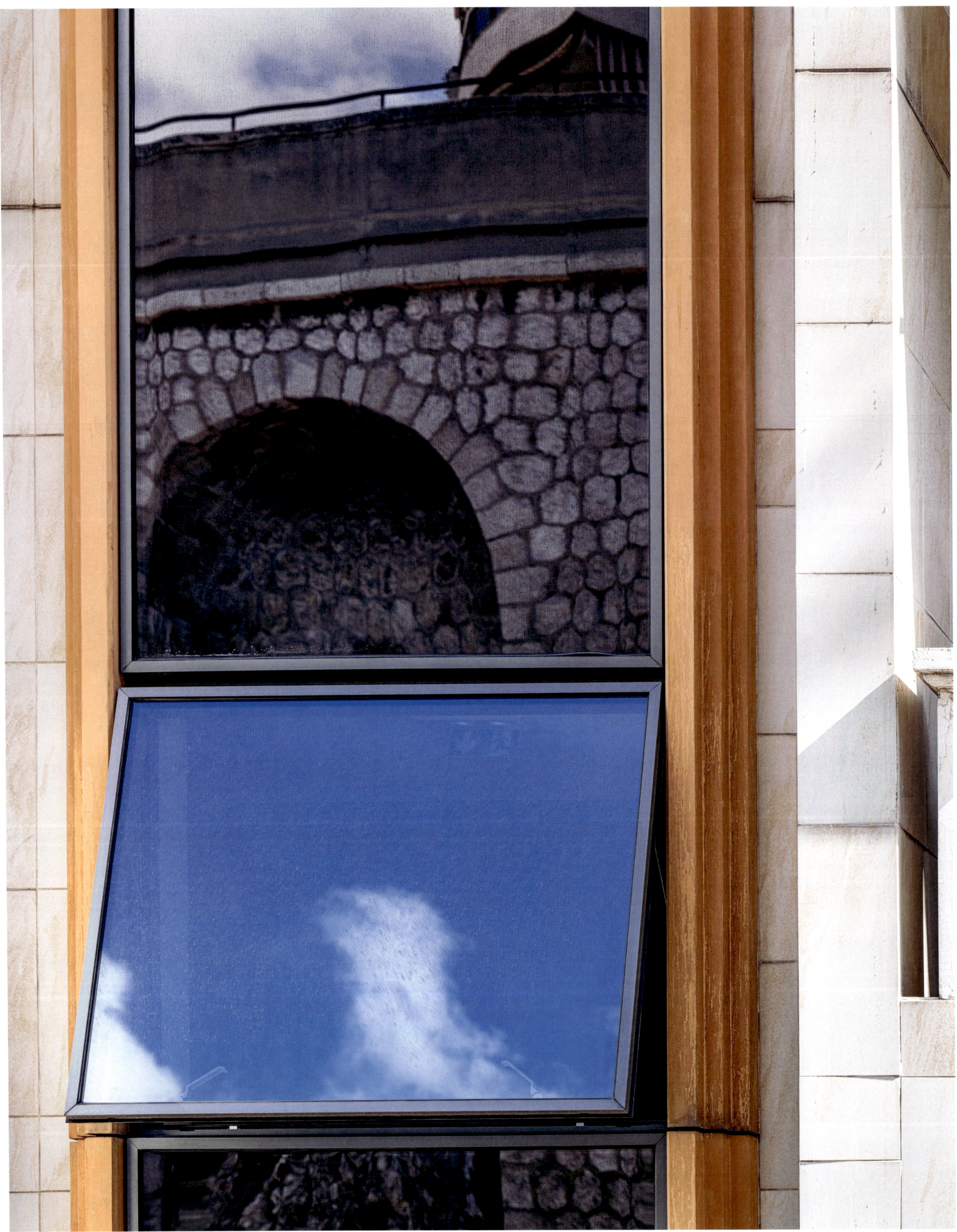

 Reflections in Window, Monaco, 2022

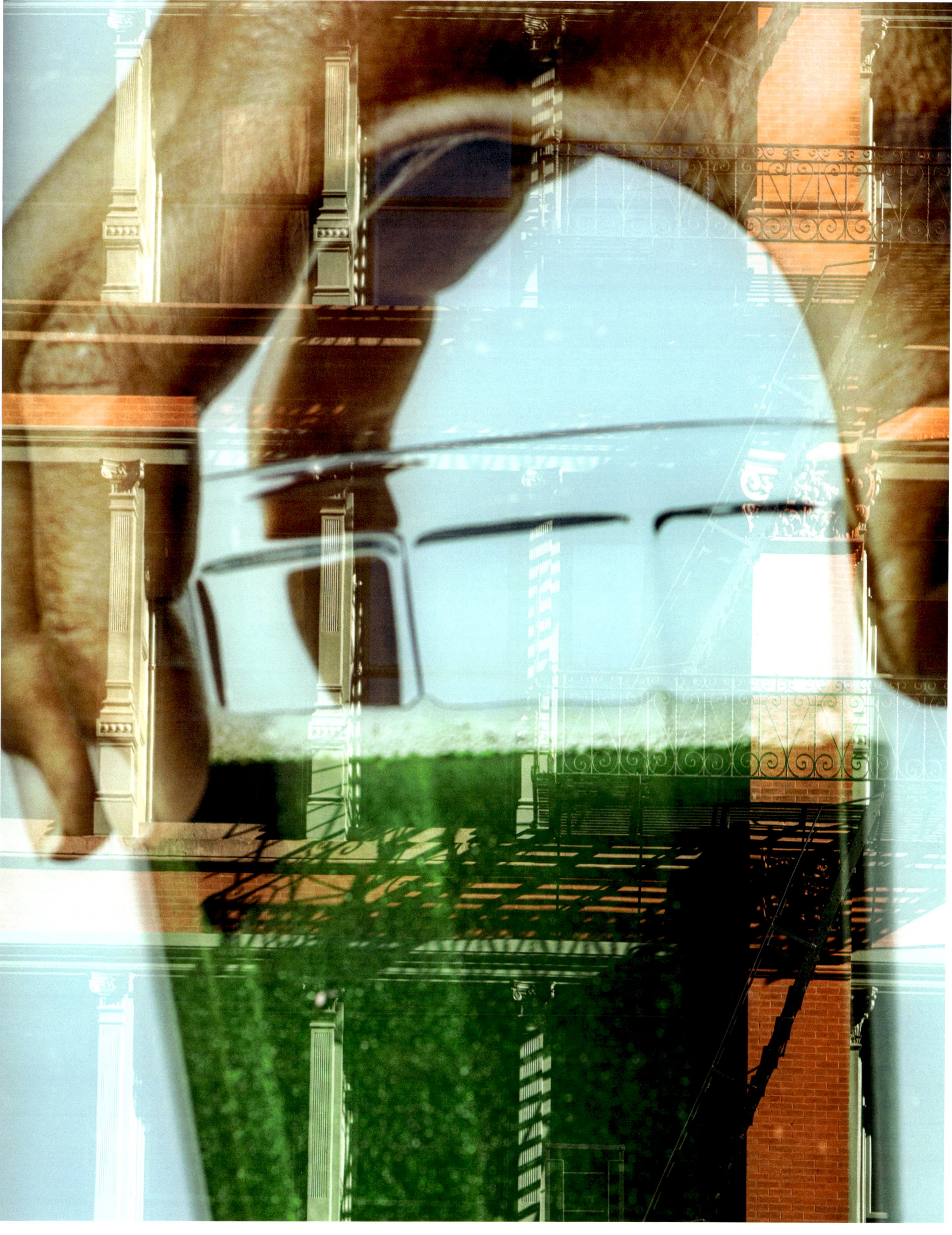

Green Juice, New York, 2021

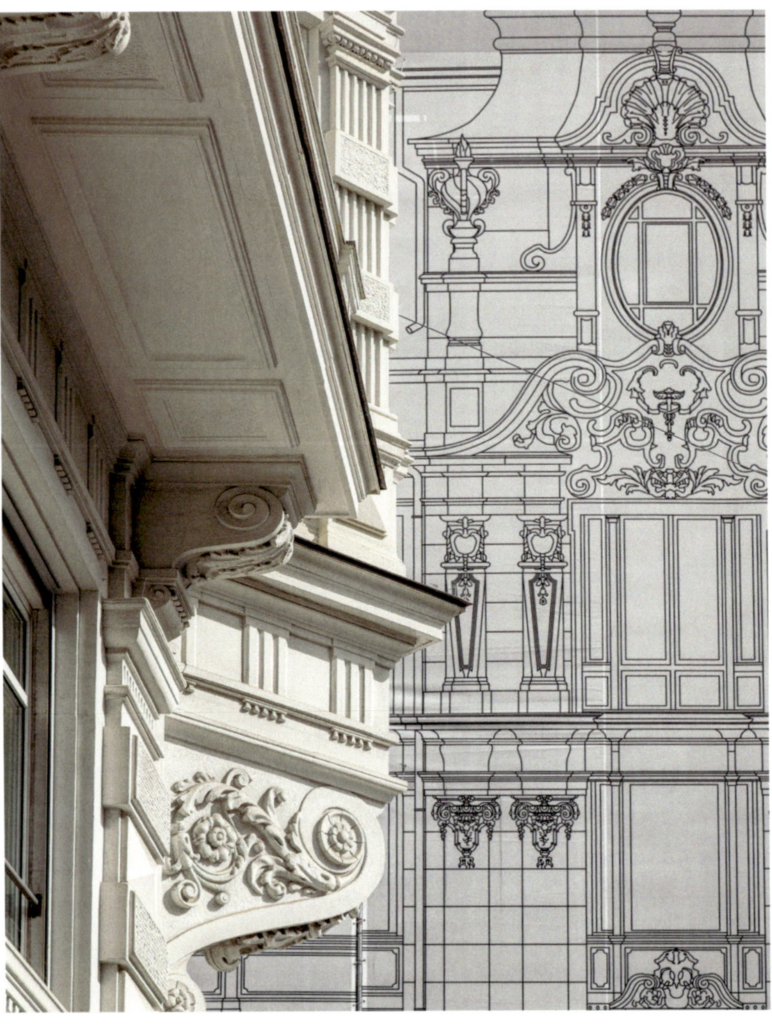

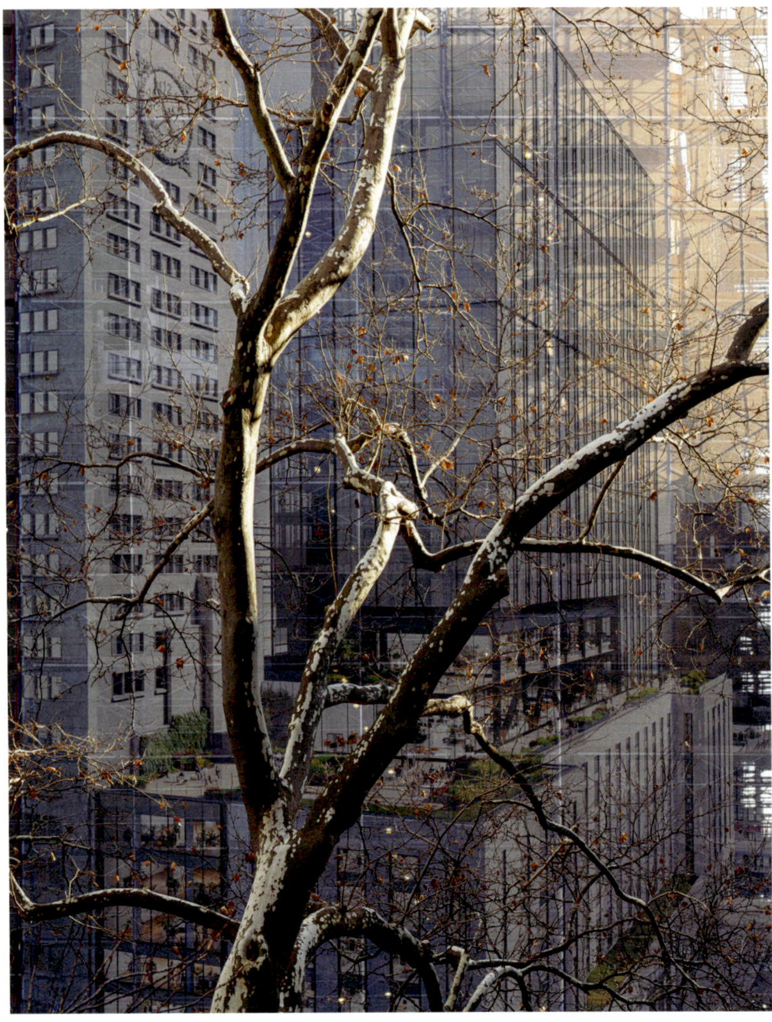

^ Facade and Printed Cover, Zurich, 2021
⌄ Skyscraper Construction Cover, New York, 2021

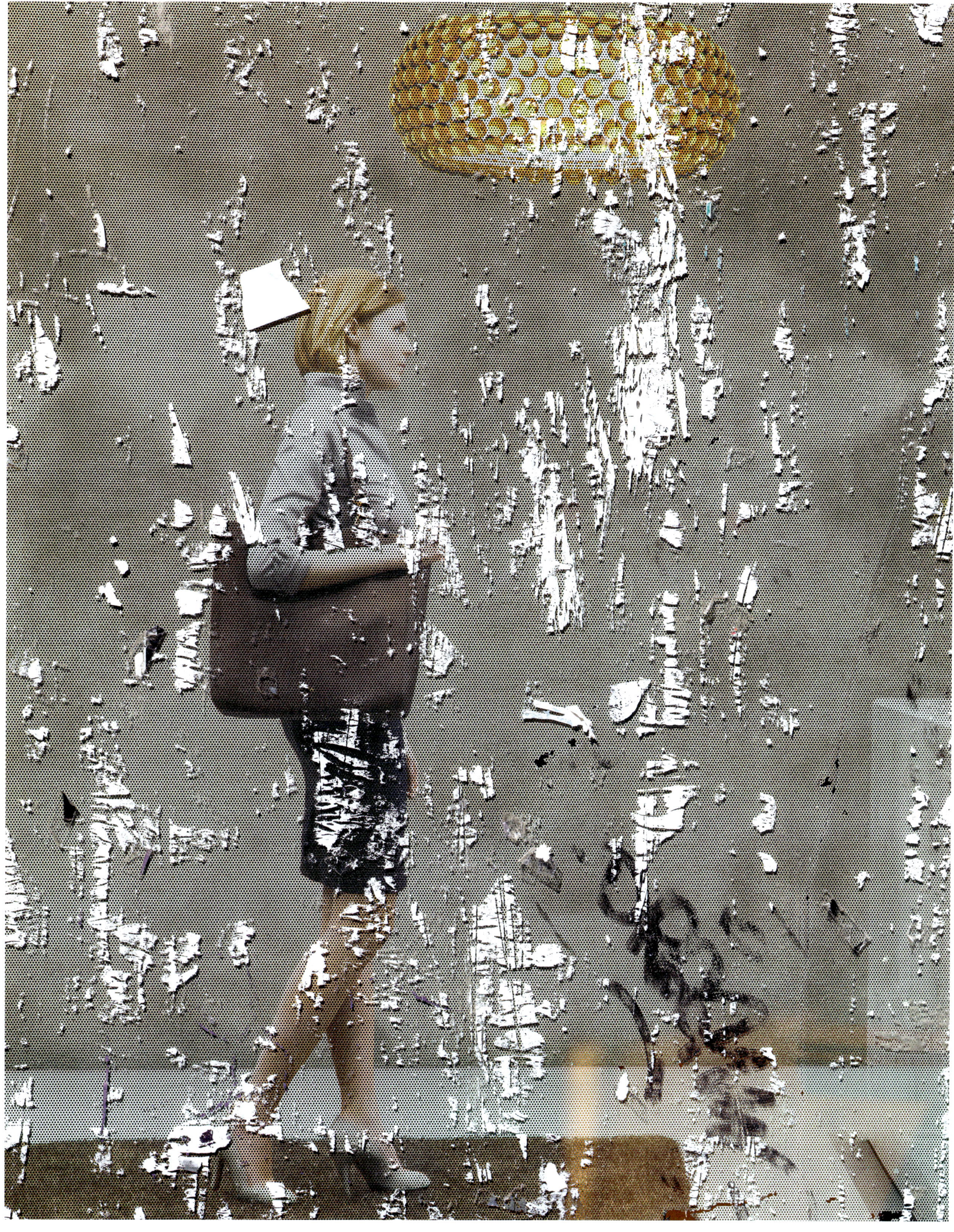

Scratched Off Poster, Paris, 2021

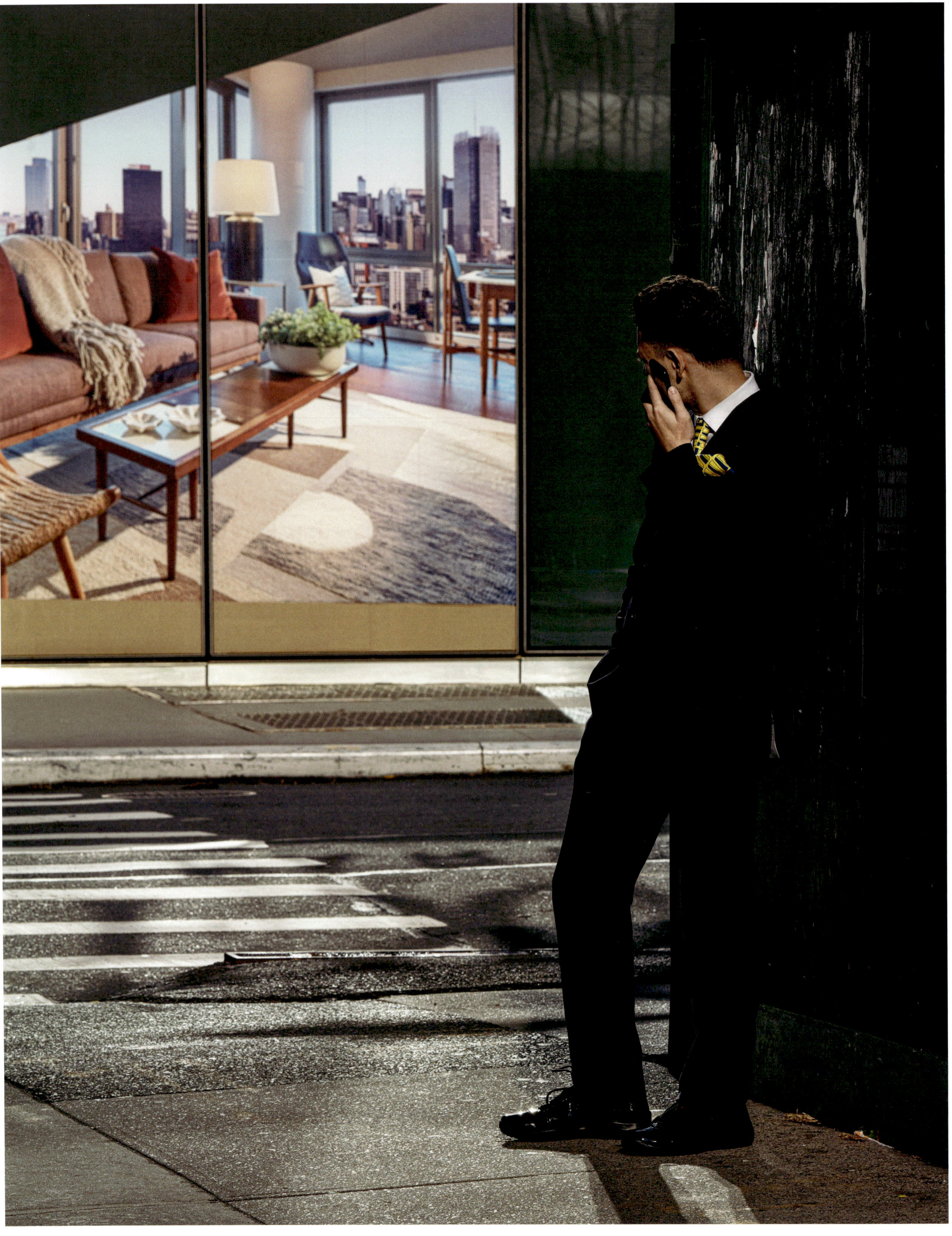

 Real Estate Advertisement, New York, 2021

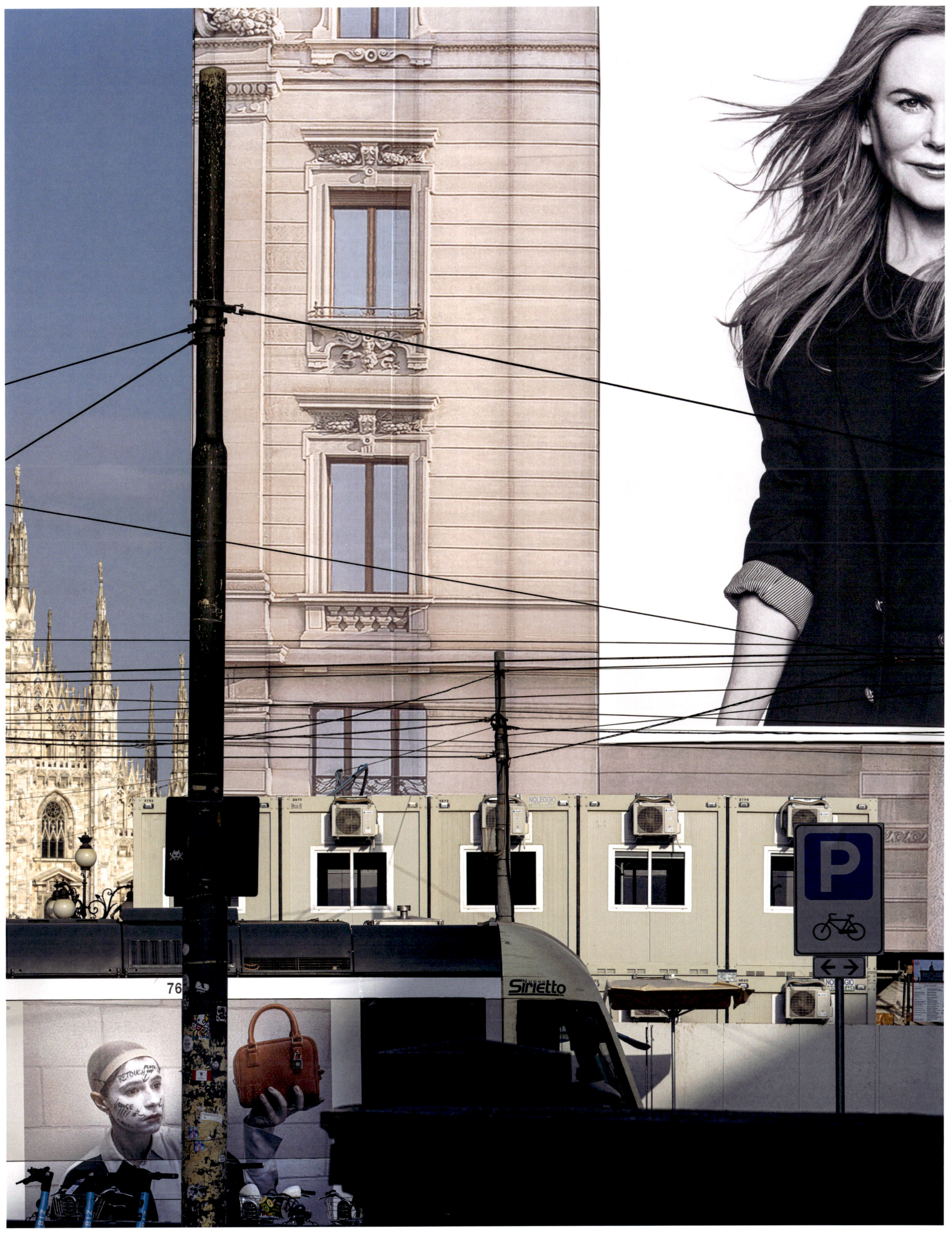

Outdoor Advertisements, Milan, 2022

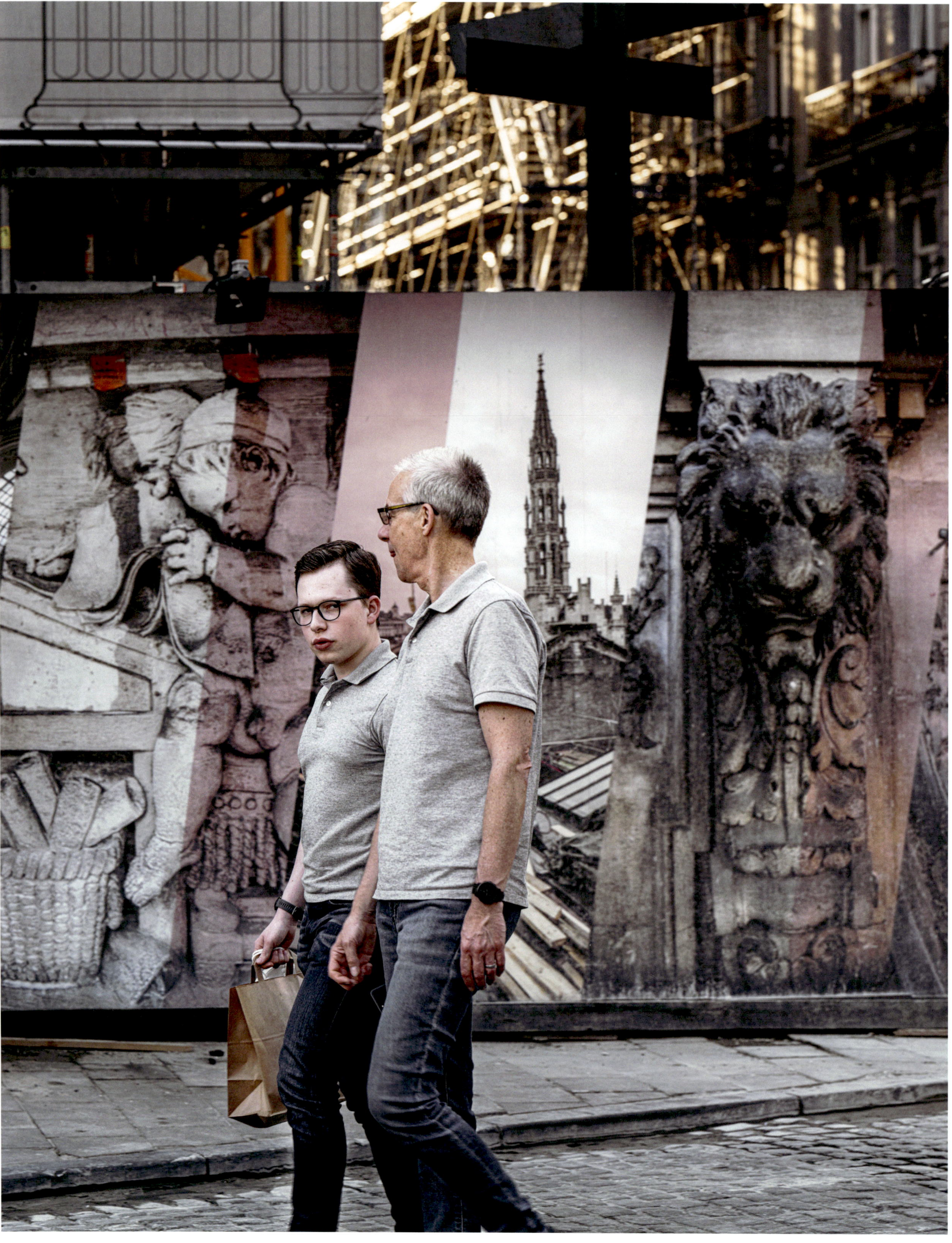

Historic Reconstruction, Brussels, 2022

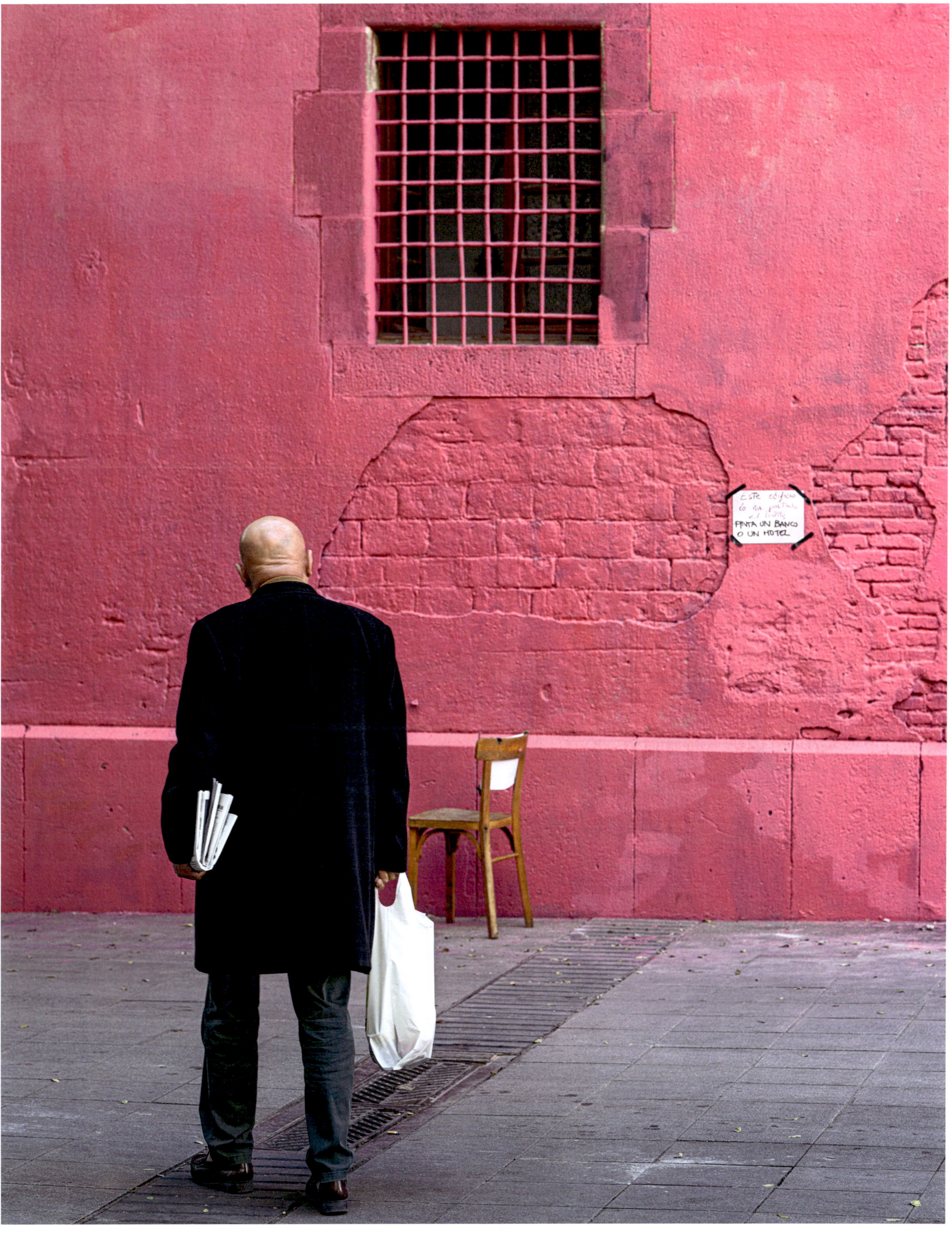

Newly Painted Wall, Barcelona, 2022

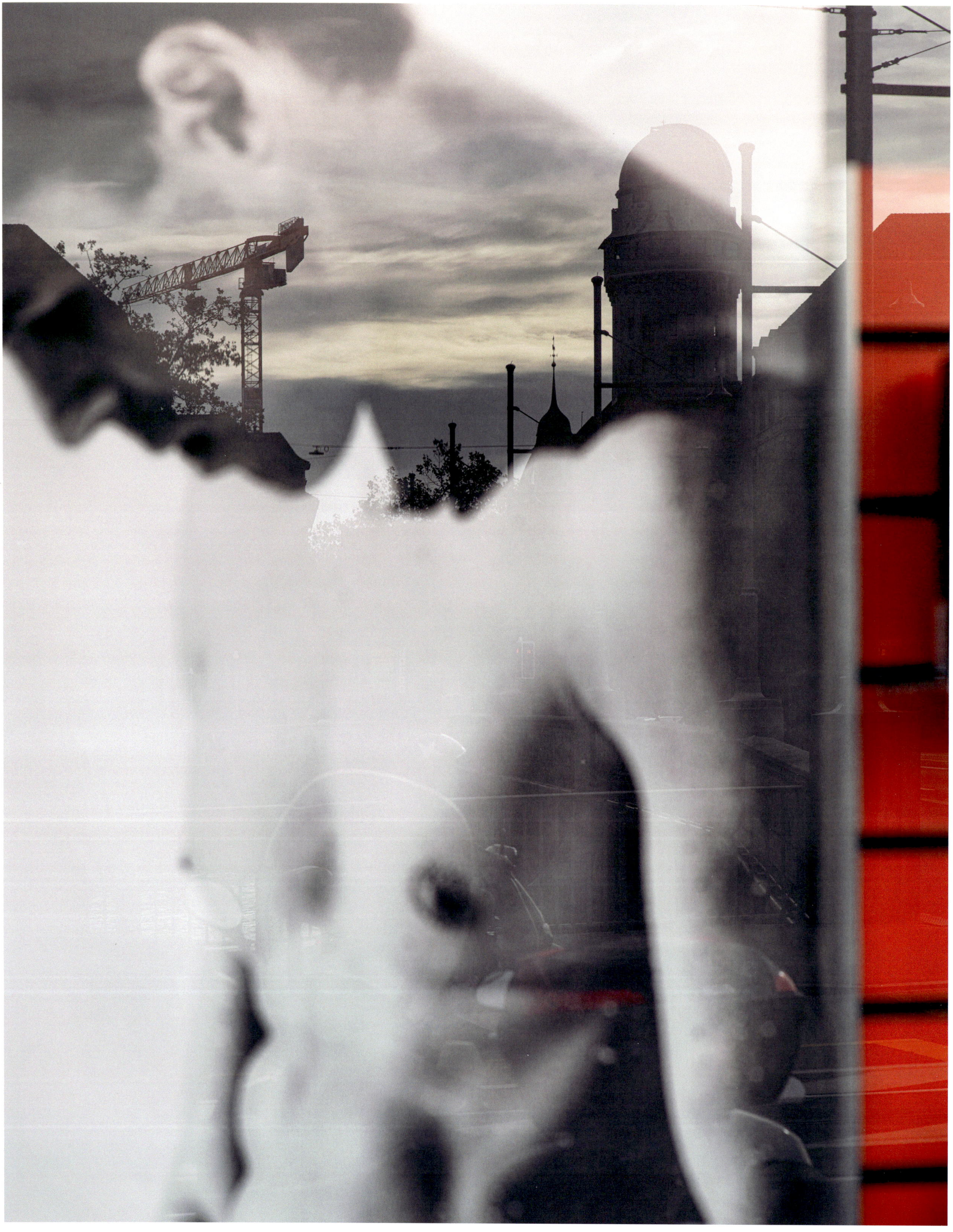

Sex Shop, Zurich, 2021

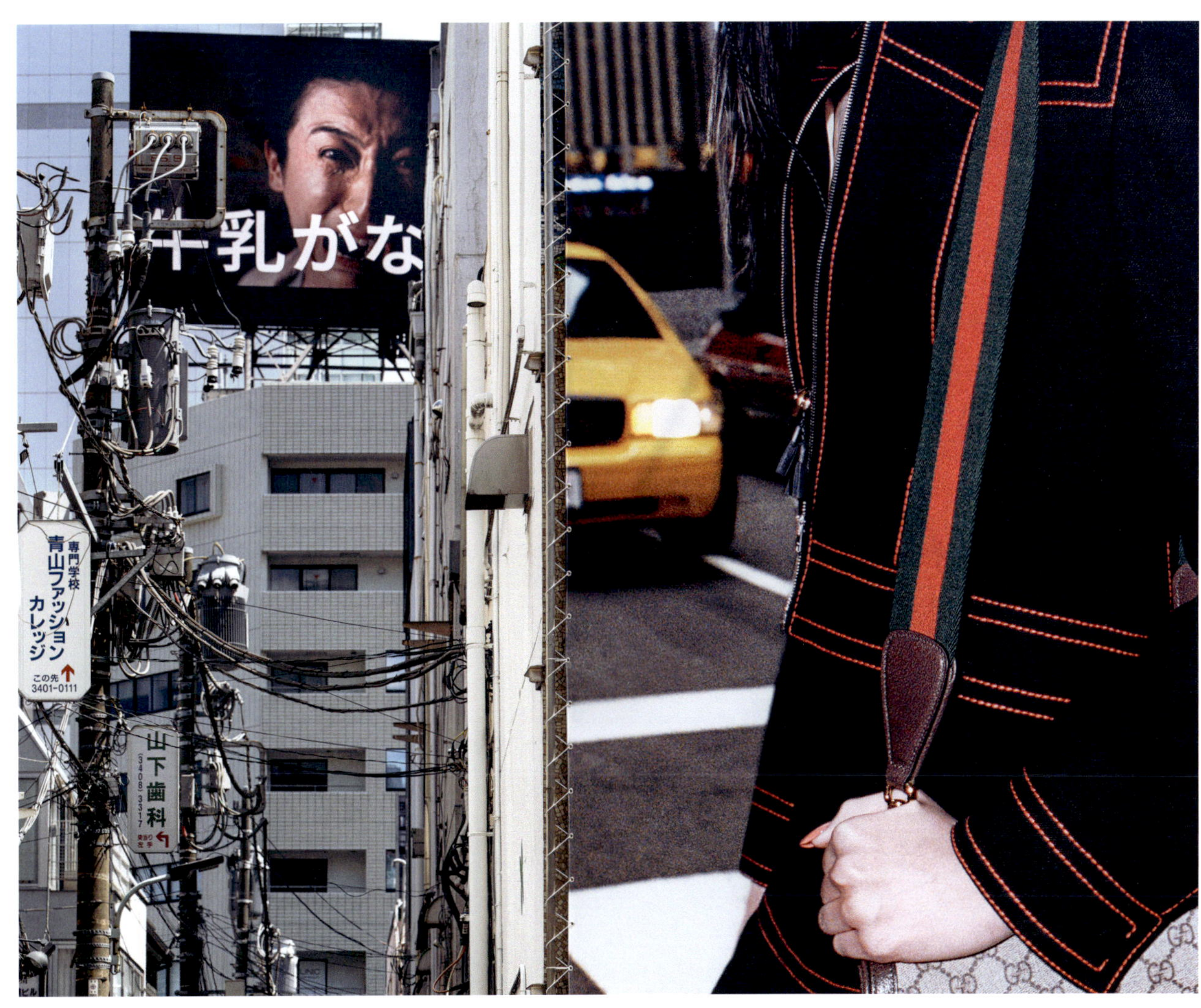

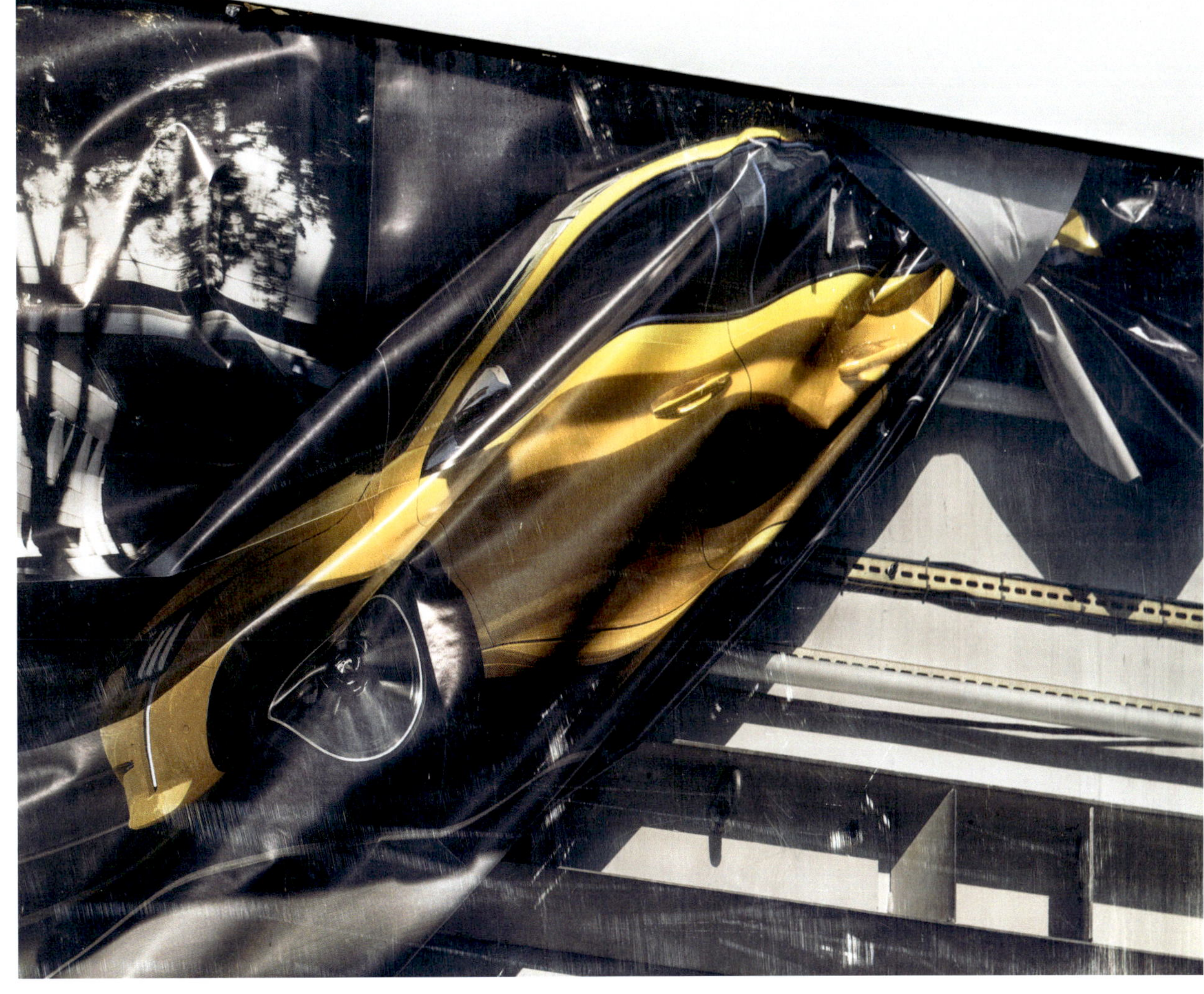

^ Luxury Fashion Advertisement, Tokyo, 2022 ˇ Stuck Banner with Car Advertisement, Monaco, 2022

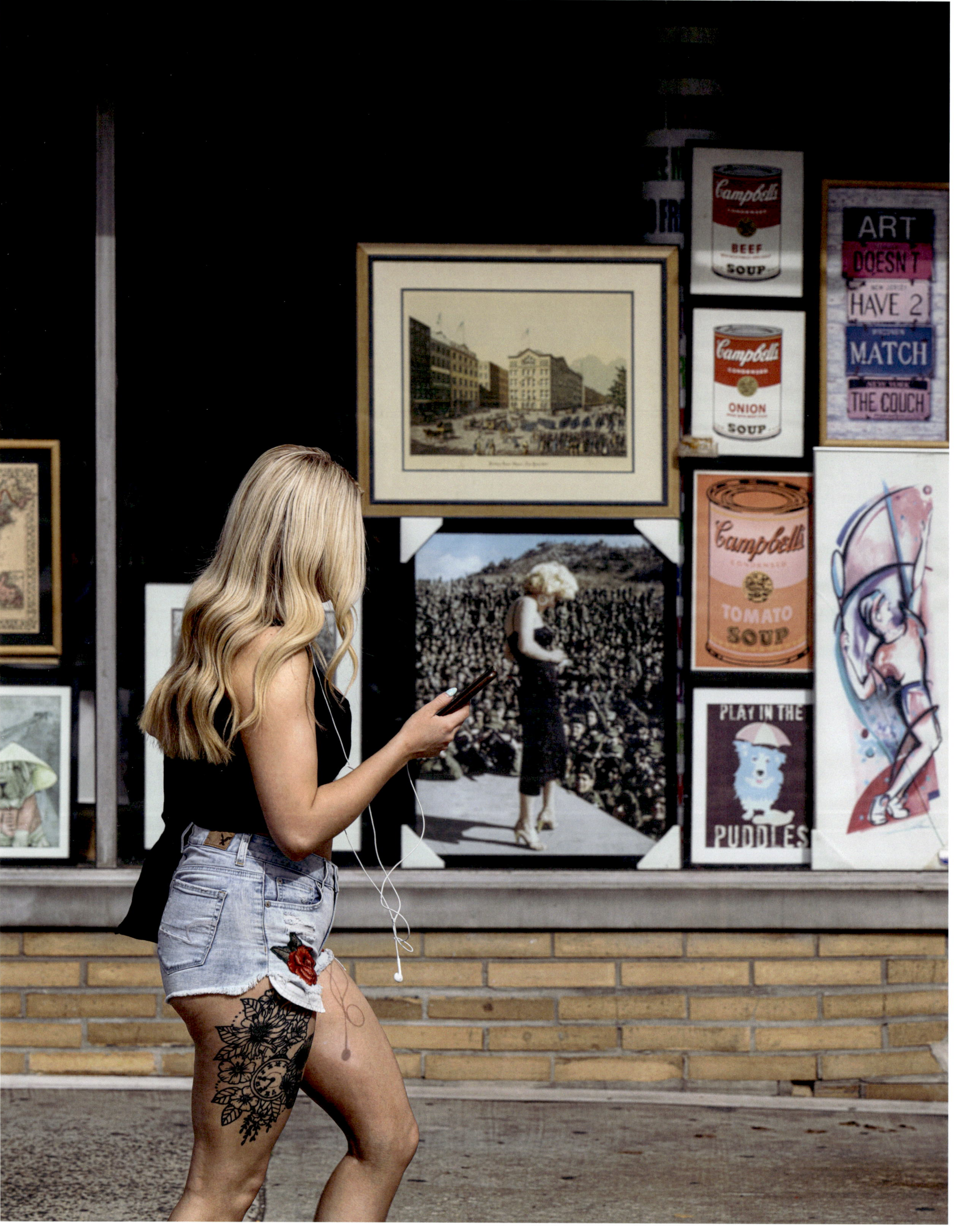

Art Store, New York, 2022

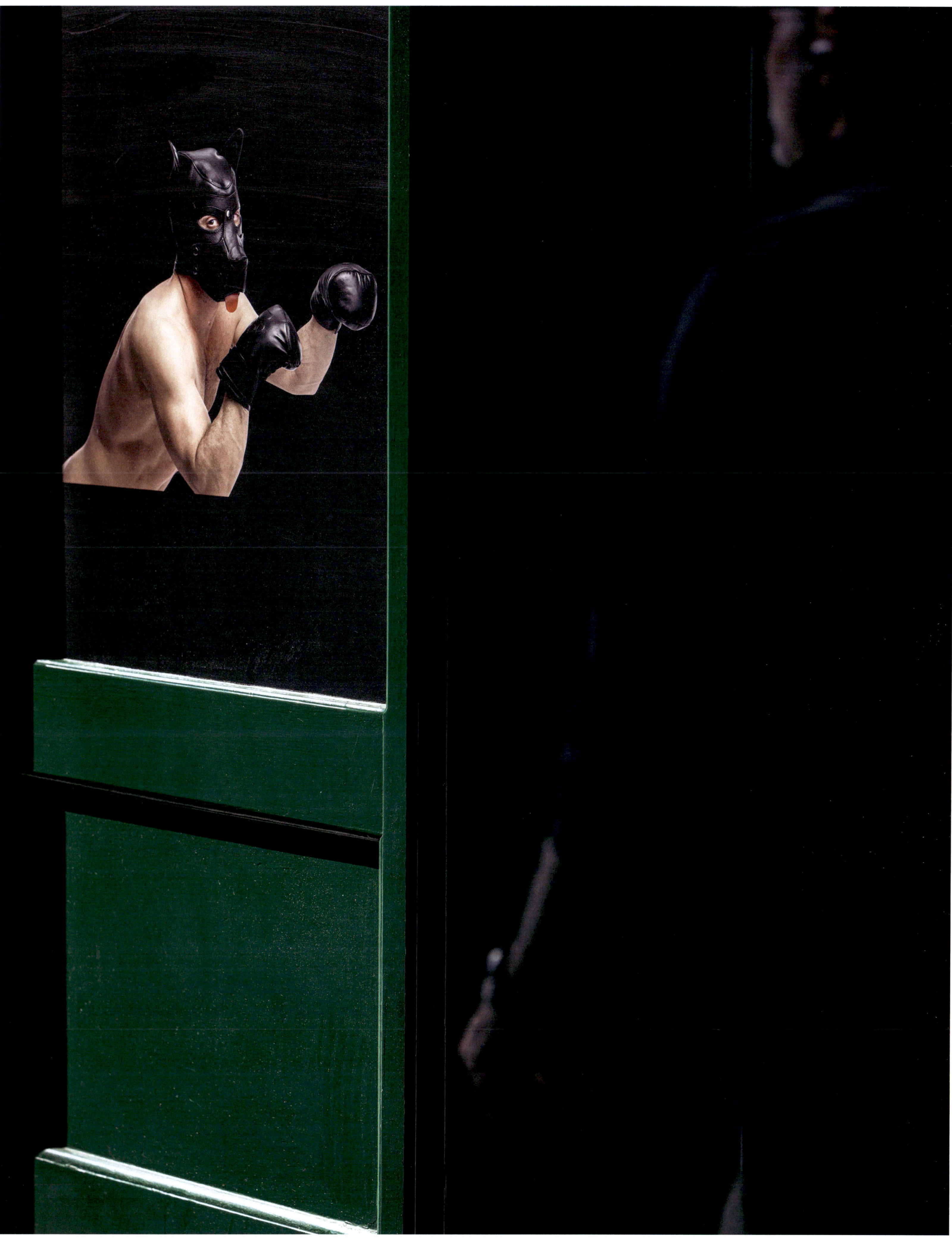

Sex Shop, London, 2022

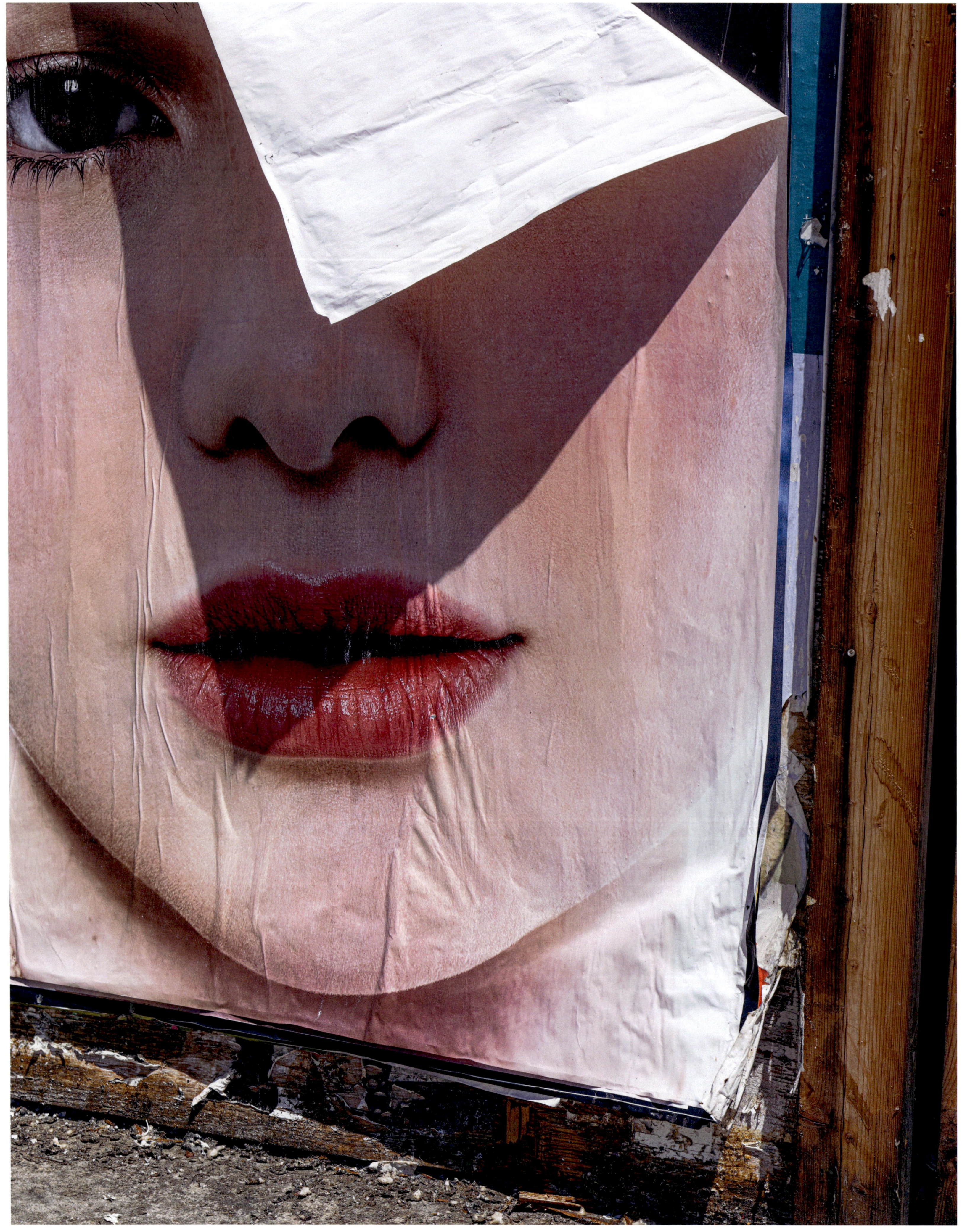

Peeling Poster, Los Angeles, 2022

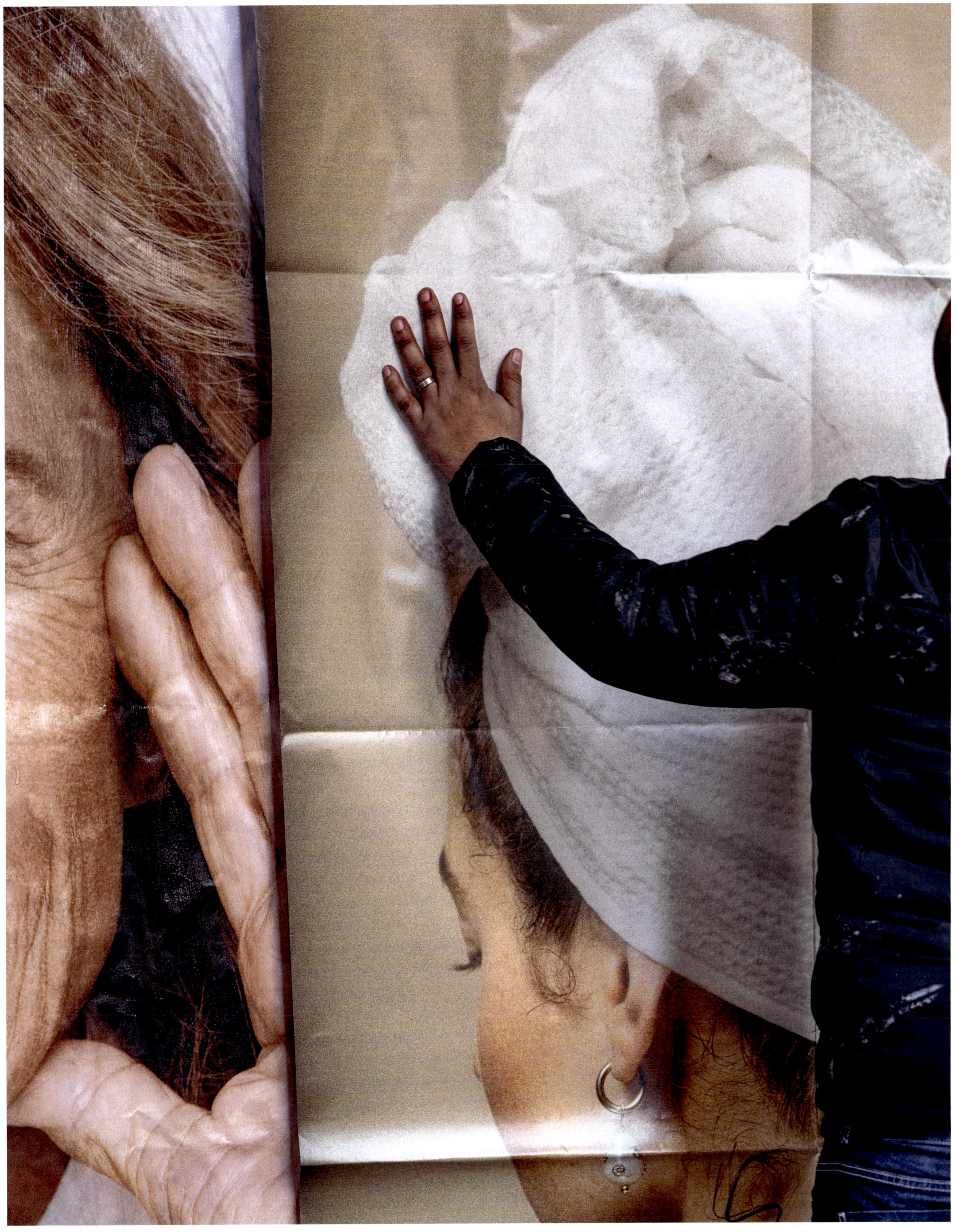

Poster Installer, New York, 2022

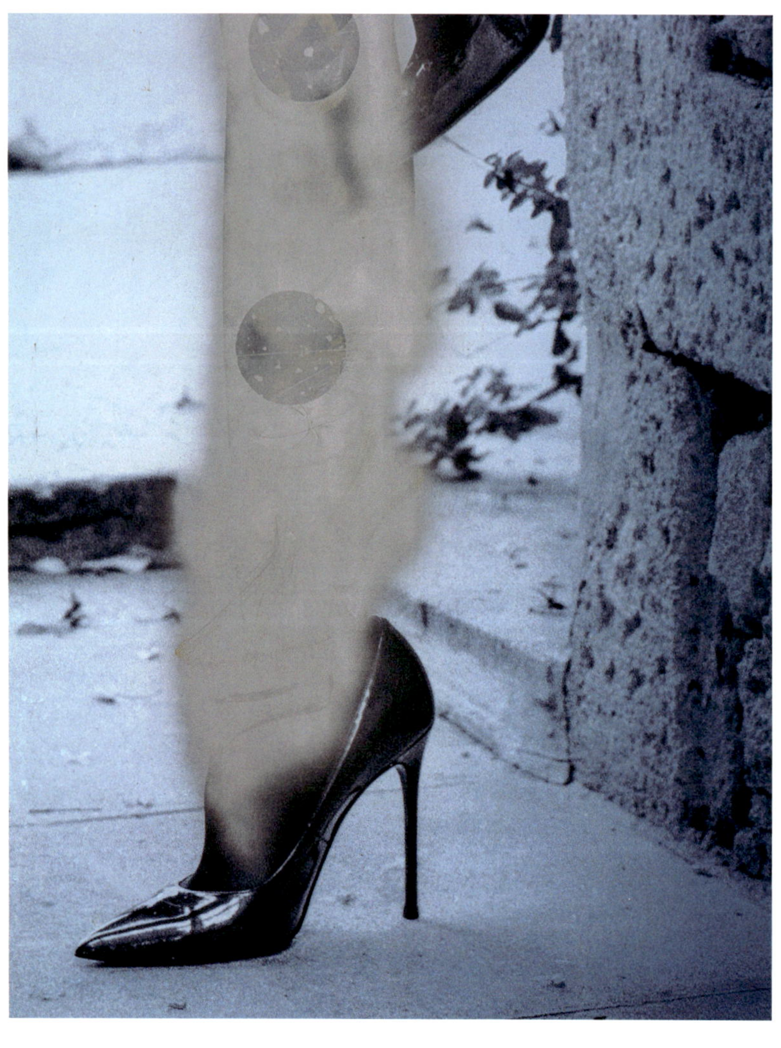

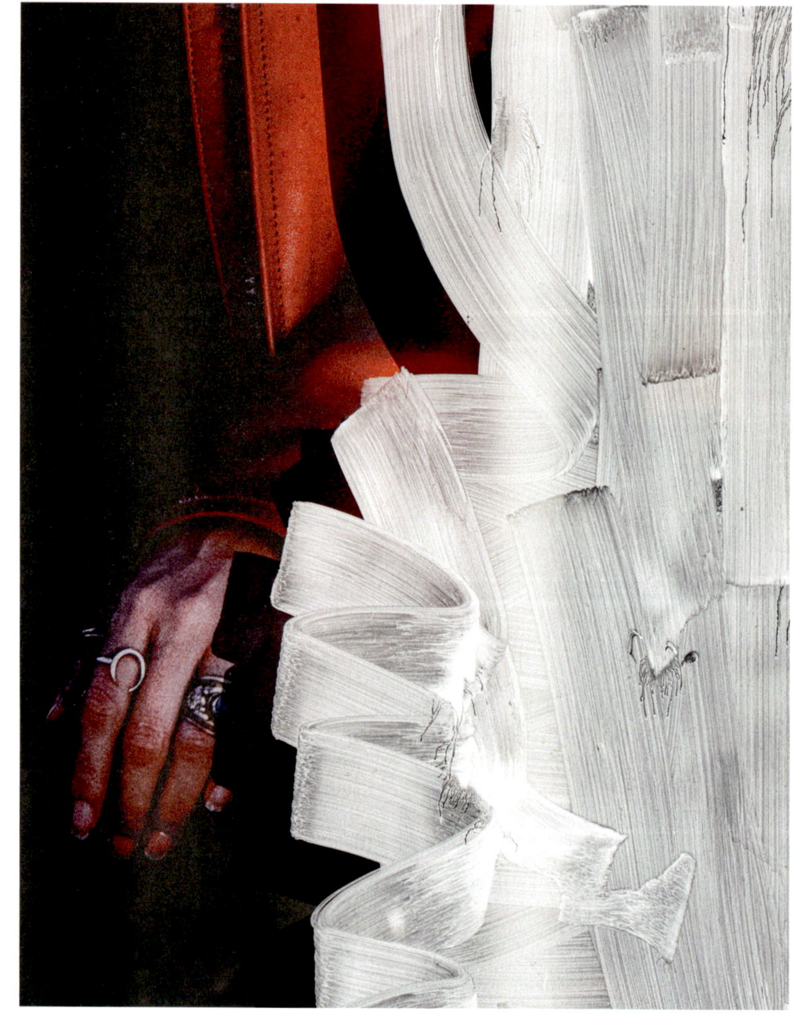

‹ Spray Paint on Shoe Poster, New York, 2021 › Overpainted Hand Poster, Paris, 2021

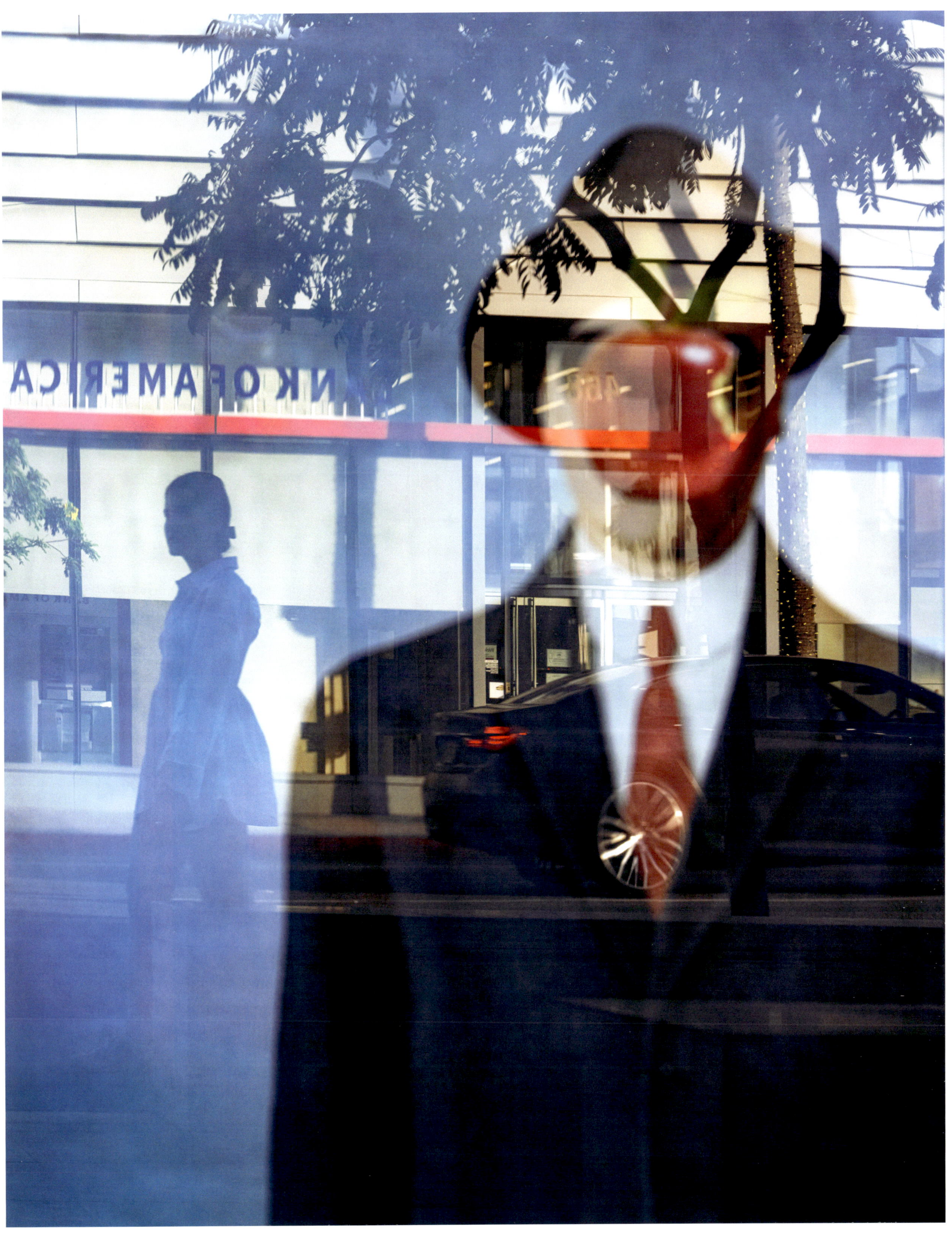

Art Poster (Magritte), Los Angeles, 2022

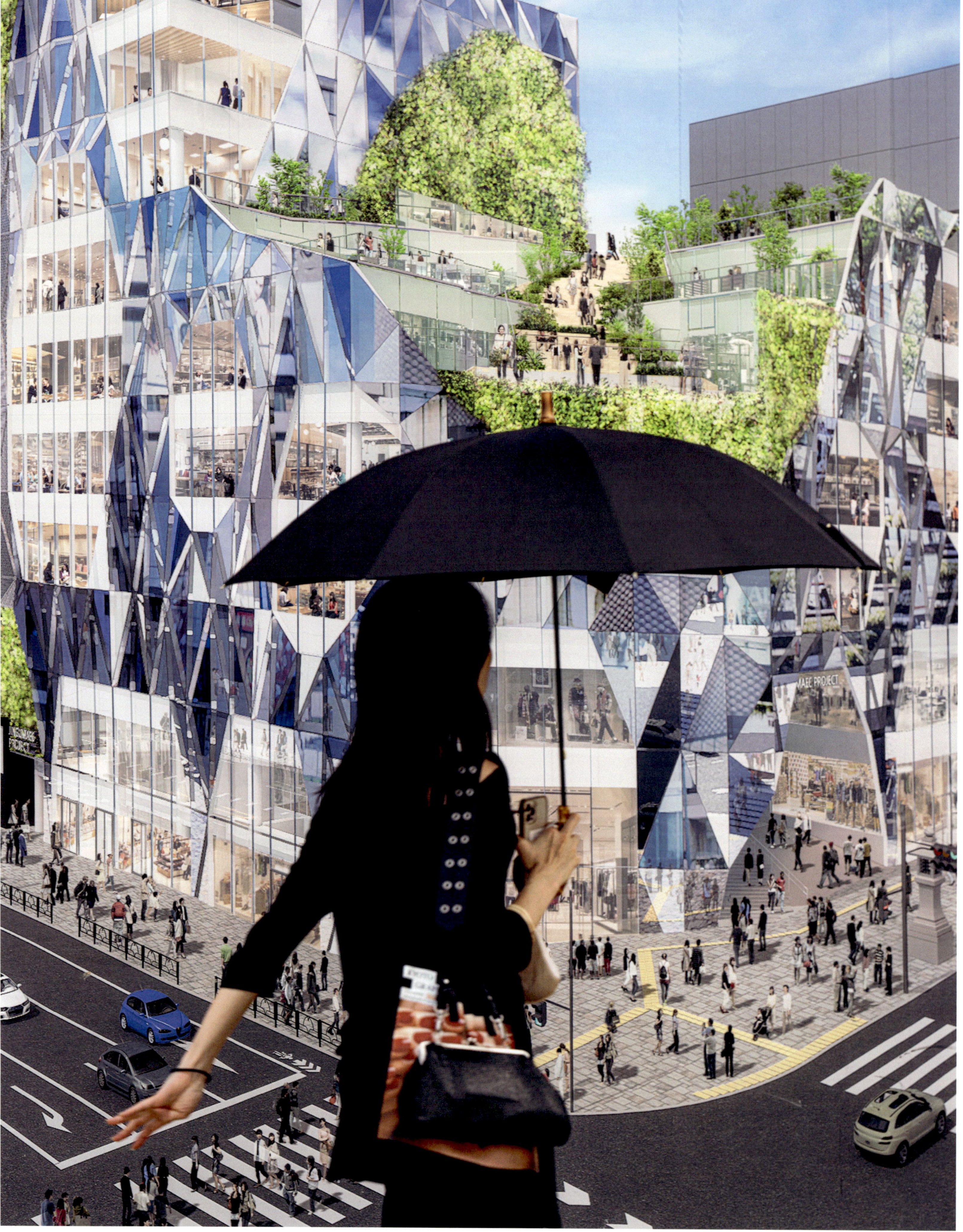

Billboard with Architectural Rendering, Tokyo, 2022

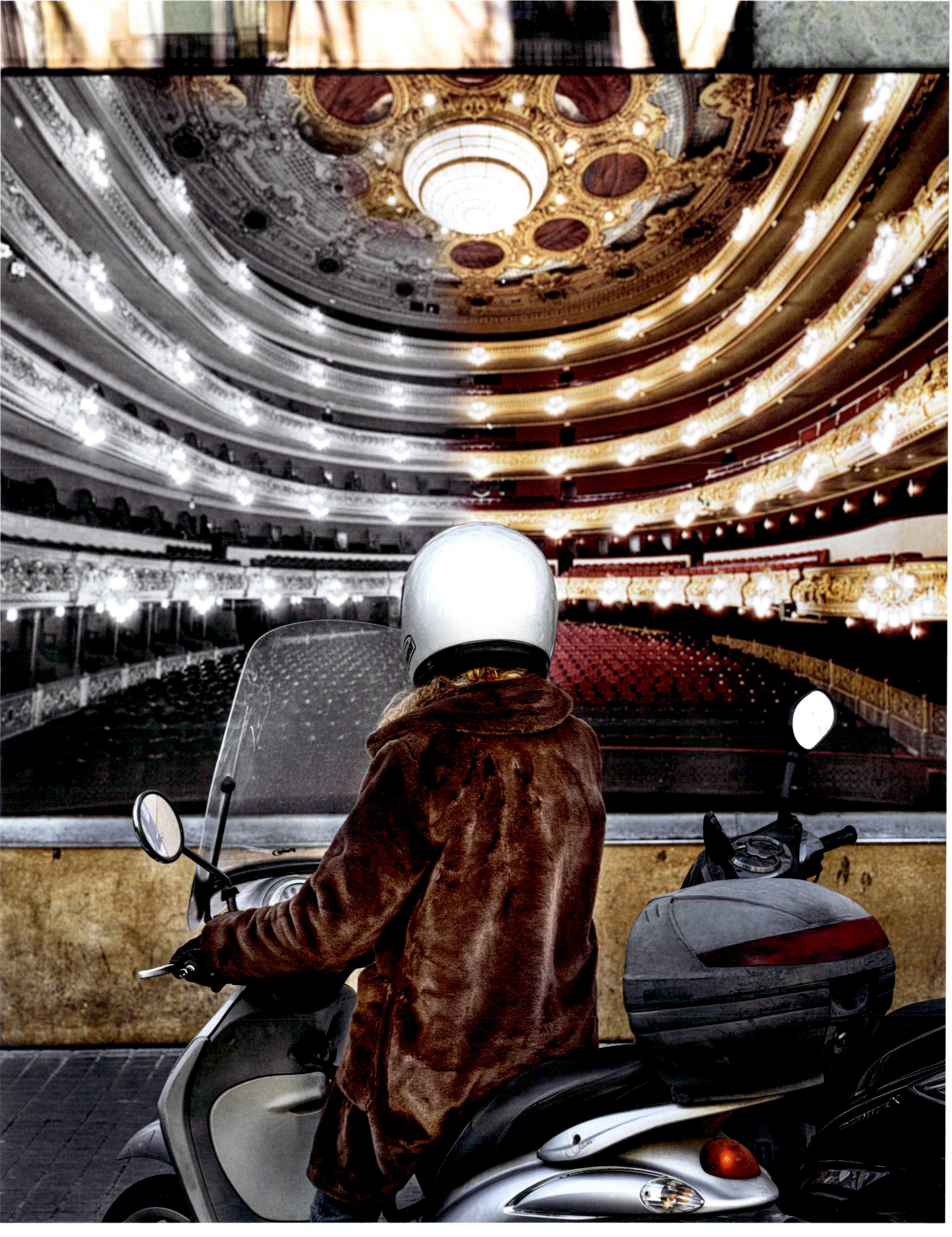

Historic Theater Poster, Barcelona, 2022

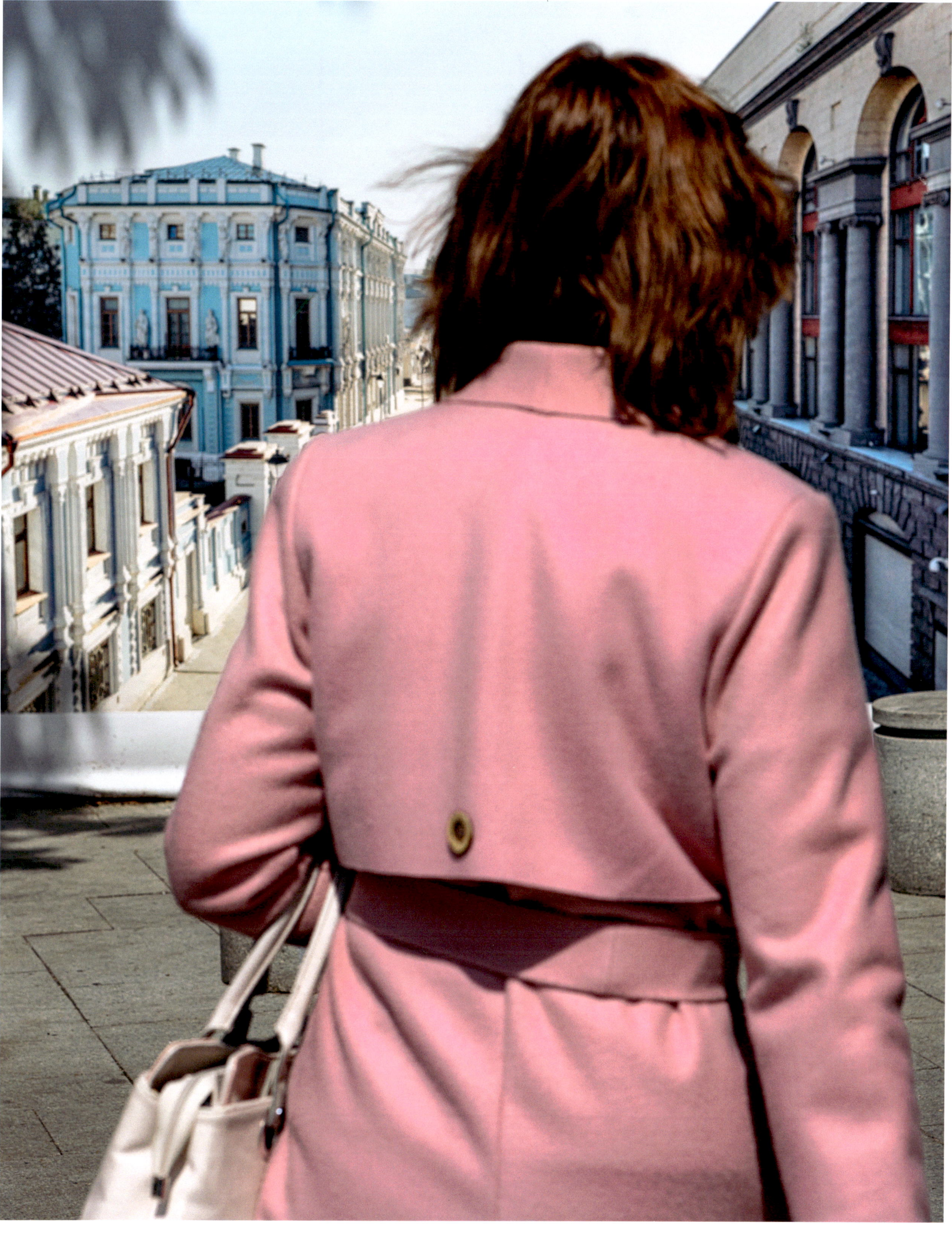

Pink Coat, Moscow, 2021

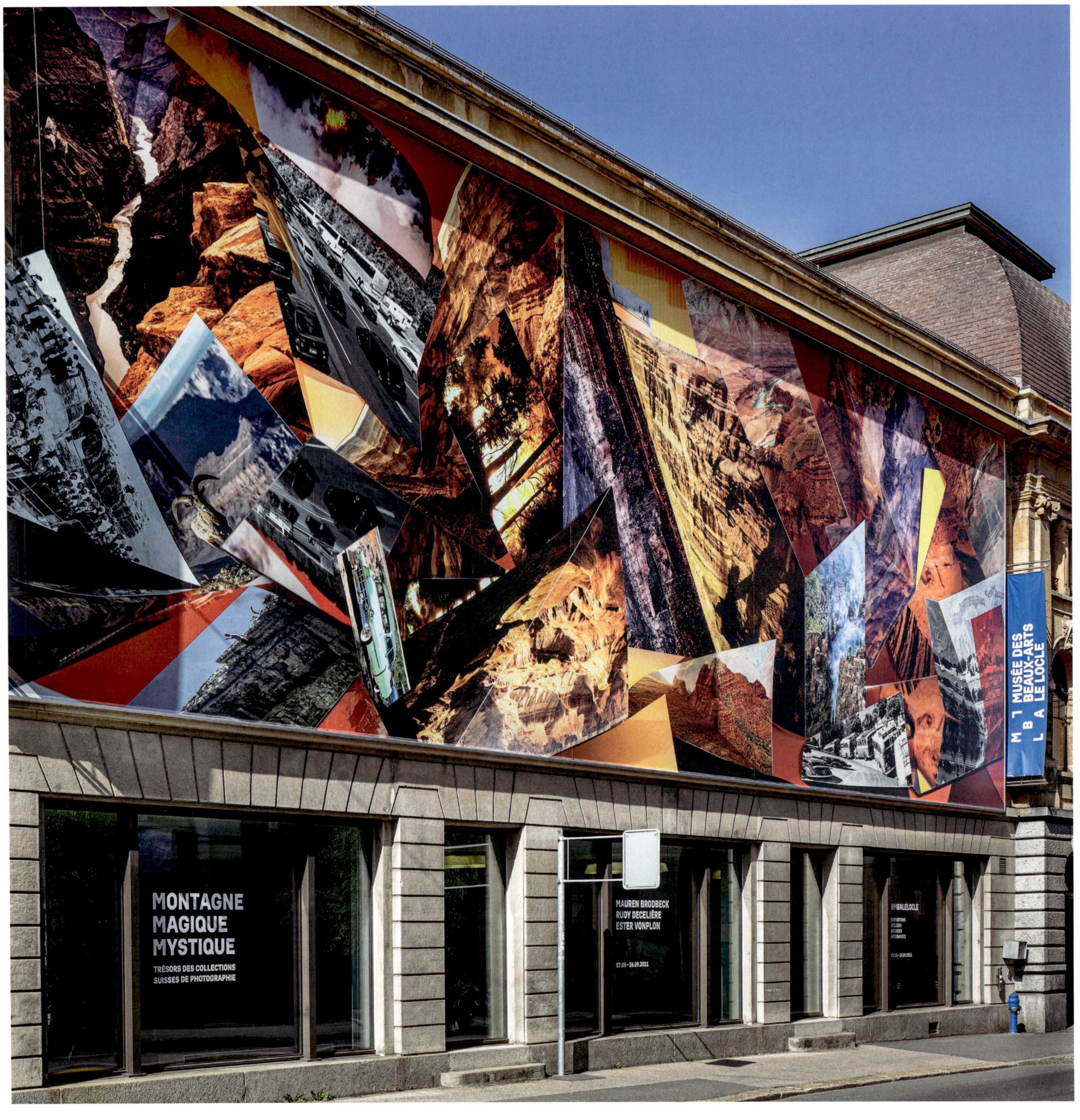

Banner from the *Landscape Sublime* project on the facade of the Musée des Beaux-Arts Le Locle, Switzerland, 2021

THE WORLD'S IMAGE

DAVID CAMPANY

You may have noticed that despite the broadly chronological layout of this book, Anastasia Samoylova's creative path has been far from linear. Beneath the orderly procession of projects is an underlying set of interests that weave and morph, as fresh and lively in the most recent work as in the earliest. Some of these interests are clear: the striking colour palettes, the intricate ways with composition and the preference for layered pictorial space. Others take a little longer to note: the persistence of collage even in the apparently 'documentary style' projects, the fascination with today's image culture, and the fine balance between visual pleasure and something more unsettling.

The formal virtuosity is attractive, while the collision of visual cues deepens the effect. It is not really a strategy, since it is not entirely calculated. Rather, a work by Samoylova achieves completeness at the point its powers of suggestion, its constellation of 'ideas' (for want of a better word), are at their most generative. Invariably, the subject matter feels contemporary, but in some ways, this is an old-fashioned kind of art. The idea of formal unity being the ground for fragmentary and even contradictory suggestion has its roots in the 19th-century modernism of Manet, for example, but it is there in much of the 20th-century art Samoylova admires, as we shall see.

The projects here cover a little over a decade, 2013–24 although again the chronology is deceptive. Most of the work was produced in an astonishingly brief five years between 2017 and 2022 (in the midst of which a year was all but lost to the Covid-19 pandemic). Needless to say, such a burst of creative vitality does not come out of nowhere. Samoylova had been incubating a hungry artistic ambition at least since her youth in Moscow at the turn of the millennium. She was born in Russia in 1984, and even childhood memories of the dissonance between fading Soviet propaganda and the emerging realities of post-1989 Russia left a lasting impression. After studying environmental design and working for a while as a high-end window dresser, Samoylova moved to the American Midwest in 2008, furthering her studies, teaching photography and making art when she could. An early project, *5000 Head* (2011), was a study of the ecological effects of intensive farming. It was notable for a formal language that already showed her fascination with the modernism and collage of the art of the 1920s and '30s.

A move in 2016 to Miami Beach coincided with an opportunity to become an artist full-time. But art, if it is a profession at all, has no guarantees, no clear 'career paths'. It was a gamble, and Samoylova won't mind my saying that there were many moments in that first year in Miami when it felt as if nothing would happen. Clearly things did happen, and rapidly. It was not exactly one project after another,

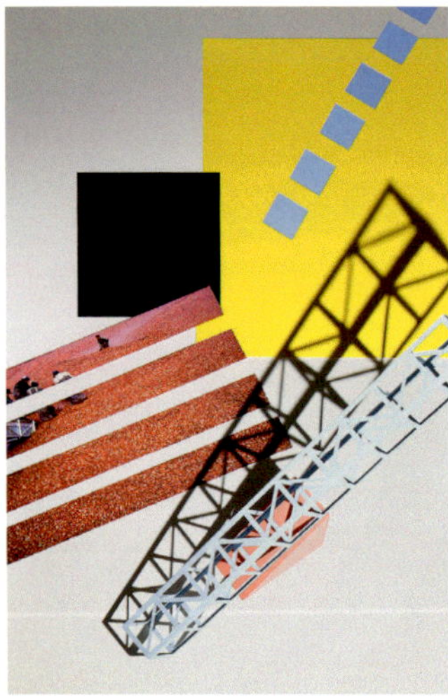

Anastasia Samoylova, from the series *5000 Head*, 2011

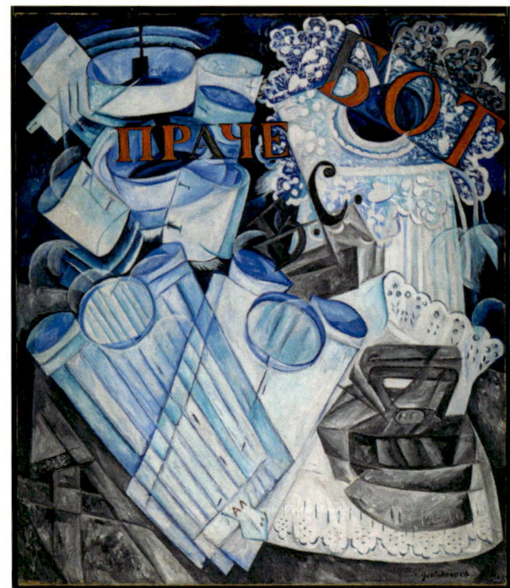

Natalia Goncharova, *Linen*, 1913

since they overlapped, and many of them are ongoing, but enough circumstances aligned. Grants and awards, residencies and commercial gallery support, along with opportunities to exhibit and publish, all enabled the making of the work gathered here. More importantly, Samoylova was ready, even if that is something we can say only in hindsight.

I have followed Samoylova's work for a number of years. I have written about it several times, edited two of her previous books (*FloodZone*, 2019, and *Anastasia Samoylova & Walker Evans: Floridas*, 2022), included it in exhibitions, talked about it with her quite a lot, and even watched her make some of her location photographs. Nevertheless, I am reluctant to say I *know* the work, if only because the art we consider significant eludes us in profound ways, and perhaps even eludes its maker to some extent. Even when editing her work, I have found a sequence of images is satisfying when it amplifies the qualities that cannot quite be grasped. Looking back, as this present book looks back, I suspect I came to see the formal aspects of her work – so strong and compelling – as the framework for its multiple and inconclusive meanings. I do not know for sure, but I suspect this is how it is for Samoylova, too, as well as for her varied audiences. Formality in art can be a tightly coiled spring, ordered and tensed before its unpredictable release.

In each of Samoylova's bodies of work, the set of themes is much easier to define than what it communicates. Exactly what are we to make of the attention paid to the endlessly formulaic internet images that are the basis of her series *Landscape Sublime*? Is it a celebration of visual populism or some kind of critique? Perhaps both, perhaps neither. Are overt judgments being made about the uneasy beauty of the fragile tropical world depicted in *FloodZone*? The classic photobooks in *Breakfasts* are admired, it seems, but they are also used as backgrounds. Does the epic *Floridas* amount to a position on that contradictory and volatile place? Is the globe-trotting *Image Cities* a polemic concerning the urban makeover wrought by corporate capital, or an allegorical dance through its ambiguous attractions? In interviews, Samoylova often expresses views that are more outspoken on climate change, on the position of women in society, on consumerism and contemporary politics than her work might indicate. This is what makes it so fascinating.

For all the effusive colours, masterly picture making and engagement with urgent issues, Samoylova's images lead to questions and openness, rather than answers and closure. This makes for more resonant art, no doubt, pulling away from simplistic messages, or activism. While it might be tempting to see this as fully intentional on Samoylova's part, a gambit to keep the work wide and accessible, my hunch is that it is guided by something else: an acceptance of the essentially open nature not only of images, but of appearance as such. Neither can account for

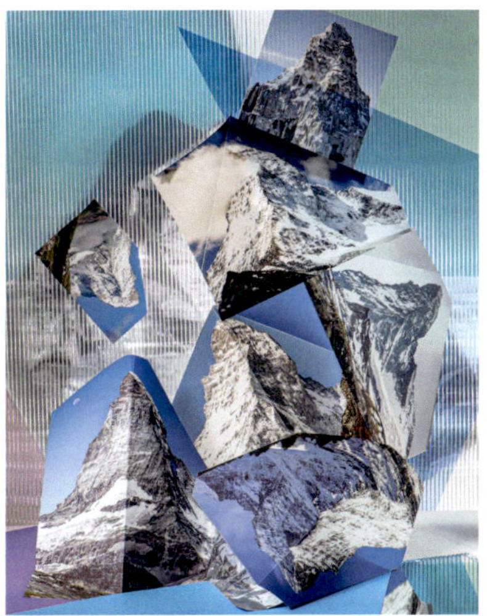

Anastasia Samoylova, *Six Real Matterhorns*, 2019

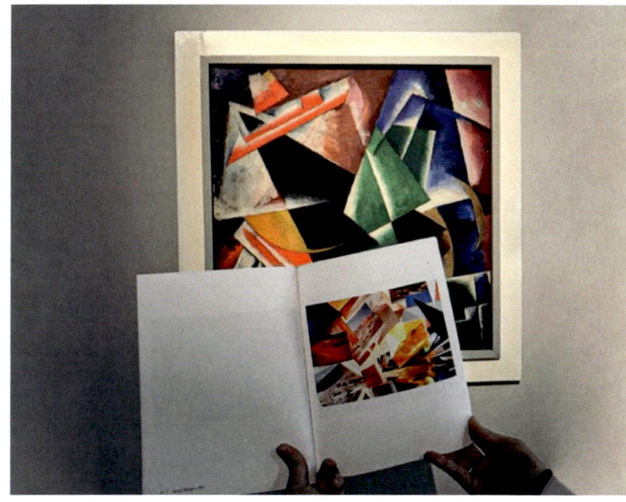

Anastasia Samoylova holding a book reproduction of *Desert Mirages* (2014) in front of Liubov Popova's *Composition* (1918), Wilhelm-Hack-Museum, Ludwigshafen, 2020. Photograph by David Campany.

much of what they show. An image, particularly a photographic image, turns appearance into a sign of itself, but an enigmatic one. Samoylova brings such signs together, and often at odds with each other, then leaves it to us.

One way into all of this is to consider the different kinds of relations Samoylova has to a range of other images, from art and popular culture to the mass media and social media. To say her work is 'image-conscious' would be an understatement. Even when it does not contain other images, she is usually photographing with a highly reflexive sense of inherited pictorial method. Her photographs describe the encountered world but they also resonate with an awareness of prior photographs, just as our sense of the world is so often predetermined by images we have seen. A feeling of déjà vu is never far away.

Certain images have been deep influences on Samoylova, at a level almost beyond conscious recognition. At other points, coming across the work of particular artists has been an affirmation of directions she has already set for herself. There are moments when her work recognizes an image or artist that is significant for her. And then there are images that she incorporates more or less directly from the countless number that thicken daily experience online or out in the world. While there may not be such a thing as a key to unlock her art, it is worth looking carefully at each of these different modes of image relation.

Our most profound influences are those barely thought about. We take them in so fundamentally that they shape how we see and make, and we notice them only when their effects surface in unforeseen ways. The curator and writer John Szarkowski put it this way: 'Artistic influence works less like a legal document than a cold virus. It doesn't convince us; it *changes* us.' Visiting London's Tate Modern in 2019, I watched Samoylova pause intently in front of *Linen* (1913), a painting by the Russian artist Natalia Goncharova. Samoylova had just completed *Six Real Matterhorns* (2019), a mural commissioned for the great facade of the Wilhelm-Hack-Museum in Ludwigshafen, Germany. Even though she knows Goncharova's art well, the uncanny structural similarity of the two works took her quite by surprise. A while later, at the Wilhelm-Hack-Museum itself, she came across *Composition* (1918) by another Russian Constructivist, Liubov Popova, and saw straight away the affinity with her own *Desert Mirages* (2014). Back at art school, Samoylova had studied Constructivism. It is a high point of modern art, made all the more resonant by the way patriarchal art history has downplayed the significance of the women artists involved, and by the fate of the Russian avant-garde in general, with its great flowering cut down and replaced by official art and propaganda under Stalin. Samoylova seemed to have so internalized Constructivism and its moment that its fundamental forms were recurring in her work a century on, and in very different circumstances. Pictorial tradition is not a matter of 'handing down', one generation

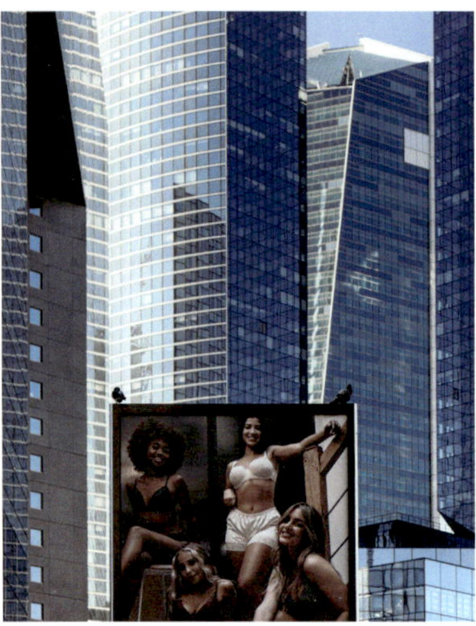

Anastasia Samoylova, *Lingerie Advertisement, Paris*, 2021

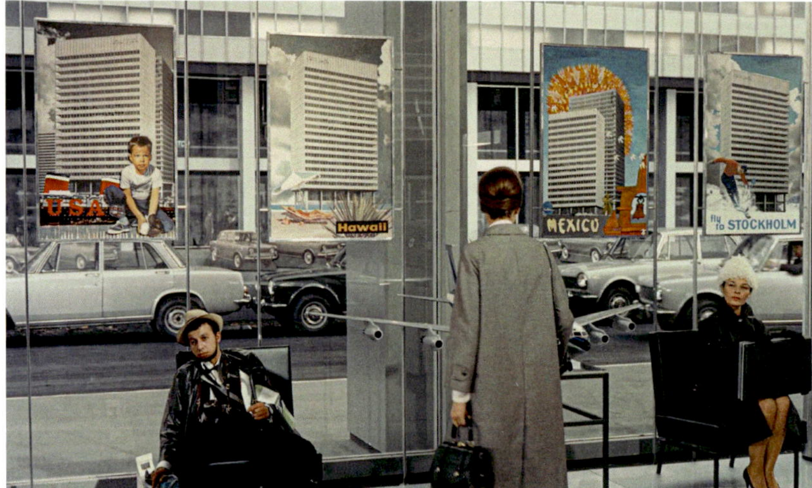

Frame from *Playtime* (dir. Jacques Tati, 1967)

to the next. It is a network of subterranean tunnels dug across time and culture, breaking through in surprising places, and welcomed when it does.

Sometimes, the impact of the art of others comes less through influence than through a recognition of kinship. In 2017, Samoylova saw an exhibition in Miami of photographs by Berenice Abbott (1898–1991) taken in 1954 along the old Route 1, from Florida's Key West up the east coast of the USA to Maine. Samoylova had already started, tentatively, to make observational photographs of the state, and was beginning to feel that the male-dominated genre of road-trip photography was a possible direction. It didn't matter that Abbott's project was already sixty-three years old, nor that it may not have been her best work. Its existence and pioneering spirit provided a timely spur. Shortly after this, Samoylova came to the little-known photographs that Abbott's friend Walker Evans had made of Florida between the 1930s and 1970s. Samoylova had already concluded for herself that the visual overload and political drama of Florida could be distilled into something like Evans's restrained yet direct vision. His work chimed with her own, becoming an important counterpoint as her *Floridas* project developed.

Affirmations of this kind are important markers in Samoylova's progress, and there have been many. In the summer of 2021 she was on an artist's residency in Moscow, and beginning to formulate what would soon become the *Image Cities* project. Nobody sees a place with greater clarity than those who have left and returned. More than a generation on from the implosion of the Soviet Union, Moscow is still a showcase city, projecting a well-groomed if dubious image of power and confidence on the global stage. But its giant Soviet-era public murals now compete with equally large billboards advertising 21st-century capitalism's brands. Samoylova had seen this phenomenon emerging in her earlier years when she worked in the city. Moscow is also enamoured with the cloaking of its new architectural projects and historic renovations in photorealistic hoardings. Such spectacle is now a common sight in wealthy countries around the world.

Samoylova was thinking through all this when, upon her return to Miami, she saw Jacques Tati's 1967 feature film *Playtime*. Shot in 70 mm, it is an almost plotless, dialogue-free meditation on the spread of the generic post-war city. Across more than two hours we watch people wander, lost and comical, through bland but oddly photogenic streets and banal lobby spaces. Tati keeps each shot long, full of endless social detail, but non-judgmental. He explores this dream/nightmare non-place while allowing viewers the freedom to come to their own conclusions. *Playtime* was a commercial flop, but today it is celebrated as a work of great prescience. At one point, Tati shows us posters in a tourist office advertising far-flung destinations, but each one features the same monochrome skyscraper, with the place name pasted over it in bright colours.

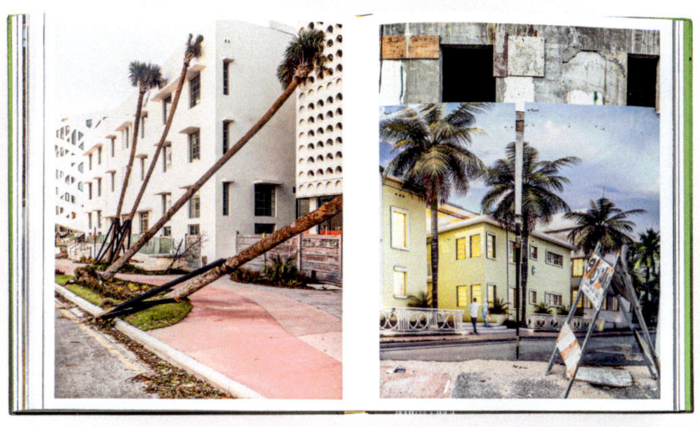

Spread from Anastasia Samoylova, *FloodZone*, 2019

USA. Hawaii. Mexico. Stockholm. Samoylova sensed straight away a connection with her own urban experience. She soon received funding for a seventeen-city shooting schedule that would make *Image Cities* a reality. In Paris, one of her key locations was La Défense, the 1980s skyscraper district to the west of the city, which many see as a striking manifestation of Tati's prediction. Samoylova even came across a billboard for lingerie that seemed to echo the scene in *Playtime*'s tourist office. The women's varied body types and skin colour signal that version of 'diversity' familiar from international consumer culture. Behind the billboard there are blue-grey facades of steel and glass that could be almost anywhere.

You get the idea. Samoylova does not so much research as *begin*, speculatively, with no precise goal beyond a strong yet open feeling for themes and forms. The image making begins to flow, often in a number of related directions. Meanwhile, curiosity about other image makers and writers, past and present, helps to consolidate some directions and open up others.

What became *FloodZone*, her first project as an observational photographer, began as a set of exploratory walks around Miami Beach in the wake of Hurricane Irma, to gather resources for her collages. It turned out to be a sidestep into documentary-style work. Samoylova knew the vital lineage of such photography in the USA, but she didn't see herself in it until she *found* herself in it, and figured things out from there. She made thousands of photographs in her vicinity, while not quite considering it a 'project', at least for a while. After six months or so, she did what many photographers do, which was to step back and sift through the accumulation with the aim of making a book, which was published in 2019. Editing and sequencing a publication is often what allows the shape and purpose of a project to assert itself.

Meanwhile, Samoylova was engaging closely with the history of the photobook. Each morning, before going out with her camera, she considered a publication by a photographer she admired. The images, sequencing, design, printing and materiality were all studied closely. Her growing library became a source of daily inspiration, and the subject of a new body of work. In a ritual way, she took to arranging cups, plates, cutlery and food on an open book spread. The set-up would then be photographed from above, with shadows from the low sun confusing the space of the book's images with the space of her own arrangement. *Breakfasts* may be her lightest and most open-hearted body of work, but even here there is a disquieting edge. The admiration of images, *iconophilia*, comes with just a hint of destruction, *iconoclasm*. The books are idealized but also shown as markers in the development of a creative life. Making *Breakfasts* is a cathartic act of absorbing an artistic lineage (rather than worshipping it) and moving forward. Samoylova doesn't get trapped in obsession with great work but, as she has written herself, imagines what

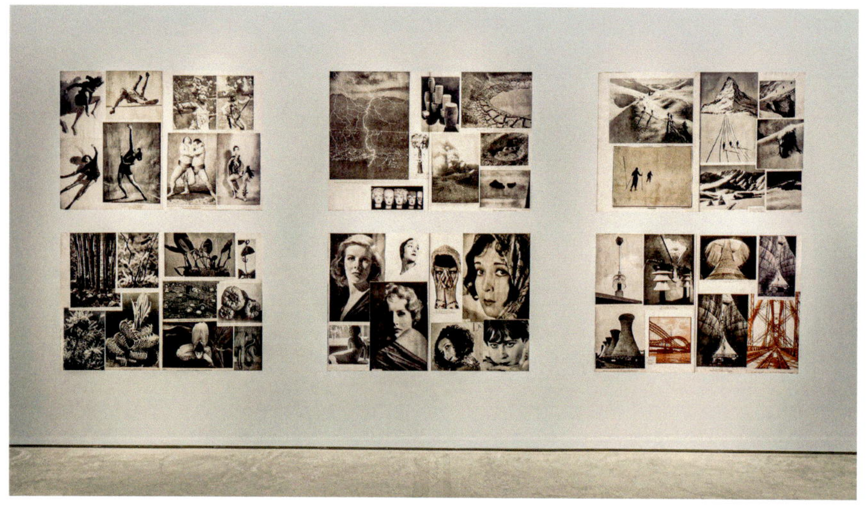

Enlarged spreads from Hannah Höch, *Album* (1933), presented in *A Trillion Sunsets: A Century of Image Overload*, International Center of Photography, New York, 2022. Curated by David Campany. Installation photograph by John Halpern.

conversations over breakfast with these canonical artists might be.

Any artist working today with found or encountered images belongs to a century-long tradition. It begins in the late 1910s–early 1920s, with the onset of what was beginning to be called the 'mass media': an ever-expanding culture of illustrated books, newspapers, magazines, cinema and images in public space. The connections between mass media and the shaping of popular opinion and value was, to some artists and writers at least, clear and dangerous. There is a politics, explicit or implicit, in the way artists began to rework public imagery. We see this in inter-war Dadaist collage, in anti-fascist photomontage and in the pointed ambiguities of Surrealism. We then see it transformed in post-war Situationism (Guy Debord's 1967 text *The Society of the Spectacle* has been important for Samoylova), in Pop art, Conceptualism, in the appropriation strategies of what came to be called the 'Pictures Generation', and in post-internet art. Moreover, the internet has not only meant the exponential production and circulation of visuals; it has also made the histories of art available as never before, including the histories of artists' engagement with mass image forms. Samoylova has been in a position to sweep up all of this and redeploy it in her own ways, not as quotation or mimicry, but as still viable responses to present-day image culture.

The series *Landscape Sublime* is particularly rich in this regard. I have mentioned already its neo-Constructivist form, but the typological approach to image culture was something the German artist Hannah Höch was working through in her collages and media scrapbooks of the 1930s. Similar images would be cut from magazines and newspapers, then gathered and arranged as a kind of visual inventory, diagnosing the tendency of the mass media towards visual standardization and thus even ideological standardization.

A second consequence of Samoylova's historically minded engagement with imagery of all kinds is the apparent coolness or emotional distance that underscores her work. Contemporary art, particularly photographic art, has been dominated for some time now by an often-spurious preference for the supposedly 'personal', 'diaristic' and 'confessional' (much of it following well-established tropes, making questionable precisely how personal it really is). This has not been Samoylova's approach at all. If there is autobiography here, it is unemphatic and filtered through a much more shared and social set of concerns. While certain facts to do with Samoylova's biography are interesting to reflect upon, it makes little sense to reduce her work to them, or to somehow see what she makes as a straightforward symptom or consequence of her life between Russia and the USA. This, too, is out of step with contemporary attitudes to art, which seem set on packaging art and artist together as one media-friendly brand. This is done in the name of 'humanizing' art and making it more accessible, but the effect is often

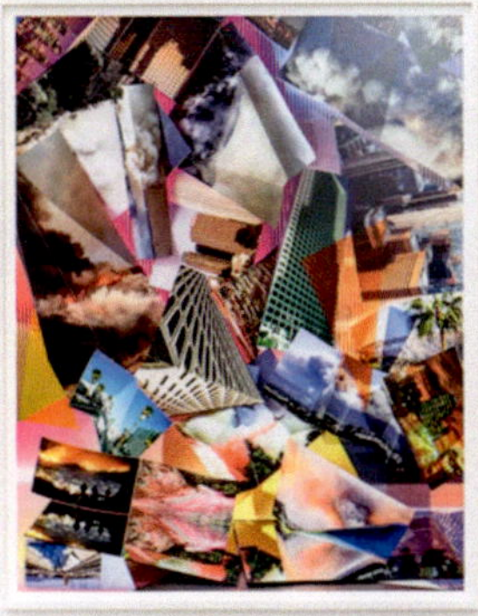
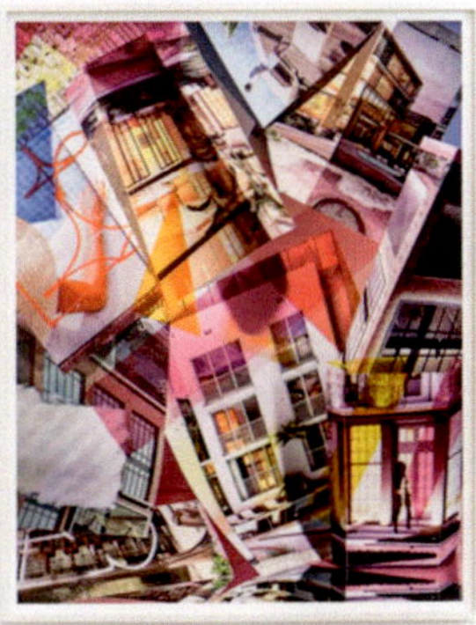

Anastasia Samoylova, installation view of *LA (On Fire)* (2020), and *New Developments* (2020), from the ongoing series *Landscape Sublime*

the reverse, reducing the bandwidth of viewers' response and interpretation to the artist's own.

Such restraint at the level of meaning ought not to be mistaken for distance, nor anything impersonal. It is an act of generosity to viewers. Meaning is *theirs*, not Samoylova's. She often remarks on the fact that most images we encounter in daily life have an 'agenda', in that they are made and intended to promote a specific set of cultural and political values, but in her own work her interest goes far beyond any agenda, leaving the door open. The wide and positive response to her work is not only to do with the accessibility and relevance of its themes; it is this handing back of agency to the viewer that has been welcomed as so refreshing. In her exhibitions it is not unusual to see discussions break out between people as they exchange views and puzzle through the possibilities together. Samoylova's commitment to making work in public spaces, in everything from hospitals and hotel lobbies to museum exteriors and festivals, is a furthering of this shared discourse.

To conclude, it is worth mentioning Samoylova's overarching preference for a kind of hyper-visibility. Her images present an almost unmanageable wealth of visual detail. Everything is clear and each square inch of the image surface is active. The light is almost always bright and illuminating, whether on location or in the studio. There are few shadows in which things might linger unseen. This is an art of *display* and *presentation*, lucid and exacting. 'Look closely,' it seems to insist, 'and consider this. Look again. Reconsider.' Visibility itself, exposure itself, is both revealing and somehow blinding. We seem to be able to see all there is to see, and yet nothing is clarified. It is all clues. Whatever there is to enjoy and think about, it is there to see, and somehow there on the surface of the world depicted. This is work that requires no elaborate captions or back story. It is not deepened by knowing exactly how it was made or why, nor by a knowledge of what the artist was thinking, or intending. For all her scepticism about images, Anastasia Samoylova remains deeply committed to them.

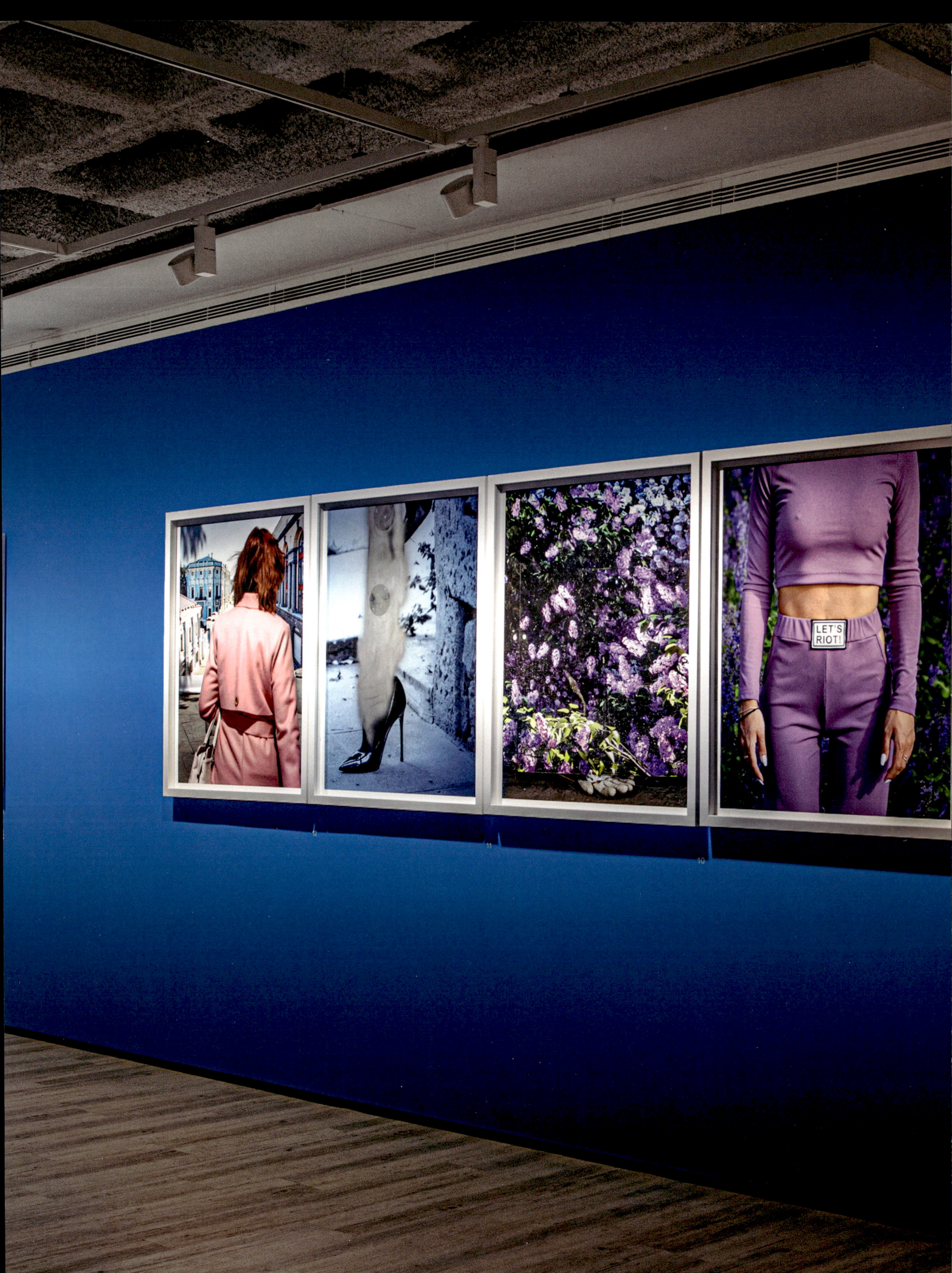
LET'S
RIOT!